# BRITAIN'S
# TOP
# EMPLOYERS

The Corporate Research Foundation (CRF) is an independent organisation that initiates, co-ordinates and delivers international research projects in business worldwide. CRF aims to contribute to a better awareness and understanding of corporate culture, effective human resource management, and the business strategies of successful enterprises, by researching the key factors behind their success and publishing its findings.

CRF represents a combined initiative of business journalists, researchers, and international publishers, and has been active since 1991 in Australia, Belgium, Germany, Holland, South Africa, Sweden, Switzerland and the United Kingdom.

Other titles in the CRF series in the UK include:

*Top ICT Companies in the UK*
*Top UK Companies of the Future*
*Top Marketing and Media Companies in the UK*

Martin Williams, Projects Director & Country Manager
Corporate Research Foundation
Kinetic Centre, Theobald Street
Elstree WD6 4PJ
Tel: 020 8387 1400
Fax: 020 8387 1410
Email: martin@CRF-UK.com
Website: www.researchfoundation.com

# BRITAIN'S
# TOP
# EMPLOYERS

## A JOB-HUNTER'S GUIDE TO THE BEST COMPANIES TO WORK FOR

### Editor: GUY CLAPPERTON

Corporate Research Foundation

KOGAN
PAGE

First published in Great Britain and the United States in 2003 by Kogan Page Limited

120 Pentonville Road
London N1 9JN
www.kogan-page.co.uk

22883 Quicksilver Drive
Sterling VA 20166–2012
USA

© Corporate Research Foundation 2003

---

**British Library Cataloguing-in-Publication Data**

A CIP record for this book is available from the British Library

ISBN 0 7494 4054 6

Typeset by Saxon Graphics Ltd, Derby
Printed and bound in Great Britain by Clays Ltd, St. Ives plc

# Contents

# Introduction

## Employment is changing

Sounds trite? Well yes, I suppose it does. But looking at the previous edition, published in 2001, there's effectively no comparison between the world of work then and the one we face now. For example, we asked at the time whether companies allowed people to work from home. A few said yes, some hummed and haa'd a bit but none said that in a world of broadband connections they actively encouraged it.

Work/life balance, although an issue two years ago, has burgeoned and is now one of the main drivers for corporate change throughout UK plc. The number of companies in this volume that have counsellors, not only for work and company matters but for life issues totally outside the professional world, is now impressive enough for the idea not to be considered extraordinary. Companies that had comfortable workplaces last time around have moved into palatial surroundings and employees have their own branches of top-notch coffee bars. Which is a nightmare if you're putting a book like this together.

Companies that scored three out of five for environment last time have a good case for being bumped up to five; companies that already had five deserve frankly more. So if you have the last edition and are comparing, please don't assume companies have deteriorated if their mark has gone down – far from it, the overall standard has increased so much we're effectively starting again with this one.

Finally a personal word: I shouldn't have edited this book. Mike Hardwidge, the editor of the previous edition, passed away prematurely during 2002. Before he fell ill he had input into selecting the writers and evolving their guidelines and the structure of the finished book. The resulting volume is for him; he should have edited this and for all I know would have done a better job. He's much missed.

*Guy Clapperton*
*Editor*

# Pay and Benefits

Since March 1993 pay increases have settled around the 3 per cent level and have maintained this historically low level throughout the decade since then. Further, they are likely to stay low – the current average is 2.7 per cent. With inflation and pay increases so closely linked, and the need to maintain the UK's global competitiveness, maintaining low pay rises is important and this would appear to have been achieved.

As this article is being written, the Iraq war is taking place. This has induced a feeling of insecurity in both the personal and business marketplaces. Individuals have maintained a surprising high level of 'feel good' in the last two years, partly as a result of the buoyancy of the housing market. This has translated into a lively retail and service sector whilst the manufacturing and production sectors have been in recession for over 12 months.

All these differing economies within the country and industry groupings naturally have different pay levels that translate into regional pay differences. Percentage pay differentials for management jobs between the UK national median and the regions show the following pattern: Eastern Counties: –7 per cent, London: +11 per cent, North East: –7 per cent, Northern Ireland: –20 per cent, North West: +3 per cent, Scotland: +1 per cent, South East: +6 per cent, South West: –5 per cent, West Midlands: –5 per cent.

When we speak of pay and benefits, we are considering the total package that comes with a job. A list of pay and benefit related items that could be included in the total package follows – other items may also feature.

**Pay:** Basic pay, bonus, commission, performance-related pay, profit-related pay, overtime, shift allowance, call-out allowance, market supplement.

**Benefits:** Holidays, sick pay, pension, company car, private health insurance, long-term disability insurance, life assurance.

Clearly not every employee would have all of these items, but many would be included and are often forgotten by the employees when speaking of their package.

If a value is placed on each of these, it can be seen that the typical package can be quite substantial and can cost the employer a large additional amount on top of the basic salary. When this is added to employer's National Insurance contributions, the costs of employing an individual are often between 50 per cent and 60 per cent above the basic salary.

As might be expected, as seniority increases so does the level of benefits: a graduate trainee's typical package might be basic salary, company pension and life assurance, possibly with profit-related or performance-related pay. A middle manager would normally have private health insurance and performance-related pay, plus life assurance increasing to about three times annual salary and perhaps long-term disability insurance. For a senior manager, a company car would typically be around 1800cc and above, but more organisations are offering contract hire and leasing arrangements, giving the individual more choice. Health and long-term insurances would increase.

The way forward over the next few years appears to be low economic growth, hopefully an improvement in the 'feel-good factor' following the Iraq war, with small fluctuations in inflation and pay levels and a drifting upwards of benefit packages.

*Steve Flather*
*The Reward Group*

# Britain's Top Employers 2003 – Caveat Emptor!

Britain's top employers may not necessarily be *your* top employers. Of course, all the organisations in this book are outstanding in one way or the other – you will probably know most of them already. A 'top employer' is likely to be large, have clear vision and leadership, excellent human resource processes, including training and career development, and will have a real point of difference in its expertise, its culture and its identity. Furthermore, it is probably likely to be a great springboard for outstanding people who form its alumni. After all, if a firm cannot celebrate achievements of those who have left, why should anyone want to join it? That is all good but thousands of successful people have not been anywhere near Britain's top employers and the purpose of this piece is to provide some self-assessment suggestions for those starting a career and, just as importantly, making job changes throughout it.

Shakespeare, as usual, said it clearly in Polonius's speech to Laertes: 'This above all – to thine own self be true; and it must follow, as the night the day thou cannot then be false to any man'. Of course, the most important person not to be false to is yourself, and I would commend four actions on the self-knowledge front:

1. Take a vocational interest test. After many years, the work of Edward K Strong Junior, one-time professor of psychology at Stanford, stood the test. Strong's idea was that if you shared the interests of successful people in any one area, you were likely to be happy there. He couldn't guarantee that you would be any good, but if you were happy in the company of people who were, that was a strong indication that you should look at it seriously. I did the Strong test when I was just 18 and on an exchange year in the United States and, given what I do in running a management communication consultancy, it was extraordinarily accurate. My top scores were for personnel director, social worker, advertising man, and, wait for it, life insurance salesman. I remember at the time being disappointed that 'president of a manufacturing concern' scored just below them. My worse scores were physicist, mathematician, veterinarian and dentist. I make this point because I wasted time at university considering becoming an accountant on the basis that accountancy

was a ticket for senior jobs. I was fooling myself. The truth about me had already been established but I didn't pay enough attention to it.

2. Understand your own verbal and numerical reasoning. It isn't mortal if your scores are low and it doesn't guarantee success if your scores are high but it remains an important consideration.

3. Take Saville and Holdsworth's occupational personality questionnaire and/or Myers Briggs personality types to discover the type you are.

4. Finally, do something I did just before leaving university. I wrote down two columns of people. The first column was people in the years ahead of me there who I liked and got on well with. The other column was people I did not feel close to. I then wrote the name of the job each had taken in both lists. Sure enough, this analysis broadly confirmed the Strong test I had taken five years earlier.

Britain's top employers in this book are great firms but the priority is you not them. I have one son-in-law who runs a company in the motion picture industry creating special effects, another works all hours for a big London lawyer and a daughter-in-law who is the first environmental manager of Britain's biggest car crusher! For them these are the best employers and the flexibility and opportunity once you have established an outstanding portable skill can equip you to lead big business as an independent.

*Simon Barrow*
*Chairman, People in Business*

# Research Team

*Bryan Betts*
Bryan Betts has nearly 20 years' experience as a journalist, covering business and business uses of technology. He has worked in a wide variety of staff and freelance roles, for publications in the UK and abroad. Originally trained as an engineer, he lives in West London not far from Kew Gardens, for which he has a season ticket.

*Frank Booty*
Frank Booty is a freelance editor and writer, contributing to many market-leading titles and books in the fields of business, IT and networking, and manufacturing. An award-winning journalist, he has also devised and chaired many conferences in the facilities management market.

*Paul Bray*
Paul Bray is a freelance business journalist who writes for the *Daily Telegraph*, the *Sunday Times*, *Nasdaq International* and other publications.

*Guy Clapperton*
Guy Clapperton, editor, is a freelance journalist of ten years' standing. He is editorial associate and columnist for *The Guardian*'s 'Business Solutions' supplement and also contributes on business and technology subjects to *The Financial Times*, *The Evening Standard*, *The Observer*, *The Daily Express*, *Director* and numerous other publications. An occasional broadcaster and speaker, this is his third book for the Corporate Research Foundation.

*Jim Dow*
Jim Dow has been a newspaper journalist for more than 40 years. He spent 23 years at *The Scotsman*, latterly as Business Editor for nine years, and now runs his own public relations/freelance journalist business in Edinburgh.

*Candice Goodwin*
Candice Goodwin has worked for twenty years as a journalist specialising in technology and how people use it at work. Based in London, she has contributed to a range of UK business and technical publications, including *The Telegraph*, *New Scientist*, *Computing*, *Computer Weekly*, and *Accountancy*. She now combines writing with freelance usability and ergonomics consultancy.

*Dennis Jarrett*
Dennis Jarrett is a professional writer, specialising primarily in IT applications and the use of the Internet. A trained technical writer, he moved into journalism and then magazine management; he has edited many of the better-known UK computer magazines. He now runs his own operation, offering marketing consultancy for SMEs, editorial consultancy for publishers, and the design and delivery of training courses and seminars for a variety of business uses.

*Jonathan Lamb*
Jonathan Lamb is a writer on business and organisational issues. He has contributed to a number of magazines, including *People Management*, *Professional Recruiter* and *People Performance*. He has also carried out client-based research in a variety of industry sectors, from automotive to print advertising. Jonathan completed an MSc in Business Psychology this year and plans to transfer his specialist knowledge into a consulting role.

*Hubeena Nadeem*
Beena Nadeem graduated with a post-graduate in journalism from London's City University in 2000. From there she went on to work for a range of titles at Haymarket before going on to edit an environmental trade magazine for a short time. Her current role involves working and writing for *Diversity Today* magazine, an Ethnic Media Group publication. She also freelances in travel writing.

*Val Proctor*
Originally from South Africa, Val Proctor has been in the world of journalism since graduating in 1987. During her career, she has worked for various newspapers in Johannesburg, done a stint in corporate PR and edited several trade publications, both in the IT and marketing fields. Now living in Hertfordshire, where she continues to freelance and work part-time for independent school, Haileybury, she is happiest exploring the rural country lanes on her bicycle.

*Rachelle Thackray*
Rachelle Thackray has written for publications including *The Independent* and *The Guardian* and last year published her first book: *20/20 Hindsight*, a Virgin Business Guide profiling start-up stories from 100 British businesses of the 1990s.

*Roger Trapp*

Roger Trapp is an experienced business journalist and corporate writer with in-depth knowledge of management issues, enterprise and a variety of related topics. He was on the business staff of the *Independent* and *Independent on Sunday* for more than a decade and – as part of his focus on enterprise – took responsibility for the *Independent on Sunday's* pioneering annual survey of fast-growing companies. He has also been a regular writer for a variety of magazines covering a range of subjects, but particularly management, finance and enterprise.

*David Vickery*

David Vickery is a freelance writer who holds an honours degree in Economics. He has worked for the advertising agencies Valin Pollen and DMB&B Financial. He has also held senior writing positions at Abbey National Treasury Services and the London Stock Exchange. As a freelance writer he has written for a wide range of blue chip companies, mainly but not exclusively in the financial sector. He is married to Angie.

# Panel of Advisors

People in Business
Reward Group

# BRITAIN'S
# TOP
# EMPLOYERS

# <sup>The</sup>Abbey National
### Group

Abbey National is a major player in the UK financial services business, with more than 15 million customers and around 28,000 staff. It is the country's second-largest mortgage lender and a retail bank, with over 750 branches; it also runs the Internet-only bank cahoot. In addition to retail banking, Abbey has two other divisions – Wholesale Banking and the Wealth Management and Long-Term Savings division. The company is centred in the UK, but it also has international operations in Europe, Australia and the USA.

In November 2002 Abbey National announced a change in strategy that will see the Group concentrate on the provision of personal financial services in the UK.

**Scorecard:**

| | |
|---|---|
| Remuneration and benefits | **** |
| Progressive attitude | **** |
| Opportunity for promotion | **** |
| Training, development and education | **** |
| Working atmosphere and environment | **** |

**Biggest plus:**
The recognition that delivering customer satisfaction in a services business depends crucially on employee satisfaction. Abbey National believes that keeping its people, and keeping them happy, will result in more and better business.

**Biggest minus:**
The danger that past actions might catch up with the company. Abbey's excursions in the turbulent waters of wholesale banking have produced substantial losses; and while not threatening the group's viability, it does make it potentially more vulnerable to takeover by a stronger competitor.

Abbey National plc
Abbey National House
2 Triton Square
Regent's Place
London NW1 3AN
Websites:
http://www.abbeynational.com
http://www.jobsatabbeynational.co.uk

# Abbey National plc

## The Business

Abbey National was the first of the British mutual building societies to seek a wider market by converting to bank status in 1989. Acquiring another major building society in the mid-1990s made the Abbey one of the country's leading financial service businesses. Despite talk of merger and takeovers, it remains independent; some City analysts do believe it needs a partner to sustain its business in the face of intense competition. However, in 2001 the DTI blocked Lloyds TSB's proposed bid for Abbey National on competition grounds. This ruling is still seen by some commentators as preventing the major UK banks taking over Abbey National.

The Abbey's strategy for growth has been based on international expansion and corporate wholesale banking (dealing in bonds and other investments), but that has proved expensive – provision for bad debt in that operation was largely responsible for the profits warning issued in 2002.

Abbey National remains one of the UK's largest companies, with a market capitalisation in excess of £7 billion. It is the UK's sixth largest bank, and the second largest provider of mortgages and savings (behind HBOS, formerly Halifax); it offers the full range of personal retail banking products via some 750+ High Street branches spread throughout the UK and through its telephone banking services; it sells life assurance, investments and pension products; it has a well developed Internet proposition (including cahoot, Abbey's separate Internet banking brand); it offers wealth management and offshore services; it has a sizeable wholesale banking operation, although the future scale of this business is under review.

Abbey National is predominantly UK based, with primary Head Office locations in London, Milton Keynes, Bradford and Glasgow. The group also has small operations in Ireland, France, Italy, Gibraltar, Hong Kong, Dubai and the United States.

*your responsibility is to deliver the expected contribution and to work continuously to improve your performance. Our responsibility is to provide you with the support and opportunity to do this and to reward your contribution accordingly*

## Company Culture and Style

Abbey National says that it has a single aim – to make life easier for its customers. There are obvious business advantages in that approach, of course, and indeed this is the company's strategy to differentiate itself from competitors. But it does imply a relaxed, creative approach that should encourage the kind of people who can apply some imagination to spotting gaps in the market and new ways to deliver value. The result, says Abbey, is a working environment that is self-assured but never self-satisfied.

One example is the award-winning 'franchising' business model that gives considerable autonomy to groups of branches in a local market. They run their own profit-and-loss accounts, and they make many of their own business decisions. The company also appears to recognise that personal circumstances can change over time, not least because it has traditionally employed a large number of women and has had to acknowledge the need for flexibility. Today it can offer various options to provide that – including an enhanced maternity package, paternity leave, flexible working, home working, and even the chance to take a career break.

Abbey has a long and honourable commitment to diversity, extending for instance to Regional Diversity Action Groups that review recruitment practices and build links with local communities. Community involvement more generally is important, and the Abbey National Charitable Trust has given £12 million to charities since 1990. The company has also run a Community Partnership programme since 1998; this provides a range of resources, including a donations programme, Matched Donations for staff charity fund raising activities (one in ten of Abbey's staff use this scheme), local staff charity committees called Community Partnership Groups, a database of volunteering opportunities for staff, Matched Time Off during working hours for staff to help local organisations which they support in their own time, and grants for practical community projects. There's also a facility for staff to adopt personal work objectives that are community-related.

Abbey National is one of the few British banks with an official environmental policy, starting from the principle that environmental considerations must be integrated into all activities.

## Human Resources

The HR function is given a good deal of prominence, part of the policy of personal development that recognises the value of employees in a people-based service-oriented business. There is considerable investment in systems and procedures for this, and HR directors sit on the group's top management committees.

Abbey National typically recruits up to 150 graduates each year, and has intensive training programmes geared to this intake. The group does emphasise that ability and competence are more important than a vocational degree, and particularly at branch level many of the managers have reached significant positions from modest beginnings in Customer Service roles.

## Career Opportunity and Development

Abbey has developed a structured but flexible approach to people management that integrates reward and development – 'your responsibility is to deliver the expected contribution and to work continuously to improve your performance. Our responsibility is to provide you with the support and opportunity to do this and to reward your contribution accordingly.'

This is enshrined in the Personal Development Plan that each employee works out with their line manager. The Plan includes targets for development as well as performance.

Training and development are central to the work environment; Abbey National has a sophisticated in-house training system for a variety of needs, delivered in a variety of ways (including e-learning and the use of external providers). The company is prepared to support staff through professional or further academic qualifications by offering study leave, payment of course fees, and other assistance.

## Remuneration

In a business like financial services, the focus on the customer necessarily means a focus on the employees who have to deliver the service: if customer satisfaction is the prime goal, employee satisfaction is not far behind.

Apart from developing an appealing work environment, the group has put together a competitive package of rewards and career development opportunities. Abbey aims to pay salaries in line with its competitors (it sees opportunity rather than merely an inflated income as the major plus for new recruits). Annual pay awards are based on performance. There's also a discretionary profit share scheme, based partly on the group's overall performance and partly on the performance of the employee's business area.

Abbey National operates a Sharesave scheme, saving money from salary for three, five or seven years. Members can cash in the savings plus a bonus, or use all or part of it to buy discounted shares in the plc. There's also a tax-efficient Partnership Shares Scheme, and occasionally the board sanctions share grants and/or purchase options linked to specific corporate milestones; they are available to all employees, and senior executives may additionally receive the usual discretionary share options.

In common with most employers, Abbey has closed its Final Salary pension scheme but operates a matched-contributions Stakeholder Pension scheme (you pay contributions of between 3 and 8 per cent of your salary, Abbey matches them).

Other benefits include free membership of Abbey's Sports and Social Club, and the company has negotiated discounts on a whole range of retail items, from electrical goods to holidays. There are also discounts on Abbey National products such as personal loans, credit cards and travel insurance. Other benefits include season ticket loans and discounted BUPA cover. New graduate recruits may be eligible for a Relocation Package worth up to £1,000.

# The Future

Abbey National saw some significant changes in its top management towards the end of 2002, and a significant shift in corporate strategy has resulted. The new CEO Luqman Arnold has very clear plans to focus Abbey National on markets where it believes it has the expertise and competitive advantage to succeed, namely addressing the personal financial services needs of the individual UK customer – expect to see more emphasis on the Abbey National brand.

A B
M B
V D
 O

Abbott Mead Vickers*BBDO is the UK's largest advertising agency, with billings of £381 million in 2001. The winner of countless creative awards, it has built an enviable reputation for innovation and creative excellence, and an impressive blue-chip client list. The firm has just under 300 staff, all based at its modern offices in Central London.

**Scorecard:**

| | |
|---|---|
| Remuneration and benefits | *** |
| Progressive attitude | *** |
| Opportunity for promotion | **** |
| Training, development and education | **** |
| Working atmosphere and environment | ***** |

**Biggest plus:**
Combines high achievement with a caring and friendly approach.

**Biggest minus:**
Times are tough in advertising, and being at the top can make it tougher still.

Abbott Mead Vickers*BBDO Ltd
151 Marylebone Road
London NW1 5QE
Tel: 020 7616 3500
Fax: 020 7616 3600
Website: www.amvbbdo.co.uk

# Abbott Mead Vickers*BBDO

## The Business

In addition to the display of current work, the reception area of advertising agency Abbott Mead Vickers*BBDO (AMV) contains a gigantic television set, a free cafe/bar overflowing with apples and bananas, and a grand piano.

AMV is by far the largest ad agency by billings in the UK (£100 million larger than its nearest rival), and has a large blue-chip client list – including the BBC, BT, Guinness, Sainsbury's, Volvo and Yellow Pages – some of whom have been with the agency for over 20 years.

AMV has won more creative awards than any of its competitors, including British Television Agency of the Year (several times), Worldwide Agency of the Year in the American Clio awards, and (according to

*We're very 'grown up' and we don't go in for stand-up rows. It's all about respecting an individual's capabilities and nurturing, not squashing, them into a performance*

Channel 4 viewers) creators of the best ad of all time: the Guinness 'surfer' ad, and most recently the Gunn Report 2002 which put AMV at fifth Best Agency in the world.

Founded in 1977 by Messrs Abbott, Mead and Vickers (Peter Mead still works there full-time), AMV was floated in the 1990s, and was bought by international media giant Omnicom in 1997. The agency now forms part of Omnicom's BBDO group, comprising a network of advertising, public relations, contract publishing and other communications firms, which often work closely together.

AMV has not been immune to recent economic storms, and had to make 13 people redundant in 2002. But the firm honoured its commitment to its graduate intake of that year, and plans to continue graduate recruiting to bring new talent into the business.

## Company Culture and Style

Lots of companies tell you they really care about both their work and their people, but in AMV's case this rings true. The quality and success of the agency's work speaks for itself, and it definitely sees itself as a big ideas company. 'Being number one in talent and creativity is much more important to me than being number one by size,' says the firm's Deputy Managing Director, Farah Ramzan.

But despite being fiercely competitive about its work, AMV discourages excessive competition between its staff. If, for example, two creative teams work on a pitch, both sets of results are often used in the presentation – unusual for the advertising business.

'We're a very collaborative culture,' says Ramzan. 'We're very 'grown up' and we don't go in for stand-up rows. It's all about respecting an individual's capabilities and nurturing, not squashing, them into a performance. We believe in performance, but not at any cost. It's one of the things our clients like about us.'

AMV takes people from any university and background, and the agency has a diversity of staff. The kind of people who flourish there are good team players who are bright, hard-working and switched-on.

They also need to be good at sharing information. 'As soon as something good has happened, we share it – write a case study, send an email,' says Ramzan. A regular forum for sharing is the monthly company get-together in the bar (where there is something stronger on offer than just apples and bananas). Ramzan says: 'People read out letters from clients, and talk about their successes – and failures. You're allowed to weep openly!'

The average age at AMV is 32 – oldish for an ad agency – and more than half the staff are women, including the chief executive and deputy managing director, so the culture is very family-friendly. Part-time working and job-sharing are encouraged, and although late nights and early mornings are sometimes unavoidable, people are encouraged to make it up to themselves and their families afterwards. At Christmas the office is converted into a grotto, and Peter Mead dresses up as Santa to distribute presents to all the staff's children.

## Human Resources

AMV gets hundreds of applications for the 6–8 places on its annual graduate training programme. Successful applicants will need ambition and talent, team spirit and personality, a good degree, and a willingness to learn. 'We have a real mix of people, we're not looking for an archetype,' says Sarah Morgan, AMV's HR manager.

Motivated people who don't get on the scheme can still join as junior staff and work their way up from the post room – as founder Peter Mead once did. There is also the opportunity of 2–4 week summer placements.

AMV is so prestigious that it seldom needs to advertise more senior appointments. There are examples of people who leave, further their experience elsewhere, and then come back, and the firm likes to stay on good terms with ex-employees, for example AMV's Development Director, who started her career in account management within the Agency, left for two years to pursue Training and Development consultancy and returned to the Agency recently as their Development Director.

Staff stay 4–5 years on average – a long time for the ad industry – and loyalty is very strong. 'We do look after our staff and we're a very friendly organisation. Our people believe in what we're doing,' says Morgan.

# Career Opportunity and Development

'As a management team, we're not just building the business – we're building the people who are building the business,' says Ramzan. She believes that to retain people, you need to develop them early, allowing them to voice their opinions, make pitches and run teams as soon as they are ready. Promotion is by ability, and takes place as rapidly as the individual can handle it – e.g. becoming an account manager after just a year – and the board numbers about 80 people, a quarter of the company.

The work of the agency divides into three streams: account management, planning and creative. Account managers specialise in client-facing and sales, making pitches and briefing the creative teams. The planning people focus on research and consumer insights, and there is quite a lot of crossover between the two streams. Creative people – the 'ideas men' (most of them are still men) who draw the pictures and write the words – tend to stay within this discipline, however.

Graduate recruits receive up to a year of structured training, both on and off the job, but AMV believes in ongoing training for all its staff, and recently appointed a full-time development director to manage it – very unusual in this industry. Reduced budgets mean most training has been brought in-house, but AMV has found this to be a benefit, and senior staff share their knowledge and experience. Staff are also sponsored to take professional qualifications, MBAs, etc.

People have a lot of say in their career development, with appraisals once or twice a year, closely linked to training and development planning. And they are encouraged to move between campaigns and clients to gain and share experience. BBDO is a large and diverse group, and staff are sometimes seconded to other group companies, occasionally abroad.

# Remuneration

AMV pays competitively and offers a wide range of benefits, including private medical insurance, life insurance, personal health insurance, and an optional contributory pension plan (4 per cent from the individual, 6 per cent from AMV, which increases on service), senior staff receive performance-related bonuses, but due to the Agency's central London location and increasing tax penalties, the agency no longer offers company cars.

There are no set grades or pay scales, but close attention is paid to external market rates and internal comparisons, ensuring fairness and consistency. The last annual pay rise (in July 2002) was 3 per cent – lower than usual owing to tough economic times.

Long-serving staff can take sabbaticals – one month after 10 years, two months after 15 years and three months after 20 years. In addition to the 20 days' annual leave, staff are given half-day holidays before bank holidays. Carrying over unused holiday is not allowed, working yourself into the ground earns you no brownie points at AMV.

## The Future

In a recession, many businesses are under pressure to cut comms expenditure. This, combined with a more general reappraisal of the advertising and comms business, means that things are unlikely to be easy for AMV for a while.

'The industry is facing enormous pressure to rethink its practices and commercial behaviour,' says Ramzan. There is a lot of pressure to do more for less money and we must constantly take the debate back to the value of our ideas and the proven return on investment to our client brands and businesses.

On the plus side, says Ramzan, 'We have an experienced management team and a disproportionate share of the best talent, which gives us an inherent ability to face the future without fear.' In addition, AMV has an impressive list of high-profile clients, who believe in advertising and have been loyal to the agency for years or even decades.

'The main thing will be to keep our sense of purpose very strong, and remember to have fun doing it', says Ramzan.

The Accor Group is one of the world's leading hotel businesses, responsible for brands including Sofitel, Novotel, Ibis and others. It covers all market sectors – budget, mid-scale and five stars, and has some 3,700 hotels throughout the world. It began life by offering the first Novotel in France in 1967 after its founders noted the success of the out-of-town hotel service in America. It now operates in 90 countries and is listed on the Bourse, the French Stock Exchange.

**Scorecard:**

| | |
|---|---|
| Remuneration and benefits | **** |
| Progressive attitude | ***** |
| Opportunity for promotion | **** |
| Training, development and education | **** |
| Working atmosphere and environment | **** |

**Biggest plus:**
The empowerment the company offers its managers.

**Biggest minus:**
The Group has grown quickly, so communications can sometimes be difficult but you're encouraged to use your own initiative and if you have a good idea you are expected to implement it.

Accor UK & Ireland Hotels
255 Hammersmith Road
Hammersmith
London W6 8SJ
Tel: 020 8237 7474
Fax: 020 8237 7410
Email: HR_UK@accor-Hotels.com
Website: www.accor.com

# Accor Group

## The Business

The Accor Group is the third largest hotel group in the world and prides itself on covering all areas of this market – the Sofitels for the luxury market, Mercure and Novotel at the middle market and five brands in the economy market: Ibis, Formule1, Motel 6, Etap and Red Roof Inns. It has grown from its humble beginnings in France both organically and by judicious acquisition. It enjoys a wide geographical spread in its business, working in all continents, while retaining an absolute commitment to its core values of customer service.

It has a history of innovation. At the time its first hotel opened, the idea of fully-serviced hotels with en suite facilities on the outskirts of a major town was virtually unheard of; it has gone further and put hotels into areas that are not widely populated by the competition, such as China, and areas within other countries that aren't near airports or International cities.

It also operates a number of other businesses – Accor Services, for example, which provides vouchers or tokens that are offered by employers and governments in place of cash payments. The majority of such schemes worldwide are operated by Accor; its main focus, however, remains the hotel industry.

*In a survey conducted among staff, 86 per cent of employees thought the company did whatever it took to satisfy customers, 82 per cent thought customer service came first every day and 78 per cent thought employees got their greatest satisfaction from customer contact.*

## Company Culture and Style

Many companies profiled in this book describe their ethos as entrepreneurial. Accor's HR Director, Philip Addison, prefers to think of Accor's personnel as responsible and empowered. Managers can make their own decisions within Accor and they absolutely have permission to make mistakes (or 'learn', to use the alternative phrase); this isn't a company in which, for example, a member of staff with a problem gets referred to the HR department; managers are encouraged to be hands-on and take responsibilty for their teams.

The company likes innovation and it likes serving customers. In a survey conducted among staff, 86 per cent of employees thought the company did whatever it took to satisfy customers, 82 per cent thought customer service came first every day and 78 per cent thought employees got their greatest satisfaction from customer contact. Tellingly, 82 per cent were proud to belong to the Group and 78 per cent of managers agreed with the company's strategy.

The co-founders still exercise a lot of influence over the culture of the business, leading to a can-do attitude. 'In the early days they'd say to someone, you're opening a hotel in Outer Mongolia, and they'd just go and get on with it,' says Addison. This is known as 'L'esprit Accor'. The business has matured but the same attitude of 'we can achieve this' permeates it, and not just if you've been with the business for ages: 'If you do your job well you won't be held back by hierarchy or anything else, they're happy for new people to have ideas,' says Human Resources Manager, Jackie Allen.

This means communications are very open and the management structure is as flat as it can be given a staff of 147,000. There is a formalised open door policy, helped along by the electronic innov@ccor, a suggestion box on the company intranet.

The other thing that it is important to understand about Accor, and which may not be apparent at first glance, is its awareness of its place in the world. As a business that operates a lot in the Far East for example, it is aware of the problems with child prostitution and is active in campaigning for and funding charities acting to eradicate this and helping its young victims; it also takes its environmental responsibilities seriously and considers this very carefully when developing new hotel projects.

## Human Resources

If you want to work somewhere in which managers can divest their responsibilities for personnel to the centralised HR department, you can basically cross Accor off your list of potential employers. Addison is determined that such policies don't work, giving management licence to shirk rather than embrace its responsibilities. Recruitment outside the Web happens at local level with the HR department supporting and facilitating.

That said, the company enacted an Ethics in Management Charter in 1990 and co-founded the Corporate Social Responsibility (CSR) network against exclusion in 1995. It was also among the first businesses to establish a European work council before it became a legal requirement. It may be largely a hands-off HR department but it is also one that isn't afraid to innovate and lead the rest of the market.

## Career Opportunity and Development

Training and career development opportunities are vast within Accor. All jobs are advertised on the corporate intranet but not all are advertised outside, as preference is given to internal candidates. Accor has a lively HR website, including AccorJobs (www.accor.com/jobs) and the Jobs Skills Guide that allows you to check the job functions for which you want to apply against your existing skills, giving you the perfect chance to make a case for more training either at your annual (as a minimum) appraisal or at any other time with your line manager.

People wanting to investigate further career progression within the Group are invited to Accor Career Days, in which job openings worldwide are discussed and made available.

Training happens at all levels, either via Accor Trainers or external bodies such as Cornell University, and the structures have been well thought out. It has a scheme called Progres, where a new employee can move through bronze, silver, gold and platinum standards of training and knowledge of the hotel trade, leading to a junior management level (and during which time they will see their salary increase as the various accreditations are added to their file). The company takes training very seriously and has its own Corporate University, the Accor Acadamie, in which it invested 6 million euros during 2001 to make it a state-of-the-art facility.

Management skills are offered by Accor Trainers in conjunction with the Acadamie Accor. The Management Development Programme offers a fast track to General Management, as well as specifics on financial management, team leadership and numerous others in a modular course – and any cynics wondering whether this is simply a matter of window dressing should note that sixteen of the UK's General Managers are in their jobs as a direct result of following this course.

In addition to core skills training, the company offers less formal courses, through distance learning on its intranet (and every hotel has a PC dedicated to the staff for this purpose) and CD-ROMs, including one introduced in 2003 on 'Welcoming Disabled Guests' – Accor being one of the supporters of the European Year of the Disabled in 2003.

## Remuneration

Clearly Accor has to be competitive to retain its staff and the packages on offer are as good as would be expected from a substantial concern in the hotel market. Salaries are competitive against the local market and bonuses are available to managers, amounting to up to 45 per cent of their salaries. Addison is quick to point out that a lot of managers actually get significant bonus payments, unlike a lot of companies in which the stated bonus has so many strings it is difficult to achieve.

Recognition of hard work is important to the business, hence the increments when people move along the Progres scale, and a good pension scheme. In addition employees get an Accor card, a discount card for very cheap rates in the company's hotels after a year's employment. Share schemes are offered in most countries, dependent on local legislation, and everyone is encouraged to own shares, and 20,000 staff members opt to do so.

## The Future

Not entirely unpredictably, Accor's aim is to grow profitably and sustainably, but also responsibly. Its environmental sensibilities, its helping clamp down on the sex tourism industry and its openness to new ideas on disability reflect a company coming to terms with the fact that it's heading for its forties; it wants to behave like a responsible, as well as a wealthy, corporate citizen and is making many of the right moves to do so.

In terms of jobs, the good news for people liking the sound of the company is that there are going to be plenty of them. In the UK alone the organisation reckons on doubling its presence, so more personnel will be required. The scope to move about internationally and between disciplines, and to move upwards rapidly if you have the drive, should make the company an attractive career option.

# ADMIRAL

Admiral is one of the pioneers in direct insurance, which enables customers to obtain lower insurance premiums through cutting out insurance agents and their commission charges. Since launching in January 1993, the privately-owned Cardiff-based company has grown from nothing to a business with 1,500 staff, 700,000 customers and in 2002 turnover of £380 million. Though it has spawned various brands designed to target certain segments of the population, the business remains focused on car insurance. The industry is highly competitive and also extremely cyclical, but Chief Executive, Henry Engelhardt, says the Admiral group remains profitable.

**Scorecard:**

| | |
|---|---|
| Remuneration and benefits | *** |
| Progressive attitude | ***** |
| Opportunity for promotion | **** |
| Training, development and education | **** |
| Working atmosphere and environment | ***** |

**Biggest plus:**
The informality and encouragement of ideas and initiative.

**Biggest minus:**
The intense competition in the industry and need to stay ahead of rivals.

Admiral Group Ltd
Capital Tower
Greyfriars Road
Cardiff CF10 3AZ
Tel: 0870 243 2431
Fax: 0870 013 2172
Website: www.admiral.com

# Admiral Group Ltd

## The Business

Admiral opened for business in January 1993 as one of the early competitors for Direct Line in the market for car insurance that enables drivers to deal direct with insurers without having to deal through, and pay commission to, agents. Originally part of a Lloyd's of London managing agent, it was the subject of a management buyout in 1999. Now, venture capitalists own about 55 per cent of the business, the management and staff hold 35 per cent and the original Names have the remainder.

Since the mid-1990s, the company has been split between two locations – Cardiff and Swansea. It has also developed subsidiary brands, with what chief executive Henry Engelhardt calls 'icon' brand names that are easily remembered, such as Diamond, for women drivers; Gladiator, for 'white van man' and other commercial users; Bell, for Credit Card payers and Elephant.co.uk, which is an internet service. The newest development is confused.com, another internet service that enables would-be customers to compare quotes from a variety of insurers before buying.

*People who like what they do, do it better...We go out of our way to make sure that staff enjoy what they do*

Engelhardt – an American who was marketing manager at another direct insurer, Churchill Insurance, before being appointed head of the management team planning what was to become Admiral in 1991 – sees it as a strength that much of that team is still in place.

As a direct insurer, the company could be based anywhere and Cardiff was chosen for the head office largely because of the support the fledgling company was offered by the local development agency. But Admiral has committed itself to the area through such community projects as sponsoring the buses on New Year's Eve and Henry's Pot, a fund to which employees can apply for a few hundred pounds towards particular needs at organisations with which they are involved in their social lives.

## Company Culture and Style

Informality is the key at Admiral. It is most obvious in employees' appearance, with a multitude of styles of dress resulting from Engelhardt's entreaties for them to be themselves. 'We hope the people we hire are intelligent enough to figure out how to dress to come to the office,' says Engelhardt, who himself favours the 'smart-casual' look. He adds that if somebody feels uncomfortable in a suit and tie, that is likely to come across in their dealings with customers.

Engelhardt also distrusts mission statements and corporate visions in that they encourage 'management by hypocrisy'. Instead, he and his colleagues adopt a simple philosophy: 'People who like what they do, do it better.' He adds: 'We go out of our way to make sure that staff enjoy what they do.'

One aspect of this policy is the 'ministry of fun' that rotates around departments organising events and initiatives, such as a 'Dress-up Friday'. There are also many social evenings and parties.

Obviously, different roles within the company attract different sorts of people, and Engelhardt also recognises that the various sub-brands will attract different sorts of people and different approaches to managing them. 'We believe in tribalism', he says. 'Different areas can be different.'

He believes that this 'small is beautiful' approach improves morale because 'nobody wants to feel like a needle in a haystack'. However, there is also a strong belief in communication, with managers charged with ensuring their staff know what is happening in the company.

About half the top team of 14 is female, with two of them working shorter weeks to accommodate their child-care needs.

The keenness to deal with work/life balance issues has also led to the company experimenting with outsourcing calls it receives in the evenings and at weekends to countries in different time zones to reduce the number of people who have to work anti-social hours.

Engelhardt reckons an illustration of the relaxed and friendly atmosphere is the number of marriages between colleagues, including one involving members of his senior team. But he also stresses that there is a sound business case for doing things this way. The emphasis on creating a carefree environment is balanced by 'making sure everything we do produces the desired effect at the bottom,' he says. 'If having all this fun meant that customers got angry we wouldn't do it.'

## Human Resources

A significant proportion of the 1,500 staff employed by Admiral work in one or other of the two call centres the company operates in Cardiff and Swansea. In addition, an operation in Bangalore handles 'out-of-hours' calls, after an experiment in routing the calls to a centre in the United States was called off due to a staff turnover rate of 100 per cent.

Keen to stress that Admiral does not operate the 'battery hen' approach of many call centres, Engelhardt says that the company's employee attrition rate is about 20 to 30 per cent, significantly below that at many similar organisations.

There are no set minimum qualifications for new employees. Instead, in common with many of today's employers, Admiral looks for enthusiasm, or a cheerful attitude, as well as in most roles an easy telephone manner. The company centres its recruitment efforts on the local area. In addition, almost every job is advertised internally and employees are encouraged to move between departments within the company. 'We're happy to promote talent, wherever it comes from', says Engelhardt.

As part of the commitment to providing 'a lot of training', a three- to four-week induction programme is followed by each employee agreeing a personal development plan with management.

The company accepts that many of the roles are carried out by graduates and school leavers for a short while before they move on to other organisations and types of work. But there is no bar on leavers returning and the company is prepared to offer flexible or short-time working for mothers and others who need help of this sort.

## Career Opportunity and Development

In keeping with its relaxed approach, Admiral has little in the way of formal career development. Instead of joining a graduate training programme, say, new employees start in an area deemed most appropriate and work their way up.

Nor does the company put a lot of effort into formal appraisal procedures. Indeed, Engelhardt points out how each individual's annual appraisal report has been reduced from two pages to just two questions – relating to performance and behaviour. This was a response to the view that managers were putting off carrying out appraisals because of the time involved in sitting down with the employees for whom they were responsible and on an individual basis working their way through a list of issues.

However, in a further sign of how Admiral allows the various parts of the business to operate in a quasi-autonomous manner, managers who were happy to use the old approach have been allowed to continue with it.

Just as he is suspicious of mission statements, Engelhardt is concerned that too much emphasis on career development can create unreasonable expectations about the speed at which individuals will be promoted or about the range of experience they will gain. However, he has said that employees are encouraged to 'better themselves at the company's expense' and the organisation takes an open-minded approach to supporting staff through examinations and other educational programmes.

With, as yet, no overseas operations, Admiral cannot offer international travel as an incentive for joining. But, as a capital city in an area rich in the arts, Cardiff offers much in the way of concerts, galleries and other cultural attractions, as well as spectator sport, while both the coast and the countryside are within easy reach. It and Swansea also suffer from less traffic congestion than other British cities.

## Remuneration

Admiral is, in the words of Engelhardt, 'as egalitarian as we think we can be'. This means no company cars, no reserved parking spaces for management (the waiting list for passes for local car parks is based on length of service), the same style of desks and chairs for everybody and even the same holidays, leave starts at 20 days and rises, with length of service, to a maximum of 28.

As a privately-owned company, Admiral does not offer employee stock options, though some management and staff own about 35 per cent of the business and there is a Staff Trust, where units are distributed for length of service and position.

The company claims to be a 'median' payer, offering market rates and monitoring them regularly to ensure they are up to date.

There is a strong emphasis on performance and, for sales staff, bonuses can represent up to 60 per cent of pay. Performance also plays a part in deciding the level of annual increases. Profit sharing has been in place for several years.

While the company does not have its own pension scheme, it matches employees' contributions to their own plans up to a maximum of 6 per cent of salary. Admiral also provides employees with subsidised gym membership and offers discounts with various local merchants.

## The Future

Engelhardt claims that Admiral is the most efficient operator in the motor industry 'as far as we can measure it'. As such, it is profitable and therefore optimistic of being able to ride the cycle of what is inevitably a cyclical industry. Its internet-based business confused.com, which enables customers to compare premiums from different providers, is an indicator of the future direction the company may take. But Engelhardt is wary of changing too much.

'We're really developing the core business. We feel we're pretty good at car insurance. Why muck it up by getting into things we aren't so good at?'

# AEA TECHNOLOGY

## RAIL

AEA Technology Rail (AEATR) provides commercial and engineering consultancy services to the transport industry. It also makes a range of hardware and software products for transport-related functions such as asset protection, signalling and operational control.

AEATR has around 1,200 employees spread across four basic lines of business: management consultancy, infrastructure, trains and systems, and products. Its engineering staff are mainly based in its Derby head office, with the management consultancy division based in central London and Warrington. It also has small overseas operations in Spain, France, the Netherlands, North America and Taiwan.

Part of the AEA Technology group, the company reported profits of £12 million on turnover of £75 million in 2001.

**Scorecard:**

| | |
|---|---|
| Remuneration and benefits | *** |
| Progressive attitude | *** |
| Opportunity for promotion | **** |
| Training, development and education | **** |
| Working atmosphere and environment | *** |

**Biggest plus:**
A climate that encourages and rewards technical excellence.

**Biggest minus:**
A bureaucratic culture persists in some areas of the company.

AEA Technology Rail
Jubilee House
4 St. Christopher's Way
Pride Park
Derby DE24 8LY
Tel: 01332 221000
Fax: 01332 221008
Website:www.aeat.com/rail

# AEA Technology Rail (AEATR)

## The Business

Despite its name, AEA Technology Rail (AEATR) provides commercial and engineering consultancy services to the entire transport industry, including road and air as well as rail. It also produces hardware and software products for transport-related functions such as asset protection, signalling and operational control.

Like its parent company AEA Technology, AEATR emerged from the privatisation of a former public sector research organisation. It was born in 1996 out of the former British Rail Research organisation. In 1998 it acquired Transportation Consultants International (TCI), and together these two organisations formed what is now a thriving and dynamic business.

Over the past couple of years AEATR has grown rapidly through acquisition, from 500 staff and a £30 million turnover two years ago to 1,200 staff and £75 million turnover today. Its strategy is to achieve superior profitability by focusing on niche markets rather than going for large market share; its 2002 profits were £12 million or 16 per cent of turnover.

*AEATR is a technically-driven company, and people who thrive there will share its commitment to engineering excellence*

The AEA Technology group, AEATR's parent, is a science and engineering organisation formed out of the UK Atomic Energy Authority. AEATR is the largest and fastest-growing operating unit, but its ability to draw on best practice and technology transfer from across the group is a major strength.

## Company Culture and Style

AEATR is a technically-driven company, and people who thrive there will share its commitment to engineering excellence. Intellectual ability is very important. A high percentage of staff are graduates, many of whom have masters' degrees, and doctorates. But as well as looking for blue-sky thinking, the company wants people who can hold their own in the commercial world and take innovative engineering products to market.

Though AEATR pays competitive market rates, this is not the place for those who simply want the highest salary, a high-profile job and an imposing title. It offers technical challenge on projects that often make a real difference to people's lives, including safety-critical development for rail operating companies, involvement in public enquiries on transport issues, and providing expert advice to government.

Though a minority – around 20–30 per cent – of its work now comes from the public sector, AEATR still retains much of the ethos of a public sector organisation, which has both positive and negative sides. On the positive side, there is a supportive approach to trade union representation and partnership. With a current policy of no compulsory redundancies, the company offers secure employment.

In the Derby head office, the culture is for technical excellence combined with commercial understanding and where staff are not measured on hours completed but quality of work, giving a healthy work/life balance. As well as the 25 days' holiday, the company enjoys additional holidays linked to public holidays. On the downside, though the culture is changing, it can still be a little slow to change.

AEATR's equal opportunities policy ensures opportunities for all and encourages applications from all sections of the community, but engineering is a notoriously male-dominated industry, so it's hardly surprising that only around 20 per cent of AEATR's staff are women. However, Managing Director, Cliff Perry, is adopting a strategy of using the graduate intake to drive culture change within the company; last year there were 12 women among its 30 graduate recruits.

## Human Resources

As already mentioned, a high proportion of AEATR's staff are graduates, many of them with higher degrees. The company takes on 30 or more new graduates a year, of which about 23 go into its engineering division.

The company approaches all universities during the recruitment milk-round, but focuses on institutions with a strong engineering or operational research background; specifically Cambridge, Sheffield, Manchester University and Imperial College, with which it has research associations but it also has strong links with Lancaster, Southampton, Newcastle and Warwick Universities. It is also taking on a growing number of graduates from outside the UK, many of them from mainland Europe.

Most of the staff AEATR recruits are engineers, but it also needs mathematicians, materials scientists, operational research and systems specialists, safety and risk consultants, project managers and economists. As the company becomes more commercially-oriented, it is looking to its graduate intake to help drive culture change within the organisation.

As well as new graduates, AEATR takes on many experienced recruits, which it finds through adverts, job sites on the Web and through recruitment consultancies. AEATR welcomes enquiries throughout the year and is happy to accept applications according to individual choice.

## Career Opportunity and Development

AEATR aims for all its engineers to achieve chartered status, and offers a structured four-year professional development scheme through the two main relevant chartered engineering institutes, the Institution of Mechanical Engineers and the

Institution of Electrical Engineers. It prides itself on having succeeded in introducing a measure of flexibility and fluidity into what have traditionally been very prescriptive schemes. Employees can also pursue certification through other industry bodies such as the British Computer Society and Institution of Civil Engineers. AEATR has also developed a Consultancy model of Continuing Professional Development designed to equip all Consultancy graduates with the necessary skills and experiences required and to meet individual development needs.

The HR department carries out a quarterly training needs analysis, on the basis of which staff may be sent on a range of internal and external courses. For example, actual or potential managers may be sent on Diploma of Management or MBA courses, while other staff may be sponsored to do masters' degrees in Rail Systems Engineering or Operational Research. The company also runs a range of internal courses covering both general topics such as stress management and specific subjects such as railway familiarisation and project management fundamentals.

As well as formal training, AEATR aims for its graduate recruits to have exposure to key knowledge domains within the industry. A system of secondment enables graduates to gain experience not only in other divisions of AEA Technology but also in external organisations, through the Engineering Passport scheme. A process is in place for identifying secondment opportunities to reflect graduates' expressed interests.

Rather than a rigid organisational hierarchy, AEATR offers a fluid structure with scope for progression within levels as well as up through management. Whereas in many organisations, the only way up is to be promoted out of the area you're good at, AEATR aims to provide an alternative career progression for talented engineers who don't want to give up engineering in order to manage. People can become technical experts with all the financial and other benefits of management status, such as company cars, without having to give up what they do best.

Conversely, the company's strategy of driving change through its graduate intake means that comparatively recent graduates who show management potential can find themselves in charge of a department of 40 people within a very short time.

AEATR's growth innovation scheme encourages staff to put forward ideas for development, and if an idea is accepted then its originator has the right to lead the development project, however junior they are.

## Remuneration

Though technical challenge, not salary, is the key driver for most AEATR staff, the company does offer above-market rates of basic pay. Salary is negotiated at local level, both on an individual basis and through the unions' collective bargaining process. As already noted, pay may reflect not only managerial status but also technical expertise; at AEATR it's possible to get paid more without having a spurious new job title.

Basic pay is topped up with a variety of bonus arrangements for all staff when company finances allow. A management bonus scheme is also in place to reward outstanding performance at senior level and appropriate sales-related incentive schemes for sales staff and management.

The company offers a competitive pension scheme and a protected share scheme called EVA – standing for Economic Value Added. The company's ex-British Rail employees also enjoy protected rights such as free rail travel for their families.

Company cars are offered to sales staff and management, with the current car policy just being changed to offer a wider range of choice. Cars can be awarded to technical experts as well as departmental managers.

Employees get 25 days' holiday a year and statutory bank holidays, and holiday allocation is flexible, with, for example, the ability to carry unused days over to the next year.

## The Future

After a series of acquisitions that have caused it to double in size in two years, AEATR now plans to enter a period of consolidation during which it will build up its business through organic growth.

Overseas markets are important to the company's future. Though the UK rail market is nearing saturation point, there's still plenty of growth potential internationally. AEATR's recent overseas acquisitions will raise its profile overseas and enable it to make the most of those opportunities.

The company is also aiming to shed its image as a rail-only specialist. It is increasingly working not just in rail but in other areas of mass transportation, which should present growing business opportunities as roads become more congested and governments here and abroad look for alternatives to the private car.

A strong believer in 'joined-up thinking', AEATR aims to work in closer collaboration with other organisations in the transport industry to develop innovative, effective transport solutions for the future.

AEGON UK has assets under management of £30 billion and is a member of the AEGON Group, one of the world's largest listed insurers. The Group companies of AEGON UK are AEGON Asset Management UK, AEGON Individual Protection, AEGON UK Services, AEGON UK Distribution Holdings, HS Administrative Services, Scottish Equitable, Scottish Equitable International.

**Scorecard:**

| | |
|---|---|
| Remuneration and benefits | **** |
| Progressive attitude | **** |
| Opportunity for promotion | *** |
| Training, development and education | ***** |
| Working atmosphere and environment | *** |

**Biggest plus:**
Ability to lead and not follow.

**Biggest minus:**
It's a financial services company.

AEGON UK plc
AEGON House
Edinburgh Park
Edinburgh EH12 9XX
Tel: 0870 600 0337
Fax: 0870 600 0338
Website: www.aegon.co.uk

# AEGON UK

## The Business

With roots dating back to 1831, AEGON UK is an interesting mix of a modern dynamic business with a UK and international dimension. It has a long history of careful, long-term husbandry of other people's money, as well as its own.

In a difficult year faced by most companies in the financial services sector it has had a good year in all its markets. Allied to its traditional outperformance in the pensions sector, the 'newer' group of activities of personal investment, institutional and retail investment sales, protection and employee benefits have all experienced strong growth.

AEGON UK is a key player in the AEGON Group, which it became part of, as Scottish Equitable, in 1994. It was a move that gave the organisation financial muscle at a time of consistent and outstanding levels of growth.

*Like any other business, you grow into it. We don't go out looking for a particular type of person. We look for people who have the potential to do the job and we invest in training so that they can do it*

The acquisition of Scottish Equitable showed, not for the last time, AEGON's aptitude for acquiring well-run, profitable organisations. The focus for AEGON UK is now on buying and building distribution capability and, to that end, it has acquired a couple of prestigious IFAs and bought majority stakes in another two. More moves like this are undoubtedly on the cards.

AEGON UK has invested over £100 million in technology in the last three years and anticipates that this will lead to a reduction in its cost base of £40 million per annum from 2003.

## Company Culture and Style

AEGON UK's continued success has had a considerable impact on the jobs market, particularly in Edinburgh.

Its growth has meant relocation within the city. In 1996 it decided to abandon its head office in St Andrew Square, which had been the home for decades of the Edinburgh life office sector but had become outmoded and technologically averse. The company moved to the outskirts of the city to a magnificent purpose-built office in Edinburgh Park, generally recognised to be one of the UK's leading business centres.

It was a radical move – others have since copied AEGON – and it had to be handled delicately in terms of staff morale, especially in the face of a growing workforce, which had to be settled in and motivated.

Around 1,400 staff moved out to the new offices but that has now grown to 3,000. The company has two major office buildings in the Park and there are staff shifts and moves between the two as the company business expands and slowly reshapes.

The group also occupies premises throughout the UK – in Lytham St Annes, home of AEGON UK Services, in Chester, the base of HS Administrative Services and in 34 Scottish Equitable branches. Outside the UK the group has offices in Dublin, Luxembourg and Italy.

A recent staff survey found that 72 per cent of the respondents agreed that AEGON UK was well led, 79 per cent agreed it was a friendly place in which to work and 62 per cent said they were satisfied with their role.

Not everybody, inevitably, is happy, and less than half the staff bothered to fill in the questionnaire, but AEGON UK says the findings will be used as part of an on-going cycle of developing, communicating and implementing plans to ensure staff satisfaction and retention.

Group Personnel Director Gareth Humphreys says: 'This survey says that this is a good place in which to work. Like any other business, you grow into it. We don't go out looking for a particular type of person. We look for people who have the potential to do the job and we invest in training so that they can do it.'

## Human Resources

The recruitment philosophy is simple enough: get people with the right skills and competence to do the work. Gareth Humphreys explains: 'We are a fair employer and do not discriminate as regards age. In a competitive market for staff you have to broaden your horizons and bring people into the industry who have not worked in financial services before.'

New members of staff take charge of their own development by working through a self-paced introductory course called Discovery, in which they learn about the group, the company's products and the market place. Further professional development is planned in consultation with employees, managers and dedicated training staff.

The age profile of the workforce is getting higher. Three years ago the company, on the basis that it is hard to replicate experience, set out to recruit over-35s and filled 150 jobs. It has since gone a step further – targeting the over-40s.

The reason: 'In the recent past we have successfully integrated large numbers of older employees into our workforce. Without doubt this has been of mutual benefit – the dynamism of the young added to the experience of the older generation is a proven winning combination.'

## Career Opportunity and Development

The selection criteria remain tough but the opportunities and rewards make it worth while. Given the growth of the company and its core position at the top of its markets, there are many promotion activities as the business expands, and the group prides itself on its training and development programmes.

The group continues to make strategic investments in distributor firms, bringing into the fold well-managed, profitable companies, which add to the skills base and create more career opportunities.

The opportunities for graduates are in the actuarial profession, investment management, business development, information systems, sales and marketing and, as the distribution arm gets longer, sales professionals. The two words to describe the kind of people in demand are 'high calibre'.

AEGON UK has an impressive track record of creating and maintaining successful partnerships. The ability to forge such relationships has provided it with the ideal platform from which to compete successfully in the domestic financial services arena.

The group believes that it forges a partnership with each employee, with talented and well-trained staff providing the bedrock on which the company builds its success.

The group says that its motto sums up its approach to its employees: 'Respect people, make money, have fun', and this is incorporated into every activity that AEGON undertakes.

Local management teams promote openness, creativity and co-operation and are encouraged to embrace change and explore the opportunities new environments offer.

Interchanges of ideas and experiences are encouraged for the greater benefit of local business operations and to engender a sense of true global community among employees.

Maximising the capabilities of employees is a constant theme and that is why there is such an emphasis on staff training and development. The recent staff survey found only 3 per cent answering 'negatively' about being proud to work for AEGON UK.

# Remuneration

AEGON UK was the first financial services company in Scotland to offer a flexible benefits package, which allows staff to tailor their remuneration package, including holidays, health and dental cover, and retail and childcare vouchers.

The package offers a wider range of benefits and levels of cover to give the employee a greater degree of control over the benefits received. Staff are also eligible for bonuses, dependent on personal and company performance, and there is a well-received pension scheme.

The remuneration varies throughout the group, depending on local market conditions, and the different needs of the staff based on their personal preferences and where they live. Horses for courses is one phrase which springs to mind. Pay and benefits generally are reckoned to be competitive and are regularly overhauled to meet the changes in the jobs marketplace.

The parent company runs an employee stock option scheme and there are seminars to explain how the system works – and it works well enough to have more than half the staff now holding AEGON stock options.

The staff survey found that 54 per cent agreed, to some extent, that benefits within AEGON were distinctive compared with other companies and about 52 per cent said AEGON was the type of company they would like to work with for a long time.

Enthusiasm for the company and working for it seems to have dimmed slightly since the previous survey; management regards staff surveys as being important and any messages coming through are always acted on so we'll keep an eye on the next one.

## The Future

Group Chief Executive, David Henderson, has set it out clearly: 'There is little doubt that consolidation in the financial services industry is going to continue apace, leaving a small group of winners and AEGON UK will be one of these winning companies. In this environment I want AEGON UK to be seen as a leader of change.'

His warning that to realise their strategic vision means becoming a 'leaner, fitter and more efficient organisation' hints at job losses in a sector where margins are being constantly squeezed and regulatory reviews move the goalposts.

There might be some squeals as the company seeks to impose what it calls a 'cost conscious culture' throughout the organisation so that it can deliver products to the market at competitive rates. Displaying its ability to spot an opportunity and take advantage of it in changing times, the company will continue its programme of buying and building distribution capacity and forging partnerships.

Air Products serves customers in technology, energy, healthcare and industrial markets worldwide providing atmospheric gases, process and speciality gases, performance materials and chemical intermediates. The company is the largest global supplier of electronic materials, hydrogen, helium and select performance chemicals. It has operations in 30 countries across the Americas, Europe, Asia, the Middle East and South Africa. Its European offices are sited in the UK, Ireland, France, Germany, the Netherlands, Belgium, Czech and Slovak Republics, Poland, Norway, Spain, Portugal and Italy. The company employs some 17,200 people worldwide and has sales of £3.4 billion.

**Scorecard:**

| | |
|---|---|
| Remuneration and benefits: | ***** |
| Progressive attitude: | **** |
| Opportunity for promotion: | **** |
| Training, development and education: | **** |
| Working atmosphere and environment: | **** |

**Biggest plus:**
The firm has an excellent approach to staff, career development and work/life balance.

**Biggest minus:**
The company's commitment to collaborative working and open communications will suit the right person admirably – but empire-builders and keepers of secrets will soon find themselves completely lost.

Air Products Plc
Hersham Place
Molesey Road
Walton on Thames
Surrey KT12 4RZ
Tel: 01932 249200
Fax: 01932 258502
Website: www.airproducts.co.uk

# Air Products

## The Business

Air Products supplies a range of industry sectors, including semiconductor manufacturing, chemicals processing, healthcare and performance industries such as paper, paints and inks. The company also designs and manufactures cryogenic and non-cryogenic equipment for air separation and other gas processing applications.

Founded in 1940 in Detroit when it was originally established to create mobile oxygen-supply equipment for soldiers, Air Products went on to establish its first UK offices in Soho during the mid-50s and diversified into chemicals, and by the early 1960s, had expanded into the rest of Europe.

Its UK operation employs over 2,000 staff, including a commercial technology centre and offices in Crewe; technology facilities in Basingstoke and an equipment manufacturing facility near Wrexham, North Wales. Its European headquarters are in Surrey. It has ISO 9001 and 9002 quality accreditations. It is quoted on the New York Stock Exchange.

*The business prides itself on its leadership in safety matters and sets consistent global standards, which often mean its safety standards are ahead of those stipulated by the local laws in some countries*

## Company Culture and Style

Air Products has a number of core values at its heart. Prime among these is the worldwide commitment to safety, health and the environment – a key matter for any company producing gaseous material. The business prides itself on its leadership in safety matters and sets consistent global standards, which often mean its safety standards are ahead of those stipulated by the local laws in some countries. On the interpersonal and skills side, the company holds integrity, respect and accountability among the most important qualities its people can have. These will typically be underpinned by a certain passion with which the employees conduct themselves and the pride they take in their performance. An ideal Air Products employee would be able to work successfully in a team environment and work collaboratively to the nth degree – mavericks and prima donnas need not apply.

The organisation is also aware of issues surrounding how it achieves its corporate objectives, and is making particular efforts to achieve true diversity by creating an environment of inclusion and respect for every employee. The popular caricature of the engineer or chemist is of a white man in a white coat; from the chief executive down, Air Products is determined to broaden its employee base and indeed has a dedicated diversity programme incorporating awareness training, skills development and communications. Evidence of this can be seen in that Air Products Europe had 73 women in managerial positions by March 2003, a threefold increase on the previous four years.

Air Products has a business-casual dress code. There are no other hard and fast rules but clearly the company employs adults and trusts their judgement as to how to dress appropriately for whom they need to meet.

In terms of creating a more flexible working environment for its employees, the company recently formalised its Alternative Working Arrangements, which give employees more flexibility on work schedules and work location when they can fit in with the company's business objectives. In this respect it can be seen that the business already outstripped the requirements of the Employment Act 2002 before it became law on 6 April 2003.

While the company demands high standards from its employees, it still believes in and supports a healthy work/life balance. The Surrey HQ offers an on-site fitness centre and subsidised access to off-site facilities at the other locations. An on-site restaurant, snack area, social club and bar are fixtures at its HQ. The social club sees a lot of activity during the summer months, in which it is used for barbecues and other family-oriented events.

## Human Resources

External recruitment happens in a number of ways and it is the HR department's task to ensure the right candidates will be aware of the vacancies. The company's website is a good starting point for would-be applicants and contains a number of details of forthcoming positions. Other recruitment routes include agencies and advertising. The HR department is also responsible for a proactive university relations programme through which graduates are welcomed into the business and sometimes earmarked for fast tracking through management training.

The HR department sees its function as very much working in partnership with the business it supports. This might sound like something all companies would claim but in this instance it is formalised through a global performance enhancement process, including performance planning, employee development, appraisals and an HR planning process. One innovation in place is an online SAP-based HR information system for all employees. Using this they can access their personal data. The overall effect is to empower managers to take more decisions by themselves without the need for reference elsewhere in the company.

## Career Opportunities

New employees get into the business in a number of ways. These include specific programmes such as the Career Development Programme (CDP), the Engineering Development Programme (EDP), and Direct Entry positions. The CDP gives the graduate entrant experience in a variety of areas by incorporating three eight-month assignments in his or her first two years with the company. A typical CDP experience might include assignments in areas such as finance, IT, sales, marketing, purchasing and human resources.

The EDP is targeted towards those working within engineering. The programme allows entrants to do three, eight-month assignments in related engineering and/or technical disciplines. The company's Direct Entry route accommodates individuals who have a specific job in mind when they join. These individuals frequently have significant prior experience and arrive with a clear career path in mind.

In terms of developing employees once they are in place, there are appraisals and periodic progress meetings with supervisors. During these sessions employees can comment on their career goals and what they need in terms of support to help them to achieve this – the managers will co-operate wherever possible whilst continuing to support the core business activities.

It is possible to progress through the company regardless of any formal qualification. Whilst a university degree is clearly a prerequisite in some of the more technical and quantitative areas of the company, nobody should enter the business and consider themselves limited by its absence – a number of successful entrants have progressed without one. Real success hinges on hard work, leadership qualities both inborn and learned, experience and the willingness to accept responsibilities.

In some companies, staff complain that their contracts and descriptions do not necessarily meet their everyday reality. Air Products says it aims to avoid this by being clear and upfront from the start, although occasionally employees will need to adapt their work to changing conditions. Air Products says it is committed to keeping as close to the job description as possible, although the reality is that change and the acceptance of it is a reality in any global business.

# Remuneration

Basic salary and variable compensation (company stock options, cash bonuses, milestone awards and team awards) are awarded on the basis of performance, linked to the company's Performance Enhancement process and/or specific company targets. Air Products encourages employees to own stock in the company and stock-based incentive schemes (deferred stock and stock options) have been a mainstay of its variable compensation programme for many years. Owning stock, the firm has observed, also encourages employees to take an additional interest in keeping track of the company's overall performance.

In terms of pensions, a variety of arrangements operate throughout Europe, but in the UK, Air Products employs a final salary/defined benefit plan. Despite many companies turning away from these plans, Air Products said it had no plans to alter its scheme as this book went to press.

Employees are entitled to a company car if it is essential for their job, or automatically at a certain level. The latter can choose between a company car or a car allowance.

# The Future

The company is planning for growth, particularly in countries where it is less established and where opportunities exist for its growth businesses. In Europe, the company expects to see continued expansion in all its core markets, especially in central and eastern Europe where its presence is still relatively small. Growth will be driven largely by its four key businesses, which are electronic materials, chemical processing, performance chemicals and healthcare.

In terms of its future staff demographics, the company is committed to nurturing an employee base that is more representative of the local populations where it operates. Granted everyone makes this claim – diversity is becoming something of a buzzword in the corporate world, but the aforementioned diversity programme puts concrete objectives around the aim. These include stronger relationships and greater innovation because of a diversity of ideas; a workforce that can relate to its local customers and the society in which it is placed; and a staff that feels truly part of the organisation for which it works. The company has made a solid start and will be pushing this policy as it continues to develop, not only as a business but as a balanced corporate citizen.

# Alliance Leicester

The Alliance & Leicester Group became a public limited company in 1997 and has a 150-year heritage as a financial institution. The bank employs approximately 9,000 people, divided between its main offices at Leicester and Bootle (near Liverpool), its contact centres at Ashford (Kent), Birmingham, Leeds and Wigan, and over 300 branches throughout the UK. Pre-tax profits in 2001 were £396 million on sales of nearly £1.3 billion. All the company's operations are in the UK.

**Scorecard:**

| | |
|---|---|
| Remuneration and benefits | **** |
| Progressive attitude | **** |
| Opportunity for promotion | ***** |
| Training, development and education | **** |
| Working atmosphere and environment | **** |

**Biggest plus:**
Relatively modest size (for a bank) and a strong customer service commitment mean committed individuals can really make a difference.

**Biggest minus:**
Will have to work hard not to be squeezed between larger full-service rivals and hyper-competitive single-product companies.

Alliance & Leicester plc
Carlton Park
Narborough
Leicester LE19 0AL
Tel: 0116 201 1000
Fax: 0116 200 4040
Website: www.alliance-leicester-group.co.uk

# Alliance & Leicester plc

## The Business

The name Alliance & Leicester first appeared on Britain's high streets in 1985, but the Group's history began 133 years earlier with the formation of the Leicester Permanent Building Society. The 1985 merger with the Alliance (founded in 1863) was, at the time, the largest building society merger ever. Five years later, Alliance & Leicester became the first building society to buy a clearing bank, when it acquired Girobank from the Post Office. In 1997, the society 'demutualised' and became a bank, listed on the Stock Exchange and part of the FTSE 100 Index.

The Retail Bank provides a full range of banking services, principally mortgages, savings, unsecured loans and current accounts. Partnerships with other institutions, such as Legal & General for insurance and MBNA for credit cards, provide the rest. Alliance & Leicester has more than six million personal customers. The Commercial Bank, which includes Girobank, focuses on cash handling, asset finance and small business banking services. Girobank handles over £80 billion a year, including a quarter of all money spent in high street retailers.

*The company has a nice mixture now, and an 'edge' and sense of urgency that it didn't have three or four years ago...Good people are progressing fast up the organisation, and being remunerated very well*

Being smaller than some of its rivals has its advantages. 'We provide the full range of banking services, but are still of a size that you can "get your arms around"', says Graham Ledward, Alliance & Leicester's Director of Group Human Resources. 'So when talented people join us, they can really make a difference.'

## Company Culture and Style

The merger of Alliance & Leicester and Girobank and the Group's subsequent flotation created huge challenges, as a building society culture (Alliance & Leicester) met a public sector culture (Girobank), and transmuted into a commercial culture. 'The company has a nice mixture now, and an 'edge' and sense of urgency that it didn't have three or four years ago,' says Ledward. 'Good people are progressing fast up the organisation, and being remunerated very well.'

Alliance & Leicester's ambition is to be the UK's most customer-focused financial services provider bar-none. It knows it will have stiff competition in this, and expects all staff to be excellent customer service providers – even on an off day! Believing that customer service begins at home, the Group has put all its staff through a customer-service training programme called 'Valuing Individual People' (VIP). This includes non-customer facing staff, who are taught to treat colleagues within the bank as customers.

'People are encouraged to bring 'the whole of themselves' into the workplace, their creativity and innovation, and we try to use this,' says Ledward. This also extends to contact centres, where the bank is moving away from strict call targets for each agent, and towards satisfying the customer, however long it takes.

Alliance & Leicester is a big advocate of the work/life balance, and its new 'brand' for staff is 'living life better'. The company recognises a number of unions. A third of staff are part-time, and a handful work from home, while branch and contact centre staff are encouraged to choose shift patterns that fit their lifestyles. Two-thirds of staff are women, and the company recently began a Women in Business programme with 120 of the most senior to help develop women's careers.

The company encourages staff to volunteer for community initiatives, such as the Right to Read scheme, helping children learn to read in Leicester, Manchester and Liverpool schools.

## Human Resources

Alliance & Leicester likes to hold onto its people, and staff turnover is falling (from 14.5 per cent in 2000 to around 10 per cent in 2002). But that still means the bank needs to recruit nearly 1,000 people a year. The graduate recruitment programme takes 10–12 people annually for a two-year management training programme, the company is starting to recruit new or recently qualified MBAs to bolster more senior management, and in 2003 it plans to start a sandwich programme for around 8–10 undergraduates. In Bootle, where the company is the largest employer, it takes on a number of YTS trainees. Applications for all jobs can be made online at the company's website.

To improve its customer service focus even further, Alliance & Leicester operates the Talent Spotters scheme, where staff can recommend people they meet outside the company who have demonstrated outstanding customer service. Three-quarters of people who apply for jobs through the scheme are accepted, and the staff member who recommended them receives £750.

The bank uses temporary staff where necessary, but prefers permanent contracts. 'We believe that if there's a permanent role we should make a permanent appointment', says Ledward. 'If we want commitment from our staff, we have to show commitment to them.'

## Career Opportunities and Development

As Alliance & Leicester provides a wide range of products and services, it can offer its staff plenty of variety and experience.

The bank likes to promote internally where possible. Jobs are advertised in a weekly bulletin and on the company intranet, and there are various promotion and reward schemes. These range from the Fledglings programme, which aims to develop talented sales advisors into branch managers and the Accelerated Leadership programme, which caters for lower-to-middle-management with senior management potential.

A reward culture operates at all levels, from Talent Spotters to Customer Service Champion Awards, which recognises employees who have consistently delivered excellent customer service to internal and external customers. Winners, who are nominated by their colleagues in the Group, are awarded a trip to Paris, the opportunity to progress in the career of their choice or a promotion in their existing role and a celebration dinner.

Alliance & Leicester operates a formal performance management process with personal development plans and regular appraisals. Competency frameworks are used to help determine promotion and rewards, and to give people a bench-mark standard. Staff are encouraged to manage their own careers and identify their opportunities.

Training combines formal classroom sessions and an increasing amount of computer-based self-learning. All new staff go through the VIP customer service programme as part of their induction. The bank also gives further education sponsorship to staff. Alliance & Leicester gained Investors in People accreditation in customer facing areas during 2001, and the majority of the Group will have achieved accreditation by the end of 2002.

# Remuneration

Alliance & Leicester is working hard to build a reward culture. Bonus schemes cover 60 per cent of staff, from senior managers to sales people. At one end of the scale are small rewards for 'going the extra mile'; at the other, some financial advisors earn 2–4 times their salary in uncapped bonuses.

The great majority of staff own shares or options, which are available through a number of schemes. 'We want staff to feel they own the business', says Ledward. The pension scheme is open to all, with contributions from both employer and employee.

The benefits package at Alliance & Leicester is becoming increasingly flexible, for example, staff can 'buy and sell' up to five days' annual holiday. Other benefits include preferential rates on healthcare and lifestyle products from eye care to holidays, and staff discounts on some of the bank's own products. Company cars are available where appropriate, and the bank is fairly flexible about what model is chosen.

Facilities at the company's main offices are wide-ranging. Bootle has a bar and social club, and both Bootle and Leicester have on-site shops, including dry cleaning services, a branch of Alliance & Leicester (of course) and a cyber cafe where staff are encouraged to use the free Internet connections in their own time.

The company believes that its total remuneration package is in keeping with its FTSE 100 status and the last three annual pay rises were inflation plus one per cent.

## The Future

Alliance & Leicester has worked hard to focus its retail banking product portfolio by offering straightforward, value-for-money products, backed up by first class customer service. This has resulted in over 700 'Best Buy' mentions in national newspapers in 2002, together with a number of awards. Alliance & Leicester expects the financial services industry to continue to be very competitive, but is confident that its strategy will deliver value to its customers, staff and shareholders alike.

# ARUP

Arup is a global firm of consulting engineers that employs over 7,000 people in 71 offices across 32 countries. In the UK, the firm has 19 offices. It is involved in a wide range of planning, industrial, building and civil projects, working in multidisciplinary teams to provide a 'one-stop' global consultancy service to clients.

**Scorecard:**

| | |
|---|---|
| Remuneration and benefits | **** |
| Progressive attitude | ***** |
| Opportunity for promotion | **** |
| Training, development and education | **** |
| Working atmosphere and environment | ***** |

**Biggest plus:**
World-class infrastructure and support services.

**Biggest minus:**
Yet to fully align working practices across all its offices.

Arup
13 Fitzroy Street
London W1T 4BQ
Tel: 020 7636 1531
Fax: 020 7580 3924
Website: www.arup.com

# Arup

## The Business

Arup is an award-winning firm of design and planning consultants that has been responsible for numerous high-profile construction projects around the world. These include the Sydney Opera House, the Hong Kong International Airport and the Sweden–Denmark bridge. UK projects include the Royal Opera House and Lloyd's Buildings – and more recently, the Millennium Bridge, the Manchester Commonwealth Games Stadium and the giant Anish Kapoor installation at the Tate Modern. In achieving its current status it has forged close links with governments and academic institutions alike.

The company was founded in 1946 under the charismatic leadership of Ove Arup. With offices first in London and Dublin, it grew rapidly over the next two decades in an era of high public spending on civil projects. Throughout its expansion, the firm has remained in private hands and is run as a trust for the benefit of its employees and their dependants.

The long-term trend for Arup has been to broaden the definition of its service provision to meet a range of client needs. Rather than focus on engineering alone, the company consults on a number of specialist disciplines: these include R&D, economics and planning, environmental, acoustics and IT. In short, whatever guidance you want on your construction project, Arup can provide it.

*Most consultants will have a cross-section of expertise, but we have a much broader range. You might find what you need in our economics department or in one of our R&D labs – whereas other firms will have simply one or the other*

## Company Culture and Style

Arup's global, multi-disciplinary identity means it was a practitioner of good knowledge management long before the term become fashionable. Wherever you work in the firm you know that if you cannot crack a problem yourself there is always somebody somewhere who will know the answer. A genuine team organisation, Arup's human resource is undoubtedly its greatest asset. As a recent example, the engineers that worked on establishing the cause of the Hatfield rail disaster brought over a specialist from Australia to help on the project.

Clive Reeder, Senior Human Resource Manager, underlines the point. 'Most consultants will have a cross-section of expertise, but we have a much broader range. You might find what you need in our economics department or in one of our R&D labs – whereas other firms will have simply one or the other.'

An important by-product of the highly-networked culture is Arup's flat organisational structure. The abundance of project work means that hierarchies are not as important as at many other large businesses. It would be an exaggeration to say there was a 'sink or swim' approach to people management but Arup is a hotbed of talent and people are entrusted with a lot of responsibility early on. The assumption is they would go elsewhere if they did not have this freedom to learn and develop their skills.

The pursuit of excellence in project work is allied to strong business ethics. The importance of this is impressed from the outset on new recruits, who have something more than a mission statement as a point of reference. Instead everyone is given a copy of a 1970 keynote speech given by the founder, which sets out the values of honesty and fair dealings that are ingrained in the organisation.

## Human Resources

Arup makes no bones about the fact it aims to recruit the top talent of the future. Over 200 graduates are taken on each year, with over two thirds of them in the UK. Once on board, they find a demanding yet richly-rewarding environment. According to Reeder, 'We throw a lot of training at them and expose them to tough experiences and top projects. We have high expectations of them and want them to adapt fairly quickly.'

The recruitment process itself is highly influenced by the leaders of the discipline in question. The firm uses 'state of the art' assessment centres, which allow interviewers to recognise elements of existing star performers in a candidate and be willing to take a chance on them, even if they do not entirely fit the prototype.

Successful candidates undergo induction during which they find out about the firm's culture and meet colleagues. Following this there is a skills week; recruits get to know their skills leader and begin their continuing professional development. They will also learn about the project work they can expect to do.

Self-governance is at the heart of Arup's corporate identity. Because it is run as a trust, it is not answerable to the City and is less vulnerable to market fluctuations. Consequently, layoffs are rare – two redundancy rounds in 2002 were the first in over a decade – and the model is one of ongoing growth. In other words, provided you have the necessary competencies, it is probable there is a place for you.

## Career Opportunity and Development

For fledgling engineers and business management professionals, career development at Arup starts with studying to pass professional exams and attain chartered status. Each employee will be assigned a mentor for the four or five years this normally takes.

Arup has an extensive range of courses available for all staff – some are delivered internally in the firm's training and development suite and some externally. This year, however, 25 new e-learning courses have been introduced through the Arup intranet. These interactive courses are available 24 hours a day to any one of the 7,000 staff around the world.

A sophisticated development course for senior staff is run in partnership with London Business School – with 24 staff on each course, they travel to take four modules in London, Hong Kong and New York. This enables team working, develops relationships and provides staff with an insight into other geographies in which Arup operates.

Reeder adds, 'We have a sophisticated competency framework which underpins our appraisal process. It has been very well received since it was introduced two years ago. There are six competency levels for most people and alongside those a number of grades and specialisms. The process is very transparent – people know exactly what they need to achieve in order to progress within the firm.'

As you would expect, a majority of Arup directors have an engineering background. In recent years, however, the firm has set about extending career path opportunities for all its professionals and in doing so has strengthened its position within the global talent market.

## Remuneration

Arup pays market salaries for engineering, design and technology staff and has a good all-round benefits package. Under its share scheme, every employee receives a set number of shares per year, based on salary and length of service. Other benefits include life assurance, car allowances, a choice of a money-purchase or final salary pension scheme and a long-term disability scheme for those incapacitated for more than six months.

As befits a true team organisation, Arup pays out bonuses each year on the basis of company performance.

## The Future

Arup's avowed aim is to strengthen its position as a key player in the increasingly globalised consulting market. It undoubtedly has the infrastructure in place to achieve this, yet its sheer reach means that it must perform everywhere it has a presence, regardless of the economic climate. From a business perspective, it would like to increase its brand visibility beyond the market in which it operates.

Its growing reach also means that it faces important decisions in its selection of work assignments. There are varying degrees of political sensitivity about engineering projects and Arup's leadership is aware of the need to reconcile any choice of partner with the high ethical standards to which it aspires. Environmental considerations, in particular, are increasingly important and a growing focus of the firm's work is on the development of sustainable projects.

Stella Littlewood, Group Human Resources Director: 'We are constantly striving for new and innovative ways in which to manage, develop and reward our staff – we never close the door on good ideas , we encourage our staff to strive for higher and higher goals – this is evidenced by our repeat business and over 75 personal awards made to our staff from commerce and industry this year.'

Founded by a group of Yorkshire farmers in 1965, Asda has grown rapidly in the last two decades and prides itself on being Britain's best value food and clothing superstore. It has 260 stores and 19 depots in the UK and employs 126,000 people. In July 1999, Asda became part of the Wal-Mart family, a move that has accelerated Asda's growth in the UK. Asda's wide range of food, clothing and general merchandise includes the George fashion range, which although founded as recently as 1990 is now an £800 million business in 220 stores.

**Scorecard:**
Remuneration and benefits:      ***
Progressive attitude:      *****
Opportunity for promotion:      *****
Training, development and education:      ****
Working atmosphere and environment:      ***

**Biggest plus:**
The way it treats its people.

**Biggest minus:**
Maintaining its high values and continually expanding is hard work.

Asda
Asda House
Southbank
Great Wilson Street
Leeds LS11 5AD
Website: www.asda.co.uk

# Asda

## The Business

Asda's first supermarket was in a former music hall in Leeds. From these modest beginnings less than 40 years ago, the company has grown rapidly to occupy a leading position in UK retailing with 260 stores across the country.

Although its position now looks assured, this was not always the case. It is an open secret that the company was just 12 days away from bankruptcy in the early 1990s, following the mishandled acquisition of 60 Gateway stores. Then as now, the company comprised very good people but they had been badly led. This changed radically with the appointment of Archie Norman as chief executive, and the company has never looked back.

From 1992, Asda's growth was the envy of its competitors. This was heightened in July 1999 when the US company Wal-Mart bought the Asda chain in a deal worth £63 billion. The match was ideal: Wal-Mart's expertise was primarily in general merchandise with a small amount of food handling; Asda's was the opposite. This allowed Asda stores to greatly increase their range of products, which now includes soft furnishings and electrical goods such as audio equipment and DVD players.

*We recognise that the people who do the job every day are quite likely to know the best way to improve how we do things!*

Furthermore, the deal brought Asda use of the Wal-Mart software systems, generally acknowledged to be the best in the retailing world. (Wal-Mart is IBM's second-biggest customer after NASA!)

Last but not least, Asda now benefits from the economies of scale that Wal-Mart's global sourcing allows. This has produced benefits to the UK customer, driving prices of goods even lower.

## Company Culture and Style

A key element of the Asda culture is 'service with personality'. It regularly wins 'Best for Friendliness' awards against its competitors. There is a genuine feeling that Asda is different among major high-street retailers in terms of helpfulness and approachability: Its service 'comes from the heart'. This in turn stems from a real desire to foster respect for individuals. Staff members are known as 'colleagues', for instance: this is not a cosmetic gesture but underpins everything that Asda does in terms of recognition and empowerment.

Asda goes out of its way to help people enjoy their work. As David Smith, Asda's People Director, says, 'We are very much one team here. We have respect for our colleagues that goes right through the organisation.' One way in which this is manifested is its flexible working, based on a response to the needs of people to balance work with life and family. Colleagues can swap shifts to cover for each other; mothers can take the first day of school off from work; grandparents can take days off to be with grandchildren; and there is even 'Benidorm leave', allowing colleagues to take a couple of months off in winter.

There is a listening culture at Asda. David Smith: 'We recognise that the people who do the job every day are quite likely to know the best way to improve how we do things!' There is an employee suggestion scheme, for instance, which has received no less than 50,000 suggestions, comments and letters from colleagues. A good 50 per cent of these have been helpful and have been put into practice. One example was the way clothing was hung. A colleague suggested an improvement to this which not only made the display more appealing but also saved considerable amounts of money.

Colleague circles meet every month in every store, and feed into divisional and national circles and ultimately to the Board. People really do seem to enjoy working for Asda – as backed by its regular 'We're Listening' attitude surveys. This constantly confirms that 90 per cent of the workforce enjoy their job, a remarkable statistic by any standards.

## Human Resources

You won't need a CV when you apply for a job at Asda! David Smith: 'We recruit purely on personality. We're not interested in paper qualifications or previous experience. We can train people in work skills, but you can't train customer service. Our people make eye contact and chat with customers. We want people who fit our culture, so introverts need not apply!'

Another interesting aspect of recruitment at Asda is its 'Goldies' campaign, targeting those aged over 50: a refreshing move in a country often accused of ageism. Asda piloted this scheme in Broadstairs, Kent, a retirement community. The results were so positive that it has since rolled it out nationwide. Hiring the over-fifties has brought three benefits: overall, they provide better service and take less absence from work; they are experienced and have often acquired valuable work skills; and they have an enhanced sense of loyalty. 'People thrown on the scrapheap by previous employers are glad to be valued by Asda,' as David Smith says.

Asda has a low staff turnover at around 26 per cent – better than its competitors. Furthermore, people who leave often return. Sometimes colleagues are lured away by better pay, but frequently find that pay is not everything.

## Career Opportunity and Development

The company likes to develop managers from the shop floor, and there are many instances of this. There is a job ladder system which colleagues can make use of. The two most important means of progression, though, are the Stores of Learning and the Asda Academy.

The eight Stores of Learning, launched in 1999, represent a £3 million investment in training for new and existing Asda managers. They have now trained almost 2,000 new managers in 29 different disciplines. Managers trained at Stores of Learning have been shown to outperform trading targets by substantial margins: and the programme won the Personnel Today 2000 Award for Excellence in Training.

The Asda Academy is a training programme based on the idea of training colleagues in traditional craft skills within Asda stores. This is another move that sets Asda apart from an industry marked by standardising. Asda has over 550 butchers, 550 bakers, 500 greengrocers, 300 vintners, 40 fishmongers and 40 florists. The Academy won a National Training Award in 1999. As David Smith says, 'If you want to be a grocery manager, you can be. If you want to a butcher, we'll help you develop the necessary skills.' In short, Asda believes in development for all, but wants it to be self-driven.

There is a quarterly appraisal programme and personal development plans in place. There is also a 'buddying' system whereby existing colleagues work alongside new recruits, avoiding the traditional 'tell and do' approach still evident in many of its competitors.

There is a graduate recruitment scheme, currently taking 75 graduates a year. These people are fast-tracked, working in areas such as logistics and finance. If they are seen as potential general managers, the store expects them to be managing stores just five years after joining.

## Remuneration

The company is a median payer. However, it has spent considerable time and effort over the last ten years building a benefits suite that it firmly believes is the best in the industry. (87 per cent of Asda staff think so, according to the satisfaction survey.)

There is a bonus scheme, where colleagues are rewarded according to the performance of the business. There is a good contributory final salary scheme (which unlike many UK companies' schemes is still open to new joiners). Colleagues have a discount scheme, which interestingly provides not only discounts on shopping in Asda stores and Wal-Mart stores outside the UK, but also on other spending. For example, colleagues can get a discount when they visit Alton Towers. This, again, was based on feedback from colleagues.

Benefits also include healthcare at management level, travel insurance and a Law Club for anyone with legal problems or concerns. A sharesave plan has been in place since the early 1990s, and has massive take-up. There is also a Colleague Share Ownership Scheme: the largest amongst hourly-paid workers in the UK. This underlines the sense of ownership colleagues feel for their company, and also strengthens their commitment to its future growth.

There is also a company car scheme, available according to job need and rank: however, around half of those eligible have chosen to take advantage of the generous opt-out cash alternative.

## The Future

Asda overtook Sainsbury's in September 2002 in terms of volume of goods sold. This made it number two in UK retailing. It was in fourth place just nine years ago – a testimony to its rapid growth.

So what does the future hold? David Smith: 'We want to be number one: but we see that as being the best we can be rather than in terms of size league tables. We want to be the best employer and the best server of customers.'

The challenge will be running a quality business, 24 hours a day, seven days a week, and maintaining its impetus in the face of fierce competition and continually rising consumer demands. Nevertheless, Asda looks well placed to do so. It created 15,000 new jobs in 2002 and is committed to opening 30–40 new stores over the next three years, an investment of over £1 billion. Its unremitting desire to deliver high quality and low prices, its excellent staff policies, and the backing of Wal-Mart, all augur well for the future.

# B&Q

The UK's leading DIY and garden centre retailer employs over 30,000 people and runs 320 stores in the UK, plus another 50 around the world. Its parent, Kingfisher, recently bought the top French DIY chain Castorama. B&Q has a turnover approaching £6 billion.

**Scorecard:**

| | |
|---|---|
| Remuneration and benefits | **** |
| Progressive attitude | ***** |
| Opportunity for promotion | ***** |
| Training, development and education | ***** |
| Working atmosphere and environment | ***** |

**Biggest plus:**
The practical, pragmatic, positive atmosphere at a company which values its employees.

**Biggest minus:**
Guilt by association – one poor-quality product or an inefficient sales response at a B&Q store can sour the consumer's relationship with the brand.

B&Q plc
Portswood House
1 Hampshire Corporate Park
Chandlers Ford
Hampshire SO53 3YX
Tel: 02380 256726
Fax: 02380 257242
Websites: www.diy.com and www.careers.diy.com

# B&Q

## The Business

B&Q has grown from a single store in 1969 to become the UK's leading DIY and garden centre retailer, currently offering over 45,000 home improvement and garden products from its 466 stores in seven countries – more than 320 in the UK, employing over 30,000 people.

In 1998 B&Q merged with France's leading DIY retailer, Castorama, to become the largest DIY group in Europe; in mid-2002 B&Q's parent company, Kingfisher plc, finally acquired Castorama outright. International operations now include nearly 50 stores from Poland to Shanghai.

B&Q has become a £6 billion business, its turnover representing about a third of Kingfisher's overall total (electrical retailing, primarily through Comet and Darty, provide most the rest). The electricals division is due to be demerged into a separate business, a process that Kingfisher has already been through with Woolworth's.

B&Q also runs a successful website operation, www.diy.com, with 24/7 access to products, ideas, expert advice, and 'how to' guides.

## Company Culture and Style

There's an informal dress code across the business, perhaps emblematic of a down-to-earth approach that is encouraged at all levels. There's a real sense of roll-your-sleeves-up hard work, with commensurate financial and other rewards. The ideal B&Q employee is probably a good team player, tending towards the extrovert, with a tenacious approach to their job and a fair degree of ambition to succeed.

*B&Q expects to open at least 20 new stores in Britain during 2003, and is looking for at least 1,000 new managers to staff them*

This is an organisation that has thought about what it does and how it does it. The big ideas include a belief in the value of its people and of its services, a commitment to minimising environmental impact, and a sense that B&Q should be seen to be doing something for the local communities in which its stores function. But it is neither didactic nor abstract about this. These high-value approaches will produce real commercial returns; the people will work better, the consumer will feel better about B&Q.

You can see some of the ideas in explicit policies. For instance, the company has a commendably responsible attitude to the environment and to the community. Since 1990, B&Q has been assessing the environmental impacts of its products and developing policies to address them. Currently this has been formalised into its QUEST Programme (Quality, Ethics and Safety) that covers not only B&Q stores and head office functions but also distribution and even suppliers.

Stores are actively encouraged to look for opportunities for environmental improvement with local authorities and others. Schemes include small-scale grants (to be spent on B&Q products) that can kick-start local environmental projects.

Larger grants for community projects are also available through the You Can Do It Awards scheme. The successful applicants get £2,000 worth of purchases from their local store; last year B&Q had a massive 4,500 applications and distributed £100,000 to 18 winners, ranging from children's theatre groups to daycare centres.

The company does not enforce a retirement policy based on age, and indeed has sometimes focused recruitment drives on the over-50s. The stores typically have a good age range among staff; the head office near Southampton has a generally younger feel, with responsibility and promotion obviously decided on ability rather than seniority.

## Human Resources

B&Q's approach is intended to respect the contribution of the individual employee and aims to let everyone make the most of their talents. With a huge organisation, that's an ambitious goal.

B&Q's public image is obviously based on the retail sites, and the company is always keen to recruit ambitious and commercially-driven managers. It is also happy to promote staff into management positions. But more than 1,000 people also work at B&Q's modern-built Head Office in a semi-rural location near Southampton.

There are dedicated online recruitment websites for stores and for head office (links from www.careers.diy.com). The application forms have been carefully designed, and will certainly help the applicant decide whether B&Q is a suitable fit for them. For B&Q, it represents a faster, fairer and generally more efficient method of finding management-level staff – B&Q says it wants to recruit a thousand new store-based managers over the next 12 months.

The online applications are an innovative and imaginative approach, and B&Q is definitely keen to make maximum use of the available technology. The company's internal website, for instance, provides good-quality in-depth information about employment and does so through an efficient and elegant interface.

Twice a year B&Q runs an employee satisfaction survey. Perhaps predictably, there is a strong correlation between the company's profitability and a high degree of general contentment amongst staff.

## Career Opportunity and Development

B&Q's mission statement proclaims that the company 'will be the best at giving people the inspiration, confidence, and solutions to create homes to be proud of'.

To accomplish that, and to meet the high customer expectations identified by their annual customer surveys, B&Q needs employees of the highest calibre. It needs to find them, and it needs to keep them. It certainly needs the staff to feel that they're valued – and this is one of the key successes of B&Q.

There is a strong commitment to training and developing staff, with an active policy of in-house promotion. Increasingly this is based on the Fast Track programme, a sophisticated and quite systematic approach to regular target-setting and reporting that can accelerate advancement. Employees have to apply to join the scheme. Currently it is producing around 40 per cent of managerial promotions.

Employees are also encouraged to add to their knowledge and experience, including the B&Q training 'university' with opportunity to take off-the-job courses (some via e-learning, which is becoming increasingly well developed at B&Q).

In general, and particularly at management level, employees have a good deal of flexibility in managing the work/life balance. Getting the job done correctly is regarded as more important than timekeeping.

## Remuneration

B&Q's growth in the last few years has produced an imaginative approach to recruitment, employment and remuneration. The company works hard at under-standing the true value of its employees, not least in terms of their contribution to sales and profits. It has developed a sophisticated approach to adding benefits and presenting them as part of a total remuneration package.

So as well as basic pay, there is a company profits bonus payable twice a year (with a guaranteed minimum and top-ups based on local performance). Employees also have a choice of pension schemes (contributory and non-contrib-utory); a Kingfisher discount card (for discount purchases in B&Q, Comet and elsewhere); life insurance schemes; a Sharesave Scheme for Kingfisher shares; a range of preferential discounts on products and services outside the group; the opportunity to apply for sabbatical leave to work on pet projects; and 25 days' paid holiday a year – unusually generous for the retail sector.

It can be easy to underestimate the total value of this, and an interesting devel-opment on the company's internal website is a prototype Total Remuneration Package calculator, which will tell people exactly how much they can expect to earn.

## The Future

B&Q expects to open at least 20 new stores in Britain during 2003, and is looking for at least 1,000 new managers to staff them. B&Q's business tracks the broad economic trend of the UK economy, especially in respect of house-buying, and both have been doing well recently. The company's core business planning for the medium term assumes that this will not change radically, which means B&Q is looking for serious expansion.

Its ultimate aim is to be the biggest ('and best') DIY retailer in the world. It already has the top spot in the UK and now in Europe too. Joint ventures in China, Taiwan and Turkey are being used successfully to test the global waters – to develop policies for local expansion, and also to extend the supplier base.

This is a company with real ambition. It has also developed the internal systems and the external policies to support that ambition.

BAKER TILLY

Baker Tilly is a leading independent firm of chartered accountants and business advisers, with clients ranging from fast-growing and owner-managed businesses, to listed and international organisations. The UK's 7th largest firm of accountants and business advisers, Baker Tilly is growing rapidly.

With fee income increasing from £32 million in 1990 to £159 million today, it has been the only new firm to break into the accountancy 'Top 10' since 1990. Its 2001 merger with HLB Kidsons continued to strengthen the UK office network, and the firm is represented internationally through its independent membership of Baker Tilly International.

**Scorecard:**

| | |
|---|---|
| Remuneration and benefits | *** |
| Progressive attitude | *** |
| Opportunity for promotion | **** |
| Training, development and education | **** |
| Working atmosphere and environment | **** |

**Biggest plus:**
Plenty of scope for individuality.

**Biggest minus:**
Rapid growth means a changing environment.

Baker Tilly
2 Bloomsbury Street
London WC1B 3ST
Tel: 020 7413 5100
Fax: 020 7413 5101
Website: www.bakertilly.co.uk

# Baker Tilly

## The Business

Baker Tilly provides all the services needed for businesses looking for continued or accelerated growth, from audit and accountancy to taxation, business recovery, growth advice and corporate finance.

In addition to core audit and business advisory services, clients have access to the range of financial products and advice through Baker Tilly Financial Services Limited and Baker Tilly Insurance Services.

With a history traceable to the late 1800s, Baker Tilly has seen particular growth over the past 12 years, and plans to maintain its growth ambitions for the foreseeable future. With fee income increasing from £32 million in 1990 to £159 million today, it has been the only new firm to break into the established accountancy 'Top 10' since 1990.

In 2001, a merger with HLB Kidsons created a firm double the size and gave Baker Tilly a significantly increased presence in many parts of the country. A truly national partnership, it now has 270 partners and over 2,000 members of staff across 34 office locations throughout the UK.

*The firm is able to demonstrate good retention of key employees, and those who leave often choose to return to Baker Tilly, discovering that a similar open culture is hard to find elsewhere*

Baker Tilly International is the 10th largest network in the world by fee income and is represented by 107 firms in 59 countries, with a global fee income of $1.4 billion and 17,000 staff worldwide. In 2001, the network experienced a 15 per cent growth in revenue.

Baker Tilly International is a network of high quality, independent accountancy and business services firms, all of whom are committed to providing the best possible service to their clients, in their own marketplaces, and across the world. All firms within the network adhere to the same high-quality standards and share skills, resources and expertise.

## Company Culture and Style

Baker Tilly prides itself on offering something a little different. The firm has always looked to take on people who, as well as being well qualified, are highly motivated and well-rounded individuals who can contribute to the organisation on a number of levels, and believes it offers people the chance to be themselves rather than just a cog in the financial machine.

People who are individualistic also fit well with the firm's diverse client base, where employees can find themselves working in a wide variety of different environments. For example, audit assignments could take in anything from TV production companies and theatrical costumiers to property consultancies.

The firm is able to demonstrate good retention of key employees, and those who leave often choose to return to Baker Tilly, discovering that a similar open culture is hard to find elsewhere. The workforce is a healthy balance between those who have been recruited and trained by the firm and those who join from the Big 4 and other firms of accountants.

By creating a larger and more geographically diverse organisation, the firm's style of rapid growth has had an impact on the corporate culture. Periods of rapid change inevitably suit some employees better than others, however, the firm is working hard at maintaining a friendly and personal feel even as it increases in size, and is determined to maintain a 'can-do' culture with a sense of drive, enthusiasm and fun.

Baker Tilly aims to recruit on an equal opportunities basis. It has a number of women at partner level – though in-line with accountancy firms in general they represent well below 50 per cent of all partners. Although, when looked at in its entirety, the workforce is more than 60 per cent female so it bodes well for future promotions. Having said that, the firm is keen to avoid complacency, and among the HR team's plans for the future is a review of the firm's recruitment and employment policies to ensure it continues to offer equal opportunities.

## Human Resources

Much of Baker Tilly's graduate recruitment is done via the Web, and would-be applicants can complete an online application and aptitude testing form that identifies promising candidates immediately.

For more senior staff, the firm often recruits using third parties: agencies and, for very senior positions, headhunters.

Baker Tilly's HR department is constantly meeting the challenges created by the firm's rapid expansion. What used to be a small firm with an individual, almost family feel, has become an important national brand; the challenge is to make the most of the opportunities while still retaining the personal touch or 'feel-good factor'.

HR plans are being put in place that will encompass pay, benefits and succession; focusing on using new communication channels to ensure that employees still feel informed and consulted as the firm grows.

A new employee support helpline is available for queries and feedback on HR issues, and since November 2002, employees have been able to access online HR information including company policies, disciplinary and grievance procedures, benefits and conditions on the company intranet.

# Career Opportunity and Development

Baker Tilly is an exciting and challenging firm for anyone looking for a high-achieving, satisfying career. Accountancy may have its origins in the dark ages but its future will definitely be characterised as groundbreaking and forward thinking. At Baker Tilly you will be given the support to achieve your ambitions.

Baker Tilly's rapid growth has certainly created new opportunities for staff: offering development and progression within the firm, challenging new roles and a range of different office locations for staff who want to move around the country. All vacancies are advertised internally before going out to external candidates.

There are also potential opportunities working abroad through secondment to the firms that make up Baker Tilly International. Whilst the member firms of Baker Tilly International are independent entities, the close relationships have provided a number of secondment opportunities in the UK as well as Baker Tilly staff taking up secondments with partners in Canada, the USA and Australia.

The majority of Baker Tilly's graduate recruits enter into a three-year training contract, leading to a chartered accountancy qualification, although over recent years, more and more opportunities have become available for graduates to train in other areas such as taxation, marketing and business recovery. The firm encourages graduates to study for appropriate qualifications whatever their field, such as the Chartered Institute of Management Accountants, Chartered Institute of Marketing or Chartered Institute of Taxation. Whatever path they choose, the firm offers support throughout their training, and pass rates are significantly higher than the national averages.

Baker Tilly also offers a programme of internal courses covering areas such as interpersonal, managerial, marketing and commercial skills. Most courses are residential, giving trainees a chance to network with their peers from around the country.

# Remuneration

Salaries at Baker Tilly are probably slightly above the norm within the accountancy profession, and bonuses are awarded to all within the firm on the basis of fee earning and profitability. This ensures that all employees share in the firm's success. Discretionary bonuses are sometimes also awarded to individuals to recognise outstanding performance. Salary progression is dependent on the individual's own performance and development, although the HR teams do maintain strong relationships with their counterparts in other firms to make sure that the remuneration packages offered are competitive in the marketplace.

The firm's benefits package incorporates private health insurance, life assurance and pension schemes. Baker Tilly is committed to the development of its remuneration and benefits policies. The firm is currently looking into additional non-monetary benefits such as more flexible working arrangements. Trial flexible working schemes are already in progress at offices in the UK.

# The Future

In future, Baker Tilly intends to carry on playing to its strengths in servicing a client base of growing owner-managed companies. Within this sector, however, it aims to grow to be number one among the middle tier accountancy practices.

The firm recognises the need to grow through merger and organic growth, believing that firms that stand still are likely to be swept away. It continues to look out for new development opportunities, but is also investing in skills, client services, infrastructure and support services, to fuel future growth.

Baker Tilly's 2002 fee income earnings put it in seventh place in the UK accountancy league table. If its current rapid growth continues, it should be on track to achieve its ambitions to be the premier firm in the middle tier.

As well as expanding in terms of fee income and locations, Baker Tilly is also looking to develop the range of services it offers to keep one step ahead of a constantly changing professional services marketplace. Recent examples of new services are its IT and e-business consultancy team and its Software Products group, gained through the 2001 merger with Harris Walters Ltd.

Barclays is one of the UK's foremost financial institutions, with interests in retail, private client, commercial and investment banking, investment management and credit cards. Based in London with major offices in Coventry, Northampton, Poole, and Radbroke, Cheshire, the Group employs 78,000 people in more than 60 countries worldwide, including Africa, the Americas, Asia and Europe.

**Scorecard:**

| | |
|---|---|
| Remuneration and benefits | **** |
| Progressive attitude | **** |
| Opportunity for promotion | ***** |
| Training, development and education | ***** |
| Working atmosphere and environment | **** |

**Biggest plus:**
Able and willing to provide wide-ranging, tailored career paths in many financial services and other corporate disciplines.

**Biggest minus:**
Still in a state of transition, which it must complete quickly and successfully to meet growing international competition.

Barclays plc
54 Lombard Street
London EC3P 3AH
Tel: 020 7699 5000
Fax: 020 7699 3721
Website: www.barclays.com

# Barclays

## The Business

Barclays has been a feature of London's financial heartland for more than 300 years, having occupied the same site on the corner of Lombard Street since its foundation in 1690. Since then it has grown into one of the UK's foremost financial services groups, as well as a major international force. 'When you are such an important part of the country's economy and provider of financial services to so many companies and consumers, you feel a lot of responsibility,' says Gary Hoffman, Chief Executive of Barclaycard.

The group has around 2,000 branches in the UK and more than 500 abroad, and employs 78,000 people in more than 60 countries. Around 67,000 of these work in the UK, mostly in the Personal Financial Services, Business Banking, Barclaycard and Private Clients groupings. The UK operation received a considerable boost when Barclays took over former building society the Woolwich in 2000.

The group's international operations include Barclays Africa, a full-service bank operating in nine countries whose origins go back to 1925; Barclays Capital, founded in 1986, an investment bank serving international corporates and institutions; and Barclays Global Investors, founded in 1995. Barclays is becoming a major force in the USA, and in 1986 it became the first British bank to have its shares listed on both the New York and Tokyo stock exchanges.

*When you come to Barclays you can tell you're entering a place with a great tradition... But it's also on the cutting edge of what's going on in the world, and it feels very fast-moving. There seems to be a new challenge every few months*

Despite its historical credentials, Barclays is also at the forefront of modern developments. It was a pioneer of automated cash machines, and its PC home banking service has gained well over 3.5 million online customers since its launch in 1997, making Barclays one of the world's largest online banks.

## Company Culture and Style

Barclays sees itself as combining the best of the old and the new. 'When you come to Barclays you can tell you're entering a place with a great tradition,' says Hoffman. 'But it's also on the cutting edge of what's going on in the world, and it feels very fast-moving. There seems to be a new challenge every few months.'

The company is less formal than of old, says Head of HR policy Karen Caddick. 'When I joined two years ago it was more formal than it is today,' she says. 'But when you meet the executive team they're not formal at all, they are very down to earth, they really engage and listen to our employees. We're not a stuffy company – you can email a senior executive and they'll reply.'

Other attitudes are being modernised, too. 'We feel increasingly customer-driven, and more externally-focused than maybe some other banks are,' says Valerie Scoular, Barclays' Group HR Director. 'We have a good mixture of old and new people, and the company is more of a meritocracy than it used to be.'

Each of the group's operations has a different personality. The branch network is very team-oriented, and branch staff realise they have a significant role in the local community – both at work and in a voluntary capacity. Barclays Capital, by contrast, feels very international, performance-driven and 'today'-based.

The group's diversity attracts an equally diverse range of people. 'When you employ nearly 80,000 people you're pretty representative of society, and we cover a broad spectrum,' says Scoular. 'We're becoming much more aggressive in equal opportunities and supporting diversity, encouraging a wide range of people from all backgrounds to join Barclays. We are very keen to ensure that we shape our workforce to reflect the locations in which they're based.'

Two-thirds of staff are women, and although they remain under-represented at senior level, Barclays is trying hard to improve matters. One key change is more flexible working, including part-time working, home-working, a job-share register, paid carer leave (eg staying home if your childminder goes sick) and increased flexibility for carers.

Just one member of staff in ten is aged over 50, partly due to a round of early retirements in the 1990s. But the Group is actively working to retain older people, with flexible retirement options, part-time working etc, and even to recruit them: 170 over-60s joined the group in 2002.

## Human Resources

Between 6,000 and 8,000 people join Barclays every year, from school-leavers and new graduates to grizzled financial experts. 'Our objective is to maximise the number and type of people who apply to Barclays,' says Scoular.

Around 90 graduates a year enter the three one-year fast-track training programmes – Business Leadership, Barclaycard Development and Barclays Capital Graduate Programme – which use placements, training and regular career interviews to groom recruits for management positions. School-leavers can take modern apprenticeships, and may transfer to one of the fast-track schemes later. More than 100 school-leavers and undergraduates do eight-week summer placements every year.

Barclays welcomes former employees who choose to return. 'We encourage people to think of Barclays as an integral part of their career, but we understand that it may not be all of it,' says Hoffman.

However, they may find they never leave. Annual staff turnover is under 10 per cent – low for a company with a lot of call centre staff – and half of graduate recruits are still there after 4–5 years.

'A lot of senior people who came into Barclays in the expectation of moving on have stayed a lot longer than they thought they would,' says Hoffman. 'About half the executive board joined straight from school or university.' Hoffman himself joined straight from Cambridge 20 years ago.

## Career Opportunity and Development

Barclays has fingers in many pies, including personal, business, corporate, international and investment banking. 'The variety of businesses brings a rich variety of career moves,' says Scoular. 'For people who want to build a general portfolio of skills, there are lots of opportunities.'

The group likes its senior managers, in particular, to have experience in several divisions, and this is being systematically extended down the company. Hoffman recalls reviewing the career of a senior colleague who, in 15 years with the Group, had never spent more than 15 months in one job. Overseas postings are quite common, especially in the Capital, Global Investors and Barclaycard divisions, and the Group is keen for its senior managers to have international experience.

Alternatively, people seeking a career in a particular métier – IT, HR, marketing, project management, change management, call centre management etc – will find structured career streams specifically for them. Career development is taken very seriously. 'As a senior team, we spend tens of days a year working on career development, succession planning, and identifying and nurturing talent,' says Hoffman. 'That's been a big change over the last 2–3 years.'

Although there are broad grading bands, promotion is by merit, taking as much account of the person's potential as their achievements to date, and people are expected to take responsibility for their own careers. Biannual reviews focus as much on the 'how' as on the 'what' of people's achievements, and are fully 360-degree, taking input from peers and subordinates as well as bosses. Quarterly sessions also take place in-between reviews to ensure that the feedback cycle is continuous throughout the year, people are really encouraged to focus upon performance improvement.

Barclays has moved away from uniform, 'sheep-dip' training. 'Our intention is that people get developed in a way that best fits their job and their personal development needs,' says Scoular. Although some use is made of international management schools, most training material is developed internally. Much of it is delivered via the Barclays University, an ambitious project launched in 2000 to deliver tailored, personal training via intranet, Internet and six metropolitan training centres.

## Remuneration

Like increasing numbers of aggressive corporate businesses, Barclays reckons to pay average basic salaries topped up with generous bonuses to those who deserve them. 'Your annual assessment decides how much money you get,' says Scoular.

Everyone is eligible for bonuses, including cashiers and call centre agents, and the Group carefully benchmarks itself against companies both inside and outside the financial services sector.

The benefits package is becoming increasingly flexible, and this trend will continue in the coming years – for example, allowing life insurance and PHI cover to be swapped for cash. Everyone gets private healthcare – from day one for senior staff – and up to 30 days' holiday, depending on seniority. You even get a couple of extra days off if you get married (though it's probably not worth tying the knot just to get that long weekend!). The top three grades get cars or a cash alternative, as do peripatetic staff.

Pension is by defined contribution (the group makes a higher contribution for over-35s), but this may change to stay competitive. Senior managers receive share options, and there is a share incentive plan and SAYE scheme open to all staff. Perks for staff include interest-free loans and preferential banking.

There is union recognition throughout the group, and almost half of staff belong to the banking union, UNIFI. Relations have improved over the years and are now very good; Barclays even helps UNIFI to recruit new members.

## The Future

As well as growing its considerable influence in the UK, Barclays aims to expand internationally, especially in continental Western Europe. Its mission is to become one of the worlds's most 'admired' financial institutions – admiration not always the obvious sentiment with which people view banks – which will be a tough task in the face of growing American competition.

The Group also knows it must continue coming up with new value propositions for domestic customers, such as the Open Plan account which offsets savings interest against the customer's mortgage, and Barclaycard's successful Nectar loyalty card.

Barclays is still in a state of transition, trying to shed its historical 'baggage' without shedding the history that goes with it. 'Some of our decision-making processes are still a bit slow and frustrating, and we still have to become more nimble', says Scoular.

But, says Hoffman: 'I've been here for 20 years, and I think we've come an enormous way in the last two.'

# Barnardo's

## GIVING CHILDREN BACK THEIR FUTURE

Barnardo's is the UK's largest children's charity, working with 100,000 children, young people and their families across the UK. It works with today's most vulnerable children and young people, helping them to address problems like abuse, discrimination, homelessness and poverty, and to tackle the challenges of disability.

As well as community projects that work directly with children, Barnardo's also runs campaigns to lobby government and heighten awareness on crucial issues. Child abuse through prostitution wasn't a noticeable issue before Barnardo's launched its campaign, changing opinions and laws so that children abused in this way are now seen as children in need.

**Scorecard:**

| | |
|---|---|
| Remuneration and benefits | **** |
| Progressive attitude | ***** |
| Opportunity for promotion | *** |
| Training, development and education | **** |
| Working atmosphere and environment | ***** |

**Biggest plus:**
The chance to make a real difference in an organisation that does so much to improve children's lives.

**Biggest minus:**
The nature of the work can be disturbing and won't be for everyone – even those not directly working with children will hear the stories from those who are. It is essential work but can be harrowing.

Barnardo's
Tanners Lane
Barkingside
Ilford
Essex IG6 1QG
Tel: 020 8550 8822
Fax: 020 8498 7031
Website: www.barnardos.org.uk

# Barnardo's

## The Business

In 1866 Barnardo's founder, Thomas Barnardo, arrived in London to train as a doctor. However, he was so shocked by the poverty and squalor he found in the East End that he decided instead to devote himself to helping these impoverished children. By 1870 he had opened his first children's home for young boys.

The organisation was founded on the Christian beliefs of Thomas Barnardo. Although it now operates independent of any church or faith, it still retains a commitment to the values, vision and purpose of its founder. Its vision is that the lives of all children should be free from poverty, abuse and discrimination, and it's purpose is to help the most vulnerable children and young people transform their lives and fulfil their potential.

This it does through a network of 300 children's projects and 300 shops across the UK, employing some 6,000 people. Barnardo's works with 100,000 UK children every year, helping them overcome severe disadvantage such as homelessness, abuse, poverty and disability. This figure includes 55,000 with whom it works regularly, a further 7,000 who are supported in one-off sessions and around 35,000 others supported through community groups.

*For the right person, the rewarding experience of seeing someone's life turn around following your team's efforts are there for the taking*

The work isn't always pretty. Barnardo's projects are wide-ranging and include, for example, working directly with abused children, with children affected by domestic violence, alcohol and drug abuse, and those living with terminal illnesses. Anyone who isn't ready to face the reality of this would be well advised to seek employment elsewhere. For the right person, however, the rewarding experience of seeing someone's life turn around following your team's efforts are there for the taking.

## Company Culture and Style

Barnardo's is influenced by a set of principles and values that are as important to it today as they were when Barnardo's was founded. Deriving its inspiration and values from the Christian faith, in today's multi-faith society these values are enriched and shared by many people of other faiths and beliefs. These values provide the basis of Barnardo's work with children and young people, their families and communities.

The charity's values are respecting the unique worth of every person, encouraging people to fulfil their potential, working with hope, and exercising responsible stewardship. It organises its services around six 'building blocks' which it believes every child needs to build a positive future: a family that can cope, protection from harm, emotional, physical and spiritual health, a sense of belonging in the community, opportunities to learn and a stake in society.

In terms of how it operates and runs its individual projects, it should be understood that the voluntary sector is very different from the commercial concerns outlined in this book. It is dependent on money freely given to it by charitable donations and to funding from local authorities. At the moment it gets 70 per cent of its funding from the Government but that can change with differing administrations and their priorities as regards public money. Effectively it starts with a zero bank balance every year. Planning has to take place in spite of this.

The culture and look and feel of the premises will vary depending on the activity. Clearly fund-raisers, who are usually home based, can wear what they want whilst running through their admin jobs but will turn up to a corporate donor suited and booted, while someone working directly with the children won't want to intimidate them with power dressing. There are no hard and fast rules; essentially the charity employs adults, and trusts them to temper their communication, verbal and visual, to the circumstances.

Overall 80 per cent of staff are female, and at senior level this falls to a 50/50 split.

## Human Resources

The HR team at Barnardo's has to deliver an up-to-date, proactive and cost-effective service in line with the organisation's strong commitment to equal opportunities and managing diversity. It has a slightly different focus from those in commercial concerns, in that it sees one of its primary goals as to reinforce the values that motivated staff to join in the first place. Whether it does so by listening when a worker is at the end of their tether or by putting formal support processes in place, the job isn't easy just because it's away from the immediate confrontation of the problems the charity wants to address.

It recruits in a number of ways – people interested in community work will already be aware of *The Guardian* on Wednesdays and *Community Care* magazine; others are advertised in specialist publications, so that HR jobs might be found in *Personnel Today*, for example. The website carries job vacancies that are being advertised externally, although not all are. The staff turnover rate is 20 per cent or so; this sounds high to people outside the caring fields but it is average for the field. As Barnardo's has been increasing in size there are around 1,500 vacancies per year.

## Career Opportunity and Development

Barnardo's is well aware of the need to develop and enthuse its existing staff, which is why not all jobs are advertised externally. Internal applicants are encouraged and anyone with access to the intranet will be able to find details.

Opportunities for training and development are not only plentiful but often obligatory – you can't work with children without both training and vetting, for example, and there are rules about the qualifications people need to work in certain roles in Barnardo's projects.

Everybody has a personal development plan and this is reviewed with a line manager periodically. People wanting a more solid idea of what Barnardo's can do for them are urged to read the leaflets the organisation produces. 'Working In Barnardo's', for example, outlines the equal opportunities possibilities, the training opportunities and the various disciplines that take employees on within the organisation – as well as the direct services for the children there are policy, fundraising, IT, finance, HR, marketing, administrative and retail opportunities.

In addition to this, Barnardo's has set up a graduate scheme for people wanting to enter the organisation in a marketing and communications role.

## Remuneration

People who want a glamorous job with big salaries and share options would clearly be poorly advised to look at the voluntary sector. However, it pays well within its sector – indeed it can't afford not to – competing with other charities and local authorities for the attention of potential employees.

Also worthy of note is the pension scheme, which has won the Pensions Week Small Scheme Department of the Year Award 2002 and Small Scheme Initiative Award 2002. The pension manager, Graham Brown, won the Pensions Management Pensions Manager of the Year Award 2002.

Other than that, all of the available money is diverted to the core services – and given that the organisation survives on donations this seems entirely right.

## The Future

In terms of future development, Barnardo's will always use its values to build on its services. It believes – and there's sadly no reason to doubt it – that its services will always be needed, and so will always need funding to operate. Immediate plans, therefore, involve building on the marketing and communications side of the organisation to make the future as secure as is possible.

It would also like to encourage more young people to join the organisation. It's easy for younger people to either assume that Barnardo's will always be there – and in the absence of funding it won't be – or for the organisation to assume people know what it does when, without constant reminders, the next generation won't understand its work.

Finally, it will focus on high-level communications with the Government and the public, where it believes it can make a difference. A recent example is Barnardo's work with children who become involved in prostitution. Barnardo's abuse through prostitution campaign is working hard to change the opinions of the Government, police and the public, who often do not perceive these children as abused and in need of help and support. Barnardo's lobbying work with the UK Government on this issue is helping to change legislation in the Sexual Offences Bill to better support these abused children. Barnardo's also runs other campaigns that lobby government on poverty, disability and youth offending.

# BENFIELD

Benfield Group is one of the leading reinsurance intermediaries in the world. With its headquarters in the UK, Benfield Group provides a range of specialist reinsurance, insurance and risk advisory services to a global customer base. In May 2001, the Group acquired US reinsurance broker E.W. Blanch, one of the leading US integrated risk management and distribution service providers. The combined company has become the third largest reinsurance intermediary in the world, with a global presence established through some 34 offices and over 1,700 employees. Key company philosophy is that all staff remain as happy and healthy as the business.

**Scorecard:**

| | |
|---|---|
| Remuneration and benefits | **** |
| Progressive attitude | ***** |
| Opportunity for promotion | **** |
| Training, development and education | ***** |
| Working atmosphere and environment | ***** |

**Biggest plus:**
The working and cultural environments.

**Biggest minus:**
Must be the right kind of person to fit in – if you are, you'll thrive.

Benfield Group
55 Bishopsgate
London EC2N 3BD
Tel: 020 7578 7000
Fax: 020 7578 7001
Email: Peopleadvisory@benfieldgroup.com
Website: www.benfieldgroup.com

# Benfield Group

## The Business

Benfield Group is the world's largest privately-owned reinsurance intermediary. With some 1,700 staff the company operates in three segments: the US business, which concerns reinsurance broking; the international business, which concerns reinsurance broking worldwide, excluding the USA; and the corporate investment group, which concerns some non-core businesses, such as Benfield Sports International (which provides consultancy services in sports sponsorship and event management, particularly motor sport), Wildnet Group (for the creation, marketing and management of interactive trading websites) and Orbit, which provides employee benefits advisory services.

In May 2001, the Group acquired US reinsurance broker E.W. Blanch, one of the leading US integrated risk management and distribution service providers. The combined company has become the third largest reinsurance intermediary in the world. The combined Group's US operations were renamed Benfield Blanch and the Bermuda-based holding company is called Benfield Group. The trading name for the reinsurance broking operation outside of the USA is Benfield Greig.

*We want to be at the leading edge in all aspects in our business – which includes the application of IT, and HR policies, as well as our dealings with customers*

The company has grown aggressively over the past five years, while the origins of Benfield Group date back to 1973 with the registration of a Lloyd's broker. A management buy-out in 1988 led to the establishment of the Benfield Group, which subsequently became one of the fastest-growing companies in any sector in the UK. Among many subsequent acquisitions was the merger with Greig Fester in 1997 to form Benfield Greig. Throughout all its activities, Benfield Group has sought to ensure all its employees are as contented and healthy as the business itself.

## Company Culture and Style

'The key point to make about Benfield Group is that we are open,' says Tracey Marshall, Global Head of HR. 'It's non-hierarchical with a flat structure. We operate with lots of teams – for example there are 90 teams in London, with on average eight per team. There is a team leader and team members. The team leaders report to an executive management group. There are no job titles here.'

The consequence of such an approach is that there is a high degree of autonomy, with people having a lot of responsibility for what they do. 'When team leaders and members discuss an issue, everyone gets heard,' says Marshall. 'The environment doesn't suit everyone. You are responsible for yourself and you must be comfortable with that. The more successful you are at Benfield Group, the more diverse your role becomes.' Moving within the company is not a problem. As stated, people are responsible for their own development – there is no framework for arranging rotations. 'You put your hand up and say 'I want to do this'. If there's buy-in, there are no barriers,' says Marshall. 'It would be a nightmare if we had to seek sign-offs and approach a dozen committees.'

The company has managed to retain a small firm feel, despite having expanded to twice its size in two years. The dress code is very much in line with City rules and regulations, and staff at Benfield Group look smart and dress appropriately for City roles. The company is male dominated, with a male:female ratio of 66:34, with 48 per cent of staff being under 35. 'This is a smart office,' says Marshall. 'How the office appears is important. We are a professional services business. First impressions are important and our approach must project that.'

When it comes to working from home Benfield Group is 'not leading the pack'. 'However, we do have a degree of flexibility,' says Marshall. 'That's arranged on an individual basis. Remember we operate in a customer services environment, and our customers expect – and get – proper cover.'

## Human Resources

Marshall regards Human Resources as 'a people advisory and development team'. There are three strands to this team – HR Ops, which is responsible for hiring staff, management information, solving problems, arranging work permits, general handholding, etc; Payroll and benefits – 'which speaks for itself'; and learning and development – where the aim overall is to provide support to staff to enjoy and thrive in the company environment. Here staff are nurtured to feel better for being part of a team and more enriched for being part of Benfield Group. 'We adopt the view that we believe we are constantly enriching the work experience of our staff in some way during their careers with us,' says Marshall. 'We encourage a thirst for learning.' That can be achieved through attendance at evening classes or dropping by the company's development zone – where there are copious supplies of relevant management videos and books, and e-learning opportunities. 'The focus is on general management and soft skills training, as well as the technical aspects of the job.'

All members of staff are able to watch and catch up with the latest news or sports events while working, via television monitors that are situated on every floor of the Group's London office.

## Career Opportunity and Development

'Once or twice a year everybody in the company participates in a learning or development event out of the office,' says Marshall. 'There's even non-business related stuff, such as contributing towards the cost of a tai chi course.'

'There are many opportunities to transfer between teams and to other offices across our international network,' says Marshall. The company also operates a performance management process called '2 Way', where individuals look to develop themselves with the support of other team members and the rest of the organisation. 'People log their development needs, making clear what they are looking for. If we can't reach consensus, which is unusual, we work out a suitable compromise,' says Marshall. 'We proactively manage the process.'

Benfield Group operates a Trainee Programme whereby external and internal candidates train for a number of roles in the organisation. 'Everyone on the scheme is recruited for a particular position. In 2001 we received, via careers fairs, some 400 applications. We personally read every single application. Whilst we obviously look for educational ability, we also look for that 'something else' that makes us want to interview the candidate.'

Aside from the Trainee Programme, Benfield Group is also beginning to run development and training schemes for all employees. 'For instance, we also have a senior leadership programme and we are looking to roll out similar programmes for all other employees within the organisation. The challenge is to pick up the middle executive layer,' says Marshall. 'We approach development of teams both vertically and horizontally – with a team or group of teams.'

'We want our people to feel comfortable while working here and therefore it's important that people understand the culture and style of the organisation,' says Marshall. Everyone has a part to play in contributing to the team effort. The formula must be working as staff turnover is below seven per cent.

## Remuneration

Salaries are highest upper quartile and 'on a par with the best in the business'. The company is soon to launch a performance-related pay scheme with a bonus depending on the profits of the business. Individuals can also expect merit increases, depending on their contribution to the company. There is a (very generous) defined contribution pension scheme, life insurance, private health care facilities and critical illness cover for all members of staff. The more an individual contributes to the success of Benfield Group, the more of an opportunity there is for reward.

'Our intention has always been to offer all employees some form of stock holding', says Marshall. There are options to purchase shares, which lapse if a person leaves the company, and shares which have to be sold if a person leaves. Over 70 per cent of the company is owned by staff members and management. Benfield Group is a private company that's highly regarded both by its industry peers and its staff. This is reflected in the company's terms and conditions.

'Instead of providing company cars, we offer significant car allowances to employees,' states Marshall. Part of the package of working for Benfield Group is the culture and ambience, which is enhanced through the offerings of such benefits as free yoga and massage sessions.

## The Future

'We have always striven to be the best,' says Marshall. 'We want to be better than we were before – we want to be the best company in our business – that's the best, not the biggest'.

Benfield Group is a great place to work if you take to the culture. 'We want to be at the leading edge in all aspects in our business – which includes the application of IT, and HR policies, as well as our dealings with customers', says Marshall. Benfield Group continues to win recognition and praise from its peers in the insurance and reinsurance industry for its innovative products and capabilities. The growing number of industry awards Benfield Group is garnering pays testimony to this.

The Big Yellow company is one of the pioneering self-storage companies in the UK, taking the idea that the consumer society is buying too much stuff, has nowhere to put it, and forging a business plan on this basis. The company was established in 1998 and has 25 stores currently trading, with a further six committed.

**Scorecard:**

| | |
|---|---|
| Remuneration and benefits: | *** |
| Progressive attitude | **** |
| Opportunity for promotion | *** |
| Training, development and education | ***** |
| Working Atmosphere and Environment | **** |

**Biggest plus:**
The culture and the people – the willingness to help and the 'can-do' attitude.

**Biggest minus:**
Low awareness of the sector among both customers and potential employees.

Big Yellow Group Plc
2 The Deans
Bridge Road
Bagshot
Surrey GU19 5AT
Tel: 01276 470190
Fax: 01276 470191
Freephone: 0800 783 4949
Website: www.thebigyellow.co.uk

# Big Yellow

## The Business

The Big Yellow Self Storage Company was established in 1998 by two property specialists. They perceived the need when they saw people moving from larger to smaller properties both in business and in the consumer space. This was to be no ordinary storage warehouse, however, and people entering a modern Big Yellow store will find friendly staff, a clean retail environment and advice on storing items large and small. Customers might want to buy a box or hire just a locker to store their valuables and they will find themselves catered for. The idea came from the US and Australia initially and Big Yellow has been instrumental in building up the market for self-storage in the UK.

In 2000 it achieved a listing on the Alternative Investments Market and in 2002 followed this with a full listing on the London Stock Exchange. The objective was to fund further growth for the business, which is predominantly in the South East of the country. It has moved into a profit position in its trading at the time it expected to according to its business plan, and although it has been hit by slow trading along with the rest of the retail market, its revenue is showing signs of continuing to grow.

*Although it has become a multiple-branch operation and intends to open a lot more of these by the middle of the decade, the ethos and feel of Big Yellow remains that of a small business*

Recognising that its growth would necessitate change, it has recruited individuals from other industries to bolster its initial management group. It would be fair to describe its growth as one of the success stories of the 1990s.

## Company Culture and Style

Although it has become a multiple-branch operation and intends to open a lot more of these by the middle of the decade, the ethos and feel of Big Yellow remains that of a small business. Business clothing is provided for the customer-facing staff and an ethos of 'business casual' pervades throughout the organisation. There is a flat management structure to the extent that if a sales assistant wants to pick up the phone to the MD they are encouraged to do so. 'We are always looking to get our people involved', says Cheryl Hathaway, HR Controller for the company.

This isn't to say that there are no formal structures within the business. The lack of bureaucracy at the top filters down to a reasonable scale of automomy at store level, where there are area and management meetings as well as staff meetings within the stores. 31 per cent of the company's management are female and the company is keen to maintain a balance throughout its stores. Flexible working is there to an extent; if someone at head office wants to work from home then it depends on the function they fulfil. Clearly, personnel at store level need to be there, and any flexible approach is at the discretion of a store manager.

Management structures aside, the company strives to be open-ended and to keep the customer in mind all of the time. This means anyone in the stores can be called upon to face a customer so anyone who is shy is likely to find a store position less than comfortable. Guidelines for dealing with customers are on offer but the main focus is on the individual; taking it as read that the company's priority is getting the work done, when you work for Big Yellow you're 'you' rather than 'employee X'. A lot of issues that will come up in the next section and the one after can therefore seem as if they're administered hap-hazardly; this isn't the case, it's just that the company is of a size at which it can deal with staff on a case-by-case basis.

The fun stuff also happens. You get your birthday (or a nearby working day) off. The company gives you vouchers as a wedding present and also on the birth of a child. There are customer service and other awards. A deal with Red Letter Days means you can have a day out by earning points. You even get an Easter egg every year!

## Human Resources

The HR department at Big Yellow continues to grow and formalise as this book goes to press. It already did a lot of unexpected things for staff though: Hathaway confirms that there have been instances in which people who are ill have had some of their medical bills paid, although this sort of action would depend on the individual and the circumstances.

Recruitment for the stores happens primarily at a local level; the local press and the London *Evening Standard* are good places to look for jobs. Graduate recruitment happens, although not in a big way – the company is going to emulate B&Q in a focus on the more mature applicant, on the basis that customers will want to know someone has had a little practical experience.

## Career Opportunity and Development

One of the fun things about working for a company in its early growth phase is that it can do slightly unorthodox things. For example, when an employee wanted to learn to drive and felt that it would benefit the company, Big Yellow contributed towards the cost of lessons – this would be done on a case by case basis rather than as a matter of course.

Most of the training to date has taken place on the job, however. The induction process for stores is thorough with a week's off-the-job training, at the end of which a full assessment takes place. They then spend weeks 2–5 studying the operations workbook and are reviewed in week four; on-the-job training continues between weeks 6–11 with a review in week 8. The overall induction is reviewed in week 11 and a personal performance review follows in week 11 or 12, then in week 13, all being well, the probationary period is confirmed as expired. Personal performance is reviewed annually thereafter, and a quarterly review of performance objectives also takes place.

At managerial level there are courses available to include recruiting for success, managing performance, training the trainer and winning ways in business. Generic standards of performance were introduced in the stores and head office specifically for customer services in mid-2003, as was a senior store manager development programme to include key operations personnel.

In addition, the company sponsors professional studies and further education for its employees, and is working towards Investors in People accreditation. If it all sounds as though it's being put in place rather than having been there forever, then bear in mind the company was established only in December 1998 – a lot has been achieved in a very short time.

# Remuneration

Packages are on the above-average side, with bonuses paid for good performance. Pay rates are linked to what the market demands, and the company takes part in research annually to ensure its employees get what they deserve. An annual review happens in April and the stores have salary bandings. Expect 20 days holiday to start with, rising to 25, but also expect your birthday off as previously mentioned!

Bonus schemes start on day one and whether store or head office based you can get up to 25 or 15 per cent respectively of your salary in this way, paid quarterly in stores and half-yearly at the corporate HQ. Head Office staff are incentivised along company performance lines as well as on an individual basis. There is a pension scheme after three months and a share option scheme for all employees of six months' standing or more.

# Future

Although the company is primarily a South East England-based operation it does have plans to go into mainland Europe within the next ten years, starting with France. In the shorter term it will continue to grow in the UK and is on course to have 50 stores open by the middle of the decade.

As an employer it will continue to put structures in place so that employees can meet their own development agendas as long as the business' needs are served first. In spite of a perceived recession at the beginning of the 21st century the company has met its revenue growth and profitability targets and there appears to be every reason to expect its success to continue.

# BLACK & VEATCH

Black & Veatch Consulting is an international multi-disciplinary firm of consulting engineers. It employs 635 permanent and 100 contract employees in the UK and overseas, and had sales in excess of £40 million in 2002. The firm is a 100 per cent-owned subsidiary of Black & Veatch Corporation in the US.

**Scorecard:**

| | |
|---|---|
| Remuneration and benefits | *** |
| Progressive attitude | ***** |
| Opportunity for promotion | **** |
| Training, development and education | ***** |
| Working atmosphere and environment | **** |

**Biggest plus:**
Freedom to make a real difference to the lives of ordinary people around the world.

**Biggest minus:**
The firm aims to work harder to meet all the creative expectations of its people.

Black & Veatch Consulting
Grosvenor House
69 London Road
Redhill
Surrey H1 1LQ
Tel: 01737 774155
Fax: 01737 772767
Website: www.bvcs.bv.com

# Black & Veatch

## The Business

Black & Veatch (formerly Binnie) Consulting has a tradition of supplying consulting services for water engineering projects that stretches back to 1890. Founded by Sir Alexander Binnie, then passed on to his son, the firm grew rapidly in the post-war era taking on many high-profile overseas projects, particularly in former British colonies.

However, privatisation of the UK water industry in 1989 radically altered the trading environment. With demand for consulting services waxing and waning according to the new investment cycle, the firm's strategy changed. In order to move from a specialist water consulting business, it opted to diversify its service provision, merging with US firm Black & Veatch (B&V) in 1995.

Now a subsidiary of the B&V Corporation, B&V Consulting has a truly global presence across six continents and specialises in four main business areas: water supply and wastewater treatment, flood defence, information and energy. Its client base ranges from privatised water companies to government environment agencies. In recent years it has drawn the bulk of its work from a small number of key clients, with whom it effectively enjoys preferred supplier status.

*Almost no one works on their own; instead new teams are formed for different projects all the time, making for a very open culture in which boundaries and partition walls are conspicuous by their absence*

## Company Culture and Style

Almost three-quarters of B&V employees are engineers and, as such, are knowledge workers in the truest sense of the word. Managing Director, David Nickols, describes them as 'strong minded, independent of thought, who love challenges and problem-solving, and who like doing so cooperatively in teams'. Given the desire to stretch themselves creatively, this calibre of individual can often be hard to manage. But so long as they do act cooperatively, opinionated individuals are welcome and encouraged.

The atmosphere in the open-plan offices is very lively. Almost no one works on their own; instead new teams are formed for different projects all the time, making for a very open culture in which boundaries and partition walls are conspicuous by their absence. This openness extends right through to a corporate and strategic level. There is contact between senior and divisional managers at information meetings held every two months. There are also a number of employee forums to provide regular networking opportunities for staff.

B&V organises a wide range of social activities for its people, and is involved in various community outreach projects. Recent examples include Engineers for Disaster Relief and Habitat for Humanity – where the firm was happy to foot the bill for volunteers to go out on-site and help build homes for people in disadvantaged communities.

## Human Resources

At a senior level B&V has made a number of key strategic hires in the last couple of years. These have occurred either through personal contacts or via search firms. Because of its pre-eminence in its field, the firm enjoys a high level of 'pulling power' and has been able to be quite targeted in such appointments.

At graduate level, the shrinking pool of engineering talent is more of a concern. Again, however, the company's profile makes it an employer of choice for many graduates at key universities with which B&V has a relationship. Graduates make up around 30 per cent of the annual intake, which – despite increasing service diversification – still varies greatly in line with the investment cycle for water companies. In 2002, for example, the firm took on over 200 new people compared to half that for 2003. B&V's status is reflected in its voluntary turnover, which stands at 12 per cent – well below the average for its immediate competitors. The biggest recruitment challenge of all, though, is in the mid-career – where compensation policy struggles to match the rising cost of living in the south-east of England.

## Career Opportunity and Development

As it has extended the range of markets in which it competes for business, B&V has sought to hone its own performance as a training provider. Three years on from a comprehensive policy review, learning and development is seen as a key strategic business partner and there is a strong emphasis on robust performance management processes.

Because of the abundance of project work, teams are regularly assembled from different areas of expertise within the firm. This means that much of the responsibility for employee development necessarily cannot lie with line managers alone. Celia Morris, Learning & Development Manager, explains: 'We are professional engineers mainly – all our staff here have one or two degrees. So they are used to the idea of coaching and mentoring as part of their professional responsibility. We are able to draw on this and build on it to actively promote a coaching and mentoring culture.'

Morris adds, 'The fruits of this strategy are already coming through. For example, we wanted to raise our profile technically so we set in place a number of measures to encourage our consultants to write and publish papers in journals. We put in the incentive of a £100 bonus and created an annual paper prize.'

There are four graduate training programmes for each of the business areas; each approved by the relevant external institution (the Institute of Civil Engineers; the Institution of Mechanical Engineers; the Institution of Electrical Engineers; and the Chartered Institute of Water and Environmental Management). For the past four years, the firm has enjoyed a 100 per cent pass rate for graduates on the first programme. It has also been innovative in its approach to the fourth stream, becoming the first organisation to produce a dual career path training scheme for environmental scientists and engineers, in order to help cross-fertilise ideas between the respective employee types.

## Remuneration

B&V attracts high-calibre individuals who are motivated by a great deal more than the opportunity to earn lots of money. That said, medium earners at the firm can expect to be rewarded in the median to upper quartile as measured against the UK offices of other international firms. Reward for high performers is in the upper decile.

Though base pay currently represents the exclusive form of compensation for employees, the firm has begun to establish a bonus pool. This is in order to bring about a more innovative approach to reward strategy and reflects a growing commercial focus at the business.

There is a defined contribution pension scheme, under which the employer's minimum contribution is four per cent as against a six per cent contribution from the employee. BUPA healthcare is provided for all staff, along with life assurance and disability allowance, and the firm pays for the membership of two relevant professional associations for staff. The company is flexible in its approach to part-time working.

## The Future

According to David Nickols, 'The future's pretty bright. We're well on the way to turning the business from one so dominated by the water industry that it was unsustainable to diversifying it to a sustainable business. We expect the rapid growth rate of the last few years to slow, but to continue nonetheless. We're ranked number one or two in water industry consulting at the moment and will soon be one or two in respect of flood defence. Beyond that we want to increase our presence in energy and information consulting. Currently under 20 per cent of our overall business comes from outside the UK and we also want to grow that share as well.'

 **THE BOC GROUP**

The BOC Group is one of the world's largest manufacturers of industrial gases, with other businesses in vacuum pumps, logistics and healthcare. Headquartered in the UK, it manufactures at well over 1,000 locations in more than 50 countries world-wide, employing over 46,000 staff, around 10,000 of them in the UK. Part of the FTSE 100 since it was established in 1963, BOC made an operating profit of £500.1 million on a turnover of £4.017 billion in 2001/2002.

**Scorecard:**

| | |
|---|---|
| Remuneration and benefits | **** |
| Progressive attitude | *** |
| Opportunity for promotion | ***** |
| Training, development and education | **** |
| Working atmosphere and environment | **** |

**Biggest plus:**
Strong traditional values and belief in teamwork are being mixed with a pacier, more results-driven approach.

**Biggest minus:**
Still rather inward-looking and process-oriented. More 'mixing' still required (see above).

The BOC Group
Chertsey Road
Windlesham
Surrey GU20 6HJ
Tel: 01276 477222
Fax: 01276 471333
Website: www.boc.com

# BOC

## The Business

BOC is a global corporation, which makes money out of thin air – literally. Its gas plants around the world produce unbelievable quantities of oxygen (mostly used to make things burn more efficiently in manufacturing) and nitrogen (used for anything from making fertilisers and freezing fruit and hamburger patties to creating an inert 'blanket' in chemical plants). Other products in its range of over 25,000 gases and gas mixtures include hydrogen, helium, argon and carbon dioxide.

BOC has become a leader in its field through its efficiency, service, and more than a century of experience. Founded in 1886 by the brothers Brin (hence its initial name, Brin's Oxygen Company – it later became the British Oxygen Company in 1906, BOC is now split into three global lines of business and two other 'specialist' businesses. Process Gas Solutions (bulk gas for industrial customers) and Industrial and Special Products (cylinders of gas, used anywhere from hospitals to hostelries) account for two-thirds of sales. BOC Edwards (another fifth of sales) supplies gases and vacuum pumps to the semiconductor industry. These three lines of business are global, manufacturing in more than 50 countries.

*We've created an entrepreneurial culture within a multinational framework, where people can drive their own part of the business*

No single country accounts for as much as a fifth of revenues, making BOC truly an international business. The two smaller businesses are regional: Gist, a UK logistics business, and Afrox Hospitals, the largest chain of private hospitals in Africa.

Despite its size, BOC is not a high-profile company, but it has been in the FTSE 100 since the index was founded three decades ago. It was shaken by a takeover bid in 2000, but emerged stronger and with a sharper, pacier outlook, and its financial results in the last three years have been the best in the group's recent history.

## Company Culture and Style

In many ways, BOC epitomises the best of a traditional engineering firm – at the forefront of its industry, with a passion for doing things well, a commitment to collaborative working, and an avuncular concern for its people.

The company retains a strong belief in processes, not just in its manufacturing operations but also in management. Some insiders chide it for being too process-oriented and not sufficiently outcome-focused, but the company is making significant changes in the way it operates, aiming to create a blend of traditional values and more flexible, modern thinking.

The management structure has become much less hierarchical in the last few years, organised as a matrix of functional groups rather than along lines of business. It hasn't always been easy (engineers like being told what to do!). But it has made the company much more nimble, says group HR Director, Rob Lourey. 'I can make a decision and say to the HR people in the divisions, "this is what we're doing"', he says. 'It makes for an effective combination of central, strategic direction and local, tactical capability.'

The matrix structure has reinforced BOC's long-standing commitment to team working, and the company is managed via what Lourey calls 'a constituency of peer-groups' – all the financial directors, health and safety managers, etc, work together to agree common standards and share best practice. This attitude extends right down the organisation.

'We've created an entrepreneurial culture within a multinational framework, where people can drive their own part of the business,' says Nigel Abbott, BOC's Group Public Relations Manager. 'It's a very rewarding atmosphere for individuals to work in.'

Those who succeed at BOC tend to be quiet radicals – smart and able to make change happen, but in a collaborative, facilitative way, not by conflict or antagonism. 'Working at BOC is fulfilling and enjoyable, because we recognise the merits of each function of the business,' says Lourey. Nobody gets looked down on because they work for a 'cost centre' rather than a 'profit centre'.

The company has a genuine regard for its people and for maintaining a work/life balance. The workforce is diverse, says Lourey, although not in sex or ethnicity – of BOC's 80-odd senior managers, just two are women and two come from ethnic minorities. The group is working hard to rectify this, by bringing more local people into management in its regional operations, so they can then be spread around the world.

## Human Resources

There is an in-joke that if you join BOC you will never leave, and staff turnover among managers is just 4–5 per cent a year. Small wonder then, that the organisation is characterised by a strong collective sense of pride. The company prefers to promote from within where feasible, and all senior and middle appointments are advertised globally within the group, so there is relatively little external recruitment at senior levels.

Nonetheless, BOC is keen to infuse new blood, and generally recruits around 60 graduates a year – 20–25 in the UK, a similar number in the USA, the rest in the South Pacific. Some are fresh from university, others are more experienced people. Graduate trainees join a rotational development programme lasting just over two years, being assessed in each post before moving on to the next. This gives them valuable experience in all aspects of the business, and avoids pigeonholing them into particular roles from the moment they join. Specialisations are generally chosen towards the end of the two years.

There may be a few ad-hoc, temporary placements organised at local level, but in general BOC has few opportunities to offer sandwich courses, summer placements, etc.

## Career Opportunity and Development

BOC is not ashamed to say that it cares about its people, and its attitude towards them is, if not actually paternal, then certainly avuncular. 'We like to give strong direction to people as they grow their careers', says Lourey. Each individual has their own personal development plan, with appraisals at least once, and preferably twice, a year. 'We work on how they can be more effective in their current role and how they can grow into new ones', says Lourey.

The company still has formal employment grades, but these are becoming less prominent and may soon be replaced with broader, more flexible bands to reflect the more meritocratic culture BOC is becoming. 'This is definitely an organisation in which cream can float to the top,' says Lourey.

In 2000, the company began an executive development programme, called Lead, aimed at developing its future leaders, devised by Columbia University and the Center for Creative Leadership. Twenty-five people a year are invited onto the 10-month programme, which combines self-learning and residential courses, and aims to promote BOC's core values and ways of working, and to develop managers' ability to operate a successful global business. Each region operates a similar programme for middle-managers.

Other training, both technical and business, is provided to all staff in conjunction with their personal development plan. The company helps staff gain further technical and business qualifications, including MBAs, often on a 'you pass, we pay' basis.

BOC's global reach is a big advantage for people who want to experience other cultures and business practices. There are seven nationalities on the executive management board (including Lourey, an Australian), and of 1,100–1,200 middle and senior managers, around 160 are expatriates, giving a 10–15 per cent likelihood of being stationed abroad at any one time. Foreign visits are even more common – part of BOC's culture of international peer-group teams.

## Remuneration

A while ago, BOC encapsulated its core values as Accountability, Commitment, Transparency (of communication) and a willingness to Stretch to deliver superior performance (which together form the handy acronym ACTS). These are the targets against which the company's increasingly performance-related remuneration is calculated, with 20–40 per cent of managers' pay being based on their performance and that of their part of the business. Combined with industry-standard basic salaries, this gives BOC an above-average level of overall remuneration, says Lourey. 'If you perform well against stretching targets, you will be well rewarded,' he says.

The company is moving towards a flexible benefits approach, where individuals can balance their salary, pension, healthcare, car and other benefits to suit their lifestyle and circumstances. As well as being good for recruitment, flexible benefits are good for recruiting the right kind of people, believes Lourey. 'They attract people who are more used to controlling their own destiny', he says.

BOC is keen for staff to share in its success, and encourages them to own shares in the group with employee purchase schemes that are open to all. Its share options scheme is generous, extending to around 1,200 of the group's 46,000 payroll – three times the scope of a typical options scheme in other companies, says Lourey.

## The Future

The gases business is, by and large, not very volatile (rather like its products), nor very cyclical (except within the semiconductor industry served by BOC Edwards). But the market for gases (over 80 per cent of BOC's business) has outpaced worldwide GDP growth by 1.5 times for more than 25 years, so the prospects are good. The competitive landscape is unlikely to change significantly, and this was the reason behind the failed takeover attempt two years ago. So BOC's declared aim of remaining strongly independent looks well based.

BOC's global reach means it is well placed to exploit opportunities wherever they arise, and it expects its Asian business to grow from 30 per cent of group turnover to 50 per cent by 2007. BOC's sense of continuity and pride in its history make it especially respected in China, where it is one of the most involved of all British companies, with 16 joint ventures.

The group's target is annual double-digit growth over the next five years – unprecedented hitherto, but achievable through improved productivity, expanding markets and judicious acquisition, believes BOC. 'I think the future is in our own hands', says Lourey.

The Body Shop has made its mark for simultaneously pioneering the use of natural ingredients in skin and hair care products and what is now known as corporate social responsibility. Having expanded rapidly through the 1980s, the company has recently gone through a troubled period. But it remains one of the best known and trusted brands in the world and has maintained its commitment to such values as supporting human rights and Fair Trade, and opposing animal testing. With a turnover in the year to March 2002 of £380 million, the company known for introducing tea tree oil and banana shampoo to the masses operates over 1,900 outlets in 50 countries.

**Scorecard:**

| | |
|---|---|
| Remuneration and benefits | **** |
| Progressive attitude | ***** |
| Opportunity for promotion | **** |
| Training, development and education | **** |
| Working atmosphere and environment | **** |

**Biggest plus:**
Working for a company that clearly stands for something.

**Biggest minus:**
The business is not always as slick operationally as it should be, with the result that frustrations can develop.

The Body Shop International
Watersmead
Littlehampton
West Sussex BN17 6LS
Tel: 01903 731500
Fax: 01903 844277
Website: www.the-body-shop.com

# The Body Shop

## The Business

The Body Shop is an internationally renowned retailer of skin and body care products. Ever since Anita Roddick founded the company – as a single shop in Brighton selling just 25 hand-mixed products – in 1976, it has paid as much attention to its 'values' as to the usual measures of business performance. Hence its 'business as unusual' philosophy.

From the start, the business distinguished itself from the cosmetics industry mainstream through such attitudes as its opposition to animal testing and its insistence on natural ingredients. These stands have developed into environmental and human rights campaigns and a commitment to Fair Trade, called Community Trade by the company.

The unconventional approach quickly won fans and the company expanded rapidly, largely thanks to its use of franchising. In 1978 a kiosk in Brussels became the first overseas franchise and by 1982 two new shops a month were opening. By 1990, only 14 years after the first shop opened, the company was trading in 39 countries.

*There's a culture of learning and development. We encourage all employees to have a personal development plan*

Much of the company's manufacturing operation has now been sold, so that the company can concentrate on retailing. But in the 1990s it launched The Body Shop At Home, a direct selling operation that involves consultants selling products through parties, typically in customers' homes. In 2000–2001 alone there were more than 100,000 parties involving nearly 1 million customers, and the operation is seen as highly complementary to the main business.

In 2001, a turbulent period came to a head with discussions about selling the company. But a new management team – led by Chairman Adrian Bellamy and Chief Executive Peter Saunders – was installed in 2002 and has pledged to rejuvenate the company so that it fulfils its potential.

## Company Culture and Style

As a global retail company with a deep commitment to its core values, The Body Shop has a clear culture and style. Long before it was fashionable, the company was non-hierarchical, modern in its thinking and informal. Though its approach has naturally evolved over the past quarter of a century, the company has a set of core values that are adhered to and are known as the 'five pillars'. These are: Against Animal Testing, Support Community Trade, Activate Self-Esteem, Defend Human Rights and Protect Our Planet.

Underlining these are commitments to community involvement, through which the company and its employees contribute to local, national and global communities; The Body Shop Foundation, which assists those working to achieve sustainable progress in human and civil rights, the environment and animal protection; and values reporting, or communicating on the company's impact on the environment and the communities in which it operates.

It follows then, that the company hires many people who are passionate about the sorts of concerns that have made founder Anita Roddick a household name. Moreover, once they are hired the lack of hierarchy means that they are not blocked from doing things that they feel fit with that passion. But, as Human Resources Director, Mark Barrett, acknowledges, this 'has its problems' – chiefly in a lack of processes that is currently being addressed. Conversely, those that do not succeed, he says, are 'people who need quite clear boundaries and rules and regulations'. Having traditionally favoured the sort of employees who take on initiatives, the company is beginning to put more value on those who do 'invisible work' and keep things going.

As might be expected from a company founded by a woman, about half of the managers in the UK and around the world are female. Moreover, some of them are mothers who work part-time. The commitment to working parents – as part of the value pillar concerning self-esteem – is also seen in the better-than-the-norm maternity rights and childcare support. At the company's Littlehampton headquarters, there is a 75-place workplace nursery, while for those who cannot use that there is a voucher system to help them to obtain the same sort of high-quality care.

Furthermore, employees can apply to work flexibly, provided they can make a strong business case, while about 70 per cent of the staff in the company's shops work part-time.

## Human Resources

As with many companies, The Body Shop's recruitment practices depend on the role being filled. People being hired to work in specialist functions at head office, say, will typically need a degree and/or professional qualification, while those joining one of the company's many retail outlets will not need the same sort of qualifications. 'It's very job-specific', says Barrett. And leavers are encouraged to return.

In general, the HR department sees its role as similar to that in most large organisations. 'We're there to do all the normal life-cycle things,' says Barrett, explaining that this means helping managers to recruit and organising and overseeing the induction process as well as running development programmes.

'The company has quite a pedigree in terms of learning and development,' he adds. 'There's a culture of learning and development. We encourage all employees to have a personal development plan.'

Less usual are the 'advocacy' initiative, under which certain employees are trained to support others when they have a grievance or some other work-related problem, and the Love – Learning Of Value for Everyone – scheme, which provides up to £100 for individuals to do a non-vocational course, such as having driving lessons, learning a language or joining a gym.

## Career Opportunity and Development

The company does not at present measure the proportion of internal promotions to external appointments. But Barrett points out that 'a lot of people get promoted'. Moreover, while moving between functions is not common, it is possible, since he himself joined the company in the finance department and moved into HR following a reorganisation.

As a company operating in 50 countries, The Body Shop has an international flavour, with corresponding opportunities to travel and to work overseas.

There is heavy emphasis on employees managing their own careers. Personal development plans are supported by succession planning and other initiatives and individuals are also encouraged to market themselves well.

One issue that the company has recently been addressing is an emphasis on long hours in certain parts of the operation. The company has responded to claims that employees were saying that they did not have enough freedom by introducing a programme called FISH. This has the aim of 'helping people to focus on customer service and bring energy and fun into the workplace', says Barrett.

## Remuneration

The company's overall aim is to pay between the median and the upper quartile. However, pay reviews can lead to some employees receiving more. In addition, various bonus schemes operate. Managers and above are subject to a scheme that is based on a combination of group and individual performance, while for shop staff it is based on their team's performance. If the shop does well, they do well. For junior employees in other parts of the organisation, the drivers depend on objectives and competencies.

In addition, there are share ownership and share options schemes. Under the government-approved all-employee share scheme, each member of staff receives an allocation of about £350-worth of shares, provided profit targets are met. Options apply to managers and above and involve an annual granting based on a percentage of their salary.

Every employee joins the company pension scheme after a year's service. The company makes contributions equivalent to 5 per cent of salary initially, rising to 6 per cent after five years and 7 per cent after 10 years. Employees are not required to contribute, but can make additional voluntary contributions. Employees can choose to have their fund invested along ethical lines.

Every employee is covered by three-times-salary life insurance from the day they join and there is permanent health insurance for all after one year. Managers and above receive private health insurance.

Holidays range from 23 days a year at the start to 33 days after 10 years' service. But – under the flexible benefits policy – it is possible to 'buy' or 'sell' up to five days a year.

Company cars are only driven by those – typically in the field – who need them for work. And all of these must meet strict environmental criteria.

## The Future

With the new senior management much more focused on retail, The Body Shop hopes to leave its recent difficulties behind it. Barrett points out that the company retains a strong brand and that this 'still has fantastic potential'.

The emphasis over the next three years, he says, will be on implementation of the strategy. Chairman Adrian Bellamy said in the 2002 annual report that the short-term focus would be on 'improving our service to our customers through better implementation in every sector of the company'. This includes driving product development and rationalisation, along with marketing, to improve growth in sales and margins and improving efficiency.

The Asia/Pacific region still has a lot of growth remaining, but the company believes it can improve sales in the mature markets of the UK and the US through continued innovation. It expects most growth to come from the traditional retail operation and the direct sales business rather than through the Internet or other channels.

But, although the Roddicks are no longer directly involved in the business (they are non-executives), The Body Shop believes its future success will depend on sticking to the values they established.

# Bradford & Bingley*

Bradford & Bingley is a leading provider of financial and property services in the United Kingdom. Its history goes back a century and a half. Having floated on the stock market in December 2000, the organisation is evolving from a mutual manufacturer of mortgages and savings products into an innovative and growing distributor of a wide range of financial services produced by a number of different suppliers. The group has about 7,000 staff and more than four million customers, who are served through a 500-strong branch network, online services, financial advisers and third-party distributors. In the year to 31 December 2001, it made a profit of £234 million.

**Scorecard:**

| | |
|---|---|
| Remuneration and benefits | **** |
| Progressive attitude | *** |
| Opportunity for promotion | *** |
| Training, development and education | **** |
| Working atmosphere and environment | **** |

**Biggest plus:**
The move towards more decentralisation creates opportunities.

**Biggest minus:**
The group is still shaking off the culture of the past at a time of intense competition in the financial services industry.

Bradford & Bingley plc
PO Box 88
Croft Road
Crossflatts
Bingley
West Yorkshire BD16 2UA
Tel: 01274 555555
Fax: 01274 554256
Website: www.bbg.co.uk

# Bradford & Bingley

## The Business

Bradford & Bingley is one of the largest high-street independent financial services groups in the UK, with more than 500 branches, 7,000 staff and more than four million customers. Formerly a building society with roots stretching back to the mid-19th century, it was perhaps best known for its two bowler hats logo and marketing campaign featuring 'Mr Bradford' and 'Mr Bingley'. However, it became a quoted company in December 2000 as part of the trend for former building societies to abandon the mutual status, by which they were owned by their members rather than investors. And, following the appointment of Christopher Rodrigues as chief executive in 1995, the business set in place a number of initiatives designed to achieve the objective of becoming a leading national provider of services relating to finance and property.

*the growing use of technology means that many of the more senior employees have begun to use lap-top computers to work at home more effectively*

From Lloyds TSB, it acquired both the Mortgage Express specialist lending operation and the Black Horse Agencies estate agency business. It also bought John Charcol, a leading mortgage broker serving the higher end of the market, and rebranded its standard services under the Marketplace name. As a result of these moves, it is able to offer a broad range of services, including insurance broking, independent financial advice and property-related services.

Conscious that there was no need for another small to medium-sized bank, Bradford & Bingley has deliberately pursued 'a clear and different strategy' based on the two separate but complementary businesses of distribution of financial products and selective lending.

## Company Culture and Style

Inevitably for a company that has grown significantly through acquisition, there is what Andrew Law, General Manager for HR, describes as a 'mix of cultures'. Employees remain highly loyal to the companies that have been swallowed up by the group.

Another issue is that a significant proportion of the old Building Society staff was in favour of the organisation retaining its mutual status and was therefore disappointed when the vote was lost.

However, Law claims there is 'a lot of belief in what we're trying to do' in moving the organisation away from being a paternalistic building society to a modern plc without abandoning too much of its past.

In encouraging this, managers are anxious not to impose a new culture from the top. Instead, they are trying to understand what are the common values and to establish the sort of behaviours by which they can live, while building on the apparent enthusiasm for working in teams.

The lack of firm direction in such matters is also reflected in the informal dress code – employees are allowed to wear what they think is suitable under the definition of 'business casual'.

Law maintains that the business 'doesn't lend itself' to a lot of formal working from home or 'hot desking'. Nevertheless, the growing use of technology means that many of the more senior employees have begun to use lap-top computers to work at home more effectively. Not that Bradford & Bingley has done much in the way of publishing guides to how such practices should be introduced. 'It's all been done in a pretty grown-up way rather than with lots of rules and regulations', he says.

In common with other organisations with a retail aspect, Bradford & Bingley has also seen the benefits of accommodating the desire – especially among female staff – for part-time working and other flexible arrangements in dealing with peak periods in the branches.

However, there are increasing opportunities to work flexible hours in head office functions, and Law points out that many people in his department, for instance, often work from home if they need to. The company has also introduced career breaks and has recently developed a policy for dealing with stress.

In an encouraging sign for women, Bradford & Bingley is one of the few leading companies with a female finance director – former Sainsbury's FD Rosemary Thorne. There are also many female branch managers. In keeping with an intent to treat its employees with respect, it takes equal opportunities and diversity seriously. The latter is especially important given the company's prominent position in an area of Yorkshire with a large Asian community.

## Human Resources

It is possible to join Bradford & Bingley in many different ways – through specialist head office functions, such as information technology and finance, or through the various different parts of the business, including financial advice, estate agency or the branches spread around the country. A first port of call for many potential recruits is the website, which has a section devoted to careers.

Once in the organisation, employees of all levels go through extensive training and development with a view to creating 'rewarding careers so that everyone can realise their full potential'. The HR department organises a range of activities, from personal development programmes through to the specialised training courses required by the regulator, the Financial Services Authority, and will also provide help for those wishing to take banking examinations and other professional qualifications.

The company seeks to attract recruits by saying the business is large enough to be complex and therefore offer a wide range of opportunities while being small enough to enable employees to feel they are making a difference.

'I think the staff do understand it's a different proposition. We get incredibly good customer satisfaction levels', says Law.

## Career Opportunity and Development

In addition to providing extensive general training and development, the company is highly committed to boosting leadership at all levels of the organisation. It has also gone beyond the succession planning for senior executives required by the FSA to develop succession plans for the top 300 managers in the company.

As part of this approach, the company has developed a system that divides employees – according to their performance – into a number of categories. These include 'evident talent', 'emerging talent' and 'solid citizens'.

The job of Law and his colleagues is to ensure that those employees in each of these groups are treated appropriately and encouraged to develop. Important as they are, solid citizens cannot stand still because the performance barrier is being raised all the time, he points out.

Moreover, high performers need to be handled properly while efforts are made to understand why others are not doing so well. Though the company will 'manage out' those that it is felt will not grow, it recognises that sometimes people do not perform because they are 'the wrong person in the wrong job at the wrong time'.

One way of dealing with this is attempting to break down barriers, or silos, within the businesses to enable good people to be spread around. Another initiative that has begun to be rolled out is a group-wide performance management system. Its starting point was the desire to identify the sorts of behaviours that characterised high performers. Through interviews with a wide range of employees, a list of attributes has been compiled and an 'attribute model' built.

Another result of the development of the performance management system is that everybody within the company should have an active personal development plan. It is the responsibility of each employee to prompt their manager if he or she is not fulfilling their part of the bargain through offering the sort of experience and development that has been agreed.

'We're trying to move employees away from traditional training and more towards coaching and mentoring, sharing of best practice etc', says Law.

## Remuneration

The company's basic approach to pay and benefits is 'nothing unusual but everything you would expect'.

As far as pay goes, the policy is to pay at the median for the sector, with high performers eligible for substantial bonuses. All employees are eligible for a share of the group profits (dependent on certain targets being met) that in recent years has equated to between three and six per cent of salary. The top 300 managers are covered by a short-term incentive plan that gives them potentially bigger rewards but tougher targets than those applying to the company as a whole.

One advantage of converting from a building society into a listed company is that staff can have shares in the company. About half of the employees own stock through a share-save scheme.

However, the old pension scheme with its closely defined benefits was closed at about the same time as the company floated. It has been replaced by an insurance-based scheme that includes, says Law, many people who have never had a pension at all before.

About 2,000 of the company's approximately 7,000 staff have company cars. However, there are three levels of company car provision. The first is for those for whom a car is integral to the job – sales people, for instance. Such employees receive fleet cars. In the middle band, the type of car is determined by use rather than the status of the employee. Then there is the senior level, where executives receive the typical status models. The company has deals with Ford and Peugeot, but at senior levels employees receive a monthly allowance and wide discretion about how to spend it.

Provision of medical and health insurance is dependent upon seniority, but the company is looking at relaxing the three years' service requirement for health insurance.

## The Future

The company intends to continue its recent policy of expanding through a mixture of organic growth and selective acquisitions.

Among the business drivers it has set out are increasing the size of the retail business, expanding the lending business, managing costs and managing the balance sheet through an active treasury function.

A key financial measure is return on equity. This is currently running at 15 per cent, but it is intended to increase this to 20 per cent over the next three to five years.

On an organisational basis it sees the need to create a better balance between centralisation and decentralisation. As part of this it has effectively split its head office into two – with administration and other service functions remaining in the traditional Bingley office and the senior executives and their support staff recently moving into a new office in Holborn, close to the institutions in the City of London.

# Brambles

Brambles is the result of a merger between the original Brambles and GKN, and as a result it feels like a much younger company than its pedigree suggests. It is a global support service group, operating under a dual-listed companies structure. Globally headquartered in Sydney with a second corporate office in London, Brambles Industries Limited is listed on the Australian Stock Exchange and Brambles Industries plc is listed on the London Stock Exchange. Over 30,000 employees in the company serve 40 countries on all five continents.

**Scorecard:**

| | |
|---|---|
| Remuneration and benefits | **** |
| Progressive attitude | ***** |
| Opportunity for promotion | **** |
| Training, development and education | ***** |
| Working atmosphere and environment | ***** |

**Biggest plus:**
The chance to meet truly motivated people who are passionate about what they do and making a difference to their clients.

**Biggest minus:**
The international nature of the company and its dual listing in the UK and Australia mean members of the board can have to spend their nights awake video conferencing in virtual board meetings.

Brambles Industries plc
Cassini House
57–59 St James's Street
London SW1A 1LD
Tel: 020 7659 6000
Fax: 020 7659 6001
Website: www.brambles.com

# Brambles

## The Business

Brambles is a support service organisation which avowedly takes on the tasks its clients will not or cannot accomplish in-house – we're talking pallet pooling management, waste management, and other non-core but essential jobs for a number of organisations. The merger that created the new company means the corporate style is that of a new organisation – just one that has upwards of 30,000 employees and numerous international locations. As this book went to print it was still pooling its resources together and rationalising CHEP and Cleanaway, the high-profile joint ventures that had existed between the two original companies.

Other operating businesses include Recall worldwide, Brambles Industrial Services in Australia, the UK, continental Europe and North America, and Meineke and Interlake in the USA. It has £4 billion in assets and 80,000 shareholders worldwide. The original Brambles was founded in 1875 while Guest, Keen and Nettlefold, which became GKN, started life in 1759. It is now listed in two countries, with 50 per cent of its revenue coming from Europe and 30 per cent from the Americas.

*Brambles feels like a very new company in spite of its size and geographical reach*

## Company Culture and Style

When summing up the look and feel of the company that is now Brambles, phrases like 'International' and 'State of the Art' spring very easily to mind. Some of the research on which this chapter is based took place between two people on opposite sides of the globe – our researcher in Brambles' London office and Chris Bulmer, Senior VP of Human Resources, in Sydney by the Opera House on a satellite video link. Such sophisticated communications are everyday elements of this company's operations.

In terms of its corporate philosophy it starts by making three basic statements. First, all things begin with the customer; second, it believes in people and teamwork; and third, it has a passion for success. The mission statement it offers centres around serving shareholders and the people who work for it, and being the best at what it does. It aims always to be a leading provider of innovative business solutions and support services – and that is common to all of the various Brambles operations described above. Prospective employees wanting to fit in will be actively looking for ways they can add value to customers the whole time.

As has already been said, it also feels like a very new company in spite of its size and geographical reach. 'When I went to my first executive committee meeting I was expecting to feel like the new person', says Bulmer. 'In fact most of the executive committee had never met each other before either.' This gives entrants into the business an exciting chance to be in at ground level and have input into a growing organisation.

And although the organisation has well-established roots, it is changing and evolving. Fourteen per cent of the top 250 managers within the company are female, which is something Bulmer wants to address. Culturally the business is diverse though; eight different ethnic origins are represented on the executive committee. Communication is another area that requires constant attention – not that there's a problem but in any service company the exchange of ideas is how the service will improve.

So, think entrepreneurial, think inclusive and think 'huge company enjoying the flexibility and freshness of a small business' and you're on the right lines.

## Human Resources

The HR function is a new one; 'old Brambles' (by which read that which existed prior to the merger with GKN) didn't have a dedicated HR function. In the short time that it has existed it has achieved much in articulating the value that was already attached to the people that comprise the businesses. For example, it has put together a series of documents on leadership capabilities, which clarify what candidates for leadership will need in terms of personal qualities that will be needed for professional/administrative people as well as at director/manager level. These aren't lists of qualifications, but behavioural indicators that will give a much more realistic idea of the candidate's prospects.

It has also set about putting Personal Development Plans in place and focused a great deal on the training and career opportunities available within the business. In addition it has recently completed its first audit of employee satisfaction with the company. It can be taken, then, that it's early yet but the HR people intend to be proactive in the extreme to deliver to the workforce. This will culminate in the delivery of what the company calls a 'people promise', which will essentially be a scheme in which employees can feed back on what they expect of Brambles and what Brambles expects of them.

## Career Opportunity and Development

As you would expect from a substantial organisation there are many opportunities to progress through Brambles, and the entrepreneurial spirit that underpins the entire organisation means people wanting to manage their own progression should thrive. The leadership documentation outlined above allows people to work on their weaknesses in conjunction with line managers. Fast tracking also happens depending on someone's perceived aptitude.

The plan is for every employee to have a personal development plan, although since the HR department has had only 18 months to equip 30,000 people with one it can be assumed that this is a process rather than a given.

It attracts employees through a variety of means including its website and will continue to do so promoting equality and recognition of people of different cultures and backgrounds. Currently it is putting formal processes into place so that achievements in a job can be recognised – not that this wasn't happening before, but on an informal basis.

## Remuneration

Bulmer is very clear that the company wants its employees to aim for more than money from the business – and its spending money on an employee survey suggests that it's serious in this aim. In terms of salary it aims to pay its senior managers in the upper quartile, and is well aware of the need to reward achievers. There are elements of performance-related pay throughout the organisation.

As would be expected of an international organisation of this nature, other benefits vary from territory to territory as the legislations and tax regimes change. It has a concept of 'total financial reward' which, once complete, will allow employees to select their benefits from a budget so that they are equal to their peers but tailored. Cars are available for essential users and finance is offered as an alternative, which can be an advantage in some territories (the UK being an example of one).

## The Future

Planning for the future takes a number of forms for Brambles. In terms of the overall look and feel of the company, clearly it has some way to go in bedding down after the merger and feeling like a single cohesive entity. The top 80 people met in June 2002 to discuss precisely that – not all in the same room, indeed not all in the same continent. It will identify managers who will become 'pillars of the organisation' and will continue to focus on identifying high-potential profit centres within the core business.

As an employer it will continue to push for diversity among its employees, but never at the expense of putting the right people into the job. Its focus will continue to be on high-performing individuals who will deliver to the shareholder and thus to themselves; this will be formalised as a total quality management project during the coming years.

Brambles is an interesting company to work for at this stage in its development. It has a long and respected history but at the same time it feels fresh and entrepreneurial, ready to take input from new and established employees alike with valid business ideas. It should be fascinating to watch its progress.

# BRITISH AMERICAN TOBACCO

Founded a century ago (1902) as a joint venture between the UK's Imperial Tobacco Company and the US's American Tobacco Company, British American Tobacco has always been proud of its internationalism. After a period as part of the diversified industrial group known as B.A.T. Industries, British American Tobacco was listed on the London Stock Exchange in September 1998 as a separate company focused purely on tobacco. Having merged with Rothmans in 1999, it is responsible for such well-known brands as Dunhill, Lucky Strike and Pall Mall. The number two tobacco company in the world by global market share (behind Philip Morris of the United States), it saw pre-tax profits rise 36 per cent in 2001, to £2.065 billion, on gross turnover of £25.7 billion.

**Scorecard:**
| | |
|---|---|
| Remuneration and benefits | ***** |
| Progressive attitude | **** |
| Opportunity for promotion | ***** |
| Training, development and education | **** |
| Working atmosphere and environment | ***** |

**Biggest plus:**
'The multicultural nature of the business. There's a real feeling of opportunity when it is so multicultural.'

**Biggest minus:**
'The image of the tobacco industry can put some people off joining.'

British American Tobacco
Globe House
4 Temple Place
London WC2R 2PG
Tel: 020 7845 1000
Fax: 020 7240 0555
Website: www.bat.com

# British American Tobacco

## The Business

As the world's second largest quoted tobacco group, British American Tobacco has a market share of more than 15 per cent. With more than 300 brands in its portfolio, it makes the cigarettes chosen by one in seven of the world's one billion adult smokers.

To meet this demand, it operates 84 factories in 64 countries, producing over 800 billion cigarettes a year. It is a leader in more than 50 markets.

British American Tobacco likes to say it was born international. This is a reference to its origins as a joint venture born in 1902, through which the Imperial Tobacco Company of the UK and The American Tobacco Company of the United States agreed not to compete in each other's domestic territory but to operate widely overseas. Ten years later, it listed on the London Stock Exchange for the first time.

Rapid expansion around the world was followed by a period of then fashionable diversification. The company became just a part of B.A.T. Industries, which at one stage or another owned retailers Argos and Saks Fifth Avenue, paper and pulp companies, a cosmetics business and extensive financial services operations, including Eagle Star and Allied Dunbar.

*In the company's social report published in 2002 – a first for the tobacco industry – the company stresses that it is concentrating on building a 'high-performance culture where talented people work well together, so that their output in the business is greater than the sum of their individual contributions'*

However, the breakdown of political barriers in the 1990s created fresh opportunities for tobacco, which had been seen as a dying market, and in 1998 British American Tobacco once again became a separately quoted company on the London Stock Exchange. A year later it merged with Rothmans, then the fourth largest tobacco company in the world, and in 2000 Imperial Tobacco Company of Canada became a subsidiary.

## Company Culture and Style

British American Tobacco employs more than 80,000 people around the world and glories in the multicultural atmosphere its presence in a range of different markets creates. Employees comment approvingly on the different accents heard in the lifts at the corporate headquarters in London and point to the fact that seven nationalities are represented on the company's board.

In the company's social report published in 2002 – a first for the tobacco industry – the company stresses that it is concentrating on building a 'high-performance culture where talented people work well together, so that their output in the business is greater than the sum of their individual contributions.'

At the heart of this effort are four guiding principles that 'describe what sort of organisation we want to be and guide us in our day-to-day working lives'. They are designed to capture the way people work together, deal with organisations, communities, partners and other companies and are key to achieving the qualitative element in the company's vision.

The guiding principles are:

1. Strength from Diversity – This means more than just understanding and respecting employees' individual differences. The company sees it as meaning that these differences are valued and harnessed as a catalyst for new ideas and truly competitive advantage.
2. Open Minded – This is an attitude that influences the way the company seeks to address regulatory issues and the expectations of stakeholders. 'We are committed to listening and to constructive dialogue; to deepening our understanding of what is expected of us and demonstrating responsible behaviour', says the company.
3. Freedom through Responsibility – This describes how the company believes decisions should be taken throughout the organisation at the appropriate level, as close to the consumer as possible, and how decision takers should accept responsibility for their decisions.
4. Enterprising Spirit – This is a recognition that 'considered risk taking' – the company's skill and confidence in seeking out opportunities and striving for innovation – is an important factor in its success.

At the London headquarters, 650 people from around the world work in a light and airy building overlooking the Thames filled with works of art, some of which are on permanent loan from the Rothmans collection, and there is a great sense of an open culture. There is no set dress code, with employees mostly dressing in the smart casual way that is becoming commonplace and 'informal opportunities for flexible working' meaning that many do at least some of their work at home.

## Human Resources

In common with many other companies, British American Tobacco sees its employees as one of its most important assets. In order to make the most of them it has created four 'drivers for global HR'. These are talent, leadership, culture and learning, and the aim is to establish standards for the whole company and, in the words of Tony Hooper, Head of HR and Facilities at Globe House, to 'substantially raise the bar in all areas'. Particular emphasis is being put on developing talent 'internally and internationally'.

HR Director, Tessa Raeburn, believes that 'people stay with us because they have a passion for the business'. She adds: 'They are excited by the diversity of opportunities we offer to make the most of their talents and broaden their portfolio of skills, but most importantly they derive personal fulfilment from what they do.'

Managers acknowledge that the negative image of the tobacco industry will put some people off working for the company, but they insist that they have 'no problem' attracting people – largely because of the challenges the work presents and the opportunities for travel offered by the international nature of the business.

Moreover, recruitment criteria are rigorous, with only about 300 graduate entrants selected from the thousands of applicants around the world each year.

## Career Opportunity and Development

Graduates who are selected join a two-year training programme, which puts them on 'fast-track career'. This entails them moving through different parts and levels of the company as part of their development.

For example, a graduate joining as a finance specialist would typically start in a junior finance role in London. Then they might move to a small operating company somewhere in the world as finance director and this would be the start of a passage through ever-bigger roles.

British American Tobacco is keen to encourage the global interaction of talent and is working on developing knowledge sharing around its international operations.

A particular initiative is the Challenge Initiative, a two-year coaching and mentoring programme for graduates seen as future managers. The programme apparently lives up to its name and tests delegates' ability to the full.

Those that pass can find themselves posted almost anywhere – a policy that means that the UK offices typically have people of over 40 different nationalities working there. Opportunities are equal and it is not uncommon for the accompanying spouse on a foreign assignment to be male.

The company has its own management development centre in Surrey and there is a training suite with teach-yourself language plans and computer programs. But much of the onus of training lies with individual employees – 'freedom through responsibility' is the attitude.

'At British American Tobacco, we're always looking for highly-talented, energetic and dedicated people who can make a real contribution to our continuing success. Whatever stage you are at in your career, British American Tobacco represents an outstanding opportunity for you to accelerate your development. This is a great place to work. We hand out responsibility early and reward flair and success', says Raeburn.

## Remuneration

In common with other international companies, pay and benefits at British American Tobacco vary from location to location, but the company always seeks to be among the leaders. In the UK, the policy is to be in the upper quartile.

For example, points out Hooper, all staff are on team bonuses. This entails each team setting objectives and then each member being rewarded according to how well they did. The objectives are all related to the company strategy.

The proportion of bonus to total pay varies according to the level of the employee in the company so that senior managers are eligible for bonuses equivalent to 20 to 40 per cent of their base salary, while for middle managers it is 10 to 20 per cent. And for those in business support the figure is likely to be 5 to 10 per cent.

Nor is it just the pay. All staff – regardless of their length of service – receive 25 days' holiday a year and all receive private medical care; those in higher grades can extend it to their families.

In addition, the company provides 26 weeks' paid maternity leave, while fathers receive two weeks' paternity leave. There is also a non-contributory pension scheme.

The staff restaurant is free and there is an active social club, which offers activities for not just employees but also their families.

## The Future

Chairman Martin Broughton made the future a central theme of the annual review in the company's centenary year of 2002.

His key aim is to achieve leadership of the global tobacco industry in terms of volume, increasing profitability and shareholder value. Pointing out that the company's market share has risen by nearly 50 per cent over the past decade or so, he believes that this goal is achievable. 'It may take several years, but we remain committed to claiming the top spot', he adds.

With market share growth in the developed world harder to achieve, British American Tobacco is looking to other markets, which were closed until recently and offer plenty of opportunities for increasing the market share that is vital for growth in a global market where total volume is largely static.

But Broughton insists that leadership is not just about selling more cigarettes. He wants British American Tobacco to lead its industry in terms of corporate practice – hence the first social report, which appeared earlier this year.

BskyB is Britain's leading satellite broadcasting group, operating from twelve UK locations and employing 13,500 people. Its headquarters are in Osterley, West London; it also has two call centres in Scotland and over 1,000 mobile installers. In 2002 the group offered more than 250 television channels via satellite dish to the homes of some 6.3 million UK subscribers, and provided programmes to millions more cable customers. Just over 36 per cent of the group is owned by a subsidiary of News Corporation. In 2002 the group was worth over £11 billion with revenues of over £2.5 billion.

**Scorecard:**

| | |
|---|---|
| Remuneration and benefits | **** |
| Progressive attitude | ***** |
| Opportunity for promotion | ***** |
| Training, development and education | **** |
| Working atmosphere and environment | *** |

**Biggest plus:**
The chance to work in a dynamic and entrepreneurial environment for a global market leader with a strong record of commercial success.

**Biggest minus:**
Relatively underdeveloped internal processes means that individuals must enjoy being self-reliant.


British Sky Broadcasting Group plc
Grant Way
Isleworth
Middlesex TW7 5QD
Tel: 020 7705 3000
Fax: 020 7705 3030
Website: www.sky.com

# British Sky Broadcasting Group plc

## The Business

Sky Television was launched in 1989 by News Corporation, headed by Rupert Murdoch, and began broadcasting four channels via the Astra satellite, supported by a management centre in Livingston, Scotland. A year later its programmes were being beamed into a million UK homes. It then merged with its rival British Satellite Broadcasting to form BskyB.

In the nineties the group, commonly known as Sky, pioneered a series of deals including exclusive rights to live FA Premier League matches and in 1996, the first Pay-Per-View broadcast: Frank Bruno's defence of the World Heavyweight Championship. Another milestone was 1998, which saw the birth of Sky Digital's 140 channels and the hiring of more than 3,000 new employees.

Craig McCoy, the group's Human Resources Director, says an entrepreneurial approach has been key to success. 'Essentially we believe in changing the model wherever possible. The origins of the company lie in a progressive, commercial proposition, which provided an environment to create something new.' In 1994 a proportion of the group was floated on the stock market and it has since risen to take its place in the FTSE 200.

*Sky wants to be 'inventive, creative, entertaining and challenging' – these are its brand values. Its employees, it says, are 'dynamic, hard-working, self-driven and change-oriented', possessing the ability to set and exceed their own targets*

With a limited subscriber market in the UK, it now focuses on driving more revenue per user through Pay-Per-View and interactivity. In 1999 it launched an interactive television offering with a four-way joint venture, Open… Sky then bought out these partners and combined Open… with the Yorkshire-based Sports Internet Group, rebranding the division as Sky Active. Subscribers can now bet, shop, play games and bank via their televisions.

Following the demise of ITV Digital in 2002, Sky launched a free-to-air service (Freeview) of 30 channels with the BBC. It has also developed a bundling proposition, offering telephony and broadband services.

## Company Culture and Style

Sky wants to be 'inventive, creative, entertaining and challenging' – these are its brand values. Its employees, it says, are 'dynamic, hard-working, self-driven and change-oriented', possessing the ability to set and exceed their own targets.

'People who work for us are imbued with a desire to innovate and work in a can-do way', says McCoy. 'As a result the company is known for being highly innovative and having extremely motivated, self-reliant people. It's a highly challenging environment. Individuals who prefer a high degree of structure will probably not enjoy working here.'

Sky says it is committed to getting staff feedback on every initiative, however pleasing or painful the results. Surveys show employees particularly value Sky's competitive attitude, although in recent times the culture has softened. 'Five or more years ago it was much more aggressive. Now it is more mature and well-balanced', says McCoy.

On the group's main campus near Heathrow there are 15 buildings and a mix of working environments. Sky Sports and Sky News are open plan; other units comprise individual offices and live television studios. In 2002 Sky won a Best European Call Centre Award for its redesigned Scottish Customer Contact Centres. It is now in the process of implementing a major Customer Relationship Management initiative, looking at how subscribers can interact flexibly with contact centre staff.

On the downside, long working hours are a prevalent part of the culture at Sky headquarters. 'There aren't many social opportunities in the immediate environment', says McCoy. 'This is an industrial part of London and people tend to stay focused on their work.' Sky provides flexible work patterns in its call centres, and is looking at how to facilitate this in other parts of the business

Sky is increasingly seeking to enable employees to participate in community programmes, including a mentoring initiative called Reach for the Sky. Recently it also appointed its first disability manager, proving its commitment to finding ways to increase diversity both in its employee base and its programme content.

## Human Resources

Sky has only one graduate scheme – for finance graduates. Plans for a company-wide scheme were mooted in 2001 but shelved due to restraints on head-count. However, 'it is definitely something we would look at again'. Most employees join Sky after first working elsewhere and gaining a track record.

The group uses around twenty main agencies to find staff for every function from temporary call centre operative to senior executive. Jobs are advertised internally via its intranet. At present Sky has no formal policy on career breaks; these are sometimes individually negotiated.

In recent years the group has focused on improving its internal processes. An 'IT transformation' initiative is currently upgrading systems and structures. 'Traditionally we have placed such a high emphasis on external platforms that some of our internal functions have been neglected', explains McCoy.

Sky is also improving its internal resources. 'We have reduced our dependence on major consultancies by increasing the calibre and reach of our own human resources team,' says McCoy. Increasingly the human resources department assumes a role of project leadership: designing organisational structures, managing change, examining employer/employee relations and developing training and internal communications.

## Career Opportunity and Development

There are many levels of training within the group. At the call centres in Scotland, more than 200 trainers guide recruits through a thirteen-week classroom-based course. In early 2003 a new customer relationship management system will enable operators to brush up on specific training during breaks. The aim is to multi-skill all operatives.

For managers Sky has a range of development programmes, largely delivered by in-house teams. News Corporation developed its own certificate and diploma in management, which managers can work to attain.

The most senior training programme is for aspiring executives, and translates Sky's four brand values (inventive, creative, entertaining, challenging) into leadership strategies: entrepreneurial risk-taking, visionary thinking, high-impact presentations, challenging the status quo. There is also a senior management development programme at the next level down which grooms managers in business strategy awareness and leadership skills, using personal development plans and a buddy system for coaching.

The group has no formal succession planning policy, but confidence, fluidity and a high degree of political awareness are essential qualities for promotion. 'It's about people pushing their ideas and trying to get recognition and mindshare from senior executives', says McCoy, who adds that Sky's rapid growth has provided fantastic career opportunities to people who have been relatively inexperienced.

Sky has a tradition of seconding top executives to other News Corporation companies, with especially strong links to Australia. Professional qualifications in finance and accounting, as well as IPD diplomas and MBAs, are sponsored on a regular basis.

## Remuneration

Payment is on a grade structure for call centre operatives and installers. Sky is also rolling out a new pay grade structure into functions such as human resources and information technology.

Generally, employees who are earning £50,000 or above are eligible for a discretionary annual bonus and also qualify for discretionary stock options. Pay is heavily performance-based, with a whole range of executive schemes for rewarding good performance at the top levels. In other areas, for example in the contact centres, there are job-specific bonus schemes and internal recognition awards (Sky Achievers, Sky Heroes) for meeting targets. It is 'a very metrics-based business'.

The group's West London headquarters has a subsidised gym for employees and everyone who works for Sky automatically gets free Sky TV – 'a very well-perceived perk', according to McCoy.

Other benefits of working for the company include a defined-contribution pension scheme, available from day one of employment, share-options schemes, family medical insurance, life insurance and disability insurance. Company cars are given to employees depending on salary level.

In 2002 Sky raised its holiday allowance to 25 days per year. Employees start with 20 days and gain an extra day for each year of employment with the company.

## The Future

While Sky does produce programmes for terrestrial television, it does not see itself turning into a production-based company. The principal drive is to evolve from an entertainment company into a leisure and lifestyle company. 'We want seven million direct-to-home users by 2003', says McCoy. Sky is also looking for average revenue of £400 per user and lower customer churn.

In 2002 less than five per cent of Sky's revenue came from interactivity and bundling; over 50 per cent comes from base subscriptions. In five years, the company will derive more revenue through leisure and lifestyle services, in addition to broadcast entertainment.

The main restriction facing the group is the limited size of the potential UK & Ireland 'Direct to Home' (DTH) subscriber base. Because of the regulatory environment Sky cannot broadcast into other jurisdictions. However, News Corporation already owns satellite television companies in Asia and Europe and has plans to expand in the States. 'The aim is to be part of a worldwide satellite TV utility and to leverage that expertise.'

Originally part of the General Post Office and latterly an independent business, then privatised in the 1980s, there has for some time now been more to BT than making the phones ring. As the main provider (in spite of the competition) of the UK's telecommunications infrastructure it was one of the main players in the Internet boom during the 1990s, and has seen its share price affected by the decline of the overall sector. It is also involved in managed systems for businesses and has a dedicated systems integration arm.

**Scorecard:**

| | |
|---|---|
| Remuneration and benefits | **** |
| Progressive attitude | ***** |
| Opportunity for promotion | **** |
| Training, development and education | **** |
| Working atmosphere and environment | **** |

**Biggest plus:**
The value the company puts on individuals is real and not window dressing – and the opportunity to carve out your own career.

**Biggest minus:**
The share schemes, which have all suffered from the downturn in the telecommunications and technology sector overall.

BT
BT Centre
81 Newgate Street
London EC1A 7AJ
Tel: 020 7356 6780
Fax: 020 7356 5188
Website: www.bt.com

# BT

## The Business

BT has a number of core markets including the obvious local, national and international telecommunications. It has four distinct lines of business: BT Retail, BT Wholesale, BT Ignite (for business customers) and BT Openworld, the Internet Service Provider. In the financial year ended 31 March 2002 – the most recently published as this book went to press – 89 per cent of the revenue came from the UK, where it had 21 million customers including both the domestic and corporate markets.

The history of its market share makes interesting reading. Since deregulation in the 1980s, during which time companies other than BT were allowed to start selling telecommunications packages, it suffered a gradual annual decline in the share of its potential market by percentage – since it would have started out with 100 per cent this is perhaps inevitable. In 2001 this stopped and subsequent years' performance suggest the business is pulling its marketing operation into order. It remains obliged to allow competitors to install equipment in its exchanges so that they may compete in matters such as broadband provision, and anticipates a lot more competition in the future. BT temporarily pulled out of the mobile market in 2001 with the demerger of $O_2$, announcing its return to the consumer mobile phone market in October 2002 with the launch of Mobile Sense, which enables customers to select their own call charge package online.

*BT has a forward-looking HR team that actively includes all individuals regardless of their age, race, gender or sexual orientation or whether they have a disability*

## Company Culture and Style

If one phrase sums up BT's culture more than any other then that would be 'enterprise agility'. The company has preached the benefits of flexible working for years, unsurprisingly since people working remotely take advantage of the BT network to keep in touch with their workplace. Cynics might care to note, however, that the organisation itself ensures that its staff are offered all of the flexibility it encourages in its customers.

Four core values, implemented by former chief executive Sir Ian Vallance, permeate the company: putting customers first, being professional, working as a single team and commitment to continuous improvement. Visiting the organisation's City HQ, one gains the impression that these are taken seriously by all BT people, who appear motivated and happy in their work. Some sort of hierarchy is inevitable with such a vast organisation but it feels like a place with a flat management structure rather than a whole series of strictures in place; there are no prima donnas in the various departments, the individuals are BT people and proud of it. Being so big it has found itself affected by Human Rights legislation in its HR policy-making, but it has prided itself on keeping ahead of the legal requirements at every turn.

In spite of the company's traditional image as a corporate, blue-chip business – which it is – it has no particular dress codes or rules about haircuts for non-customer facing people. 'We employ adults', says director of people networks Caroline Waters. 'We trust them to use common sense about how they should look.' The same goes for the approach to the work undertaken, in that BT is among the crop of businesses that pays its workers to get results rather than to be behind a given desk for any length of time. Staff work flexible hours and from various locations as long as they produce the goods professionally and on time. Likewise there are no rules about coming back to work for the company for those who resign – it's accepted that people's lives change and different employers can be right for someone at a different stage. BT's overall aim is that someone should be motivated to come back when it's right for them – like any forward-looking company it's happy to take advantage of experience people get in the outside world!

## Human Resources

BT has a forward-looking HR team that actively includes all individuals regardless of their age, race, gender or sexual orientation or whether they have a disability. It has run workshops on what it's like to be a gay customer to ensure that its customer experience is every bit as inclusive as its employee experience. Some 98 per cent of women on maternity leave return to work after having their baby, which is an astonishingly high number regardless of criteria, and real evidence that BT's forward thinking people policies are really having an impact.

The inclusivity starts at recruitment level, with advertisements being put into places in which they're likely to catch the people who are underrepresented throughout the company. The right person for any job within the company will be driven primarily by goals and by the customer, and will be rewarded by employment within a company that is well aware of the need for career/life balance and planning. Much of this is managed through the company intranet, through which people can build their own attendance package.

## Career Opportunity and Development

BT has a number of career councils, which help identify and support talent at all levels within the company, but it's worth stressing that the company welcomes self-starters and people wanting to develop their own career path. It will put people through appropriate training for formal qualifications, in connection with which it works with the Institute of Electrical and Electronic Engineers, and also the WES (Women into Engineering and Science) scheme, amongst many others.

BT has an active youth recruitment process through which it attracts hundreds of Modern Apprentices and graduates each year. All Modern Apprentices benefit from BT Career Start, a structured approach to their career, which includes a formal apprenticeship and training both on the job and in a formal academic sense. A personal development plan is evolved for all employees with their line manager and the company has its own virtual corporate 'university', the BT Academy. This allows for both technical and professional development through structured e-learning programmes developed with the individual to suit their learning style and needs.

## Remuneration

Working through BT's employee benefits is very much a process of checking off the 'usual suspects'. Private health insurance, a good pension and other benefits that would be expected of any multinational of any size are all present and correct.

The stock purchase scheme has clearly enjoyed mixed fortunes as the entire· telecommunications sector has suffered. It remains committed to this as a long-term benefit, however, and conducts all the usual market research to ensure that its packages are competitive.

There are other benefits including a profit-share scheme, save as you earn option plans, average holiday entitlement of 25 days per annum, discounts with a number of companies and, of course, the inevitable discounts on BT products. In addition, BT has negotiated discounts with a number of other companies so that employees can get, for example, cheaper holidays than their non-BT friends. Overall the aim is to make life less expensive for people working for BT, and to embrace BT's technology to enhance their quality of life in ways that might not be obvious. Staff retention is incredibly high as a result at less than three per cent turnover per annum.

## The Future

It's all too tempting to predict 'more of the same' for BT's future when 'same' actually encompasses a colossal amount of corporate change and re-engineering. Certainly the flexi-working, goal-focused BT of today bears little relation to the one that existed ten years ago and, as long as the technology continues to develop, there's little reason to expect the version that's around ten years from now to be in any way predictable from the present day's vantage point.

What can be said with utter certainty is that the company will continue its focus on growth through its people. It has made a solid staff on being as inclusive as it can become, but it is unlikely to be satisfied for a long time yet. It will continue to develop and foster policies that will encourage people at all levels of the company to participate and push the company forward, feeling that it is their organisation rather than a faceless employer.

On the way out of the interview our researcher noticed that the lifts had floor numbers not only in numerals but also in Braille and that the lift 'talked' passengers through the floors. This wasn't a surprise, but as evidence the company was putting money behind its claims it was reassuring.

# BUPA

BUPA (the British United Provident Association) continues to be the UK's market leader in private health and care, employing some 42,000 people in this country alone. Its range of care and funding products include homes for the elderly and a network of 36 hospitals. BUPA owns Sanitas, a healthcare provider in Spain, and has also become active in Australia and Asia-Pacific with two significant acquisitions. Worldwide, it has eight million customers in 190 countries. BUPA Wellness centres offer a range of medical services, both to corporate and personal customers. The group, which as a provident association reinvests its profits, had a turnover in 2001 of £2.4 billion and annual profits of £104 million.

**Scorecard:**
Remuneration and benefits        ****
Progressive attitude        *****
Opportunity for promotion        ****
Training, development and education        ****
Working atmosphere and environment        ****

**Biggest plus:**
Continues to maintain high-quality services and places priority on exceeding its customers' expectations.

**Biggest minus:**
Ability to grow in the UK is limited because it has become dominant in some markets.

BUPA
BUPA House
15–19 Bloomsbury Way
London WC1A 2BA
Tel: 020 7656 2000
Fax: 020 7656 2700
Website: www.bupa.com

# BUPA

## The Business

In 1947, 17 provident associations were brought together by an Act of Parliament to form BUPA, providing private health care for the general public in Britain. At the time, 38,000 people registered. Today the group has eight million customers worldwide.

In the early nineties it admits it was poorly-managed and needed to transform itself into a well-run and financially sound organisation – a goal it believes it has now achieved. Bob Watson, Group Human Resources Director of BUPA, says: 'Five years ago we decided we had to be much more customer focused. We started relating everything we did and every job role to that aim. We're now at a stage where if you look at key indicators such as financial performance and customer and employee satisfaction, we have improved hugely.'

Structured into five core business units, BUPA is best known for private medical insurance cover, with 42 per cent of the UK market (including company schemes) and a premium income of £1 billion.

*Creating an environment which people like to work in is essential – it's a major way to make sure we attract and keep those much-needed skills*

The group also controls 36 private hospitals, and a significant development has been the Government's announcement of a joint venture between the National Health Service and BUPA, under which it will convert and operate a hospital near Gatwick for NHS patients.

BUPA runs more than 200 care homes under the name BUPA Care Services. A rapidly expanding area of business is its Teddies daycare nurseries, providing care for pre-school children: it has more than 30 such centres and plans to buy or build up to 12 per year. Concurrently, it has taken the decision to divest itself of smaller non-core businesses in dental care and home care.

The group's overseas business has also grown. Two recent acquisitions – of a large private medical insurance business in Australia, from AXA, and Vista, a healthcare company based in Singapore – have given the group a foothold in new markets, including eye care clinics in China.

In Britain, BUPA raised its profile in 2002 with its sponsorship of the Commonwealth Games in Manchester.

## Company Culture and Style

The BUPA vision is 'taking care of the lives in our hands' and the group is deeply committed to treating employees as individuals and ensuring they benefit from a healthy work/life balance. Four years ago the group launched One Life, which took employees out of their working contexts to help them to engage with the vision of treating customers with individual care and respect. This was followed by a managerial course, Leading One Life, which more than half the group's 3,000 managers have completed. In 2002 BUPA proved it was top of the pack in work/life balance by winning an industry award for its introduction, following a pilot with 80 employees, of flexible working practices for all staff in its UK membership business.

BUPA people tend to be dedicated and hard-working, recognising that there is more to life than simply taking home a pay cheque. The organisation aims to foster an inclusive, open culture in which people feel they can express their views and are recognised for the contribution they can make. The working atmosphere at head office is informal and friendly, while on a front-line level, employees say they benefit from seeing differences made. The graduate scheme, for example, gave one worker 'insights into all sorts of different areas, from high-level analysis right down to front-line in hospitals... I could see the impact that people's work directly has on our customers'.

The group says it is keen to find graduates who can put the customer at the heart of everything they do, who are commercially aware and want to deliver business results. It looks for graduates who can provide inspirational leadership and management, who can take responsibility and like to use their initiative, and who have the confidence to come up with new ways of working.

But Bob Watson adds: 'We have so many roles here and because there are national shortages in a lot of the areas we work in, we need to be able to compete for people with a high level of skill. So creating an environment which people like to work in is essential – it's a major way to make sure we attract and keep those much-needed skills. We set a large store on organisational stability.'

BUPA also conducts a service organisation profile each year, which allows the company to benchmark itself against other companies. Each member of staff completes a questionnaire expressing how they feel about the company. 'We use it as a development tool for managers', says Bob Watson. 'Our aim is that every manager concentrates on and improves in just one area each year.' Employees recently rated BUPA as being up with the best in its adaptive ability.

## Human Resources

BUPA advertises every job vacancy internally, and uses agencies, websites, professional journals and recruitment fairs to find new staff. BUPA Nursing is one of the UK's leading nurses agencies, recruiting nurses and care workers for a diverse range of clients, while its Strand Nurses Bureau places nurses and carers specifically in London.

The group's graduate recruitment scheme is now in its fourth year and offers three programmes: group general management, finance and information systems. By the end of the year's scheme, graduates will have seen both healthcare delivery and healthcare funding practices, and are expected to benefit from a group-wide understanding of the business, to have experience of working in diverse business areas and to have developed a network of contacts across the business. In 2001 there were 18 places on the graduate recruitment scheme.

Four years ago, BUPA sought to formally recognise outstanding contributions by employees, by establishing an awards programme, with the top winners attending an awards dinner. It is also keen to build relationships between different parts of the business, particularly as the group continues to grow. 'A key focus is to connect across different businesses', says Bob Watson. 'We have created forums where people from different parts of the group can get together. BUPA is quite unique – but we probably haven't yet found the most effective way to release the value of the synergies.'

## Career Opportunity and Development

BUPA continues to encourage its employees to drive their own careers but has started to focus much more on its own succession planning methodology. 'Each year we are identifiying individuals and assessing them against a competency framework', says Bob Watson.

The group's recent acquisitions in Australia and Asia-Pacific have meant that there are more opportunities to work for BUPA overseas, as well as people coming from abroad to work in the UK for the group. All vacancies are advertised on the group's intranet, and generally employees will embark on a two-year fixed placement abroad.

If you are prepared to be proactive, says one graduate trainee at BUPA, opportunities do open up. 'You benefit from working in different teams, on a variety of projects. As a graduate trainee you have a lot of freedom to move around and experience a variety of business areas so you can gain an understanding of the entire group.'

After a year's employment any BUPA employee can move within the group in the UK in order to develop their career, and the group says it strongly encourages professional development, to the extent of funding part or whole courses of study. 'We are very supportive about continuing professional education,' says Bob Watson. 'If someone is taking a course of study, providing it's relevant to their development within the company, the usual thing is that we will fund 75 per cent and pay the additional 25 per cent as and when they finish.'

## Remuneration

BUPA offers its graduates a starting salary of between £19,000 and £22,000, plus a rent allowance, life insurance, free health advice, an interest-free season ticket loan and 25 days' annual leave.

Other jobs are benchmarked, with market surveys conducted for each post and location to keep pay competitive. Salaries are reviewed annually and are based on performance. In addition, some staff will receive a bonus based on BUPA's overall results. For managers, this bonus is usually 25 per cent of salary or above.

All staff benefit from access to a pension scheme, although from October 2002 BUPA says it will run a defined contribution scheme – as opposed to its former defined benefits scheme – for new employees. 'We will continue to fund pensions at a very competitive level', says Bob Watson.

Every BUPA staff member, except those who work in care homes, benefits from private medical insurance cover. Mid-level managers and above are given company cars. Many BUPA sites have gyms and sports and social clubs; those which do not have them offer employees subsidised membership of local fitness clubs.

## The Future

In the next five to ten years BUPA is looking to double its revenue. Within the UK it aims to do this by further developing its health and care offerings in areas such as health screening, corporate health programmes, daycare nurseries and care homes, although Bob Watson admits 'in some of our businesses it's difficult for us to grow because of Competition Commission constraints in certain markets, such as hospitals'. He also points out that 'three quarters of people in care homes are funded by local authorities and funding has been starved – consequently it's very difficult to make reasonable margins'. BUPA says it is open to new ventures with the NHS, should they occur.

In early 2002 BUPA launched a major new programme for its top 80 executives, called Inventing Our Future, which looked at the topics of business innovation, technology and transformation of organisations. It kicked off with a series of masterclasses given by leading academics from around the world, and was followed by residential workshops.

From overseas BUPA is seeking a greater percentage of revenue. 'We have pretty specific strategic plans about where we want to go,' says Bob Watson, 'but having said that, we very much believe that a strategy is a living thing rather than being cast in stone. We're very interested in establishing a greater presence in some countries such as Australia, and this is now beginning to happen.'

Cadbury Schweppes plc is the group that owns a number of the world's best-known confectionery and soft drinks brands, which are manufactured and distributed in almost 200 countries around the world. The company currently employs more than 40,000 people across its five geographic regions of: Americas Beverages, Americas Confectionery, Europe, Africa and the Middle East Confectionery, European Beverages and Asia Pacific. In revenue terms the group is primarily a soft drinks company in the US (Cadbury Schweppes is the world's third largest soft drinks company) and primarily a confectioner everywhere else (it's currently the world's fourth largest confectionery company).

## Scorecard:

| | |
|---|---|
| Remuneration and benefits | **** |
| Progressive attitude | **** |
| Opportunity for promotion | **** |
| Training, development and education | ***** |
| Working atmosphere and environment | **** |

## Biggest plus:

Cadbury Schweppes has a strong set of corporate values, combining business ambitions and community responsibility, that is well thought-out and communicated effectively – this is an organisation that knows where it is going, and wants all its staff to share that sense of direction.

## Biggest minus:

Like any consumer-based business, competition is tough and at times brutal. Keeping up with the ever-changing desires of consumers and ahead of the competition is a constant challenge.

Cadbury Schweppes plc
25 Berkeley Square
London W1J 6HB
Tel: 020 7409 1313
Fax: 020 7830 5200
Website: www.cadburyschweppes.com

# Cadbury Schweppes plc

## The Business

Cadbury Schweppes plc is a publicly quoted operation that can trace its origins back over 200 years – Schweppes was founded in 1783, Cadbury in 1824, and Dr Pepper (the basis for its US expansion) in 1885. Today it's a thoroughly modern multinational with some of the world's best-known brands, including Bassett's Jelly Babies, 7 UP, Snapple and Orangina as well as those associated with Cadbury and Schweppes.

The Group's current resurgence is attributed to a strategic analysis started in 1997 under the label Managing for Value, a system of developing and meeting business targets that necessitated a thorough understanding and allocation of resources – including the group's brands, but also its people. In the past few years Cadbury Schweppes has cut back on some non-core businesses while actively pursuing international acquisitions (among them Snapple in the States, Hollywood chewing gum and Orangina in France, La Casera in Spain, plus interests in Poland and Turkey).

After hitting a tricky patch in the mid-1980s, the Group is back on course and delivering strong growth. For its last financial year Cadbury Schweppes reported turnover up seven per cent at £5.3 billion, *Cadbury Schweppes feels that it now knows how to manage its business, so sustainable growth is the new priority* with profits five per cent higher at over £1 billion. It recently announced the proposed strategic acquisition of the Adams sugar and gum confectionery business. When this deal is cemented in April 2003, Cadbury Schweppes will be the world's leading confectionery business and add a further 14,000 plus employees to its family. It will also add significant confectionery presence in the Americas.

## Company Culture and Style

At present the company is evolving from the Managing for Value phase, a value-oriented strategy based on understanding and leveraging the group's strengths and setting clear financial targets based on them. The current focus is on growth. Cadbury Schweppes feels that it now knows how to manage its business, so sustainable growth is the new priority.

Marketing in general and brands in particular are the main focus, but Cadbury Schweppes also recognises the impact of its personnel policies on the bottom line. In building a definable corporate culture for a diverse group of operating entities, Cadbury Schweppes has developed five themes to describe the experience of working at the Company.

They are the opportunity: to be an individual; to make a difference (Cadbury Schweppes is not a people-heavy organisation, and it wants every voice to be heard); to grow with the company; to gain from its success: the 'working together' sense of shared values and the sense of passion and commitment embodied in 'join our world'.

The central HR department has developed programmes to communicate these messages and to monitor them, though individual businesses can decide how exactly to implement them.

The working environment at Cadbury Schweppes has been described as both challenging and rewarding: it's difficult simply to keep your head down and coast, and if you want to push yourself you can expect Cadbury Schweppes to recognise your ambitions. Team players are valued, contribution is encouraged, and there's a definite policy of encouraging personal development – for instance, you can apply for time off and financial support for further education and qualifications such as MBAs.

Community involvement is something Cadbury Schweppes believes in and gives a lot of support to, last year the group invested over £1.8 million in the community in the UK alone. Volunteering and community projects are seen as a legitimate way for individuals to develop valuable skills, and there are active programmes to encourage employees to get involved. Typically this will involve mentoring and involvement in school-run business games as well as hands-on work such as ground clearance. There is also a biennial Chairman's Award for Employee Community Involvement, a trophy plus cash for a chosen charity, which last year was won for the individual's work in drug rehabilitation.

## Human Resources

Cadbury Schweppes has an active central HR function with an explicit brief to attract, motivate, retain and develop the Group's employees. This has produced a set of policies and procedures, which individual operating units can adopt in a manner appropriate for their business.

The Group has a graduate recruitment programme that provides a substantial number of the people who move into middle management with Cadbury Schweppes.

## Career Opportunity and Development

Cadbury Schweppes runs an impressive selection of learning and development activities – self-paced study, coaching and classroom courses in everything from language skills up to professional qualifications. As a result there is no standard training programme – Cadbury Schweppes expects that training will be tailored to the individual.

There is considerable emphasis on improving the skills of managers, in particular with coaching programmes that aim to help them get the most from their staff.

Cadbury Schweppes is also trying to build multi-dimensional managers, with movement between operating units and even between countries to give extra experience.

The Sales and Marketing Academy is a two-year programme that aims to identify core principles of consumer marketing and apply good practice. As with many of the group's strategic exercises, the result should be a common approach and a common set of tools for all the different Cadbury Schweppes businesses.

## Remuneration

Individuals get two performance reviews a year, one essentially retrospective and the other for future development. Specific objectives are set and pay reviews do take performance into account. It is a meritocracy.

Remuneration policies vary from one business unit to another, but Cadbury Schweppes aims to have competitive salary levels. In most cases there will also be an annual incentive plan for managers, with a bonus based on company and personal performance. The levels are decided locally, and there are no guarantees about the size or availability of a bonus in a given year – it all depends on business and individual performance.

The Group's share option scheme, intended to recognise those who have made a significant contribution, is focused on senior corporate management, though it is being extended further down the hierarchy. In addition, there is a Share Save scheme based on a three, five or seven-year saving plan that buys shares at a 20 per cent discount on the prevailing price. Around two-thirds of the group's UK employees are in a Share Save plan.

Cadbury Schweppes operates two pension programmes, a well-established traditional final-salary scheme and for newcomers since July 2001 a defined benefits career average salary plan.

## The Future

Cadbury Schweppes' corporate management takes a long-term view. It is clearly essential to maximise returns in the short term, both to maintain investor confidence and to provide a positive cash flow for the business. But acquisitions, emerging geographical expansion and the development of new brands are all being pursued actively. The Group is committed to growth for the future; and the good news for employees is that its people are acknowledged as one of the drivers for growth. Cadbury Schweppes sees an investment in its staff as an investment in its future.

# *Capital* One®

Capital One Financial Corporation is a financial services company whose principal subsidiary, Capital One Bank, offers consumer lending products. The organisation is a publicly quoted company listed on the NYSE. Capital One is a top-10 credit card issuer with more than $56.9 billion in managed loans and over 48 million worldwide customers. Capital One employs over 20,000 people as a group world-wide with more than 2,000 of these based in the UK.

**Scorecard:**

| | |
|---|---|
| Remuneration and benefits | **** |
| Progressive attitude | ***** |
| Opportunity for promotion | ***** |
| Training, development and education | **** |
| Working atmosphere and environment | ***** |

**Biggest plus:**
All the advantages of working in a consultancy or blue-chip company, with all the benefits of working in an achievement-oriented environment.

**Biggest minus:**
Two Starbucks coffee bars and two restaurants equals temptation – both have an adverse effect on staff pockets and waistlines.

Capital One
Trent House
Station Street
Nottingham
Notts NG2 3HX
Tel: 0115 843 3300
Website: www.capitalone.co.uk

# Capital One

## The Business

Capital One Finance Corporation is a financial services company whose principal subsidiary, Capital One Bank, offers consumer-lending products. The organisation is a publicly quoted company listed on the NYSE. Capital One is a top-10 credit card issuer in the US and in the UK, with more than $56 billion in managed loans and over 48 million world-wide customers, serviced by more than 20,000 employees globally, with 2,100 of these in the UK.

In 1996, Capital One launched its first overseas operation in the UK where it currently offers Visa and MasterCard credit cards to UK customers, under the company name Capital One Bank (Europe) plc. Capital One currently has more than two million UK customers, serviced from the European headquarters in Nottingham. The company describes itself as 'an information-based company specialising in financial services'. The expansion into the UK preceded other moves into France, Canada and South Africa, with more expansion planned. Most of the staff (some 93 per cent) claim to feel good about the ways the company involves itself with the local community. Capital One is the winner of many community awards, the most prestigious being the 'Business in the Community Award for Excellence'. The company invests in the local district via financial donations but is not just a cheque giver – it also offers the skills, attributes and time of its employees – associates – to influence the community positively. Each Capital One associate has the opportunity to dedicate at least one day a year of work time to community work.

> *unlike at most companies, where mainly executives hold shares, all Capital One associates can be owners in the company*

## Company Culture and Style

At the core of Capital One's culture is a strong ownership philosophy. Unlike at most companies, where mainly executives hold shares, all Capital One associates can be owners in the company. Associates can participate in share option and purchase programmes or, equally importantly, display ownership behaviours such as being flexible about job scope and tasks, spending the company's money 'like it's your own', and seeking continuous improvement. This ownership behaviour extends throughout the company's work and the belief is upheld that, as owners, associates change positively the way they view their jobs, each other, and Capital One. Owners are committed to excellence and willing to go the extra mile to get the job done.

The ownership philosophy means employees are referred to as 'associates', because everyone within the business contributes on equal terms to the company's success. The aim is to create a stimulating culture, where associates engage in problem solving, make positive contributions, become owners in the company, share in financial success, develop new competencies and grow in their careers. The company expects associates to work hard and believes in rewarding effort with celebration and fun. This takes the form of anything from all-associates events and parties to launching key projects in an innovative and fun way. How many other companies would 'resurrect Elvis' to help launch an IT system called DISCO or set aside £50 per head, per quarter, to spend solely on having fun?

The approach is reflected in the physical surroundings. Capital One's latest building Loxley House was opened in March 2002 by HRH the Prince of Wales and provides a £60 million extension to an existing refurbished building. The new facilities are adjacent to a canal and include such distinctive features as a suspended decking terrace for a restaurant and kayak racks for anyone wishing to paddle to work. The only glass ceiling at Capital One is in its five-storey atrium. Note, too, that if you wear a suit and tie everyday here, you will be sent home to change into something more comfortable (not strictly true!!!). The company firmly believes it's cracked it, in that it offers a unique and rewarding working experience that delivers first class business performance.

## Human Resources

Successes in operations overseas and in the UK are attributable to the fact that Capital One tailor-makes credit cards and services to suit its customers. The recruitment policy mirrors this information-based strategy approach. The company hires people to enable it to achieve its business goals. There are no hard and fast recruitment rules – the requirements of a senior executive will be different to a call centre associate. However, all associates go through a series of tests, relevant to the job for which they are applying. Depending on results, candidates are required to attend interviews and further testing days, which can range from three to seven meetings.

With graduate recruitment, the company looks for a 'good degree' (2.1 or above) in any discipline, including 22–26 UCAS points, and maths. The company seeks demonstration of exceptional analytical skills, leadership potential, motivation and good interpersonal skills for when associates interact with all areas of the business. Further, the company is interested in people who have passion and energy to get things done. Away from recruiting, the HR department handles consultancy, management development, compensation, benefits and payroll. Independent endorsements of Capital One's position of being an excellent employer have enabled high-quality candidates to apply and subsequently be influenced in their decisions to join the company.

# Career Opportunity and Development

Many organisations quote the age-old adage that 'people are their most important assets' – Capital One maintains it goes beyond merely paying lip service to the philosophy by making it integral to all that it does. Associates are regarded as a key aspect of the company's stakeholder model, alongside customers, shareholders and communities. Capital One prides itself on being at the forefront of many innovations when it comes to associates' development. The company has: an in-house development team; departmental training specialists; a progressive performance management and development cycle; weekly performance meetings between associates and their managers; development action plans to plan an individual's growth; and 360-degree feedback sought twice a year through the performance management process. All provide a systematic process to challenge associates to take ownership of their continual development and success.

At an individual level each associate has four to six objectives that are set between themselves and their manager every year. These relate directly to departmental priorities and corporate goals. Objectives are reviewed in one-to-one meetings with managers at least once every two weeks, which allows associates to gauge their progress individually and in relation to company-wide performance.

An internal vacancy scheme (VacancyOne) advertises most new positions within the company before they are advertised externally, and the educational assistance programme funds tuition fees for a range of work-related courses across many educational levels. To aid associates' personal development and work/life balance, the company has launched 'Learning Zone', a library facility where associates can borrow free-of-charge books, CDs, videos and DVDs to aid learning on any subject from accounting to cooking with Jamie Oliver.

Externally, Capital One believes the development of its associates' skills via community work is vital. By developing its in-house professionals in this way, Capital One believes it is able to tailor their skills to new and challenging scenarios.

# Remuneration

Valuing and supporting a culture that empowers each associate to think and act as an owner is a real part of life at Capital One. Consequently, the company's compensation packages align with both the efforts and value the associate brings to their individual role and any growth in shareholder value. This is seen to provide an opportunity for Capital One's staff to truly share in the company's successes. Running alongside a base salary exists a comprehensive range of other solid benefits including:

- non-contributory pension scheme, although associates can choose to increment company contributions;
- health insurance;

- performance-related bonus;
- 25 days' holiday (pro rata for part-time associates);
- long-term incentives;
- share purchase plan;
- Educational Assistance Programme;
- employer of choice subsidies, eg nearby Holmes Place health and fitness club discounts;
- life assurance and accidental death and disability cover.

There is a subsidised restaurant and interest-free commuter travel loans. Alongside all these benefits is the culture of the organisation, plus the physical benefits close by of a wealth of good pubs, clubs, restaurants and shops. The location of the Nottingham HQ is well-suited for access to other parts of the UK, something that contributes much to the work/life balance so eagerly sought by workers today.

## The Future

Over the next five to 10 years, Capital One's aim is to develop its UK brand while continuing to grow its European business. Capital One would like to further develop its reputation as an employer of choice and, from a community perspective, continue to play an active role in supporting and interacting with its local partners.

The company remains committed to its policy of recruiting, retaining and rewarding the best people and harnessing its powerful information-based strategy to understand the needs of all its stakeholders and customers. Following these guidelines should influence positively its ability to achieve its corporate and community objectives. Indeed the company's founders – Rich Fairbanks and Nigel Morris – are continually seeking more industries to which their strategy can be applied. Having cornered credit cards, what's next?

# CAPITAL RADIO GROUP

Readers of a certain age will remember Capital Radio as one of the first independent radio stations to emerge after people other than the BBC were allowed in during the early 1970s. The Capital Radio Group remains proud of that heritage and the radio stations that bear its name, but the business has expanded into many other areas over the years as well. It is now the UK's leading commercial radio group with 20 analogue and 43 digital radio stations across the UK.

**Scorecard:**

| | |
|---|---|
| Remuneration and benefits | **** |
| Progressive attitude | **** |
| Opportunity for promotion | **** |
| Training, development and education | *** |
| Working atmosphere and environment | **** |

**Biggest plus:**
The people and their commitment.

**Biggest minus:**
The fast-moving, changing and competitive environment won't be for the fainthearted.

Capital Radio Group
30 Leicester Square
London WC2H 7LA
Tel: 020 7766 6000
Fax: 020 7766 6100
Website: www.capitalradiogroup.com

# Capital Radio Group

## The Business

The Capital Radio Group has, since its inception, been a bastion of independent, commercial broadcasting. It now owns 20 analogue and 43 digital radio licences including a number of immediately-recognisable brands in music radio; The Capital FM Network, Capital Gold, XFM, Century, Capital Disney and Life. Launching with the single 95.8 Capital Radio Station in 1973, it was the second legal commercial radio station to air (LBC pipped it to the number one slot by a week).

Listed on the London Stock Exchange and employing just under 700 people, it would be wrong to bracket the business as if it were any other company serving customers. For Londoners especially, Capital has become part of the backdrop of daily life and adds a number of support services from which it does not make any money directly. Its main charity, Help A London Child, and its broadcast events around it predate Live Aid, Comic Relief and a thousand other potentially life-saving projects. Its flatshare line, designed to help Londoners find somewhere to live, has no direct commercial bearing on the organisation but has a clear value to its participants. And of course the broadcasters it has employed in the past – Kenny Everett, Michael Aspel among others – read like a Who's Who of the 1970s, no matter which generation you're from.

> *The Capital Radio Group is a big part of the lives of the people who work here...They have Capital running through them like a stick of rock!*

It doesn't limit itself to broadcasting, however; it has a music label of its own named Wildstar, which boasts Craig David among its recording artists.

Underpinning all of these diverse activities is a committed and loyal staff, and it is in wishing to join these that you should consider approaching the business direct.

## Company Culture and Style

'The Capital Radio Group is a big part of the lives of the people who work here', says Tracey Reid, Director of Human Resources. 'They have Capital running through them like a stick of rock!' As would be the case in any creative environment there's a buzz about the business' Leicester Square HQ, and not just because of the obvious allure of the Central London location. The average age of employee is 27 but that may change in the future since employee retention is high. In fact, trying to pin down exactly who'd be a good fit at Capital is made tricky by the sheer diversity of the requirement; the technical staff will be different from the sales force.

What they all share in common, says Reid, is dedication. 'They're amazing in a crisis; we've had people coming out overnight when there's a serious problem, without having to be asked.' Core to Capital's values is integrity – not only from one's own point of view but in dealing with other people. There's no room for prima donnas or people who favour histrionics as their preferred means of debate; mutual respect is how the company operates. This isn't meant in a sentimentalised way – the company doesn't expect all 700 employees and the near 400 free-lancers/presenters to be best mates; it does expect people to knuckle down and produce the best radio possible no matter how far removed from the end product someone's immediate role may appear.

It's perhaps surprising, then, how relaxed the atmosphere appears to be – or maybe not, considering the nature of the business. Even at a sales level, this isn't a suited and booted environment (although if you're in sales and meeting a corporate client you can expect to use common sense and dress for the occasion). Work/life balance is important, but not to the exclusion of all else; this isn't one of the colossal consultancies or former public utilities so people have to fit their needs around those of the business to an extent. In terms of being ahead of statutory requirements on maternity and other rights, however, the company behaves better than a number of corporations several times its size – allowing adoptive leave as well as parental leave, for example.

## Human Resources

The Capital Radio Group is active in recruiting to all aspects of its business including programming, sales and marketing, support functions including finance, technology and HR and administration. The selection criteria are strict and centre around the competencies required in each individual post on offer and the company's core values.

There are no outmoded rules about people who have previously left rejoining, other than the common sense ones applying to people whose departure was over a disciplinary matter. The benefits offered by HR include the aforementioned training and the resulting chance to manage your own career – don't expect HR to come and tell you you're due for a promotion, for example, you'll need to be enough of a self-starter to decide this for yourself. Ideas are welcomed and rewarded from anyone in the organisation.

## Career Opportunity and Development

The thing to note about the Capital Radio Group is its primarily flat management structure, which is extremely visible in the sexual balance of the management board (50:50, not due to any positive discrimination or similar efforts but due to the right people for the various jobs being available at the opportune times – and there being no glass ceilings).

Ideas, in fact, are welcomed from anyone at any level of the company, as might be expected from a business of Capital's size. Self-management is encouraged, although people who want their own way all the time should bear in mind the business is there to make money rather than to provide their personal career trajectory. As long as that is understood, the opportunities are considerable and training where appropriate will be forthcoming. Likewise flexibility in the business' approach as an employer is considerable where it's likely to be mutually beneficial; staff have arranged extra leave time around the aforementioned charity work to extend their voluntary activities and the business has welcomed this. As the website says, each of the radio stations it operates is involved with its local community and this has characterised the company since it began.

## Remuneration

The Group offers everything that might be expected of a competent, modern employer in terms of remuneration. In a competitive field such as radio a decent salary goes almost without saying; health insurance, pensions and other benefits come in tow as standard.

What's probably the most fun about working for Capital in terms of the remuneration, however, is the perks. Staff get two free tickets for places at Capital's Party In The Park and other public events, for example, and these are understandably very popular. There are other musically-themed perks alongside the more serious issues surrounding the allocations of company cars (which exist) and career management.

## The Future

As this book was being written, the first few digital radio sets were coming onto the market and selling out immediately; digital radio stations were starting to emerge into the public eye (or ear) and the success of the medium, if not in doubt long term, had yet to be measured. For this reason asking for specifics on the future of the Capital Radio Group was difficult.

However a number of elements are clear. First, that by acquisition and organic growth, Capital will aim to remain at the forefront of popular music radio and to build on its existing brands. Second, the investment in a record label isn't a coincidence – nobody is saying much about building on it but if it discovers another couple of Craig Davids you could reasonably speculate that more will follow. The next year will be spent driving the new performance management system to ensure maximum employee potential, both as contributors to the business and as fulfilled individuals in their own right.

# CHESHIRE
## BUILDING SOCIETY

The Cheshire Building Society is a successful, independent, regionally based society with a strong commitment to mutuality. It has a branch network extending throughout the North West of England and includes 51 building society branches and 13 property service branches. The Cheshire employs around 1,000 staff and ranks 11th in size out of a total of 67 UK building societies. In addition to the branches, the offices in Macclesfield are the base for a number of teams, including the customer contact centre, mortgage services, marketing, human resources, IT, e-commerce and financial planning.

**Scorecard:**

| | |
|---|---|
| Remuneration and benefits | *** |
| Progressive attitude | **** |
| Opportunity for promotion | **** |
| Training, development and education | **** |
| Working atmosphere and environment | **** |

**Biggest plus:**
The Cheshire invests a lot of time and money in its staff, providing clear direction for career progression and training to fulfil skills needs which meet business objectives.

**Biggest minus:**
Because it has such a localised business footprint, there are no overseas opportunities.

Cheshire Building Society
Castle Street
Macclesfield
Cheshire SK11 6AF
Tel: 01625 613612
Fax: 01625 502462
Website: www.thecheshire.co.uk

# Cheshire Building Society

## The Business

Established in 1870 in Macclesfield, the Cheshire was one of the first Permanent Societies, which started a revolution in personal finance. Today's Society is the product of 13 mergers, which began in 1969 when the Cheshire merged with the Northwich Building Society. This was followed by a series of smaller mergers through the 1970s and 1980s.

The Cheshire entered the estate agency business in 1989 by initially establishing this service within some of its existing branches. This enabled it to enter the market with minimum expenditure, while maintaining control of quality and customer service. An expansion in 1997 led to it launching a House Letting Service.

After its launch in May 1997, the Society's offshore subsidiary, Cheshire Guernsey Limited, has gone from strength to strength, providing investors with even more choice. To make its promise of a global perspective a reality, the Guernsey company devised a website so that new and existing customers can keep up to date with developments in the offshore investment market.

> *a recent staff survey showed that 90 per cent of employees like the work they do (compared to a 79 per cent industry average) and 87 per cent of staff say they feel part of a team*

Since the arrival of current Chief Executive Colin Whittle, the Cheshire has been through a significant change management programme. Its already broad branch footprint in the northwest – including Derbyshire, north Wales and Lancashire – will be extended into cities such as Manchester, Liverpool and Preston. Wider, national markets are served through the Society's call centre, its e-commerce facilities and its intermediary business team, who manage mortgage business across the country.

## Company Culture and Style

The friendly, warm and open atmosphere is apparent the moment one walks into the Macclesfield head office. This feeling is obviously not put on just for visitors as a recent staff survey showed that 90 per cent of employees like the work they do (compared to a 79 per cent industry average) and 87 per cent of staff say they feel part of a team.

'We pride ourselves on having a happy, team-spirited environment', says Maryam Herin, Head of HR.

The Cheshire has become far less hierarchical over the past few years, and the use of an intranet means that any staff member can ask the chief executive questions any time – publicly – and receive an answer back online as well.

Whittle is also very much seen on the ground, ensuring he visits all branches as regularly as possible. This leads to the staff feeling well-informed, and they are aware of where the company is going and what the long-term goals are. Once again, the staff survey backs this up, with 73 per cent of people reporting that they feel secure and happy in their working environment, which is significantly above the industry benchmark.

'Our culture is about involvement, communicating with each other and being flexible,' says Herin.

'Cheshire Life' is an online internal chatline, which staff use to talk about anything from sharing a joke to sharing views on company policy and asking each other for advice on holidays, local tradesmen etc. Herin says it's never abused, and is fired up automatically on everyone's PCs when they log in in the mornings.

The Cheshire's values centre on customer focus, professionalism, communication, teamwork, the ability to act with integrity and honesty, and to be progressive and proactive.

People who can deliver without too much supervision will flourish here. In addition, people who enjoy dealing with customers will also fly. This, says Herin, comes back to the organisation being friendly, open and knowledgeable.

Because of the team culture, the company allows for all types of people to deliver and there is much sharing of experience, much learning and a very supportive environment in which to work. However, she emphasises that there's no pressure for staff to participate in things they don't want to. 'It's all about respecting individuals and accepting personalities', she says.

'We have been able to facilitate career progression through promotion opportunities and we are prepared to invest in their training. We believe in our people and our people have delivered and we continue to gain experience and learn as we move forward delivering what our customers need and achieving results.'

The Cheshire used to have a dress-down policy on Fridays, but it was so popular that now the dress code is smart casual all the time. Of course, front-line staff in the branches have uniforms, and the staff work with chosen suppliers to select and test designs.

As with many companies, the Cheshire still has a way to go with top female managers – two of the executive team of eight are women, while the next layer down is 40 per cent female. One board director of 10 is a woman.

## Human Resources

The Cheshire recruits across the spectrum ie school leavers, students in a gap year, parents who come back to work after having children, those wanting the flexibility of evening work or those wanting to work from home.

The company has recruitment days and evenings at head office, both as a means to recruit new staff and also to publicise its brand.

Staff turnover is lower than the industry average – 12 per cent as opposed to 16 per cent of the national figure – once again indicating that the majority of staff are happy in their work.

Degrees are not essential, although there are some jobs where particular qualifications are needed, and the Society is prepared to support staff in gaining qualifications for their job. Generally, though, the company rather looks for a right attitude and a culture fit.

The HR department invests substantially in training and development, arranges networking groups, refresher courses, continuous development and updating programmes, etc. It also recently introduced a performance management reward scheme, which links individual, team and corporate successes against a company scorecard.

Long service – from 10 years upwards – is recognised and a special dinner with the chairman and CEO is arranged for eligible staff.

The organisation is also very happy to accommodate job share and those who want to work part-time. 'We are proud of our flexible approach because it encourages people who have different requirements from work to get involved with us. If we can accommodate people who want to work over lunchtime, in the evening or just at weekends we will match this against our business needs.'

## Career Opportunity and Development

The Cheshire is very much a business that has grown from the inside out. Many people in the organisation have been seconded or promoted in the last couple of years. And, contrary to the general trend, there have been no redundancies, but the company has achieved growth of 100 people each year in the last three years.

These figures show great potential for development, and also demonstrate that the Cheshire not only retains skills but also develops them. Comprehensive training – both technical and developmental – is very much part of life here.

'One of our new initiatives is the launch of a career development partnership, which will make is easy for staff to manage their own career but this will, in turn, be overseen by a mentor. In this way, we can identify and manage top talent who will need mentoring. It's a kind of tailored form of training but will not be elitist because it will be open to everyone to apply and places will be allocated on merit', Herin says.

The Society provides advice, opportunities, facilities, resources and financial support so that all employees can acquire the skills, knowledge and qualifications needed for their work, and so they can develop their potential fully.

Staff are also encouraged to study for professional qualifications as well as computer-based training to improve IT skills, which is a very flexible and convenient method of learning for its staff.

The Management Development Programme provides an excellent start for new managers as well as providing an opportunity for experienced managers to update their knowledge on the latest management thinking.

The company has a good working relationship with retailer John Lewis, so staff from both groups can learn from each other.

New staff participate in a comprehensive induction programme where they receive a good overview of the Society. The Chief Executive presents the corporate strategy and meets all new staff, targets are explained and an overview of what is expected of them is given, and so on.

'There should be no surprises for new staff here – knowing our people, they'd let me know if they were unhappy about anything and they are encouraged to do so via a number of different channels', says Herin.

## Remuneration

The Cheshire has the usual set of benefits including competitive pay, bonus schemes, private healthcare, permanent health insurance, pension schemes and company cars for managers. There is also what it classifies as 'cafeteria benefits', where Cheshire staff are able to take advantage of special discounts for gym memberships, holidays, retail offers and so on.

Bonus payments are based on performance, with three levels in the bonus scheme. The corporate level, based on corporate objectives, is up to a maximum of six per cent, the team bonus up to four per cent and individual performance is up to four per cent.

The bonus scheme is reviewed every year and paid annually. There is no stock because of the Society's mutual status.

## The Future

The company's immediate future was shaped with the appointment of Colin Whittle as Chief Executive four years ago. Since then, there has been a lot of investment in infrastructure, technology, people and policies. Now is the time for us to capitalise on that for the benefit of our staff and our customers, says Herin.

This will include expanding the number of branches to a small extent and within its existing footprint of the northwest. There will also be continued controlled growth both in terms of traditional markets and being able to provide other financial services, eg credit cards, loans, travel.

It has also been working on using developing technologies to provide members with better service, but has been careful not simply to bolt on an e-commerce solution to existing technology. Rather, it has undergone a root and branch restructure of all its internal systems. Indeed, the Society was one of the first to enable customers to apply for a mortgage online – since then, it has seen a 160 per cent increase in value of loans coming across the Internet.

'We have been investing in a modernisation programme for some time now and in 2002 the business saw real benefits through significant growth. The Cheshire, now with its Contact Centre, e-commerce facility and intermediary channel, means that we have a national distribution strategy which enables us to meet our business objectives in a cost-effective and efficient manner', Herin concludes.

Churchill is the UK's fifth largest general insurer, employing 8,000 people at 47 sites in the UK, Ireland and India. In 2001 its turnover was nearly £2 billion, and it had pre-tax profits of £56.3 million. Today it administers over seven million active polices for its customers in the home, car, travel and pet insurance markets.

**Scorecard:**

| | |
|---|---|
| Remuneration and benefits | **** |
| Progressive attitude | ***** |
| Opportunity for promotion | **** |
| Training, development and education | ***** |
| Working atmosphere and environment | **** |

**Biggest plus:**
Strong commitment to training and self-improvement.

**Biggest minus:**
Rapid growth means that integration of new business areas remains a challenge.


Churchill Insurance Company Limited
Churchill Court
Westmoreland Road
Kent BR1 1DP
Tel: 020 8313 3030
Fax: 020 8313 5361
Website: www.churchill.com

# Churchill Insurance

## The Business

Churchill Insurance was founded in 1989, when it employed 88 staff and sold 36 car insurance policies on its first day. Since then it has grown swiftly and in the process, transformed the way insurance is sold in this country. Today, the Churchill Group sells policies for the home, travel, car and pet insurance markets, and is a credit card and loan provider.

The spur to the launch of the business was a belief on the part of its chairman and founder, Martin Long, that existing methods of insurance delivery were out-of-step with other more customer-oriented industries. Funded by Credit Suisse subsidiary Winterthur, he established a direct insurance provider whose fundamental aim was to take the hassle out of buying insurance and making a claim.

Growth has been organic, by acquisition, and through strategic partnerships. Key acquisitions include the NIG Group (a broker-based business focused on the private and small commercial market), Devitt Insurance Services (a specialist in caravan and motorcycle insurance) and Inter Group (the UK's premier travel insurance administrator). In 1996 a software development subsidiary was established in New Delhi, India. More recently it entered into partnership with AMP to underwrite Pearl Assurance products. At the end of 2001, Churchill acquired Prudential's general insurance business. During this period, Churchill also became a partner to a number of the UK's blue-chip companies, including Lloyds TSB, Nationwide and Standard Life.

*Martin Long has gone on record to say if anyone comes up with an idea that makes the company £1 million he will buy that person a house*

## Company Culture and Style

Unparalleled customer service delivery is at the core of Churchill's vision and underpins all its working practices. Yet although the company has already set standards across the insurance industry, there is a strong adherence to 'kaizen' – the Japanese philosophy of continuous improvement. Accordingly, employees are encouraged to speak out if they see ways to better existing methods and there are cash or other prizes for the best suggestions. Indeed, Martin Long has gone on record to say if anyone comes up with an idea that makes the company £1 million he will buy that person a house.

In any business where a majority of employees spend most of their time talking to customers there is a danger they will lose sight of the organisation for which they work. Not so at Churchill, which is a company that likes to communicate, regularly and often. This is due to the influence of its chairman, who spends up to 70 per cent of his time talking to people within the business at all levels. All staff have a regular one-to-one meeting with their manager and performance reviews take place every eight weeks. And for senior managers, there is an opportunity each month to spend half a day working in another area of the business. The fresh pair of eyes each executive brings is intended to generate new solutions and constructive observations – and it does. What is especially striking, according to Karen Sharpe, Head of Group Communication, is the absence of territorialism or departmentalism in this respect. 'I've never worked for a company that is as open and ready to change,' she says.

One reason for Churchill's flexibility is its relatively young age as an organisation. Without the long tradition of other big insurers, it is not wedded to the idea of the 'tried-and-tested'. Far from it, the business was constructed on the notion that change was both good and necessary for the industry. The attitude of its leaders remains that those closest to the customers have a valuable role in shaping the business and that in this respect every individual, regardless of job title, is important to the company. This is a powerful motivating tool for many of the call-centre based workforce. They are made aware that their ideas and contributions matter and they respond to this.

The company commits to ensure the call-centres are as pleasant a working environment as possible. The rationale is that this is the way to ensure the sales and claims handling operations function most effectively. Naturally, a great deal of attention is paid to ergonomics and health and safety issues. At the heart of the approach, though, is a belief in the value of other people and the role of teams. Teams are formed of ten members, who as well as supporting each other in the workplace are encouraged to socialise together after work. The friendly nature of the company is also revealed by numerous social events and fundraising activities that take place on the premises. 'We are a real fun company', says Karen Sharpe. 'We do work hard here but we also really look after our staff.'

## Human Resources

Churchill has grown significantly since its launch and has integrated a number of different workforces. However, the common denominator in everyone it looks to recruit is a strong personality. Above all, a strong desire to give of your best whatever your circumstances is paramount. Though a decent education is desirable, there is no graduate trainee programme; really, it is attitude that counts. New recruits will find colleagues revelling in the opportunity to 'go the extra mile' – sometimes literally, as those who drive to work have been known to drop off an insurance certificate on their way home if a customer needs it urgently. Nor is devotion to the cause allowed to go unnoticed either: the actions of those who wow! customers are always publicly recognised.

The company holds open days for the recruitment of call-centre employees. Applicants take a telephone interviewing test, sit personality tests and are then formally interviewed. In its early years, Churchill had a policy of hiring mainly from outside the industry. This was because it wanted to establish a different culture to the one that existed in traditional insurance providers. The result is that a high proportion of managerial appointments have been made internally, though in recent times more appointments have been made from outside. Some of these occur through the acquisition of other businesses; others are less expected, such as two recently appointed ex-forces executives.

Because there is a round-the-clock commitment to the customer, Churchill employs a large number of part-time, flexible workers and home workers. Shift patterns vary but are dictated in the main by call-centre staff themselves. For some, the job may entail a conventional five-day working week; for others it may mean three 12-hour shifts over consecutive days.

## Career Development and Training

Once people are on board there is a 'phenomenal' amount of training and development, according to Sharpe. She says, 'There is a huge focus on career paths because in a call-centre environment people need to know where they are going. At every stage of your progression in the company if you meet the challenges you face, you can go to your line manager and tell them you are ready to move on and they will put in place a training and development plan for you to get there.'

New recruits undergo a comprehensive three-week induction process, the first day of which usually includes a personal discussion with Martin Long. Once the induction is completed, people 'buddy up' with another colleague until they are proficient at everything for which they are responsible within their job description. From that point on, they can take responsibility.

A career plan is mandatory for everybody and there is a performance review every eight weeks for people to benchmark their progress. In all there are a total of eight levels within the organisation; though it sounds a lot, employees can greatly influence the speed of their development. Much of the training takes the form of e-learning which can be carried out at the individual's own pace – but there is also some practical training around areas such as negotiation skills. In addition, Churchill will provide financial support for anyone who wants to acquire relevant professional qualifications, offering financial rewards for those that gain, for example, the Chartered Institute of Insurers certificate.

As the group has grown in size and scope there has been a corresponding increase in movement around the business. Enhanced opportunities within the organisational structure and the long-standing commitment to training and development are evidenced by a turnover level that is well below the average for call-centre-based businesses in the UK.

## Remuneration

Churchill expects a lot from its people and rewards them accordingly. In March 2002, it was voted one of the top 25 companies to work for in a survey by the *Sunday Times* and was identified as demonstrating best practice in remuneration policy. On basic pay, it aims to pay in the upper quartile, while the benefits package includes a non-contributory pension scheme, private healthcare and life assurance cover.

Fringe benefit provision is always under review, in the sense that the company tries to be innovative in its approach. There is a long service award of £150 after three years, and an online shopping facility was recently introduced for those employees too busy to go shopping after work. Though the takeup was ultimately not sufficient to justify its continuation, it provides a good demonstration of the company's concern for the welfare of its employees.

## The Future

Having come so far in such a short space of time, Churchill is not about to make radical changes to its business model. The aim has always been to develop the capability to offer customers any type of insurance or related product, at any time, by any method. This integrated package has almost been achieved. Further acquisitions may be made but there are no plans to diversify; this is a company that believes in concentrating on what it does best.

Business models aside, the company will continue to place a premium on sourcing the right people to attain and retain a loyal customer base. Sharpe says, 'The chairman is very fond of saying that it's people you bet on, not strategy. He's right. When you open a new call-centre you can have all the right processes in place, you can project manage it, but in the final analysis it'll be the people sitting there at three in the morning who actually make it happen for you.' At Churchill, people have and will continue to make the difference. And at a challenging time for the insurance industry, it could be the difference that matters.

# C L I F F O R D
# C H A N C E

Clifford Chance was formed in 1987 with the merger of two London-based law firms, Clifford Turner and Coward Chance. In 2000 it became the first fully-integrated global law firm when it merged with partnerships in the US and Germany. It now leads the market in London, New York, Europe and Asia, providing advice across numerous jurisdictions to multinational companies and financial institutions. Run by some 665 partners, the firm employs 7,500 people – nearly half of them lawyers – in offices around the world.

**Scorecard:**

| | |
|---|---|
| Remuneration and benefits: | **** |
| Progressive attitude: | ***** |
| Opportunity for promotion: | *** |
| Training, development and education: | **** |
| Working atmosphere and environment: | **** |

**Biggest plus:**
The quality, interest, depth and challenge of the work.

**Biggest minus:**
Client needs are paramount, which may mean long working hours.

Clifford Chance LLP
200 Aldersgate
London EC1A 4JJ
Tel: 020 7600 1000
Fax: 020 7600 5555
Website: www.cliffordchance.com

# Clifford Chance

## The Business

In 1987 two London law firms – Clifford Turner, large, non-traditional and with a strong corporate practice and international network, and Coward Chance, a more traditional banking-based City firm – began talking about international co-operation, and combined to form Clifford Chance. The new firm started looking at ways to differentiate itself from its competitors and by the end of the 1990s had 20 offices, including one in New York, and 4,000 staff.

From there it was a short step to a three-way merger with US firm Rogers & Wells and German firm Pünder, Volhard, Weber & Axster. 'At that point, in 2000, it ceased to be a London-based international firm and became an integrated global law firm', says Alistair Dawson, the UK's group head of human resources.

Today Clifford Chance has more than 30 offices worldwide and concentrates on high value, complex activities, working for companies that operate across a variety of jurisdictions. The group attracts clients such as Merrill Lynch, Coca-Cola, Volvo, Siemens, GE Capital and Goldman Sachs. 'These are companies that think like us and often they come to us because if they are going to do something, they don't want it to go wrong', explains Mr Dawson.

*There is a difficulty in describing what someone from Clifford Chance is 'like'. The firm's lawyers are often those who come up with an independent or non-conformist view*

In 2001/2 Clifford Chance expanded its footprint in California, recruiting 70 staff to work from offices in Los Angeles and San Francisco. In the same year, the London operation turned over more than £400 million. Overall, the firm charged fees of £1 billion, of which 28 per cent came from continental Europe; 23 per cent from the Americas and 7 per cent from Asia.

## Company Culture and Style

If you walked into a room full of City lawyers, it might not be easy to spot the people who work for Clifford Chance; they are a diverse bunch. The organisation values expertise and intelligence. The people are bright, quick, analytical and creative; there's a pace of intellect there. There is also a common view about quality of output, client issues and professionalism. But there is a difficulty in describing what someone from Clifford Chance is 'like'. The firm's lawyers are often those who come up with an independent or non-conformist view.

In London, operations are structured into five main departments: finance and capital markets; corporate; litigation; capital markets; tax, pensions and employment; and real estate. Each practice area is divided into smaller working groups, with up to 40 partners, lawyers and trainees in each group. Those who flourish at Clifford Chance will enjoy the collegiate environment, possessing 'self-aware-ness, self-confidence, and persuasion and influencing skills'.

The firm favours candidates who have held positions of responsibility or achieved in an area other than academia. It tends to attract people who have their own high standards in delivering an outstanding level of service to clients.

There are opportunities to take a break from billable hours: the firm engages in a proportion of *pro bono* work, so that employees can be involved in offering legal advice to projects helping under-privileged people in Tower Hamlets and elsewhere. Clifford Chance also runs charity events, matching amounts raised with its own contribution. Staff at City headquarters benefit from a shop, a gym and evening meals.

As for dress, Clifford Chance has adopted a business-casual code; staff are encouraged to wear 'appropriate' clothing depending on the environment – more formal in Europe than the US, for example. The male:female ratio among graduate trainees at the firm is now about even, although only 18–15 per cent of partners are women.

## Human Resources

Clifford Chance makes extensive use of the university milk-round to recruit undergraduates in their final year of study. It also uses agencies to hire qualified lawyers, and the Internet. When candidates are invited for interview they are given access to one area of the firm's electronic intranet, which gives details about the interviewer. If a job offer is made, the candidate can view terms and conditions. Following acceptance, he or she can log onto details of courses.

In 2002 almost two thousand undergraduates applied to win a two-year training contract at Clifford Chance. Just 120 were selected; 40 per cent were studying subjects other than law, and all were expected to achieve a 2:1 degree or higher. The firm also runs a two-week vacation placement scheme, open to undergraduates.

Clifford Chance has a 'flexible working' policy and equips all lawyers with laptops and mobile telephones so that they can operate remotely and log into the firm's intranet and systems.

The firm has begun to use technologies such as web-streaming to provide information about company policies and practices to employees via desktop computers. For example, new trainees are sent a video message by the UK managing partner, who also makes a point of meeting them face-to-face.

## Career Opportunity and Development

Clifford Chance is proud of its reputation as one of the UK's most progressive law firms. In the late 1990s the firm established a training centre in Amsterdam and uses the name The Academy as an umbrella term for all the training programmes it runs.

As in other law firms, trainees embark on a training contract, which is structured into four 'seats', giving experience with a variety of clients and colleagues. Formal training events are mixed with informal mentoring and development meetings, which happen every three months. The firm aims to encourage all staff to develop their careers and to access training; its legal support secretaries, for example, are provided with their own specially-tailored 'Profile' guide.

With a solid international network and a US operation significantly bigger than other British law firms, Clifford Chance offers many opportunities for career development. At any one time, 40 or more trainee lawyers will have been sent abroad to work on secondment. A trainee might be sent on a due diligence exercise, for example, and be posted to Bermuda for six months.

After four years, qualified lawyers are sent on a development course, which helps them to work on non-legal skills, including management. In common with other City firms, a major challenge for Clifford Chance lies in persuading its employees to remain at the firm long-term. The firm tries to give meaningful careers outside of that structure – for example in professional support, which is well-paid and interesting work. But one of the difficulties is in using the phrase 'average' because people in the firm are used to being 'better than average'.

One of the ways in which the firm is tackling this issue of churn is to make its processes more transparent. They are now much more open about who their partner candidates are, and use an assessment centre approach. Lawyers can ask 'am I on partnership track?' and they are told if there are prospects or not.

Clifford Chance is also working to improve the management and mentoring skills of its partners and has hired Harvard professors to run in-house programmes teaching partners about managing within a professional firm.

## Remuneration

In 2002 Clifford Chance offered a starting salary of £28,000 to its trainee lawyers. This figure rises to £32,000 in the second year of training and to £50,000 when a graduate qualifies as a lawyer, and thereafter on a sliding scale. Other staff have varying pay scales, which are in the upper quartile of comparable City-type firms.

A year post-qualification, Clifford Chance lawyers can expect an annual bonus of up to 10 per cent of their salary; this rises to 20 per cent in the next two to three years, and to 40 per cent three years after qualifying. Bonuses are based on performance, in terms of both ability and personal contribution to the firm.

Lawyers can earn more in total remuneration here than in any other UK law firm; they see competitors as being US law firms and banks. The firm tries to remunerate its lawyers sensibly but with sufficient scope to reward the high performances.

After a short qualifying period, all staff at Clifford Chance are eligible for private medical insurance, which includes partners and dependants. The firm operates a non-contributory pension scheme and a money-purchase scheme under which the employer contributes 5 per cent up to the age of 35, and 10 per cent thereafter.

All staff benefit from 25 days' holiday per year, with the ability to buy or sell five additional days.

## The Future

In 2003 Clifford Chance will move all its UK operations into a 30-floor tower at Heron Quays, Canary Wharf, an initiative which the firm says will enable every employee to work above ground with access to natural light. The site is to be equipped with flat-screen computers and will feature glass walls to maximise light.

In the UK there is a major initiative to improve client focus in the short term, with training programmes that have already been attended by three-quarters of staff at all levels. Human resources objectives include improvement in partners' mentoring and coaching abilities and, also for partners, a new awareness of performance by means of upward feedback. For employees, the focus is on improving take-up of existing training and education packages.

Longer-term, the firm will focus on developing its corporate practice through cross-border activity and leveraging synergies. Global development will continue; the firm wants a larger presence in the US and expects that in five years' time UK operations will provide only a quarter of the group's fee revenue.

*Coca-Cola Enterprises Ltd*

Coca-Cola Enterprises Inc is the largest franchised bottler of The Coca-Cola Company. Listed on the New York Stock Exchange, it operates in eight markets: the US, Canada, Great Britain, France, Belgium, the Netherlands, Luxembourg and Monaco. In 2001, it had unit case sales of 4.2 billion, and total revenues of $15.7 billion.

**Scorecard:**

| | |
|---|---|
| Remuneration and benefits | **** |
| Progressive attitude | *** |
| Opportunity for promotion | **** |
| Training, development and education | ***** |
| Working atmosphere and environment | **** |

**Biggest plus:**
Excellent opportunity to thrive in a successful manufacturing company.

**Biggest minus:**
Not a great deal of scope for innovation.

Coca-Cola Enterprises Ltd
Charter Place
Uxbridge
Middlesex UB8 1EZ
Tel: 01895 231313
Website: www.cokecce.com

# Coca-Cola Enterprises Ltd

## The Business

Established in 1986, Coca-Cola Enterprises Inc (CCE) produces, distributes and sells a range of carbonated and non-carbonated non-alcoholic beverages on behalf of The Coca-Cola Company – it also manufactures and distributes product for a number of smaller brand owners. CCE remains the biggest of The Coca-Cola Company's bottling franchisees, covering 80 per cent of the North American market, as well as Great Britain, France, Monaco and the Benelux countries. The company employs 72,000 people in total – 5,000 of them in Great Britain.

Less than 20 years ago the bottling of Coca-Cola products was greatly fragmented. CCE was created in 1986 in order to bring many of the US bottlers together and so allow for greater coordination of distribution activity. It assumed control of bottling operations in Great Britain in 1997 when it acquired The Coca-Cola Company/Cadbury Schweppes joint venture operation then responsible for such activities.

'Coca-Cola' may be among the world's most recognised brands, but CCE's aim is to remain highly attuned to local markets, both at a national and regional level. Its high profile association with football is an example of the former. An example of the latter is its sponsorship of tourist initiatives in the Lake District in the wake of the foot-and-mouth epidemic in 2000.

*Previously, the emphasis was on consistent profit growth. With CCE we have broadened this so that along with consistent growth in profit we are also focusing on ever-improving quality standards together with year-on-year volume growth*

## Company Culture and Style

Communication and planning are two key features of a decentralised business within which there is a high level of mobility. The company's strong local focus led to the creation of eight sales regions. Each region has its own field sales team responsible for placing product, local trade marketing and achieving sales and distribution targets. These activities are coordinated nationally by a central marketing team.

Needless to say, the interface between the central and devolved elements of CCE is fundamental to optimum business performance. Field-based employees execute against arrangements made well in advance by category and channel planners. Every time the company introduces a new product or runs a promotion, the onus is on them to ensure it and the associated marketing material reaches supermarkets and other distribution outlets for launch date.

CCE enables its strong 'act local' approach to business through its infrastructure and the premium it places on effective logistics and supply chain management processes. As well as the regional offices there are six factory sites, attached to each of which, in turn, is a distribution centre. Each region has a director and a dedicated HR, finance and marketing team, as do the manufacturing arms of the company. In effect, they are semi-autonomous businesses.

Since the company's acquisition by CCE, there has been development of strategic thinking at the company, according to Simon Brocket, VP Human Resources. He says, 'Previously, the emphasis was on consistent profit growth. With CCE we have broadened this so that along with consistent growth in profit we are also focusing on ever-improving quality standards together with year-on-year volume growth. We are also looking hard at what it takes to be successful in an organisational sense as well as a commercial sense.'

With this in mind, CCE recently carried out an internal SWOT analysis and regularly conducts employee opinion surveys. Employees identified one of the biggest strengths of CCE as the collegiate working atmosphere; there is a strong sense of a team environment in which the contribution of everyone is respected and valued. People also fed back that they had a clear understanding of what was required of them. This has helped to create a very strong sense of focus; it also fosters self-responsibility, executional excellence and pride in personal accountability.

## Human Resources

CCE recruits around 400 people each year into its major functional areas: manufacturing, distribution, field sales, support services. The company recruits graduates and non-graduates and holds internal careers days at each of its regions and is a regular participant in the university milk-round.

Around 2,000 people are employed across the factory sites, which, because they have a big presence in local communities, often attract the interest of friends and relatives of existing employees. Between 40 and 60 young people are recruited onto the Skillstart programme each year. This is a two-year training scheme providing an introduction to manufacturing, distribution and business. About half that number are hired for a Modern Apprenticeship Scheme which combines study and practical skills acquisition over a three-year period.

## Career Opportunity and Development

CCE is proud of its commitment to training, which comes out above average against a number of external benchmarks. Prior to 1997 this kind of investment had to come out of local budgets, as people were trained to do what was needed to fulfil their job description and little more. Now there is a genuine focus on people development and more resources – currently £3 million annually – are directed in this area.

All newcomers to CCE are likely to be struck by the commitment to helping raw recruits and quickly feel part of the identity of the company. Induction is based upon a set of tools called Targeted Organisational Planning, which collectively informs recruitment and selection, objective setting, and orientation. Early on everyone receives a two-day overview of the business as a standard orientation, then undergoes an orientation to the site or region at which they are based. The aim is to define clearly what is expected of them in their role within the context of both the immediate and wider business environment.

Talent development committees are an important feature of the organisational structure. Each region has its own committee, which is made up of the director and his or her senior executives, with the aim of planning for future business needs against the available pool of talent. Needless to say, high-performers can expect new doors to open along their career path. By way of example, Brocket comments, 'Currently there is a major Corporate project being led out of the US, which is about re-engineering core business processes. It's a great opportunity for people from CCE GB to work in the US in multifunctional teams to help create a blue-print for how this organisation will work in the future.'

# Remuneration

Given the company's association with soccer it is no surprise that HR uses an analogy in respect of remuneration. 'We identify ourselves with other large national FMCG companies and within that segment we would position ourselves in the Premier League', says Brocket.

CCE remains competitive in variable as well as base pay, and prides itself on a flexible benefits package through which life assurance, health, travel, pet, car and long-term disability insurance can be arranged. The company can also help to secure a good deal on mortgages and other loans. The unashamedly paternalistic attitude in respect of reward policy is also reflected in pension provision. At a time when company pension schemes are under close scrutiny, CCE has a commitment to continue to operate its defined benefit scheme and, at the time of writing, was planning to introduce variable rates for contributors in 2003.

There is also an employee share plan, open to anyone who has been with the company for at least six months. There are two subsets in the plan: a matching share scheme in which the company gives each employee a free share for every one they purchase through contributions of up to three per cent of their pay; and a partnership share scheme under which employees can buy more shares that will remain unmatched.

Finally, there are cash allowances for two types of company car: a business needs car that is necessary for an employee to fulfil his or her job requirements; and a benefit car, to which most managers are entitled.

# The Future

Although the company has the largest share of the soft drinks category in which it operates, consumer tastes are changing and demand for new flavours is growing. With this in mind, getting the right marketing mix is crucial. Right now, carbonated drinks form by far the largest part of CCE's portfolio – however, to reflect changes in consumers' tastes CCE expects non-carbonated drinks to grow in importance in the next few years.

The recently increased investment in training and development of employees has meant they are now very well informed about the contribution they make to CCE and understand the 'local' focus of its operations. In the last year, especially, the level of internal communication has risen greatly, with the result that increased business awareness is generating more curiosity about activities outside Great Britain. The company views this as an opportunity to deepen the involvement of more of its people in the way it shapes its future.

According to Brocket, 'We're ready to take another step in the evolution of the company over the next couple of years. We will develop our talent pool, making our organisation more effective and change the way we work and make our business processes more efficient. We will use our market knowledge to improve the way we interact with customers and use insights within production organisations to manufacture increasingly more difficult brands to high-quality standards. In short, we will reinvent many aspects of the company whilst keeping hold of the underlying values and characteristics which have made us successful so far.'

## Computer Associates*

Computer Associates is the world's leading business software company, providing mission-critical software solutions that run businesses. Annual turnover is about $3 billion, gleaned from its territories in over 43 countries. The company's products are used by 95 per cent of Fortune 500 companies, while the company itself is enthused over by its staff. At the European HQ in the UK, for example, employees' children are cared for superbly in an on-campus Montessori Child Development Centre. The company puts a strong emphasis on community relations and family-friendly practices. It's a company where hard work and good benefits go hand-in-hand.

### Scorecard:

| | |
|---|---|
| Remuneration and benefits | ***** |
| Progressive attitude | **** |
| Opportunity for promotion | *** |
| Training, development and education | **** |
| Working atmosphere and environment | **** |

### Biggest plus:
Family-friendly and community-oriented workplace that mixes serious hard work with performance-oriented rewards.

### Biggest minus:
Although there is a pervasive caring and benevolent image, it would be easy to believe the company is a 'soft-touch'. Beware, it is not.

Computer Associates UK Ltd
Ditton Park
Riding Court Road
Datchet
Slough
Berkshire SL3 9LL
Tel: 01753 577733
Fax: 01753 825464
Website: www.ca.com

# Computer Associates UK Ltd

## The Business

Computer Associates (CA) delivers the software that manages eBusiness, with solutions addressing all aspects of eBusiness management through industry-leading brands, covering infrastructure/enterprise management; security management; storage management; portal and business intelligence; application life-cycle management; data management and application development; and object-oriented database technology. CA brands are designed to work together seamlessly, which means they should be well positioned to meet the next generation of computing and business challenges.

Founded in 1976 in New York by entrepreneur Charles Wang, CA serves organisations (including 95 per cent of the Fortune 500 companies) in over 100 countries, with offices in 43 of them. With some 16,000 employees globally, fiscal revenue for 2002 was $3 billion. CA in the UK employs about 1,000 people with most based at the European headquarters in Ditton Park, close to Heathrow Airport. Satellite offices are located throughout the UK and Ireland, in Altrincham, Dublin, Edinburgh, Leeds, London, Slough, Nottingham and Taunton.

*We aspire to be a clear leader in the software markets in which we choose to focus by building enduring customer partnerships that deliver tangible value*

Computer Associates leads the way by being the first and only enterprise software company so far to meet the exacting standards of ISO 9002 Certification by achieving Global Certification

Over the past three years CA has invested $2 billion in R&D, while in the financial year 2002, R&D represented 23 per cent of revenue. In a departure from industry practice, CA's current business model enables its customers to license software on a subscription and month-to-month basis, and allows them to vary their software mix as their business and technology needs change. The whole business style is backed with CA's near unique approach to considering employees' work/life balance. In sum, CA is a hard-nosed contender with a caring image.

## Company Culture and Style

First impressions of CA are very good. The European HQ at Ditton Park near Slough is modelled on the New York worldwide HQ. It's three storeys and 23,230 square metres of glass and steel, surrounded by acres of immaculate parkland, complete with water features and sports facilities. The pristine building is constantly accessible, with a permanent security presence. The atmosphere is hard-working high-tech meets caring, but firm, employer. Ian Williams, Regional HR Manager points to CA's five core values as espoused by Sanjay Kumar, President and CEO:

'We aspire to be a clear leader in the software markets in which we choose to focus by building enduring customer partnerships that deliver tangible value. We will: put customers first in every interaction; build a success-oriented culture to attract and retain the best talent, through performance; exhibit a passion for quality and innovation in all we do; work as a team, focusing our collective resources on our market goals; and do all of this with the goal of maximising shareholder value. These are the five points we need to remember and act on.'

There's a cross-section of every type and personality in the company, where the average age is 'mid-30s' for both male and female and dress is 'business casual'.

A good work/life balance is possible with CA. Facilities include free breakfasts and all-day free tea and coffee. An on-site gym is open round-the-clock, with instructors present from 7am to 7pm. A Montessori creche is available for children from 3 months to school age, and parents can visit at any time. There's also a holiday club for children from 5 to 15 years. Staff can shop online with Waitrose and have goods delivered to work with no delivery charge. It's part of a package to keep staff happy and 'having nothing of concern that's preventative to work'.

CA is keen to stress its community relations – each staff donation to charity is doubled by the company. There's active encouragement to work on charitable causes in company time. A green travel plan operates, with staff who wish to cycle to work being provided with a company bicycle.

## Human Resources

Easy movement is possible between centres of the CA empire – a person in a UK sales role might want to work in Spain, for example, and discusses the possibility with his/her immediate manager. While CA recruits internationally, advertising is handled locally as much as possible. Staff can be sought in a variety of ways – the Internet is most popular, there's traditional newspaper advertising and through a preferred list of agencies.

'What's most promoted is the employee referral route,' says Williams. 'Team members receive US$3,000 for each employee successfully introduced. There are many advantages – it's less costly and has good quality control. What's selling us are our employees.'

'Most senior positions are filled from within – we have 16,000 employees and from that number there should be the talent within to fulfil the majority of management roles,' says Williams. 'People can also transfer between departments – we have someone who moved from marketing into legal, did a degree and is progressing very well. Anything is possible.'

This is a firm with a family culture permeating through everything it does. Anyone who leaves the company will not be able to return. 'There are exceptions to the rule but if someone leaves the fold, they have left the family.' For all the benefits offered, this is no soft-touch company.

## Career Opportunity and Development

'Everybody at CA manages their own career', says Williams. 'As already discussed, someone sitting in finance, say, could decide he/she would like to move into a selling role and would seek to gain any skills they didn't have.' Managers discuss individual performance with staff during a twice-a-year appraisal process and complete and online summary of that discussion which, in turn, feeds a training needs analysis system from which the HR department can extend all training needs. Interestingly, there's an HR-held budget for training. 'Managers have no qualms about coming to HR and saying "this is the training that's needed for these staff members"', says Williams.

Managers worldwide also have to endure an appraisal process, handled electronically and anonymously. Staff reporting to a particular manager can record their views against a set of criteria. Appraisals for managers are processed in both directions, from above and below. 'No one escapes.'

A leadership course is run in-house for every manager, covering many topics of management. The course is administered by HR and delivered by an external training company where appropriate. More than £1 million is set aside each year for investment in training for the UK business alone.

Career opportunities are offered in a number of critical areas: software development, software sales, field services organisation, education services, HR, marketing, finance, child development centres, technical support, global information services, and facilities and global administration services. The UK R&D group is the hub of CA's software development activity throughout Europe, and is its largest development site outside the US. Any new graduates joining this group attend a 10-week 'bootcamp' training course in the US, for software engineers to assimilate facts on current operating systems and hone development skills.

As Sanjay Kumar presents CA's career opportunities: 'With the right people, the right technologies and the right strategy in place, the sky's the limit.'

## Remuneration

Salaries are performance-oriented, with no rate for any one job. Benefits are numerous and there's a money purchase pension scheme, where staff pay 1, 2 or 3 per cent of pensionable salary (basic salary at 1 July plus 100 per cent of bonus/commission paid through payroll in previous fiscal year) and CA pays twice the selected level. Staff may also pay AVCs. Holidays are 20 days, rising to 25 after five complete years of service. Private healthcare is available for all staff, spouses/partners and dependants at no cost, immediately on joining, as is a dental plan. Accident and Emergency cover is provided in addition. Group life assurance (lump sum of twice annual salary including 100 per cent of any bonus/commission) and group personal accident (permanent total disablement or death after an accident provides lump sum of twice gross annual earnings) are effective immediately on joining the company. Voluntary life cover can be added to total four times base salary. There's a group income protection scheme (monthly benefit of percentage of salary less single person's state incapacity benefit).

Company cars or allowances are available for eligible staff. Staff can buy shares at a 15 per cent discount. After 10 years' service staff receive a Rolex watch. A further benefit is educational assistance – any staff member wanting to study for degree, diploma, NVQ or other qualifications will be sponsored if the course is relevant to the member's role or personal development.

## The Future

'The emphasis now and in the future for CA is "customers first", and flexibility in what we offer to customers. CA's business model now provides flexible month-to-month licensing. We allow shorter contracts to help customers mitigate the risk inherent in technology implementation. We are committed to conducting business in a different manner that truly benefits customers.'

CA focuses on retention of quality staff. Churn rates are low, and some of that is undoubtedly due to the good work/life balance, although critics would argue the state of business globally and generally – and of the computing sector in particular – is not as hectic as it has been.

CA has grown by acquisition (today's ratio of CA-to-acquired staff is 50:50), although there's not been an acquisition in the UK for nearly three years.

What'll definitely help are CA's community relations and much-valued appreciation of – and focus on – family life and child development.

# Deloitte & Touche

Deloitte & Touche is a global professional services firm, providing assurance and advisory, tax, and consulting services through its member firms around the world. It operates in all major industry areas, including consumer, energy, financial services, government, manufacturing, technology, media, technology and travel, tourism and leisure. In the UK, it employs 10,000 people, 600 of whom are partners. It had revenues of £713.6 million for the financial year ended 31 May 2002.

**Scorecard:**

Remuneration and benefits ****
Progressive attitude ****
Opportunity for promotion ****
Training, development and education *****
Working atmosphere and environment *****

**Biggest plus:**
Strong sense of engagement with a large and growing population.

**Biggest minus:**
Managing organisational change very quickly is a challenge.

Deloitte & Touche
Stonecutter Court
1 Stonecutter Street
London EC4A 4TR
Tel: 020 7936 3000
Fax: 020 7583 1198
Website: www.deloitte.co.uk

# Deloitte & Touche

## The Business

Deloitte & Touche is one of the UK's so-called 'Big Four' professional services firms. Within its business are three main service lines: assurance, which is the main audit practice; tax – encompassing corporate tax, international tax, and indirect tax; and consulting and advisory services, within which corporate finance, business consulting, corporate restructuring and forensic services are prominent. In addition, there is a HR consulting practice and an actuarial business (B&W Deloitte). The large support infrastructure that surrounds these operations exists to serve both the internal and external activities of the firm. As an example, the IT department has been responsible for the provision of extranets to client organisations.

The structure has undergone two important changes recently. Following the break-up of Arthur Andersen's global network, Deloitte & Touche acquired the bulk of its business in this country, adding an additional 3,500 people in the process. In addition, the firm has shed Deloitte Consulting, its consulting arm, which focused on providing IT services to audit clients. This will be rebranded as Braxton and run under separate management. Those consultancy services that remain do so as part of an integrated service package within each of the main advisory businesses.

*In essence, what we're looking for are talented people who will thrive in an environment which empowers them to take responsibility early on and gives them an opportunity to accelerate their careers at a pace which suits them*

## Company Culture and Style

Deloitte & Touche has undergone significant structural change as a consequence of a changing regulatory and business environment. Deloitte's decision to separate Deloitte Consulting, one of its consulting capabilities, was primarily driven by market perception and a greater scrutiny of the consulting market in the wake of high-profile cases of accounting irregularities in the US.

Yet, if the environment has become more challenging, the company's values remain unchanged. According to Steve James, a partner in human resources, 'Our core values are still built around our commitment to our clients and our commitment to our people – those things are fundamental. So, too, are our integrity and commitment to cultural diversity at a global level. Probably the impact of the market has just brought an even sharper relief to our core value of integrity. We also remain committed to technical excellence in everything we do.'

Deloitte & Touche has, however, implemented significant structural and cultural change over the last couple of years. This has ranged from the introduction of accelerated career path opportunity to greater flexibility in reward and remuneration. In order to maintain its corporate identity the aim has been to align the needs and aspirations of individuals with those of the company. This policy of genuine engagement with its workforce is seen as highly important by Deloitte & Touche. 'We definitely see our people as being 10,000 brand messengers and what they have to say about the firm is as important if not more important than any advertising campaign', says James.

The leadership has sought to manage the change process by increasing the level of intra-firm communication. How else to retain the high level of commitment they trumpet? It seems to be working. A few years ago, less than 30 per cent of employees said they were happy with the level of communication they received about the business as a whole. Today, three-quarters are satisfied and the extended range of communication is helping to boost both productivity and the level of value-added service to clients. The company is particularly proud of a new intranet facility. It is updated daily and is used by chief executive, John Connolly, to answer questions from anyone, anywhere in the business.

## Human Resources

Deloitte & Touche is one of the largest graduate recruiters in the country and regularly hires between 500 and 700 such young people each year. Last year (2002) was no different, despite the Arthur Andersen transaction and adverse market conditions.

James explains that the firm has effectively honed the competency model it is seeking in graduates. He says, 'In essence, what we're looking for are talented people who will thrive in an environment which empowers them to take responsibility early on and gives them an opportunity to accelerate their careers at a pace which suits them. Accordingly, they will deliver early and continue to deliver and add value progressively over a career span within the context of technical excellence and quality work.'

The main qualities looked for in graduates are: potential technical excellence; management effectiveness (in respect of time, workloads and project work); leadership (with regard to teams); and strong client service (through the use of good interpersonal skills). These attributes are believed to underpin the future competitiveness of the firm and form the basis for a psychometric selection test, used in conjunction with structured competence-based interviews.

As the business continues to grow and diversify, there is an additional need for more experienced hires. Intake levels will vary according to internal and external factors but the number for 2002 was not far below that of the graduate intake. Finding such people is always challenging, even for a firm of Deloitte & Touche's standing, but recent investment in e-recruitment channels has helped to extend and improve its reach.

## Career Opportunity and Development

A majority of graduate recruits will study for the ACA – the main qualification for accountancy-based professionals. Assuming this is gained, there is considerable scope for career progression within Deloitte & Touche. The chance to become a partner is a particularly big motivation for many to plot their development within the firm, rather than look outside.

In the last couple of years there has been a move to reduce the bureaucratic structure that once surrounded career paths. The result is that there are fewer grades in the company hierarchy and less adherence to fixed timespans in roles. The attitude is: 'if you're good enough, you'll be promoted', rather than an insistence people remain where they are for a certain duration.

The company has also opened up new career options for specialist directors, who might not be on a standard path to partnership but will still have high value to the firm. So, as a retention tool, new types of promotion and rewards have been put in place.

As with e-recruitment, there has been a comparable investment in e-learning provision, the fruits of which are still being rolled out. However, there is a strong belief that most of the core learning occurs on the job. Skills vital to a successful career at Deloitte & Touche, like negotiation and teamwork, are achieved through the relationships that are formed within the business and through client interface.

## Remuneration

The company's reward strategy is to match the market in which it operates and to be competitive at every level. In order to retain the top talent, Deloitte & Touche is well aware it must pay at least as well as the other big three professional services firms, as well as other large corporate businesses, such as actuarial consultants and investment banks. Tellingly, the firm claims not to have lost a partner to a competitor organisation in over five years.

Within the compensation structure there now exists considerable differentiation, to reward on the basis of talent, performance and delivery. Base pay salary ranges are very broadly defined in order to attract and retain market talent. Bonuses are another key retention tool, with high performers eligible to earn up to 70 per cent of their salary value.

## The Future

Until recently, global consultants were highly visible in the corporate landscape – but the mood has now altered. Deloitte & Touche has been swift to adapt to changed circumstances and its hiring strategy is a demonstration it does not fear what lies ahead. There is, however, caution.

According to James, 'The regulatory environment has not concluded its deliberations and I think that will drive more change. Clearly the market has gone through a challenging time: the number of transactions has diminished, amount spent on consulting services declined. We expect things to improve but we don't know when. Despite difficult market conditions we are still the fastest growing of the big four professional services firms by revenue growth.

'In terms of our people we need to be operating as one firm, one population, engaged and committed to the Deloitte philosophy. We took a strategic decision to put everyone together as quickly as possible. We believe that all our people need to work together in a common culture in which all 10,000 of them belong. We will achieve this through strong leadership and adherence to our core operating principles; these are the two ingredients that will make it a success.'

# ◗ DENTON WILDE SAPTE

Denton Wilde Sapte is one of the leading specialist legal firms in the City of London. It specialises in sectors including banking, energy, technology, telecommunications and media. It is the result of a merger in February 2000 between Denton Hall, which was particularly strong in the energy, technology, media and telecoms areas, and Wilde Sapte which specialised in the Banking and Finance sector. These were two of the oldest firms in the City. It operates internationally in Europe, Asia, the Middle East and Africa through its own offices, formal alliances and close working relationships with other firms. The merger was intended to capitalise on the sector strengths of the two practices and to grow the international operations.

**Scorecard:**

| | |
|---|---|
| Remuneration and benefits | **** |
| Progressive attitude | ***** |
| Opportunity for promotion | **** |
| Training, development and education | **** |
| Working atmosphere and environment | **** |

**Biggest plus:**
The people. Don't be fooled by the crusty image of City law firms – people here are easy to talk to and the hierarchy is relatively flat.

**Biggest minus:**
The size of the business means that communication and cross-fertilisation between the different departments can be difficult. This is something the company is constantly working to improve.

Denton Wilde Sapte
5 Chancery Lane
Clifford's Inn
London EC4A 1BU
Tel: 020 7242 1212
Fax: 020 740 40087
Website: dentonwildesapte.com

# Denton Wilde Sapte

## The Business

Denton Wilde Sapte is a specialist legal firm with particular focus on three areas: banking and finance, energy and infrastructure and technology, media and telecommunications. It employs 1,700 people throughout the various territories in which it works across the world, 1,300 of whom are in the London and Milton Keynes offices. Half of these people are fee earners, with the rest composed of support staff. Opportunities for both categories of employee are listed frequently on the company website.

In addition to its core activities centering around corporate governance, dispute resolution and other legal areas, it publishes a number of detailed legal briefings through its website.

## Company Culture and Style

The key to understanding what it's like to work at Denton Wilde Sapte is probably to abandon any preconceptions about what a City law firm would be like, unless you already have insider knowledge. A glance at the company website tells you that this is a business with a sense of humour – the graduate recruitment page, for example, is headed with the 'WLTM' (would like to meet) tag so beloved of lonely hearts ads. This doesn't mean this isn't a serious company, but it sees no harm in enjoying what it does well.

*The atmosphere is vibrant and entrepreneurial and the best of the values of the previous companies have been retained*

It actually feels like a younger company than it has any right to, partly because of its relatively recent establishment as a merged entity – combined culture is still evolving but a few things are already clear. The atmosphere is vibrant and entrepreneurial and the best of the values of the previous companies have been retained. These include respect for each other as employees, being responsive to each other, building the brand and maintaining the highest professional standards. Within that, there are a number of positives for any potential employee. The company encourages staff to take the initiative and positively assesses the lessons learnt from all ventures, although the rewards for success give people plenty of incentive to succeed. Openness and transparency are key watchwords for the business, and the result is a true meritocracy – if you're good enough and you have the ambition to become a partner there's a good chance you'll do it. It's not just work though – the sports and social side of the company is lively enough to merit a page on its website.

The other area to watch for is the technology. The clients want a company that will be available 24/7 and, as a result, the resources such as teleconferencing and video conferencing are widely used in daily working, as well as the more standard intranet technology through which employees can communicate.

## Human Resources

Recruitment happens in a number of ways, and as has already been mentioned the website is a good place to start if you're interested. The firm has strong relationships with a number of recruitment consultancies, staff are rewarded for introducing candidates directly, and advertising in the legal journals is another means of getting fee-earners into the organisation. Staff are very well-regarded in the recruitment market. A team of 30 people are dedicated to human resources and training.

The HR team regards it as its job to support staff in carrying out their jobs as efficiently as possible, and to empower them in doing so. It does this by arranging training (see next section) as well as a variety of other stimuli for staff at all levels: it appoints trainee representatives so that even the least experienced of the staff will get a say in the way they are handled, and nominates charities for which the company works in any given year.

As well as jobs specifically advertised through the various channels, the company welcomes speculative applications from suitably experienced people.

## Career Opportunity and Development

First, the bad news – graduate level entry criteria are as strict as you would expect from a leading City firm. Anyone with less than 2.1 at degree level, or expecting less than that, needn't apply; interpersonal skills are, of course, essential and languages an advantage.

Once someone has joined, Denton Wilde Sapte is well aware that the calibre of person it wants will need the stimulation of a continuing learning programme if they are not to stagnate, and career appraisals are therefore a vital part of the business. It has a policy of 'upward appraisals' so the partners are assessed not just by the board but by the people with whom they work – this is done independently and anonymously by a third party talking to staff, so that a realistic picture of the input someone needs will emerge.

Every job has a competency formula attached, with staff measure against this as a metric. Typically for graduates, the first couple of weeks with the company are spent on familiarising ones-self with the business, and during the first two months they complete two modules for the PSC, which is taught in house. They then complete training seats, and are appraised continuously on their performance during this period. Development continues throughout the company at higher levels as well, focusing on both business and legal competencies.

Trainees at all levels speak highly of the company. To get an idea of the views of the more junior staff it's useful to look at the company's website, where graduate trainees are given the chance to air their views.

## Remuneration

Scales of pay are competitive – in this field they need to be. As this book went to press the HR team had been researching a flexible benefits scheme which would give employees the opportunity to tailor individual benefits such as holidays, private healthcare insurance and life assurance and to purchase additional benefits such as childcare or shopping vouchers.

The overall package is under review but the HR team has undertaken that the current value of the benefits package will not reduce if the new scheme is implemented.

Once someone reaches partner status the rules change somewhat; there is a 'lockstep' system, through which people progress over a period of time, and a merit award. The merit award won't just depend on someone's ability to pull in money but also on their contribution to their department and the overall performance of the company.

## The Future

Denton Wilde Sapte's immediate priority is to establish its brand as the leader in its markets throughout the whole of EMEA. In terms of the company's development as an employer you can expect to see a lot more work on personal development plans and a will to build on the entrepreneurial flair that already permeates the business.

At a time of economic downturn it arguably faces a difficult task, and is already encouraging partners to be creative about their approaches to clients – not simply to sit back and wait for the approach to come in. It has the right balance of newness as a recently merged company and pedigree from the parent companies to pull this off, even in a difficult market. This should be a company to watch in the future.

# DIAGEO

Diageo is the world's leading premium drinks business with an outstanding collection of beverage alcohol brands across spirits, wine and beer categories. These brands include Smirnoff, Johnnie Walker, Guinness, Baileys, J&B, Captain Morgan, Cuervo, Tanqueray, and Beaulieu Vineyard and Sterling Vineyards wines.

Diageo is a global company, trading in over 180 markets around the world. The company is listed on both the London Stock Exchange (DGE) and the New York Stock Exchange (DEO).

**Scorecard:**

| | |
|---|---|
| Remuneration and benefits | **** |
| Progressive attitude | ***** |
| Opportunity for promotion | **** |
| Training, development and education | ***** |
| Working atmosphere and environment | **** |

**Biggest plus:**
Diageo is a leading British blue-chip company with all the pride and power that market leadership and instant brand recognition can provide.

**Biggest minus:**
Diageo operates in markets that are sensitive both to fashion trends and to general economic conditions. Both represent pitfalls that will require careful negotiation in the future.

Diageo plc
8 Henrietta Place
London W1G 0NB
Tel: 020 7927 5200
Fax: 020 7927 4638
Website: www.diageo.com

# Diageo

## The Business

Diageo Plc is a world-leading premium drinks company, originally formed from the merger of Guinness and Grand Metropolitan in 1997 but now forging a distinct identity in a hotly competitive business. Diageo's brands – around 250 of them, including Johnnie Walker and J&B whiskies, Jose Cuervo tequila, Guinness, Smirnoff, Captain Morgan, Baileys, and Tanqueray – are sold in some 180 countries around the world. Diageo also owns a third of French champagne and cognac producer Moët Hennessy.

For its last full year, to June 2002, Diageo reported revenues of £11.3 billion and operating profits of £2.1 billion, up eight per cent and nine per cent respectively on the year before. Diageo has finally sold off the US food firms Pillsbury and Burger King. This completes the goal of becoming a focused premium drinks business. Diageo also owns 34 per cent of Moët Hennessy (spirits).

*few companies can offer Diageo's breadth of experience and opportunity in consumer goods, and Diageo is particularly acknowledged as a great source of marketing education and skills – understanding consumers and servicing their needs is the group's mantra*

The company has warned of difficult trading conditions, especially in Latin America, but Diageo looks sufficiently strong and sufficiently innovative to weather the storms. As with most large companies, its pension fund has a deficit that increased last year to nearly £1 billion, but again Diageo is probably better placed than most in being able to top up pension contributions.

## Culture and Style

Diageo isn't a business that constantly invents new products – R&D typically equates to less than one percent of sales, and while new products are fed into the mix the group's growth will generally come from increased focus on high margin brands in their most important markets. But it is a business that has to stay right on top of its market, and that translates into a deep understanding of consumers and a focus on brands.

A distinct Diageo culture has developed to blur the inevitable distinctions and demarcations within formerly separate organisations. It helps that there was already good deal of synergy – a good fit for brands and geography, but a helpful similarity of approach that emphasised consumer marketing.

Diageo has developed a vision and set of values and systems to help bind a diverse business together. The company's core business philosophy is summarised as 'Managing for Value', primarily in terms of shareholder value: but that is realised in particular by emphasising the value of Diageo's brands and Diageo's people.

Certainly Diageo takes the view that everyone in the organisation can help to create, maintain and add to value. Other key phrases used within Diageo support the point: 'Passionate about consumers' is at the heart of caring about brands; the consumer lies at the heart of Diageo's business. 'Be the best' is the group's aim for its products; the value also urges continuous learning, setting high standards and delivering results by beating the competition. 'Proud of what we do' suggests a continued sense of integrity, sensitivity, diversity and social responsibility – caring about the company, its brands, and the way it operates.

There's another message of relevance here: 'Freedom to succeed' is all about creating an open, challenging culture based on teamwork and trust. Branding doesn't exist in isolation: it needs consumers, but it also needs commitment and management from the group's own people. Diageo takes the view that great brands need great people to manage and grow them.

More recently, 'New ways of working' has been developed. This is being rolled out to individual operating units, and will be implemented in different ways by local managers, but essentially provides the management and IT tools for a flexible working environment. Managers set objectives and monitor them, for instance, but individuals might be encouraged to decide where and when their individual goals are delivered. More prosaically, office layouts and IT systems can be redesigned to provide for hot-desking with more meeting areas, more team days, more home working if that's appropriate.

The management structure is inevitably quite hierarchical, given the product range and the geographical spread. Even so the CEO is quite approachable, and 'skip level meetings' are a normal way of by-passing the nominal chain of command.

Diageo also places commendable emphasis on what it terms 'corporate citizenship', a portfolio of issues that includes ethics, corporate governance, employee relations, customers, consumers, suppliers, pensions, communities, health and safety, the environment and many other areas of business activity. Diageo is involved in all these areas, and in many of them is happy to benchmark itself against a relevant peer group.

One example is the Diageo Foundation, a charity that commits one per cent of the group's profit to social investment and other community programmes.

## Human Resources

Diageo acknowledges that its long-term growth depends ultimately on the ability to inspire its key staff, to support them and to enable them to realise their full potential.

Finding, keeping and developing the people who drive Diageo has placed considerable demands on the HR function, and so has the development of a characteristic Diageo culture within which they can work. The group recognises the importance of the Human Resources function; and HR has a high profile in the organisation, with a seat on the plc board and good access to the key decision-makers via an executive member on each divisional board.

Key HR processes include People Performance Management, a continuing performance review for employees with their line manager; People Development Reviews and 'Be The Best', development planning programmes to identify personal priorities and match them to the company's needs; and High Performance Coaching, a specific two-day intensive course for managers. Well-developed processes like these help the company get the best out of its employees – and vice versa.

## Career Opportunity and Development

Diageo is a huge and diverse organisation, but it does emphasise its overriding concern to recruit and keep the best people. It has certainly invested considerably in employee development principles and programmes, including 'a framework of processes and behaviours that commit us to winning through people' called The Diageo Way of Building Talent.

An attractive feature of any large organisation is the range of careers and the opportunities that it provides. But few companies can offer Diageo's breadth of experience and opportunity in consumer goods, and Diageo is particularly acknowledged as a great source of marketing education and skills – understanding consumers and servicing their needs is the group's mantra.

For management there's a good deal of coaching to find high performers who are committed to living the group's values. The Management Development Programme, which targets around 200–300 high-potential people typically in their late 20s and early 30s, has become a major factor in this development approach.

Diageo is a global company that offers excellent career progression within an environment that expects every individual to make a difference.

## Remuneration

Pay and benefits remain highly competitive, with total remuneration for any grade generally in the top 10 per cent of payers, and bonus systems enable Diageo to reward individuals according to their contribution. A new incentive structure is also being introduced to provide a direct link between the creation of value for shareholders and the way in which senior managers are rewarded.

For top managers Diageo operates a bonus system based on three-year targets for profit improvement; each manager's annual bonuses are 'banked', to be paid out over a number of years – a process which ensures that performance is sustained. For its most senior executives, Diageo also has a Long-Term Incentive Program that compares the company's performance against a peer group of 19 other businesses.

# The Future

Diageo is coming out of the first four years of a fairly traumatic birth, with cost savings from the merger of two very well established companies being offset by the inevitable operational hiccups and many issues of policy to be decided. Last year was probably a real turning point, both for Diageo's business – concentration on premium spirit brands, development of more innovative mixed drinks like Smirnoff Ice and Archers Aqua, continuing promotion of the traditional seller Guinness in new markets – and for the implementation of a Diageo culture with its own aims, style and systems.

The company has recently warned that its targets look 'increasingly challenging' in the immediate future, given world events and a generally more difficult global economic environment. Even so, Diageo is still expecting to increase annual sales by 8 to 10 per cent for the next few years.

Diageo looks like a confident, well-resourced operation that has the ambition and the imagination to handle temporary hiccups. It wants more of the world's drinks market, and it will use both existing brands and novel developments of them. Already in No 1 or No 2 position in most of its priority markets, the company looks a good bet for the long term.

# Dixons Group plc

The Dixons Group covers a number of strands – the Dixons High Street stores, Currys, PC World, PC World Business and The Link in the UK. These are household name retail operations but it is important not to overlook the other employment opportunities within the group. People with skills in logistics, buying and administrative support will find opportunities within the organisation. It is publicly traded and has over 30,000 employees in the UK alone.

**Scorecard:**

| | |
|---|---|
| Remuneration and benefits: | **** |
| Progressive attitude: | **** |
| Opportunity for promotion: | **** |
| Training, development and education: | **** |
| Working atmosphere and environment: | **** |

**Biggest plus:**
The longevity and strength of the brands.

**Biggest minus:**
The fast-changing market – innovation is needed constantly and ideas can be swallowed up and look dated very quickly.

Dixons Group
Maylands Avenue
Hemel Hempstead
Herts HP2 7TQ
Tel: 01442 353000
Fax: 01442 233218
Website: www.dixons.co.uk

# Dixons

## The Business

Dixons Group plc is one of Europe's longest-established specialist electrical retailers. The company that started as a single photographic studio in 1937 now has retail operations in 12 European countries. The Group includes Dixons, Currys and PC World in the UK and Ireland, The Link in the UK, PC City in France, Spain and Italy, Elkjop in the Nordic countries, Uni Euro in Italy and Electro World in Hungary and the Czech Republic. The Group also owns a Brussels-based commercial policy development company, CODIC, operating in Belgium, France, Germany and Luxembourg. The Group is listed on the London Stock Exchange.

Its Hemel Hempstead head office in Hertfordshire houses 2,000 staff working in Finance, Buying, Marketing, Human Resources, Legal and Corporate Affairs. A further 1,000 people handle UK-wide customer service for all four chains and telephone sales and help-lines for Coverplan and Freeserve in Sheffield. PC World Business, a small business-focused direct sales operation turning over more than £170 million a year, has its 500-strong headquarters in Bury, Manchester. The European businesses are headquartered in Paris, Madrid, Oslo, Stockholm and Monticello D'Alba. The Group has more than 1,350 stores as well as distribution centres and head office functions in all countries of operation and an international buying office in Hong Kong. In the year 2001/2 the Group turned over £4.8 billion and made profits of £278 million.

*The retail business is exhilarating – whether you find this exciting and stimulating or plain exhausting will depend on the sort of employee you are*

## Company Culture and Style

The retail business is exhilarating – whether you find this exciting and stimulating or plain exhausting will depend on the sort of employee you are. Electrical retailing is particularly competitive and Dixons brands aim to set the pace for the competition. The company has thrived on the philosophy that there are few prizes for retailers that settle for second place. The Group articulates its principles in a corporate 'Being the Best' statement that includes tenets such as operating with honesty and integrity, giving outstanding service to customers, continuing improvement and solid teamwork. Essentially, if you're not prepared to work in a customer-facing environment then Dixons is probably not for you.

It's a philosophy that the company strives to maintain across the business – yes, it's fast-paced and challenging but it's a business that thrives on team work and mutual support. You'll be required to take decisions and be accountable – and sometimes you'll make mistakes but this is a business where people have space to learn from their mistakes.

Store staff have uniforms (recently updated after staff consultation) while non-customer-facing staff wear casual dress. The diverse workforce reflects a Group whose customers are 8 to 80 and come from every background. Dixons people regularly clock up long service records of 25 and even 40 years – recognised in company-wide celebrations every year.

## Human Resources

If you've got what it takes, there are training and development packages at every level and in every function as well as Group-wide general management training to help you find the right career path.

The Company recruits throughout the year at every level. Store staff are recruited internally and there is also a partnership arrangement with JobCentre Plus to recruit new employees where it is opening a new branch or associated operation. Store managers are developed from our internal pool of talent, with most having experience in more than one chain at deputy manager level before they get their own store. A talented motivated manager running a store can effectively find him or herself driving a business worth anything from £6 to 16 million a year by their mid to late 20s.

There's an entry point for a wide range of levels of educational attainment. The Group recruits people without post-16 qualifications provided they can attain the Company's standards of numeracy, literacy and has have the inherent skills to provide excellent customer service. In Head Office there are many roles that will require GCSE or A Level or post university qualifications.

## Career Opportunity and Development

The breadth of the organisation allows high achievers to move about the different areas of the Group gaining a wide range of skills and experience. A finance manager in Head Office may move into chain finance management, buying, marketing or service and support general management. Potential chain managers, area managers or future directors may spend a spell in Head Office in central buying, marketing or forecasting functions. Many who leave the Group return after a few years with a competitor or another organisation and are able to leverage both Dixons Group and external experience to build their career thereafter. As the Group has expanded there are increasing opportunities in France, Spain, Italy, Scandinavia, Central Europe and the Far East as well as the UK.

The Group is committed to being an Employer of Choice. All employees receive opportunities, pay and benefits to match their skills and ambitions.

Individual performance reviews lead to bespoke training and personal development for all employees in an environment that is enjoyable, diverse, flexible and challenging.

Whether you work in its UK or European Head Offices, one of the 1,300 stores, Call Centres, Distribution Centres or Service Centres you will experience a team and people focused culture. Dixons has grown from a small business to a market-leading European retailer. It attracts some of the best retail talent due to the nature and variety of the challenges and the rewards and recognition that successful individuals receive. Recent Dixons alumni include the Chief Executive of Woolworths, the Chief Executive of Argos and Chairman of Homebase, the Marketing Director of Matalan, the Chief Executive of BBC Worldwide and the Finance Director of BT.

The Group's competency framework focuses on developing excellence in business management, people and personal performance. This framework forms the basis for the Group's recruitment, training and development and performance assessment processes.

All training and development is designed to meet both the business and an individual's needs. Subjects covered are as broad as the business. Everything from in-store selling skills to advanced negotiating skills for buyers. There are also tailor-made development programmes, which are provided by Ashridge and Henley business schools. The Group's development uses a variety of approaches in delivery of training. This may take the form of modules, interactive CDs, training workshops and a dedicated e-learning Intranet service delivered to locations throughout the UK.

## Remuneration

In addition to competitive rates of pay, the company offers a wide range of employee benefits from innovative nation-wide gym membership in the UK, car leasing, to life insurance and a company pension scheme, to which the Dixons Group will contribute up to 8 per cent of your salary. The company offers career breaks, a Medical Benefits Plan and share ownership schemes to allow every employee to share in the success they help to generate. All employees are entitled to staff discount on all Dixons Group products and services and there are special staff offers on high technology products from time to time.

In addition, there are a number of employee awards available for high achievers, adding not only to employee incentives but to the fun of working for this established but still competitive company.

## The Future

Dixons is one of the leading brands in its space, to the extent that people don't refer to buying things from electrical stores when they need something, they think of buying things from Dixons. This has its advantages but also means it has set itself something of an act to follow.

Its plans, those that it can discuss as a public quoted company, include further growth into Europe and consolidation of its position as a leading electrical retailer. This means a continuing eye on whether its stores look up to date; a continuing refreshing of its stock and the sorts of goods and gadgets its customers are likely to require. Its multi-channel policy has been a success and it remains one of the more prominent brands on the Web as well as in the High Street or trading estate.

Underpinning all of this is the continuing conviction that the people make the business what it is, and the customer experience will determine the success or failure of the company and all of its ventures in the future – people with ideas on how to innovate in that area will be welcomed!

Named 'Law Firm of the Year 2002' and 'Insurance Law Firm of the Year 2002', DLA is unusual among UK law firms in that it is nationally integrated, so whichever office a client goes to, it is all the same practice.

This allows DLA to provide the same level of service in each location, as lawyers in a local office are also part of a focused national team. DLA is expanding into continental Europe both by association and by merger, its latest acquisition being in Madrid. The firm has around 2,800 people, including over 315 partners, with annual turnover having grown by 46 per cent in the last three years and more than doubled from £100 million to £203 million in the last five years. Fee income has also risen over the last five years at a compound annual growth rate of 14 per cent.

**Scorecard:**

| | |
|---|---|
| Remuneration and benefits | **** |
| Progressive attitude | **** |
| Opportunity for promotion | **** |
| Training, development and education | **** |
| Working atmosphere and environment | **** |

**Biggest plus:**
Working for a driven and ambitious organisation with global ambitions and a participative culture.

**Biggest minus:**
The firm expects people to be willing to work hard in a demanding environment.

DLA
3 Noble Street
London EC2V 7EE
Tel: 08700 111111
Fax: 020 7796 6666
Website: www.dla.com
Email: recruitment.graduate@dla.com

# DLA

## The Business

DLA is a commercial law firm, providing professional advice in areas such as labour relations, buy-outs, technology and media, litigation, real estate and business restructuring, to corporate, financial and public sector clients.

According to Nigel Knowles, Managing Partner (awarded Managing Partner of the Year 2002) 'At DLA we are in the business of law. And like any successful business, we have to combine clarity of vision with a strategic focus that will deliver the financial performance to fund our growth plans. At the heart of our success is an absolute commitment to client service, and a belief that every single person within DLA has a role to play in adding value for our clients.'

*We have created an environment within our organisation which is energetic and participative and, I believe, unique in our profession. It enables great people to work together to deliver great results to our clients*

DLA is the only integrated UK commercial law firm, operating in both English and Scottish jurisdictions. It also has offices in Brussels, Hong Kong, Singapore and Spain, and is the founding member of D&P, an international legal grouping with firms in Belgium, Denmark, France, Germany, Hong Kong, Italy, The Netherlands, Norway, Singapore, Spain, Sweden and, of course, the UK.

DLA is a partnership, but operates as if it were a corporate entity and benchmarks itself against other professional service organisations, rather than other law firms. It is also a little unusual in that it grew out of practices in the north of England and then opened up in London, making it a lot less London-centric than many firms that started in London.

## Company Culture and Style

DLA's relatively flat organisational structure encourages teamwork and demonstrates the firm's values, which include mutual respect, building reputations and careers, taking responsibility, and striving for highest quality, according to Robert Halton, Human Resources Director. 'All organisations have values, but many never articulate them,' he says. 'We are looking for people who are inclusive', he says, adding that the firm regards all its people as professionals and team members, not just the fee-earning lawyers.

Reinforcing this Knowles outlined 'We have created an environment within our organisation which is energetic and participative and, I believe, unique in our profession. It enables great people to work together to deliver great results to our clients.'

'The managing partner's door is always open, so we look for people who want that kind of environment. We look for a willingness to get involved, personable people with good communications skills who are able to celebrate successes and have a laugh.'

DLA's geographical diversity enables people to join a global firm with a local feel. Wherever people operate they are in vertical groups, as part of a larger team with more resources: the firm is made up of groups of fee-earners organised by function, eg banking, litigation, corporate. Teams for specific projects can also be formed by combining staff from different groups, and from clients.

There is no formal flexible working strategy, though the start and end hours are flexible, and there is 24-hour working in some areas, primarily on the support side. The working week has been cut from 37.5 hours to 35 hours, with no loss of output. Halton says that people work long hours when necessary, but are more effective when they do not overdo it: 'The EU working time regulations gave an opt-out option, but we didn't take it. We said these regulations make sense, so watch your hours.'

The firm has an active Corporate Social Responsibility programme, with an in-house team paid to coordinate it. DLA works with the Prince's Trust, sponsors an art award, does charity fundraising, and has a number of partners and other lawyers who provide time and expertise to charities and local organisations.

As Nigel Knowles says 'As a major employer we know we have a significant role to pay in the communities in which we work and live. It is an obligation we take seriously and one which we pursue with energy and enthusiasm.'

## Human Resources

The firm recruits at a number of levels, including support staff, graduates as trainee solicitors, and also from other law firms. The main intake is 85 graduates per year across the UK – having so many offices gives DLA access to more universities. DLA maintains relationships with their local universities.

'We recruit lawyers two years in advance', says Halton. 'We interview them in their preferred office, then they go to an assessment centre where they'll be tested for logical thinking, analysis, presentation, team working, social skills and so on – ensuring a similar high standard in the intake from every location. We are not just looking for academic qualifications; although these are important, we look for individuals who will fit into the DLA culture.'

Trainees join on a two-year contract. DLA recruits a proportionately low number for its size because it aims to retain more of them when they qualify. The target is 90 per cent, and Halton says that in recent years it has managed 95 per cent to 96 per cent. Summer vacation placements are also available.

# Career Opportunity and Development

DLA recognises that in a people-dependent business such as law, retaining and motivating its people is essential, and that this requires more than just spending cash: it must also reinforce its stated values with career and lifestyle benefits. Knowles says, 'The quality and loyalty of our people is key to our success, and attracting and retaining high-calibre people is a priority within our business.'

'We had a bad reputation for turnover in the past, but no more,' Halton says. 'We surveyed the leavers and got a 24 per cent response – the problem was how people were treated and respected, and career development. People weren't being managed properly.

'I think now we give people more responsibility earlier on. We make sure people have reviews, and tell us if they don't. And we're less stuffy than some law firms – it's more like a grammar school than an Oxbridge college.'

The firm has invested heavily in both printed and online resources to help people progress in their careers. It has a performance management process whose aim is not merely to determine current performance but to plan an individual's future career development, and a behavioural competency plan, which explains what it expects people to be competent at, at the different levels of trainee, team leader, manager, and director/partner.

In April this year, DLA received 'Investors in People' accreditation, recognising the success of their development programme and the engagement of people throughout the organisation in delivering strategic goals.

# Remuneration

As a partnership, DLA is owned by its partners, who receive a proportion of its profits, calculated on their total contribution to the business. Employees are paid a salary and receive benefits including private health cover, a contributory pension scheme and life assurance. The starting salary for a graduate trainee ranges from £16,000 to £28,000, depending on the region of the country.

The firm operates incentive schemes to reward long service and to build loyalty, for example instead of a bonus there is a service holiday award on top of the basic 25 days annually. 'We decided against a bonus scheme as it can be divisive', says Halton. 'Time is critical in our business, so it is precious. In recognition of that, we have introduced a scheme where you can get extra leave with service. For every three years' service you get an extra 10 days leave to be taken over the next two years.'

There are no company cars, but people are eligible for a car loan scheme; London staff can also get interest-free season ticket loans while other offices have a discretionary car parking assistance scheme.

The latest additional benefits are a telephone information and referral service for all DLA people and immediate relatives, and the pilot of a concierge service. The latter offers help with such things as finding household services, gift shopping and holiday planning, and while users must pay for the services delivered, the firm covers their membership of the scheme which it hopes will make life easier for working mothers in particular.

## The Future

DLA's stated aim is to become a top five European full-service law firm, with a significant Asian presence, within three years. It plans to achieve this is part by alliance and merger with other D&P members, on the basis that clients in each country will prefer local lawyers to imported foreign ones.

As part of this, it is continuing to develop its HR strategy as an important means of differentiating itself from the competition. Says Halton, 'HR is about assembling a jigsaw, and not about individual initiatives. I believe people want to be in an organisation that's going places,' and according to Knowles 'The DLA brand symbolises an organisation that is going places'.

# egg™

One of the pioneering Internet banks, Egg started life as part of the Prudential in 1998 as a telephone-only service for savings. It later expanded into the emerging online world and serves a group of affluent customers with credit cards and loans as well as the initial savings service. It remains a vibrant, lively place to work and puts a great deal of focus into motivating people in its call centers as well as its head office personnel. It achieved a listing on the London Stock Exchange in its own right in June 2000.

**Scorecard:**

| | |
|---|---|
| Remuneration and benefits | **** |
| Progressive attitude | ***** |
| Opportunity for promotion | **** |
| Training, development and education | ***** |
| Working atmosphere and environment | ***** |

**Biggest plus:**
The company was set up with a view to improving the lives of its customers and continues to aim to make a contribution to society by making their finances easier to manage.

**Biggest minus:**
More of a frustration than a drawback, but as a bank the company has to adhere to a number of controls and regulations that could appear to clash with its laid-back but efficient culture.

Egg plc
1 Waterhouse Square
138–142 Holborn
London EC1N 2NA
Tel: 020 7526 2500
Fax: 020 7526 2665
Website: www.egg.com

# Egg

## The Business

Egg is a brand in its own right and a major one at that; it offers credit cards, loans and savings accounts, mortgages, investments and insurances. It is dedicated to improving the quality of its customers' lives by making their financial management simpler. It does this both through telephone accounts and the Internet. On the Net not only can someone look at their Egg accounts but they can set up their other bank accounts so that they can be seen through the Egg website, enabling an immediate look at a whole financial picture. It is independent of its parent company the Prudential, which still owns the majority of the shares but it is traded on the London Stock Exchange as Egg.

Egg has always committed itself to becoming a profitable international business of scale, and it recently (November 2002) launched its first product in France (where it trades as Egg France), although the products are clearly subject to the individual legislations within the different countries – for example in the UK it offers 0 per cent interest for credit transfers to new holders of its credit card, whereas in France this would not be legally possible. The guiding principle remains to allow customers to cut through a lot of the financial complexities they might otherwise face and to get a better deal. It employs just over 2,000 people, 1,000 of whom are at its Derby call center – and don't be put off by phrases like 'call centre', it is brightly lit, has a lot of plants and mood/relaxation rooms and is a far cry from the poorly-regarded call centres that hit the headlines during the late 1990s. It has done well by valuing its employees; some 10 million customers (and increasing) use the services it offers.

*Hierarchically there is the flattest of structures – if a call centre partner has an idea they can put it to whoever they want and it'll get serious consideration*

## Company Culture and Style

Egg sees itself as an innovator and this is reflected at every level of its operation. It is avowedly a digital banking and financial services company and aims to make the most of every opportunity the technology allows, although this can bring with it certain constraints; for example, mortgage applications cannot be processed entirely online at present, for legal reasons.

On visiting the London HQ, you are struck by an immediate air of informality. The directors happily wear jeans and there are no rigid codes about appearance further down the food chain – you are there to do a job and enjoy it, and as long as you can fit in as part of the team you're welcome. Hierarchically there is the flattest of structures – if a call centre partner has an idea they can put it to whoever they want and it'll get serious consideration. Chill-out zones are built into all of the premises and it's a surprise to find a table football game in the middle of a bank's head office! It's easy to forget that you're at the heart of a financial institution in the City of London, but of course you are – and underpinning the laid-back surface attitude is a rigid application of all of the security and regulatory measures a customer could want.

So, potential employees can expect a number of things. First, you don't have to buy a new suit except for the interview. Second, once your induction period is over you'll be working for someone interested in you as well as your output: you're not a drone. Third, you'll be vetted within an inch of your life and must sign the Official Secrets Act – and if you're a customer as well you should be pleased to hear that. The atmosphere within the company is candid – people are deliberately encouraged to communicate, and if you have a problem there's no value judgement against you if you need to ask for help. A follow-on from this is that you absolutely have the right to fail, this is seen as part of learning although, of course it shouldn't be habit-forming!

## Human Resources

Egg's HR department is in many ways very forward looking – it has a 'Chief People Officer' rather than anything as austere as an HR director. Its intention is to steer the company towards 'value-based revenue', which means getting a fast buck out of a customer is a lot less important than looking after them so they're encouraged to stay with the company for another ten years or however long.

The rules in HR reflect the rest of the company's ethos. Training is taken seriously enough to allow for the development of an 'Associates Alumni' group, made up of the call centre personnel who have achieved certain standards. If you leave on good terms your application to come back will be welcomed, although be warned – the Egg you left four years ago won't be the same as the Egg to which you would be returning now.

Remember when you're being interviewed that you can expect the unexpected – they want to know how you'll deal with it. One enthusiastic manager had a clown walk into an interview on a few occasions, and judged people's gumption on whether they'd actually ask why someone was dressed like that in a bank!

## Career Opportunity and Development

Tied into the HR function is the scope for training and development, an area on which Egg is currently putting a lot of focus. As a company it is only a few years old and is now keen to address the developmental needs of its staff. It has always been keen to motivate, hence the 'associates' tag for the people who work in its call centres, and it now wants to build on its solid start.

None of which is to say that it is lacking in the basics. Periodic appraisals and assessments of personal development plans happen regularly as might be expected in any substantial organisation, but more than this the company wants to build people's life skills up. 'In business people can have the technical knowledge but not the personal skills to make a deal happen', says Chief People Officer Andy Craggs. 'We're talking about coping skills and life skills.' This holistic view is designed to bring the best out of every individual, and employees are encouraged to put themselves forward to re-skilling in these areas when they believe it would benefit themselves and the company.

Call centre associates are taken seriously as regards their training needs. They are trained and then 'buddied' for at least two weeks so that if they need any further input there is a structure through which they can get it informally. With these and other support structures in place employees can then manage their own careers as far as is possible whilst serving the company's own business requirement. It's the last bit that's the killer: Craggs admits to having to say 'no' more than he'd like for the moment.

## Remuneration

Egg believes in offering more than just top dollar to its associates and other employees, but it does all the usual market surveys to ensure it remains competitive in its payments. Pay is partly performance-related but its definition of 'performance' is different from a number of similar operations; for example, other companies might pay their telephone operatives for the number of calls they manage in a particular day. Egg believes this encourages associates to get rid of callers quickly to make up their quotas, so it pays more attention to the quality of advice and help given on the phone ('advice' here in the most general sense rather than any sort of regulated independent financial advice).

Many employees have Egg shares and half the staff have options. The varying fortunes of the Stock Exchange have dictated that this can be a mixed blessing but the staff are aware that this isn't a short-term perk but an evolving benefit. Of course as a company with strong affiliations to the Prudential, there are some excellent financial products on offer to the staff at extremely reasonable prices; pensions, life assurance and other benefits need to be state-of-the-art to be taken seriously.

## The Future

Egg will continue to work towards shareholder and customer value in everything it does for the foreseeable future. It wants to retain its image of doing everything slightly differently and innovating wherever possible, and focusing on its core 25–45 year-old market in doing so.

It will continue to foster an entrepreneurial outlook throughout its employees and aims for a reputation as an exceptional company to work for, something it already has in a number of circles. It will continue to respond to its customers' needs – for example when most companies talk about credit they talk about an APR; Egg's anecdotal evidence suggests not all customers know what an APR is, so its associates are encouraged to keep the selling simple on the phone.

It will always stick to its core mission of making a difference to society by helping people understand and manage their finances painlessly, whilst also giving them a market-beating service or market beating product. Short of actually giving cash away (and actually it does – its 0 per cent interest card for 6 months still gives 0.5 per cent cashback to customers!), it has made an excellent start in a short period of time.

# GALLAHER GROUP Plc

Gallaher is the world's fifth largest tobacco company. Gallaher's shares are listed on the London Stock Exchange and its ADRs are traded on the New York Stock Exchange. Gallaher is headquartered at Weybridge, in the UK, and has leading positions in many Eurasian markets, including Austria, Germany, Greece, Hungary, Kazakhstan, the Republic of Ireland, Russia, Sweden and the UK. Gallaher's comprehensive brand portfolio includes leading international brands such as Benson and Hedges, Silk Cut, Mayfair, LD, Memphis, Sobranie, and Hamlet. The Group employs around 10,000 people worldwide – 2,100 of whom work in the UK – and has manufacturing plants in the UK, Russia, the Republic of Ireland, Kazakhstan, Austria, Sweden and Ukraine. Gallaher engages in the business of manufacturing, distributing and marketing tobacco, knowing that its products are controversial. The Group is openly and fully aware of its responsibilities ,as it seeks to sell its tobacco products to informed adult smokers, people who have chosen to smoke knowing the risk associated with smoking.

**Scorecard:**

| | |
|---|---|
| Remuneration and benefits: | ***** |
| Progressive attitude: | **** |
| Opportunity for promotion: | **** |
| Training, development and education: | ***** |
| Working atmosphere and environment: | ***** |

**Biggest plus:**
An innovative and dynamic Eurasian tobacco company, which retains a family feel.

**Biggest minus:**
Operating in a controversial sector.

Gallaher Group Plc
Members Hill
Brooklands Road
Weybridge
Surrey KT13 0QU
Tel: 01932 859777
Fax: 01932 832508
Website: www.gallaher-group.com

# Gallaher Group Plc

Gallaher was demerged from American Brands, Inc. (now known as Fortune Brands, Inc.) in May 1997. Management believed that the demerger would benefit both companies as they had different financial and operating characteristics, and different investment risk and return profiles. Since 1997, Gallaher has been transformed from a predominantly British and Irish company into a leading Eurasian tobacco group.

Demerger enabled Gallaher to focus on expanding its tobacco business overseas. In 1999, the Group established a factory in Kazakhstan, and in 2000, Gallaher acquired the Russian cigarette manufacturer Liggett-Ducat.

In 2001, Gallaher acquired Austria Tabak. Austria Tabak is the cigarette market leader in Austria and Sweden. In the same year, the Group also acquired a small cigarette factory in Ukraine.

Gallaher's Continental European operations are now based in Vienna, and Commonwealth of Independent States operations are based in Moscow. An international central marketing division has been created in the UK to serve all of the Group's locations.

*My impressions before I joined have been borne out. It's a well-led, well-directed company, on both a financial and strategic level. It knows what it wants and how to achieve it*

Gallaher has delivered consistent growth since demerger. Between 1997 and 2001, earnings per share before amortisation of intangible assets increased at a compound annual growth rate of 10.9 per cent.

In 2002, Gallaher's international expansion strategy was furthered by the acquisition of Gustavus, a small Swedish snuff manufacturer; joint venture agreements with R.J. Reynolds in certain European markets, and Sampoerna in Malaysia; and a letter of intent with the China National Tobacco Corporation for the on-shore production of a Gallaher brand in China.

## Company Culture and Style

What impresses everyone who comes into contact with Gallaher is the enthusiasm shown at every level of the business. Jonathan Donovan, Head of Employee Relations, left a senior HR role in the financial sector to join Gallaher in 2002. He notes: 'My impressions before I joined have been borne out. It's a well-led, well-directed company, on both a financial and strategic level. It knows what it wants and how to achieve it.'

In an impressively short time, Gallaher has become a truly international business. Despite this growth, the commercially rigorous culture of the Group is still tempered by a family atmosphere. As a result, people genuinely enjoy working at

Gallaher – a fact underlined by its strikingly low staff turnover. The Group prides itself on looking after its people.

To flourish at Gallaher, you need to be a go-getter with energy and talent, and have an interest in driving forward the business. As to those unlikely to succeed, Donovan suggests that anyone looking for an easy ride is advised to look elsewhere: tobacco companies are locked in an aggressively competitive world and Gallaher wants people unafraid of hard work and commitment.

In line with its commitment to communicating with employees across the Group, Gallaher has launched *Dialogue*, a magazine published in English, German and Russian; it is one of a number of initiatives helping to provide a genuine Group identity.

## Human Resources

HR at Gallaher is a strategic function that works very much in partnership with the Group's management. Its purpose is to drive the integration of the business, to develop staff, and help them deliver.

The HR strategy is about boosting employees' contributions through robust policies and processes. This has become even more important recently. Donovan says: 'We are a sizeable FTSE-100 company with significant international interests. The HR role is increasingly sophisticated. We need to be integrated at every activity – from business strategy through to the incorporation of new businesses into Gallaher's culture.'

Gallaher recruits around 10 UK graduates a year. The right attitude is more important than a degree when it comes to success at the Group.

## Career Opportunities and Development

Gallaher is clearly a different company now than in the 1990s. Today there are people within the Group with broad international responsibilities, and career opportunities exist that were not dreamed of five years ago.

The Group has a strong commitment to training at every level – and seeks to balance this across internal and external courses. There is widespread support for those wishing to continue their professional development, and this is now often supplemented by visits to the Group's overseas operations. Thanks to the recent major acquisitions, there are greater opportunities for overseas working and travel than ever before. Language training is available for those whose posts require it, mainly in German, Russian, French, Italian and Spanish.

There is a well-established management development function at Gallaher. The aim is for employees to work to 'smart objectives', against which their performance is measured. Multi-skilling is something that has been successfully introduced at many levels: in the factories, for instance, Gallaher's people are highly flexible.

All vacancies are advertised internally on Gallaher's Group intranet, and recruitment from within was traditionally highly valued at Gallaher. This remains the case, coupled with the recognition that external recruits can bring a different perspective and experience to the Group. This has led to a rise in the number of people joining from outside, particularly in specialist positions.

## Remuneration

Gallaher is an upper quartile payer; it wants to get the best people, and is prepared to pay for them. In addition to basic salary, UK employees benefit from a profit-related pay scheme. Managers can also participate in a performance-related pay scheme.

Sharesave and Share Purchase schemes are available at every level of the Group.

In terms of pension plans, Gallaher is committed to high-quality pension provision.

Gallaher operates its own health insurance scheme in which spouses are included, as well as children below the age of 18. There is also a death-in-service life assurance benefit for employees in the UK.

In the UK, company cars are offered to all managers, and others, where required for the job. Vauxhalls and Saabs are available, with Mercedes for senior executives. There is a cash option for those who prefer not to incur the tax penalties.

## The Future

Gallaher's strategy is to develop a balanced portfolio of interests in established and emerging markets with growth prospects across Eurasia – organically, and through acquisitions, strategic alliances and joint ventures.

Donovan sums up the Group's future plans: 'Our ambition is to re-inforce Gallaher's position as a major Eurasian player. I am convinced that the people at Gallaher have the energy, enthusiasm, effectiveness and efficiency to achieve this.'

GlaxoSmithKline

GlaxoSmithKline is a world-leading research-based pharmaceutical company with its headquarters in the UK and with a total of more than 100,000 employees around the world. The company was formed in a merger, completed on 27th December 2000, between Glaxo Wellcome and SmithKline Beecham. The resulting company has bedded down and retained its market leadership, holding 6.9 per cent of the world's pharmaceutical market. It is a leader in four major therapeutic areas: anti-infectives; central nervous system (CNS); respiratory; and gastro-intestinal/metabolic. It sees its mission very much in improving the quality of life for its customers.

**Scorecard:**

| | |
|---|---|
| Remuneration and benefits | **** |
| Progressive attitude | ***** |
| Opportunity for promotion | **** |
| Training, development, and education | **** |
| Working atmosphere and environment | ***** |

**Biggest plus:**
The opportunity to contribute to the creation of one of the world's biggest pharmaceutical and healthcare companies.

**Biggest minus:**
Press coverage sometimes makes the pharmaceuticals industry the default 'bad guy' when, in fact, GSK is making concerted efforts to be an environmentally and socially responsible company.

GlaxoSmithKline
New Horizons Court
Great West Road
Brentford
Middlesex TW8 9FF
Tel: 020 8975 2000
Website: www.gsk.com

# GlaxoSmithKline

## The Business

GlaxoSmithKline has spent the years since it came into existence bedding down as a cohesive entity with its own culture rather than as two separate companies, and has met with a lot of success in this respect. It has over 100,000 employees worldwide, 40,000 of whom are in sales and marketing and over 42,000 of whom work in research and development. It spends £2.4 billion on R&D per annum and its 2001 results showed sales of £20.5 billion and pre-tax profit of £6.2 billion.

GSK is among the top three companies worldwide in both over-the counter medicines and oral healthcare products, owning ten oral healthcare and nutritional healthcare brands. Overall, the company has household name brands in 130 countries. GSK's powerful research and development capability encompasses the application of genetics, genomics and other leading-edge technologies.

*Flexible working has arrived in a big way and improved the quality of life for a number of employees who don't need to make the trek to Brentford every day to be effective*

It leads the world in anti-infectives, central nervous system, respiratory and gastro-intestinal/metabolic areas, as well as developing a growing portfolio of oncology products. It is pioneering affordable medication internationally and is working on AIDS-hit communities with Unicef.

## Company Culture and Style

GSK has spent two years building up its new corporate culture, which is based primarily around becoming a centre of excellence in every clinical area in which it operates, which encompasses most of them. Flexible working has arrived in a big way and improved the quality of life for a number of employees who don't need to make the trek to Brentford every day to be effective. Dominic Johnson, Director of Policy and Employee Relations, points to two planks underpinning the culture: integrity in everything the company does and entrepreneurial spirit. This facilitates continued adherence to the statement put out by Chief Executive, Jean-Pierre Garnier, when the current company launched:

'Our mission – why we are in business: our global quest is to improve the quality of human life by enabling people to do more, feel better and live longer. Strategic intent – our business goal: We want to become the indisputable leader in our industry. Our spirit – the individual and organisational qualities that will enable us to turn our opportunities into achievements.

We undertake our quest with the enthusiasm of entrepreneurs, excited by the constant search for innovation. We value performance with integrity. We will attain success as a global leader with each and every one of our people contributing with passion and an unmatched sense of urgency.'

In 2001 the business moved into its new HQ, GSK House. This is a 13-storey tower block dominating a multi-building campus. In addition to the tower block, five five-storey buildings are arranged around an enclosed street area with pedestrian link bridges crossing at various levels, Staff facilities include a gym, shops, cafés and restaurants, all grouped along the central 'street'. Intended to house nearly 3,000 employees in its state-of-the-art buildings, this is one of the largest business developments in West London since the Second World War. On entering the feeling is of cleanliness but also of wide open spaces and employees being allowed to relax in comfortable zones when they're on breaks – the coffee shop, for example, looks like a proper coffee shop rather than some of the tokenistic efforts made by some employers.

## Human Resources

If one word can be said to sum up the staff at GSK then it is 'diversity' – and this doesn't simply mean an effort to employ people from different racial backgrounds, important though this is, but a concerted effort to invest serious money in services that will benefit employees with different needs at different times in their lives. These include child and eldercare information services, flexible working options and enhanced maternity and paternity provisions. Operational Excellence remains a buzz-phrase, with the company recognising that supporting employees is an essential part of achieving this.

The human resources department continues to look closely at the way in which it serves staff. As well as 'generalist' human resources departments supporting the businesses, a number of 'shared service' specialist teams have been running for a couple of years to cover pay, benefits and recruitment.

Internal surveys suggest the policies have gone down well, with 88 per cent of employees agreeing they are proud of the corporate culture. The HR department will continue to look at ways of improving this still further by simplifying some of the processes that have arisen over a period of time.

## Career Opportunity and Development

GSK, as a major UK pharmaceutical and healthcare company, places great importance on the recruitment of graduates and postgraduates, not just in the UK but throughout Europe. Accordingly, shared services recruitment has placed an immediate emphasis on internal job posting on the company's intranet, external recruitment via the Internet, and building on existing links with European business schools.

GSK has one of the world's largest sales and marketing operations in the global pharmaceutical industry, with about 43,000 sales and marketing personnel world-wide. Because the world is changing so rapidly, both organisations and the people they employ need to be versatile and flexible. Healthcare is a global business and career opportunities at GSK can be global too. Inter-business transfer is common and, depending on cost/benefit evaluation, may involve moving between the UK, the US, and Europe.

GSK aims to offer stimulating and rewarding careers, particularly while the merger integration process is building the new organisation. However, GSK also recognises that staff may make many career choices in their time, and may want to move on from the company. Therefore, the company aims to maximise individual contributions when people are there, while in return offering the means for employees to improve their personal saleability and acquire new skills. Like many other organisations, GSK has moved to a 'flatter', less hierarchical, more informal structure – the chief executive has an intranet page with space for comments from everyone.

While this may mean fewer chances at traditional promotions, this loss is balanced by an increased emphasis on giving staff the chance to enhance their skills and manage their own careers. The company offers programmes for self-study, internal and external training and development, covering leadership development as well as more specifically job-related competencies. One of the first GSK initiatives, launched in April 2001, was a new global performance development review programme covering staff at all levels in the business.

## Remuneration

Under a scheme called TotalRewards the company hopes to take employee benefits beyond the simply financial. The scheme to help employees with the need for care for elderly relatives has already been mentioned and much other personal help is available; in terms of hard cash, though, the average salary is £40,000 and share savings schemes work throughout the business. Clearly there are different legislative frameworks in different territories but wherever possible ideas like 'buy one share get one free' schemes abound.

Beyond financial rewards, GSK aims to provide an 'employee experience' that creates the right environment for people to do their best work, providing exciting development opportunities, and helping people to build resilience and achieve a comfortable balance between life and work. The idea is to build a framework in which an employee can thrive as an individual, and inevitably give of their best to the company as a result.

## The Future

Today, change in the pharmaceutical industry is being driven prmarily by three forces: rapid advances in science and technology; the growing importance of marketing power and the emergence of patients as consumers. GSK is very strongly placed to benefit from the exciting opportunities emerging from these changes in the pharmaceutical industry and will continue to underpin this with a serious amount of resource thrown at community initiatives. It will also grow its R&D and it will develop Centres of Clinical Excellence for Drug Development (CEDDs) – it has one for respiratory illness already and plans to open more.

The company believes it will have the financial strength, scientific expertise and marketing power to capitalise on all of its opportunities, and it intends to generate enhanced growth and shareholder value in the short, medium and long term. It expects to continue to be a market leader for many years to come.

HBOS was founded in September 2001, when the Bank of Scotland merged with the Halifax. The Bank of Scotland was founded in 1695, a year after the Bank of England, which makes it the second oldest bank in the UK, and the Halifax was founded in 1853. Until June 1997, when it became a bank, Halifax was the world's largest building society.

This £28 billion union created a new force in the financial world – in fact, a number of new forces. The first annual report of HBOS announced proudly that it is a new force in retail banking, insurance and investment, business banking, corporate banking and treasury.

It was, unusually for organisations of such size, constructed as a 'merger of equals': one of Scotland's leading newspapers has given its verdict: 'Bank of Scotland's marriage with Halifax just keeps on looking better.'

**Scorecard:**

| | |
|---|---|
| Remuneration and benefits | **** |
| Progressive attitude | *** |
| Opportunity for promotion | **** |
| Training, development and education | **** |
| Working atmosphere and environment | *** |

**Biggest plus:**
The power and skill from two complementary businesses forming a fast moving customer responsive financial giant.

**Biggest minus:**
Still to convince its home-based Scottish public that Bank of Scotland has not been taken over.

HBOS
The Mound
Edinburgh EH1 1YZ
Tel: 0131 243 8697
Website: www.hbosplc.com

# HBOS

## The Business

The Bank of Scotland has never been afraid to dip its toe into new waters. But after its failed bid for NatWest it dived into the water from a great height and is now doing some powerful synchronised swimming with the Halifax. The merger has not seen the sacrifice of any important brand names and HBOS is the holding company.

The result is that the Bank of Scotland and Halifax are now part of a powerful organisation with assets of £355 billion, 25 million customers and a stable of brand names such as Intelligent Finance, Clerical Medical, Capital Bank, The Mortgage Business, St James's Place Capital and esure.

Bank of Scotland Corporate Banking is the UK market leader in MBO financing, bank finance for social housing, PFI/PPP and public to private financing. Bank of Scotland Business has increased its business customers in the UK, as well as increasing joint venture business and is the UK's largest contract hire operator.

## Company Culture and Style

There are no employees. They are all 'colleagues'. This is to reinforce the message that they are all part of the same team. First names are very much in, even with the boss himself, James Crosby.

In his annual report James Crosby stated: 'Earning the advocacy of all 60,000 HBOS colleagues is a tall order. Listening to colleagues' views through regular monthly polling and detailed annual surveys and then acting on their feedback is very much part of how we ensure the two-way flow that builds commitment to our company and its goals.'

*There are no employees. They are all 'colleagues'. This is to reinforce the message that they are all part of the same team*

Two different cultures do not merge overnight. Sir Peter Burt, outgoing deputy chairman and seen as the main architect of the merger, says that takeovers are usually easier to manage: there is no dubiety or argument as to which culture is going to dominate.

The real problems in a merger, he states, come from ensuring that people work together and that corporate cultures fit. The difference here is that the Bank and the Halifax had worked closely together for many years and the two businesses were largely complementary, with very little overlapping.

Clarity of management and businesses that complement each other have top importance. Hierarchical lines have been stripped away and those who can do the job have been empowered so to do.

The merger has meant a significant amount of restructuring. HBOS says that much of the merger process is virtually complete and that it has all gone remarkably smoothly, with the two businesses sharing a common philosophy of value for shareholders through customer satisfaction.

## Human Resources

Merging two diverse teams into one has not been easy but the job is almost over and HBOS says that creating a merged team has been delivered with very little acrimony. Staff turnover numbers have been relatively small and the focus on putting the best people into the jobs that suit their skills has not meant staff being transferred unwillingly to Halifax or Edinburgh.

The vast majority have been redeployed and re-trained, job losses have been minimal and every effort has been made to keep up staff morale in what has been a time of momentous change for them – but also a golden career opportunity as part of a large, ambitious and determined organisation.

HBOS is passionate about promoting dignity at work and is determined to create the most friendly, most motivated workforce.

The mantra, according to the first annual report of the merged business: 'We recognise the diversity of our workforce and are committed to remaining at the forefront of progressive companies in our work life policies.

'We aim to achieve a workforce that is reflective of our current and potential customer base to better serve the changing communities.'

## Career Opportunity and Development

Opportunities abound and so does the internal competition. HBOS has already recruited 1,500 people in Business Banking, many from the other Big Four banks and it is looking to take on many more as it launches its attack on the SME market.

Skills are recognised and nurtured. Independent and team performance is valued and people – colleagues – are helped to develop their full potential in what the Bank calls an 'open, honest and non-hierarchical working environment'.

The development programmes range from job-related training and graduation induction courses through to MBA style management courses at Harvard and secondments to enterprise bodies and charities.

In seeking advancement in such a vast organisation it has to be assumed that staff will have to be prepared to move to where the jobs are but HBOS points out that, while it has a UK-wide mobility clause, it is rarely imposed. It believes that there is little to be gained from forcing someone to make a 'geographical move' if they are not happy with it.

In such a vast organisation with five main strands, a portfolio of top brands and a long list of strategic objectives there are attractive career paths for those who are keen to go down them, no matter where it takes them.

James Crosby, makes this point in the annual report: 'The bottom line is that good performance is rewarded, poor performance is not and exceptional achievements are rewarded exceptionally.'

## Remuneration

The clear view at the time of the merger was that if certain crucial issues are not addressed quickly in any merger there are strong chances that the merger will fail. One of these issues was staff remuneration: removing perceived inequalities in a staff of 60,000 and incentivising the staff to take the enlarged company forward. A lot of hard work is being put into this and with considerable success.

HBOS aims to be an employer of choice and recognises that the remuneration package must provide real value to recruit and retain quality staff, particularly in view of the extremely competitive market for financial services staff.

A structured approach to salaries, bonuses, share ownership plans and benefits designed to provide a strong framework ensures that rewards are directly linked to performance.

HBOS's flexible benefits plans give staff the chance to tailor their benefits package to suit their lifestyle and the majority have opted for flexibility.

Other incentives are short-term cash bonuses, based on the business parameters they can influence through their actions and longer term by share ownership plans based on added value to shareholders.

In addition, staff can invest some or all of their short-term cash bonus in HBOS shares, with an enhancement of one free share for every two bought if the shares are held for three years. A long-term share option plan has been developed and will provide most employees with options to buy HBOS shares during a set period.

## The Future

For successful, ambitious companies, reach should exceed its grasp – that is the view of the now-retired Deputy Chairman of HBOS, Sir Peter Burt, who, as the man at the helm of the Bank of Scotland, was one of the main figures in the merger.

Whilst missing out on taking over NatWest when that bold move was trumped by the Royal Bank of Scotland, the move showed the Bank of Scotland could think big and that led to the merger with Halifax.

And there is no doubt that HBOS will continue to think big. As an enlarged group it will take advantage of all the skills, expertise and contacts which Bank of Scotland and Halifax bring, and continue its UK and international expansion.

# Hewitt Bacon & Woodrow

Hewitt Bacon & Woodrow is a global consultancy and outsourcing firm delivering a complete range of human resources management services. It is the UK and Ireland business of Hewitt Associates, a US-headquartered human resources solutions company which operates in 37 countries around the world, and which generated $1.5 billion of net revenue during its fiscal year 2001. Hewitt Bacon & Woodrow employs around 1,800 staff across 10 locations in the UK and Ireland.

**Scorecard:**

| | |
|---|---|
| Remuneration and benefits | ***** |
| Progressive attitude | ***** |
| Opportunity for promotion | *** |
| Training, development and education | ***** |
| Working atmosphere and environment | **** |

**Biggest plus:**
A structure that helps people develop as individuals, and can reward them very well.

**Biggest minus:**
The rigorous client focus makes this, in effect, a professional service industry, where staff must build and maintain good client relationships.

Hewitt Bacon & Woodrow
St Olaf House
London Bridge City
London SE1 2PE
Tel: 01372 733000
Fax: 01372 733218
Website: www.hewittbaconwoodrow.co.uk

# Hewitt Bacon & Woodrow

## The Business

Hewitt Bacon & Woodrow was formed in June 2002 by the coming together of Hewitt Associates Ltd and Bacon & Woodrow. Hewitt Associates was founded in Illinois in 1940, initially as an insurance brokerage company, which specialised in financial planning for business executives and professionals. It quickly evolved by 1950 to provide actuarial and related services to help other companies develop employee benefit and compensation schemes.

Formed in 1924, Bacon & Woodrow had become one of the UK's leading actuarial and consultancy firms. The joint history and brand value in both names and organisational histories has been seen as a prize to be valued in the transition, and for the foreseeable future the joint name will be used in the UK and Ireland.

*We encourage our associates to learn another core-European language – we have difficulty persuading people to move within the UK, but have quite a few on assignment between countries*

One significant change in the last year has been incorporation: formerly a partnership, Hewitt Associates is now listed on the New York stock exchange. All of its employees received an allocation of shares and at present around 20 per cent of the company's stock is owned externally.

Hewitt Bacon & Woodrow provides services in strategic pensions consulting and administration; benefits delivery and HR consultancy.

In the HR market, not only must companies attract staff, but they must retain them too. 'Large organisations are struggling with huge staff turnover in the first year', says Jered Stifter, practice leader for Hewitt Bacon & Woodrow's client development group. 'We are finding that what candidates are told during the recruitment process doesn't match what they find when they get there.'

## Company Culture and Style

Collaboration and teamwork are the key words for Hewitt Bacon & Woodrow. This makes the working environment rather different from many other consultancies, because its teams are not status-orientated and there is no 'star culture'.

That focus on teamwork means that, whilst its consultants still need to be academically bright and quick thinking, they also need good communications skills, both to deal with clients and with their colleagues. Today's consultants need to be agile and adaptable, so they can put themselves in the client's shoes and understand why the client works the way they do; they also need to know when to challenge the client's preconceptions and prejudgements.

In the past, activities such as pensions consulting were primarily handled by actuaries, but this is changing as the company has worked to broaden the experiences of its consultancy, for example their investment consulting team includes some people who have worked in the City as investment managers. This team does not directly manage any money, but it works with pension fund trustees, Finance Directors, Pension Trustees and Managers to make the right strategic investment decisions for their funds.

Diversity in the team is important too. Despite the traditional male-dominated actuarial and consulting workforce – Hewitt Bacon & Woodrow has a 60:40 gender split, and around 30 per cent of the company's management are female.

As a sign of how much the actuarial business has relaxed, the dress code is relatively informal too. In keeping with many City firms the Human Resources Director, Paula Cook, admits that it is has proved necessary to tighten the definition of 'business casual', and advise some younger members of staff how to dress and act smartly for client meetings.

The merger with Hewitt has also accelerated the flattening of the old Bacon & Woodrow hierarchy. The new organisational structure is a matrix with relatively few job titles, as the company believes that an individual's specific experience and expertise is more important than their title.

'We want people who are worldly-wise, they need to be able to build relationships with clients and they need to understand our clients' business issues', says Paula Cook. 'We need a balance of humility and pride, but when some people come to us, they are incredibly bright and are used to always having been top of the class, so we see a lot of arrogance – we don't recruit people who cannot demonstrate a balance of self-confidence and empathy for others. We want people who spark off each other and build collaborative relationships.'

## Human Resources

Each side of the company recruits somewhat differently to reflect its skills profile and needs. Pensions consulting prefers to grow their own actuaries by recruiting graduates and supporting them through a 3 to 5-year actuarial qualification. Although there is always a number of people who join part-way through qualification. Pensions and benefits delivery administrators are less likely to be graduates, instead requiring well-developed administrative and client service skills.

The HR consultancy team need experienced people with a good HR track record and practical skills in consultancy, which, of course, graduates are unlikely to have. Other teams in the HR area need practical skills and experience in areas such as organisational change, reward consultancy, staff and organisational communications (eg newsletter, handbook and website design).

In the past, anyone who left the company was not welcome back, but this has changed. Today, the company recognises that people may actually have more to offer when they return than when they left. It also has a good track record of women returning to work after maternity leave.

There is also a degree of flexibility on working hours, with staff encouraged to have outside interests even if they would impact on the normal working hours, for example sitting as a magistrate. Some offices have as many as 50 per cent of their staff working on non-standard patterns.

The important thing is that people should genuninely want to go to work, says Cook: 'Our people are telling us that their drivers are feeling able to influence or affect events, plus needing space for intellectual and creative thinking.'

## Career Opportunity and Development

Training and development starts as soon as someone joins the company, although professional actuarial training is only one of several strands. Another is training in business and personal skills, for example not only do managers need to understand how to manage people, but associates need to know how to receive and understand feedback, and how to ask for clarification where needed.

In addition, although most pensions legislation is country-specific, today's consultants need a greater knowledge of how these things work in other countries. Not only are areas such as financial management becoming pan-European, but it may also help them understand a client that is the UK office of a French company, say.

Competency structures are in place for each business line, plus there are development centres for people at different stages in their careers. However, the company no longer has fixed training targets for people once they get past their first few years, as it found that this structure had become too rigid.

'Not everything fits a structure, so our philosophy is that any learning is good learning', says Cook. 'For example, we encourage our associates to learn another core European language – we have difficulty persuading people to move within the UK, but have quite a few on assignment between countries.

'Community involvement can be a very good learning experience too, helping to build confidence and teaching communications skills such as listening and relationship-building. It can also teach leadership skills through charitable work such as school governorship.'

## Remuneration

'We don't pay the highest salaries in the industry, what's more important is to reward people fairly, with robust performance management', says Stifter. This means that while basic salaries are unexceptional, the addition of an annual incentive scheme and a global profit sharing scheme make it possible for the total reward package to be much higher.

The annual incentive scheme assesses organisational and personal goals, 50 per cent is based on the individual contribution and the rest on the performance of the team and the market. The company uses 360 degree appraisals, seeking feedback from all members of a team as well as managers and clients, to find out how performance could be improved.

As an HR advisor to other companies, Hewitt Bacon & Woodrow also chooses to take innovate steps in its own HR policies. For example, it implemented a newly-designed Flex benefits package, which includes some new initiatives in pension choices and leave options.

Flex makes a few core deductions from salary and then allows employees to 'buy' extra benefits, such as a higher level of medical or life insurance, a bigger pension, or additional leave for a long holiday or sabbatical break.

## The Future

The company's target is to become the leading consultancy provider in the people business, so that clients will come to it without it needing to pitch for their business. It is operating in a benefits delivery market place that is seeing strong growth and changes in work practices. The pensions consulting business is also experiencing significant change – providing an exciting, if somewhat challenging, time for clients and consultants alike.

At the same time, the market is increasingly multinational, and the company's clients are continually reshaping themselves. This means there are no constants, and its consultants are always having to rebuild their client relationships.

The aim therefore is a stronger integration of the services brand across Europe, and the acquisition of more complete clients – clients who take two or more services. The company's brand is its staff, though, so its biggest challenge is the availability of enough sufficiently talented people.

With some 160 branded outlets around Britain and Ireland, HMV is a major player in the music, video and games business. It employs around 400 people at its London head office and ten times that number in its stores, with more stores opening every year. It also sells over the Internet via a retail website. During 2002, HMV Group's European business showed an operating profit of £74 million on sales of £784.4 million, most of this Britain and Ireland.

**Scorecard:**

Remuneration and benefits ★★★★
Progressive attitude ★★★★
Opportunity for promotion ★★★★★
Training, development and education ★★★★★
Working atmosphere and environment ★★★★

**Biggest plus:**
Working with a product you love and serving people who love it too.

**Biggest minus:**
Working in a fast-paced retail environment will not suit everyone.


HMV UK Ltd
Film House
142 Wardour Street
London W1F 8LN
Tel: 020 7432 2000
Fax: 020 7432 2134
Websites: www.hmv.co.uk
www.hmvgraduates.com

# HMV

## The Business

The first HMV shop opened on London's Oxford Street in 1921. However, although the brand is over 80 years old, today's HMV is young. It is part of a company that was formed as HMV Media Group in 1998 by a management buyout supported by venture capital.

The new company acquired the HMV and Dillons stores from EMI, and Waterstone's from WH Smith. It then floated on the London Stock Exchange as HMV Group in May 2002.

HMV is part of the group's music retail arm, while all the book stores now operate under the Waterstone's brand and have their own management and head office. There are also HMV stores elsewhere in Europe, in North America, and in the Asia/Pacific region, but these do not come under the London head office.

The company has managed to continue growing, which has helped combat increasing competition, especially from price-squeezing channels such as supermarkets and online resellers. It competes in the latter area itself, with its retail website.

*As a young organisation it also aims to create a youthful buzz in its stores, while remaining aware that its customers are a much more diverse age group*

Although music remains the company's mainstay and music sales continue to grow, video, DVDs and computer games are increasingly important parts of the mix. In 2001/2 they represented nearly half of HMV sales.

## Company Culture and Style

HMV UK is first and foremost a retailer. It has over 160 stores and expects to open another 20 to 25 during its 2002/3 financial year. 'With stores opening all the time, we recruit over 1,000 staff a year and there are great opportunities for employees to progress their careers with HMV', says Liam Donnelly, Human Resources Director.

Operating in the entertainment business, HMV has a significant advantage over retailers in many other areas in that it can legitimately expect its staff to love and thoroughly engage with what they sell. As a young organisation it also aims to create a youthful buzz in its stores, while remaining aware that its customers are a much more diverse age group.

That lively buzz is an important part of its motivational team-building – it expects its staff to be individuals but work as a team, sharing knowledge, developing training at branch level and also having fun while they work.

'Customer service is one of the key areas we can differentiate ourselves from the competition so we focus hard on this area. We position ourselves as "the" specialist retailer, which means we offer a fantastic range of product and great product availability. But the key ingredient to delivering this proposition is the staff – they need to have very good product knowledge and genuinely want to work with our customers, and in return we can offer talented people a fantastic career in retail', Donnelly says.

The retail environment demands hard-workers, and Donnelly adds that HMV expects a lot from its people: 'There is no getting away from the fact that retail is hard work. Our staff need to be passionate about the product, sparky and bright, they have to be teamworkers with a sense of humour, they have to be fairly resilient and driven and focused on doing well.'

HMV is also very focused on fair play, and opportunities and development are based on merit alone. HMV does employ more men than women in its stores, but Donnelly says that this merely reflects the fact that music retail seems to attract more men. He estimates that as many as 70 per cent of the applicants for jobs at sales assistant level are male, adding that there is nothing in the business to stop women getting through on merit, to the extent that a third of HMV's regional managers are female.

There is a company dress policy, in that retail staff wear uniforms, but the only guideline in other respects is that they look tidy and customer-friendly. As well as encouraging staff to socialise together, HMV supports music industry charities and likes its staff to do the same, for example raising money for children's music therapy.

## Human Resources

HMV has no minimum academic criteria for recruitment, as it is primarily looking for people who want to work in retail, have product knowledge and the ability to deliver great customer service. However, as well as recruiting non-graduates, it also has a very successful three-year graduate training programme; initially this offered 25 places a year but this figure has been doubled to 50 to support the business' growth plan.

The aim is that a graduate trainee will become an assistant manager in a year, and be a store manager in three years. Applicants for the graduate scheme are assessed on key competencies such as commercial understanding, customer focus and people management, and on product knowledge. They are asked about their previous experience and also their mobility, because trainees and managers may have to move around the country.

The working week is a standard 37.5 hours, with Sundays paid as double-time. Working in retail means working a lot of weekends and although the company uses some part-time staff who want to work at weekends there is still a requirement for all employees to do the same. 'Sunday is a big day now for retailers so we need the right quality of staff available', Donnelly explains. Temps are also used to ease the load of the full-time staff at specific times of year, for example HMV expects to recruit over 1,500 for the Christmas season.

## Career Opportunity and Development

Retail staff need a determination to succeed, not just for themselves but for their team and store, and for the organisation as a whole. Conversely, HMV realises that in order to attract and retain good staff, an organisation must fully commit itself to motivating and developing its people. As Donnelly says, 'We need to keep the right people once we have them, and we need to grow our own management because we are a specialist retailer with an aggressive growth strategy. With over 160 stores, we also have to train our managers to ensure they in turn can coach, develop and motivate their teams in each location.'

Career development begins with a company induction: all new staff get one day of training off-site plus a handbook covering company history, the support they can expect from head office, personnel issues, etc. This is also their training workbook and must be signed off every three months.

The training is split into levels, according to staff grades, and is workbook-based. Different threads cover everything one needs to know in order to run a store, for example, inventory tracking, people management, finance, operations, and the role of head office. In effect there is a very clear career path for sales assistants, with associated development opportunities, right through the organisation to senior management levels.

In addition to the graduate scheme, HMV operates a range of Fast Track programmes aimed at identifying those recruits with the highest potential, from managers right down to sales assistant level, and pull them out for accelerated progression. Some 200 sales assistants were picked out during 2002 for additional development.

The company works with academia too; it already uses Oxford University's Templeton College to develop the high-level leadership skills of its regional and senior managers, and it is launching a management diploma in association with Ashridge Business School in 2003, which will see 30 employees selected per annum to complete a recognised three-year diploma.

To help staff understand their career options, HMV has graded its stores into 10 categories, from the giant flagship London store on Oxford Street to shops with just a handful of staff. Each has a manager, an assistant manager and a team leader, plus other staff; each employee has a role definition, so they know what the next level is and what the career development requirements are to get there.

## Remuneration

HMV makes considerable use of incentives, with prizes and an annual awards ceremony for top-performing staff, and a quarterly performance-related bonus scheme for all employees. Teams and stores are assessed by managers and mystery shoppers on the basis of sales and customer service. There is also a share scheme, following the company's floatation in May 2002, and a company pension scheme.

The company runs an annual competition, appropriately named Top of the Shops. Each of HMV's 16 regions nominates its top store, and these then compete for a cash prize to be shared out among its staff – a minimum of £1000 per winning employee. The stores are reviewed against a rigid set of sales and back-office criteria.

The standard paid holiday entitlement is 23 days a year, although the company asks that staff do not take holiday in December as this is its busiest time of year. HMV also offers a 30 per cent staff discount on purchases, and staff moving between stores are eligible for relocation assistance.

HMV's aim is to be upper quartile on retail pay, once bonuses and basic pay are included, and measures itself against quality retailers – Liam Donnelly says that in past years it has been one of, if not 'the', top payer, ahead of many other retailers often associated with good pay levels.

## The Future

Like its customers, the company is adapting to new technologies and sales channels as they come along, for example its Internet site is successful and already offers music for download. HMV takes the view though that whatever happens, people will always want to shop, and that there is plenty more growth to come in the business.

It recognises though that, while a wide product range and high-quality customer service are essential, shoppers need more than that: they also want to be entertained and rewarded by the shopping experience. In short, they need to be given an added reason and incentive to visit a particular retail location. This might mean live performances by bands, or access to music in whatever format they require, perhaps including downloading facilities in-store.

'Many of today's outlets already offer advanced sampling facilities, but in five to ten years time increasingly sophisticated technology will allow a greater degree of customer interaction – presenting an option to locate, preview and sample every title in stock or to automatically order titles which are not', says Donnelly.

# The world's local bank

HSBC is one of the world's largest banking and financial services organisations. HSBC's international network comprises 7,000 offices in 81 countries and territories in Europe, the Asia-Pacific region, the Americas, the Middle East and Africa. Its British position was strengthened when it acquired Midland Bank in 1992; and in September 1999 Midland Bank was renamed HSBC Bank plc.

**Scorecard:**

Remuneration and benefits            *****
Progressive attitude                 ****
Opportunity for promotion            ****
Training, development and education  *****
Working atmosphere and environment   ****

**Biggest plus:**
Its focus on people and its consistent strategy.

**Biggest minus:**
In such a large organisation, change takes time.

HSBC Bank plc
HSBC Tower
8 Canada Square
London E14 5HQ
Tel: 020 7992 3823
Website: www.hsbc.com

# HSBC

## The Business

The HSBC Group is named after its founding member, the Hong Kong and Shanghai Banking Corporation Limited. This was established in 1865 to finance the growing trade between China and Europe.

The inspiration behind the founding of the bank was Thomas Sutherland, a Scot who was then working as the Hong Kong superintendent of the Peninsular and Oriental Steam Navigation Company. He realised that there was considerable demand for local banking facilities in Hong Kong and the China coast, and helped set up the bank. Then, as now, the Hong Kong and Shanghai Banking Corporation's headquarters were at 1 Queen's Road in Hong Kong. HSBC Holdings plc is headquartered in London.

Throughout the late nineteenth and early twentieth centuries, the bank established a network of agencies and branches mainly in China and South East Asia but also in the Indian subcontinent, Japan, Europe and North America. In many of its branches the bank was a pioneer of modern banking practice. From the outset, trade finance was a strong feature of the bank's business, with bullion, exchange and merchant banking also playing an important part. Additionally, the bank issued notes in many locations throughout South East Asia.

*Collective management is the best way to describe HSBC's culture; and as a result, those who flourish are teamworkers rather than individualists*

In the UK, HSBC is represented by the former Midland bank, once one of the 'big four' British banks, which it acquired in 1992. Now named HSBC Bank plc, it offers a comprehensive range of financial services.

## Company Culture and Style

It is fair to say that HSBC's style is denoted by quiet confidence rather than brashness; it is certainly not an organisation that shouts from the rooftops. Its brand stresses words such as 'modest', 'human', 'honest', 'open-minded' and 'knowledgeable'. Another key word is 'multicultural': in London, the board and all layers of management below it include representatives from many races and ethnic backgrounds.

HSBC's branding is 'the world's local bank', and it strives to be exactly that wherever it operates. It also draws on its vast global network in order to find the best practices and share them across the group.

Collective management is the best way to describe HSBC's culture, and, as a result, those who flourish are teamworkers rather than individualists. This is seen at all levels at the bank. There is a strong sense that the bank's thousands of offices are in fact one office; and it is not unusual to find workers in London chatting to their opposite partners in New York or Delhi about how they handle procedures.

Banking in the UK still retains some air of being a male bastion. Of its top executives in London, HSBC Bank plc has three females, and another three on the Group board. However, there are many more at the next level down – tomorrow's top executives – which is an encouraging sign that the old bastion is crumbling at HSBC.

There is a good balance between work and life at the bank. Major locations in the UK have worksite nurseries, and there are partnerships with external nurseries elsewhere. HSBC has around 83 per cent of females returning to work after pregnancy, around 30 per cent higher than the national average. This is aided by flexible working patterns, help with care for the elderly, disability care and others, and there is an in-house employee assistance scheme through which employees can get help with problems concerning health, divorce and much more. Perhaps the real reason for the high return rate, though, is the fact that HSBC is a great place to work. Its culture is vibrant, stimulating and rewarding, but without the arrogance and coldness seen at some banking organisations.

## Human Resources

There are opportunities at many levels to work for HSBC in the UK. This starts with local recruitment for cashiers, rising through an 'A' level entrant scheme, a UK management trainee scheme and a global graduate scheme.

Graduates enter a fast-track management route. Beginning with a six-week training course in the business, they follow this with four six-month placements in different departments, one of which is the branch network. After that, the graduates take on a management position, usually in one of the departments already trialed, and they have a degree of choice about where they work. Thereafter, the bank encourages them to take professional qualifications and provides support for them to do so. It has programmes at the London Business School and Warwick Business School, which provide two to three-week case-study residential courses.

The 'Make a Difference' programme encourages all staff to be innovative. People with useful suggestions are put in touch with the person who runs the area and they work together on it. In the UK, senior management make huge efforts to canvas opinion: Bill Dalton, the Chief Executive, lunches with clerical staff every month to get a feel for the issues they face.

## Career Opportunity and Development

HSBC stresses a mix of training and learning for all its employees. The bank's philosophy is that learning is important and it wishes to encourage it at all levels. Sue Jex, Head of Diversity and Employee Support in HSBC's London head office, said 'Classroom training is just one part of a bigger learning programme. We have 120 learning centres around the UK, and a 'Leap' library, which offers employees information on a wide range of topics, which they can order from their desktop.'

Given HSBC's truly global scale, it is not surprising that there are many opportunities to work overseas. It has an international managers programme, which UK employees can apply to join. This is intended for those who wish to work overseas for a long period, perhaps for their whole career (although they can opt out of the programme at any time). The postings can be to any country and generally last from two to three years per posting. Support is provided, including language training.

Everyone in the bank has a development plan. This examines the skill set required for the current job and also looks ahead to the skills needed for the next role. Both the individual and the bank have input into the planned career route.

## Remuneration

In the UK, the bank has a programme called 'Let's Reward Success'. Pay is calculated for each job and each grade within that job, then a bonus is paid on both personal and corporate performance. The bonus can add up to 20 per cent of salary.

Share options are given both for good performance and for those the bank wants to keep long-term: for instance, some secretaries at HSBC have them. These can generally be exercised between three and ten years after receiving them. The bank has its own stock broking arm, which makes converting the options cheaper as well as easier.

New entrants have a defined contribution pension scheme to which both the company and the employees contribute; existing employees are in a final salary scheme, which was closed to new entrants in the 1990s. There is also a healthcare scheme, which covers both staff members and their immediate family.

Cars are offered to certain levels of management within the bank, and also if needed for the job. Increasingly, many people choose to take the cash option rather than the car. There is a death-in-service life cover scheme for all employees, which pays four times salary. Holidays are generally 28 days a year, rising to a maximum of 30 days according to length of service and job level.

## The Future

HSBC is determined to be the bank that understands its customers best. Jex: 'We believe that success comes from understanding both our customers and our employees. So we want to know our customers, be on their side and provide the services they want – and do exactly the same for our people.'

In recent years, the bank has made a significant investment in its customer relationship management systems and is seen as a real market leader.

Further global expansion remains a possibility, and indeed HSBC are currently expanding their presence in both Mexico and China. This growth leads to further opportunities to learn about new markets, different cultures and economies and forms part of the exciting mix that makes HSBC a great place to work.

J D Wetherspoon owns and operates pubs and hotels, and is one of the fastest growing companies in the UK. It employs over 15,000 staff, most of them in the 600-plus J D Wetherspoon pubs and Lloyds No.1 bars throughout the UK, including several in Northern Ireland. Some 260 staff are based at its head office in Watford. For its 2001/02 financial year it reported an operating profit of £70.1 million, up 20 per cent on the previous year, on sales that rose 24 per cent to £601.3 million.

## Scorecard:

| | |
|---|---|
| Remuneration and benefits | **** |
| Progressive attitude | **** |
| Opportunity for promotion | ***** |
| Training, development and education | ***** |
| Working atmosphere and environment | *** |

## Biggest plus:
The variety of challenging work and the strong training opportunities.

## Biggest minus:
The 24/7 nature of the pub business, where most roles are expected to work evenings and weekends, will not appeal to some.

J D Wetherspoon plc
PO Box 616
Watford WD1 1YN
Tel: 0870 2438243
Fax: 01923 219810
Website: www.jdwetherspoon.co.uk

# J D Wetherspoon

## The Business

Tim Martin opened his first pub in North London in 1979, gradually expanding the group and floating it on the London stock exchange in 1992. The company has attracted fans for its policies of supporting real ale, providing non-smoking areas, offering low priced drinks and food, and banning canned music in its pubs.

Two years ago it acquired the Lloyds No.1 chain of bars, which attract a different clientele by providing a trendier environment, which does include music. As well as expanding the Lloyds No.1 chain, Wetherspoon has also moved into the hotel business, opening a number of Wetherlodges around the country.

The company is credited with having created 10,000 new jobs during the past five years, and says it plans to create another 30,000 in the next ten years. It has well over 600 pubs and bars, and is opening at least 80 more per year, the new pubs being larger than those opened in previous years. Wetherspoon pubs are individually designed and several have won national design awards.

*The biggest thing is a can-do attitude. We want people who will try anything, get things done, are open to development both self-development and in the company, and are looking for better ways to do things*

Area, pub and shift managers make up around 3,000 of its 15,000 staff, with the rest being hourly paid associates, such as bar staff and team leaders. On average, each pub has 25 associates and five shift and trainee managers.

'A lot of pub work is routine, but there is a lot that can change day to day', says Su Beacham, Wetherspoon's Director of Personnel and Training. She adds that the nature of the business is changing too, for example food is now 25 per cent of turnover, yet diners require more space than drinkers and take longer. During 2002, Wetherspoon began opening its pubs one hour earlier, at 10am, to sell coffee and breakfasts.

## Company Culture and Style

Company Chairman, Tim Martin, remains very influential. He has a fortnightly meeting to discuss the business with staff of all levels, including some bar staff. 'In some ways he's our own worst critic', says Beacham. 'Tim says the company is like a shark – it must move forward or it will die.'

Constructive and objective criticism is encouraged, and Martin works to avoid complacency and keep the culture open, for example seeking feedback on proposed marketing campaigns from staff at the sharp end. Indeed, he believes that staff feedback is more important in many ways than customer feedback. An example was the introduction of oversized lined glasses: praised at the time by consumer groups, it proved a nightmare for pub managers, thanks to a minority of quarrelsome customers who demanded a full glass whatever its size.

Although the company is popular with investors, it has had criticism from some in the City for spending too much on staff and making less profit as a result. Wetherspoon's response is that, because the pub business depends so heavily on the availability of high-quality staff, it needs to invest in them to build a long-term business.

Pub staff are provided with a uniform shirt, to be worn with a skirt or trousers. They are also subject to the normal health and safety restrictions where food is concerned, so long hair must be tied back, and it may be necessary to remove jewellery and piercings. Area managers have an image to project so are expected to dress smartly.

'Work/life balance is a challenge in a business where your busiest time is when most people are not at work', says Beacham. 'We try to limit late nights, and rotate people's weekends off. Wetherspoon was the first pub group to get down to a 48-hour average working week, and is working to reduce it further. There are also opportunities for fixed shifts to allow for study, childcare, and so on.'

Each year, Wetherspoon chooses a charity to sponsor and encourages every pub to try and get as many staff as possible involved, publishing a league table of the highest pub and individual contributions.

## Human Resources

Associates are recruited through general advertising, including adverts in pubs and on the company website. In a recent staff survey, 86 per cent said they would recommend the company to family and friends. There are no specific educational requirements or qualifications needed, however.

'The biggest thing is a can-do attitude. We want people who will try anything, get things done, are open to development both self-development and in the company, and are looking for better ways to do things', says Beacham.

'We are quite open to recruiting disabled people where possible. Obviously a wheelchair would not be safe behind the bar, but there are other jobs, and people can and do adapt.' She adds that while only one of the four board members is female, the gender split among pub managers and senior management is close to 50:50.

'We have everyone from school leavers through ex-military to an Olympic medallist. You have to genuinely like people, but when we tried to work out what makes a good shift manager we came to the conclusion that there is no specific profile or target group.'

## Career Opportunity and Development

Internal progression is very important to Wetherspoon: for example, all of its pub managers were originally shift or trainee managers, the company does not recruit pub managers from outside. Of the 60 area managers, half were pub managers, and all the company's stocktakers were pub managers. In total, 65 per cent of managers were promoted from associate level, and, in addition, half of the head office staff have pub experience.

While there is a strong career progression, an employee may also choose to stay in a role, for example as a pub manager. 'We have to recognise that people aren't perfect in a new job on day one and may need time to grow. And a few have been over-promoted – we have to have the honesty to admit when something is not working', Beacham notes.

Over the years, Wetherspoon has worked out what people need to know in different jobs, so there is a standard training route for each role (although the head office is less structured). For example there are three shift manager grades, each with its own training schedule followed by an assessment.

The company's recruitment brochures explain the training process, and new staff receive a company handbook and training handbook. Its training has won pub industry awards for its thoroughness and practical nature.

'Training is embedded in the company culture. It is about attitude and trying all the time to improve things', Beacham says. 'Training is also about how you treat your employees. If you treat them poorly, then they won't do a good job or be nice to the customers.'

Wetherspoon uses 360 degree appraisals, and is now working with Leeds University to map the company's training onto professional qualifications.

## Remuneration

Wetherspoon is the only pub operator where every employee is eligible for a monthly bonus. An associate's bonus is on a sliding scale dependent on assessment scores, with the average being nine per cent extra per month. The bonus is paid monthly so even short-term staff see the benefit very quickly. Managers get more (15–25 per cent extra) because they also get a profitability-related bonus.

Pubs are assessed on four key factors: cleanliness, beer quality, service, maintenance. The company uses 'mystery shoppers', recognising that real customers will often not report problems, managers may also visit each other's pubs to do assessments, and Tim Martin spends three days a week visiting Wetherspoon pubs.

All employees have share options after six months; there is also a SAYE scheme which comes out of gross earnings and can be spent after three years on buying shares at the price set when the scheme started.

There is a stakeholder pension, and some managers are eligible for free medical cover, while associates can buy it at a discount. Pub managers get free accommodation, rented off-site where a pub does not have it; alternatively they can choose to take the value of the accommodation in cash instead. Spare pub accommodation may be rented to staff at a discount.

Employees who need to travel for work have company cars. Employee feedback produced the option of trading up or down in car class.

Staff get 50 per cent discounts on food while working, and 20 per cent discounts on drinks and food at other times for them and their guests. Discounts are also available at the company's Wetherlodges.

The company runs a number of incentive and prize schemes, such as an Associate of the Year prize, which is based on speed of service and has a car as the top prize. The aim is for everyone to get at least one reward of some kind each year, from a bottle of wine upwards.

## The Future

Wetherspoon's 10-year goal is to own and operate 1,500 pubs and become the UK's largest independent pub operator. It says that this will require solid finances and around 45,000 employees, and that the biggest problems facing it are therefore finding enough sites, and finding and retaining enough high-quality people.

Tim Martin has also been one of the leading opponents of increased regulation of the pub trade by the British government. In particular, he has vocally opposed plans to transfer responsibility for liquor licensing from magistrates courts to local authorities.

# JM⊗
# Johnson Matthey

Johnson Matthey is a world leader in advanced materials technology, applying the latest techniques to add value to precious metals and other specialised materials. The group now has four divisions: catalysts and chemicals; pharmaceutical materials; precious metals; and colours and coatings. Though British in origin, Johnson Matthey is a multinational company that sells its products around the world and has operations in 34 countries. Of its 8,100 employees worldwide, some 3,000 work in the UK. During 2001 it reported operating profits up 10 per cent to £193.3 million on turnover of £4.8 billion.

**Scorecard:**

| | |
|---|---|
| Remuneration and benefits | **** |
| Progressive attitude | **** |
| Opportunity for promotion | **** |
| Training, development and education | ***** |
| Working atmosphere and environment | **** |

**Biggest plus:**
A friendly company that retains the personal touch despite continued growth and expansion.

**Biggest minus:**
A few of the traditional values still remain.

Johnson Matthey plc
2–4 Cockspur Street
London SW1Y 5BQ
Tel: 020 7269 8400
Fax: 020 7269 8477
Website: www.matthey.com

# Johnson Matthey

## The Business

Johnson Matthey (JM) is an established British company that has successfully made the transition to successful global performer. Established in Hatton Garden in 1817, the company's origins are in precious metals processing, and its precious metals technology is still unique within the UK. Over the years, however, its activities have deliberately been extended to include a wide range of advanced materials. It now carries out pioneering research in areas such as pharmaceuticals and environmentally-friendly fuel cells and, in 2000, won its second Royal Academy of Engineering MacRobert Award – the UK's most coveted prize for engineering innovation – for an innovative pollution control system.

During 2001 and 2002, JM made three major acquisitions in the pharmaceuticals area, establishing pharmaceutical materials as a division in its own right, and also acquired two chemical companies. The company's four divisions now deal with manufacture of catalysts and pollution control systems; manufacture of pharmaceutical compounds; refining, fabrication and marketing of precious metals; and making colours and coatings for the ceramics, glass, paint and plastics industries.

*The type of person who flourishes at JM is bright, sparky, quick-thinking and action-oriented. JM likes to employ people with character – definitely not clones*

While JM diversifies into new materials, however, there's still plenty of growth potential in its well-established precious metals and catalytic systems businesses.

Chief Executive, Chris Clark, demands a 20 per cent return on assets in all businesses and is bent on continuing to deliver the profitable growth for shareholders that has characterised the company in recent years. The company turned in record results in 2001, and entered the FTSE 100. This year its growth was hit by a decline in metal prices and the ceramics industry recession, which hit ceramics manufacturers in the Midlands and resulted in the closure of one of JM's factories in Stoke. Even in this difficult climate, the company still succeeded in increasing operating profits by 10 per cent.

## Company Culture and Style

JM has a proud history and a reputation for integrity. Its traditional values remain – business standards and ethics are rigorously observed – but under Chris Clark's leadership the company is also progressive, unbureaucratic and a lot slicker and faster in its dealings than it was 20 years ago.

JM today is characterised by individual leadership, fast decision-making, getting things done, and local responsibility. As an advanced technology company, it places a heavy emphasis on innovation in the widest possible sense. The type of person who flourishes at JM is bright, sparky, quick-thinking and action-oriented. JM likes to employ people with character – definitely not clones. The company's directors are strong, individual characters who value the same variety in employees.

The headcount at JM's head office overlooking Trafalgar Square is a mere 70 people, reflecting a hands-off approach to day-to-day operations. The four divisions are fairly autonomous and globally managed, reflecting the business organisation of their customers.

Though a truly multinational business, JM prides itself on its ability to retain a personal touch. The company is highly communicative, both to external and internal audiences. Its directors go to great lengths to get to know people in the organisation, and employees find that it's easy to get noticed. The charismatic Clark himself is highly visible to staff and, having been with JM for 40 years, is personally familiar to many of them.

JM is an equal opportunities employer in fact as well as in theory. In what used to be a traditional male stronghold, some 35 per cent of all employees are women, including the group's financial controller. A combination of old and new ideas has been the key to building a modern business for the future. This vision has been clearly communicated and subscribed to by employees.

## Human Resources

Throughout Johnson Matthey, tremendous emphasis is placed on people. The company strongly believes that far too much talent from 'UK plc' is diverted into the City or the Civil Service and away from British industry. The company has therefore established very close and personal links with leading UK universities in its quest to attract the cream of British graduates. JM recruits around 25 graduates annually from UK universities, out of around 1,000 applicants, while the number recruited in the US has risen to around 50.

JM is a technology and science-driven company, with its reputation for technical excellence driven right from the top; in 2002, Chris Clark was awarded the Society of Chemical Industry's centenary medal, awarded to figures of distinction in science-based industry or commerce. Inevitably, many of its recruits are specialists such as chemical engineers and materials technologists, but the company also takes on non-specialists. It looks for people who are practical, flexible and ready for the modern business world. Foreign language skills are also highly sought-after in this increasingly multinational company.

Each JM division has its own human resources function and director and its own management development processes, culminating in annual presentations at Trafalgar Square to all group executive directors.

The head office HR function is mainly involved in setting high-level policy and dealing with senior employees. Its Management Development and Remuneration Committee, made up of non-executive directors, meets three times a year to establish remuneration for the company's senior executive directors. Every other month, all executive directors meet at the Executive Development Committee, which plays an operational role in encouraging and facilitating cross-divisional moves, assessing vacancies across the group and the pool of available talent, and implementing development and training programmes.

## Career Opportunity and Development

Training and people development planning takes a high priority at JM. The company considers senior management succession carefully, creating an impact that flows right down the organisation. Graduates and other promising employees go through an annual business training course, while fast-track middle managers join the management development programme, which is mirrored in the UK and US. Senior managers may find themselves on courses at INSEAD, Wharton and Harvard.

High-potential people have personal development interviews at appropriate intervals. Demonstrating the board's commitment to recruitment and development, all high-potential graduates recruited since 1992 have informal meetings with directors as part of a 'get to know you' bridge-building exercise.

There is perhaps more emphasis than previously on bringing in new blood from outside the company, but JM still retains a strong tradition of developing from within. The company's recent series of acquisitions and consequent expansion have created new opportunities for both existing and potential employees.

Over the past two years, the bulk of these acquisitions have been within the UK and Ireland; the addition of Scottish pharmaceutical company Macfarlan Smith, for example, brought in an extra 260 jobs and the acquisition of Northern-based Synetix from ICI, an extra 400 jobs. As a result, of Johnson Matthey's 8,100 employees worldwide, some 3,000 are now based in the UK.

Although JM doesn't expatriate people for the sake of it, it is a multinational group with divisions organised globally, and for those who want to rise to the very top, willingness to move around the world is pretty much mandatory. All its senior executives have spent some time working abroad.

For those who actively want to travel, there are frequent overseas and cross-divisional opportunities. Essentially the question asked is 'who's the best person for the job?', underlining the importance of acquiring portable skills.

## Remuneration

JM is very competitive on pay and benefits, ranking alongside the best in the FTSE 100 index. With average salary increases of 4.7 per cent within the group over 2002, salary levels compare very favourably with other chemical industry companies. A December 2001 survey by *Management Today* ranked the company at number one within the Chemicals and Plastics sector for, among other things, ability to attract, develop and retain top talent.

Through its management development and remuneration committee, the company receives regular advice from consultants on its pay and incentive arrangements among JM's peer group in each country in which it has operations. JM is proud of its highly-rated, upper quartile company pension scheme.

Incentive arrangements are prevalent throughout the business. Annual performance-related bonuses for senior executives are assessed centrally; below this level, individual businesses are encouraged to handle their own incentive arrangements. A share incentive plan, capped at 2.5 per cent of salary, is also available, with the company providing a 2 for 1 match.

Company cars are awarded to those whose jobs require it and to the upper management quartile. Arrangements are flexible in that up- or downgrades of model may be arranged – these are reflected in either direction by up to 20 per cent of salary – or a cash alternative may be taken instead. UK holidays are 25 days a year.

## The Future

Staying in world-leading positions is often harder than getting there, and JM is increasingly competing on the global stage. However, the company's diversified interests act as a hedge against recession in any given area; its growing strengths in autocatalysts and its recent expansion within the pharmaceutical sector, for example, have softened the impact of the downturn in the ceramics industry.

Expectations are ambitious. 'In five years', says Peter Garfield, 'I expect us to have grown in size, with about £250 million profit, and I'd expect our total number of employees to have risen to more than 12,000.'

In this climate of growth and innovation, there is a real need for people who can deal with the inherent pressures and, quite simply, be better than the competition. Such people are naturally in short supply, and it is recognised that recruitment, training and development are fundamental to having the right people for the right jobs.

While JM clearly cannot guarantee jobs for life it can, and does, offer its people enhanced skills and greater employability. It backs this with a real commitment to open communications, team working and personal development, empowering employees but leaving them in no doubt that they must take control of their own careers.

'It works', concludes Clark, 'and I have every intention of making sure it goes on working.'

JONES LANG
LASALLE℠

Jones Lang LaSalle is a leading real estate services and investment management firm, operating in 33 countries on five continents. It provides comprehensive integrated expertise, including management services, implementation services and investment management services on a local, regional and global level to owners, occupiers and investors. It also offers property and corporate facility management services. LaSalle Investment Management, the company's investment management business, is one of the world's largest and most diverse real estate investment management firms, with $23 billion of assets under management. There is also a hotel and tourism division, which delivers advisory, transaction, financial and management services in the hotel real estate industry.

**Scorecard:**
Remuneration and benefits ****
Progressive attitude ***
Opportunity for promotion ****
Training, development and education ***
Working atmosphere and environment ***

**Biggest plus:**
The professional environment and team spirit.

**Biggest minus:**
The image of the real estate services can be variable in spite of the dedication of the personnel.

Jones Lang LaSalle UK
22 Hanover Square
London W1A 2BN
Tel: 020 7493 6040
Fax: 020 7408 0220
Website: www.joneslanglasalle.co.uk

# Jones Lang LaSalle

## The Business.

Jones Lang LaSalle was formed by the 1999 merge of LaSalle Partners Inc and Jones Lang Wootton, which had its beginnings in 1783. Today, it is one of the world's leading real estate services and investment management firms, operating in three geographic regions – the Americas, Europe and Asia Pacific – with regional headquarters in Chicago, London and Singapore.

In the UK, the Jones Lang LaSalle Group has offices in London, Birmingham, Leeds, Manchester, Norwich, Glasgow and Edinburgh and a staff of over 1,000.

Clients include institutional investors, property companies and developers, banks and financial organisations, corporate occupiers, retailers, hoteliers, national and local government and private concerns. The company's job is to offer advice and imple-

*Professional and driven are the two words that sum up the working environment at Jones Lang LaSalle*

mentation on every facet of development, marketing, sales and leasing, acquisition, investment, asset management, landlord and tenant matters and valuation.

## Company Culture and Style

Professional and driven are the two words that sum up the working environment at Jones Lang LaSalle. There is a strong emphasis on career development, but at the same time, it encourages an entrepreneurial, team-based spirit.

It is also a friendly company, where nobody stands on ceremony despite a fairly rigid hierarchy. 'People are accessible', explains Ruth Mundy, HR Director. 'Our office layout is mostly open plan for reasons of easier communication. We all work in a pressured, fast-paced environment, the level of which only depends on the area in which you are.

'We believe in working hard and playing hard but have done a lot recently on being more flexible in the way we work. We are starting to encourage people to work from home and have taken steps to enable hot-desking.'

The company is also trying to encourage more women into the business to detract from the masculine image that property investment has. The success of this is borne out by the fact that 50 per cent of the company's graduate intake this year is female.

Values are centred strongly on servicing the customer and extensive work is being undertaken on client relationship management. 'We are making sure we get feedback from clients and, more importantly, that we act on it', says Mundy.

The company likes to attract a broad range of personalities, wanting to be more diverse in bringing different skills in. It does, though, depend on the kind of job involved. They are also beginning to recruit more mature students onto the graduate programme in a bid to get away from the idea of graduates always being straight out of university.

'Mostly, our staff need to be resilient, able to take pressure, like being team players, and in possession of analytical problem-solving skills', she sums up. 'They should also ideally have a strong track record in best practice organisations and there is a lot of emphasis on people who can manage and coach others.'

At director level, 12 per cent are women, although Mundy stresses the company would like it to be more and are taking steps to address that.

The company has been a bit slow off the starting blocks on the work/life balance but has taken an innovative approach to it. 'We believe that each person will have a different balance', says Mundy. 'It all depends on what stage you are in your life – younger, single staff are happy to work longer hours while those with children will obviously have a different focus. We try to accommodate all perspectives.'

## Human Resources

Jones Lang LaSalle has fairly strict criteria for most jobs and draws up skills criteria for each grade. Technical jobs have particularly strict sets of rules. The company does a lot of training of their interviewers to look for particular skills and this has been successful.

For the graduate programme, the minimum grade is 2:1 and there is also a requirement for 20 'A' level UCAS points. Languages are of great interest to the company too, as career opportunities in other European countries often arise.

Each section of the business has its own HR manager so that there is an intimate understanding of how each job area works and what skills are needed.

There is a thorough graduate recruitment process specifically designed to recruit the right people. However, they do see it as a two-way process, so they ensure throughout the recruitment process that candidates meet various levels of employees, from current trainees to senior international management. This provides them with the opportunity to assess the people and the environment as much as they are being assessed.

In the last few years, the HR department itself has seen a strong shift away from a purely administrative welfare role to more working strategically with the business. This encompasses more strategic training and management coaching.

## Career Opportunity and Development

This is one of Jones Lang LaSalle's strongest areas. The company believes that its training schemes provide a solid foundation on which to build a career in property. All graduate trainees participate in an in-house designed financial skills training course. The schemes last for between one and two and a half years depending on previous education and experience.

Trainees are allocated coordinators, supervisors and counsellors, depending on the level they are at. Mundy says senior staff place great stake in this system and ensure that it works and that they fulfil their various mentoring roles.

There is currently strong emphasis on what happens once people have qualified. Often, the mentoring simply stops but Mundy believes this needs to continue, with even senior staff needing mentoring programmes.

Being a global organisation, there is extensive overseas opportunity and the company is encouraging more staff to take transfers, even if it's only for a few months.

There is an official international staff exchange programme where key people with potential are found roles for a year on another continent. However, this is only for a small number of people because of the difficulties in facilitating it.

In terms of managing careers, Mundy says she is also working on this more. 'We're a complicated organisation so it can be difficult for people to see where they are and where they are going.'

To address this, workshops are being run to explain what career management and development means in the company. 'We want to move away from people thinking development simply means going on a course – they need to understand that so much development actually takes place in the office.'

There are clear policies on what to do to be promoted and everyone has annual performance reviews, as well as mid-year assessments to talk about goals and what could improve, what development needs to take place and what to do to be promoted.

So, what's not in the contract? Mundy admits that the complexity of the organisation (its wide range of services and the consequent need for many different skill sets) takes people by surprise. 'As long as you're prepared for that, you'll be ok', she says.

# Remuneration

Jones Lang LaSalle benchmarks its pay with the market but often finds this difficult as it is involved in such a variety of markets!

'Generally, we pay median-based salaries but we are in the upper quartile or higher for performers', she explains. It's very much a performance-related company where bonuses can be substantial in certain areas.

The bonus pool is related to the performance of both the corporate and the individual. 'Within our market sector, we are seen as one of the best places to work', Mundy stresses. 'One of our stated aims is to be the employer of choice.'

The company also has a 'save as you earn' scheme to enable all staff to purchase stock. There is a certain amount of stock that is distributed to key performers, and it is an area they would like to extend. The health cover scheme now includes everyone throughout the organisation, as does the pension scheme and life cover. There are also season ticket loans, while other benefits like car allowances or company cars depend on the grade at which the employee is.

Graduate trainees receive a welcome bonus on joining, primarily to help with student loans, and all Royal Institution of Chartered Surveyors fees are fully paid.

## The Future

The company's stated aim is to differentiate itself by offering quality service built around a strength of skills in the business and by bringing these skilled teams together to work for clients holistically.

In the words of President and Chief Executive Officer, Christopher Peacock, 'results for 2001 and the opportunities we have identified ... serve as welcome confirmation that our integrated global platform is working effectively for our clients, while setting Jones Lang LaSalle apart from competitors'.

Concludes Mundy: 'We've identified what we need to do so it's now a matter of keeping on track to achieve it, to listen to our staff and shareholders and respond appropriately.'

KPMG is a leading global network of advisory firms, which aims to turn knowledge into value for the benefit of its clients, people and communities. In the UK, where it has around 10,000 people, KPMG saw five successive years of double-digit growth up to 2001, and – despite tough market conditions – held fee income firm in 2002 at £1,018 million. It also successfully disposed of its consulting business. In the wake of corporate turmoil, it has worked with the Government and others to develop a new regulatory framework. KPMG is dedicated to attracting and retaining a talented and diverse group of people and aims to offer a stimulating environment, work/life balance and effective training. Strong values lie at its heart, including a commitment to ongoing corporate social responsibility programmes.

**Scorecard:**

| | |
|---|---|
| Remuneration and benefits | **** |
| Progressive attitude | ***** |
| Opportunity for promotion | ***** |
| Training, development and education | ***** |
| Working atmosphere and environment | **** |

**Biggest plus:**
Huge opportunities and the collective will for people to succeed with a shared set of values.

**Biggest minus:**
Heavy demands from clients potentially impose great strains on a work/life balance.

KPMG
8 Salisbury Square
London EC4Y 8BB
Tel: 020 7311 1000
Fax: 020 7311 3311
Website: www.kpmg.co.uk

# KPMG

## The Business

The firm's roots go back to the 19th century, but the modern KPMG was formed in 1987 with the merger of two leading firms, Peat Marwick International (PMI) and Klynveld Main Goerdeler (KMG). It has since emerged as one of the world's leading businesses, providing assurance, tax and financial advisory services and, through its associated firm KLegal, legal services.

The UK operation is part of the firm's EMA region, which covers 103 countries. Although there are strong links between countries, fostered by shared goals and investment, the UK firm operates autonomously and counts 24 per cent of the FTSE 100 as clients.

Despite the downturn in the British economy, which impacted on the volume and profitability of some of its client work, income for the year ended September 2002 held up at £1,018 million. Ian Robinson, UK head of human resources, says: 'In a market which has seen such turmoil, this is quite an achievement. Our success comes from ensuring that we not only maintain existing client relationships but increasingly develop new client relationships.' However, the tough climate took its toll with some 1,000 UK people made redundant in two tranches.

*Spotting the leaders of tomorrow is an ongoing and developing programme*

In August 2002, KPMG UK fulfilled its promise to dispose of consulting interests, selling KPMG Consulting to Atos Origin. Meanwhile it trebled the size of its legal services division KLegal, merging it with Scottish law firm McGrigor Donald.

The majority of the workforce is based in the south, though there are substantial offices in hubs such as Birmingham, Edinburgh, Leeds and Manchester.

## Company Culture and Style

Those who thrive at KPMG are ambitious for collective rather than individual success. Potential partners possess the ability to engage with clients at the highest level, on top of rock-solid professional skills. In recent years, opportunities to join at partner level have increased. Recognising diversity as a key strategic business issue, the firm has a team examining issues surrounding gender and ethnic origin, and is looking to increase its ratio of women partners.

During 2001 the firm's leadership recognised the need for a fundamental shift in the way it operated. This resulted in darwin, the largest change programme in KPMG's history, which aimed to engage all of its people through consultation, and included debates on issues such as leadership and the working environment. 'What we now have', explains Robinson, 'is a change programme which will evolve over time'. Results include flexibility in the design of working space, and simplifying and dovetailing existing structures and systems.

Five years ago KPMG drew up a 10-point 'Values Charter': these values are so important that the reward structure encourages all partners and staff to fulfil them. One is to 'respect our people's need to balance personal and business lives'. But maintaining a work/life balance does not sit easily with a client-facing stance. 'Clients place incredible demands on our people. The need to balance that will always be a challenge', says Robinson. 'We don't think we've cracked it, but we are increasingly alive to it.' Ian is looking at establishing flexible or even seasonal working patterns. The firm also wants to be flexible about career breaks, particularly in a time of economic uncertainty. While working from home is not a particular focus, KPMG is aware of the need to make it easier for employees to work from all remote locations, such as client bases.

KPMG has remained committed to communities, investing £5.2 million in volunteer time and other resources, and directly benefiting more than 500 charities.

In addition to regular internal surveys and featuring in external surveys, KPMG consults staff representatives on issues such as pensions and redundancy. There is an open e-Discussion forum where people can lodge grumbles and suggestions, and a regular business-focused 'discussion of the month'.

## Human Resources

While the firm recruits professionals at all levels, graduate recruitment is a priority. Like most top employers it looks for at least a 2:1 degree, but it is also interested in work experience and general motivation. Its graduate recruitment team holds presentations at a small core of the 80 universities from which it recruits.

Most graduate entrants will train and take exams in a specific discipline over a three-year period, but one small group of graduates is recruited onto a Business Foundation programme, spending six months in each of four parts of the business. When offered a place, graduates may specify which UK office they wish to join. All graduate entrants are linked with a 'buddy' before they join – an informal support network.

Last year more than 500 recent graduates were hired through an online recruitment system. Extending its use to other areas has allowed KPMG to negotiate with agencies and cut hiring time and cost. In 2002 the firm also streamlined its human resources function, bringing administration staff into one location and freeing up advisors to work closely with their internal clients. It now operates a helpline, aiming to answer 80 per cent of queries over the phone.

## Career Opportunity and Development

KPMG places a high priority on developing its people, making extensive use of coaches. 'We expect everybody to be able to coach other people because on-the-job training is key to everyone's development', says Robinson.

Community service is seen as a valuable form of development: a departmental away-day might include a team community project such as building a garden or renovating a property. KPMG people are engaged on an individual level in activities such as mentoring head teachers and helping children read. In 2002 more than 1,600 people were active volunteers.

In 2002 the firm established an interactive website to help people to access the resources needed to develop and succeed within the firm. The firm's performance management system involves goal-setting for business and personal development through mid-year and annual reviews, and 'learning paths' have been developed for each grade. Teaching takes place in classrooms and via the computer – with an increasing emphasis on technology-enabled learning.

While trainees are encouraged to take the initiative, KPMG also fast-tracks its best people. 'Spotting the leaders of tomorrow is an ongoing and developing programme', says Robinson. Selected senior managers – the group from which partners are drawn – attend an assessment centre, where competencies and development needs are identified. The firm is looking to increase 'out of the box' experience for all senior managers: any wishing to become partners usually work for six months outside the firm. However, the firm is also aware of the need to give non-partners the chance for an enjoyable and rewarding career. Globally, it runs two internal MBA programmes and sponsors employees on part-time external MBA courses.

Opportunities for overseas transfer are plentiful, although graduates must first pass their qualifying exams. KPMG has a global opportunities website, and there are client-led openings. Secondments are normally for a fixed term. In addition, there are opportunities for secondments to clients, government bodies and other offices nationally.

## Remuneration

KPMG has developed a reward philosophy under which all employees can earn bonuses depending on performance. Despite the tough conditions which meant that the firm's targets for 2002 were not met, funds were still set aside to enable bonus payments to be made.

While graduate starting salaries may be marginally higher at companies that recruit smaller numbers, KPMG offers other benefits such as help with repaying student loans and a free lunch worth £2.45. In addition, it offers a car scheme at manager level, a private health scheme, free eye tests and access to a number of sports and social clubs.

Benefits are delivered through Flextra, a flexible rewards package that allows employees choices in shaping and distributing their entitlement. It includes options such as a computer leasing scheme. MyPensions, part of the website, was used to launch a new, flexible, contemporary stakeholder pension scheme – a money purchase scheme offering a choice of employer/employee contributions and investments.

# The Future

KPMG sees the future as presenting 'a tremendous opportunity at a time of great change' – the opportunity to develop its offering to companies who are not currently clients.

The extraordinarily exciting and demanding world markets of the last decade have made its leadership highly sensitive about finding people with broad enough experience to take over in the next five years. 'There is an ever-increasing need to invest in the development of our leaders of the future, to take advantage of opportunities', says Robinson. To that end, it is developing a programme with its US firm and Harvard Business School, structured around e-learning modules, for its senior managers. 'That is the group we need to invest in, so that we have people hitting the ground running as partners. The challenge is to develop faster, because there is less time and expectations are higher.'

Over the next decade, notwithstanding the changing business and regulatory environment, KPMG sees itself emerging as one of the world's leading multidisciplinary practices in the advisory field, implementing global strategies on a local basis.

## london&quadrant housing group

London and Quadrant is a housing association dedicated to providing homes for a wide variety of residents. Its mission is: creating places where people want to live. Around eight families a day are relieved of homelessness by the organisation, which speaks eloquently of the dedication of the teams involved. It has its roots in the 1960s but has the look and feel of a much younger, professional organisation. It has diversified into low cost home ownership and targets key workers as well as providing supported housing for vulnerable residents.

**Scorecard:**

| | |
|---|---|
| Remuneration and benefits | **** |
| Progressive attitude | ***** |
| Opportunity for promotion | ***** |
| Training, development and education | ***** |
| Working atmosphere and environment | ***** |

**Biggest plus:**
Job satisfaction – reflecting that at least eight homeless families or single people are housed by the time you finish a working day has to be excellent.

**Biggest minus:**
The profile of the sector can make it difficult to attract the best managers. Once people are in, however, they rarely want to leave.

London & Quadrant Group
Human Resources Department
Osborn House
Osborn Terrace
London SE3 9DR
Tel: 020 8557 2022
Website: www.lqgroup.org.uk

# London & Quadrant Housing Group

## The Business

On 16 December 1966, the BBC screened a drama called 'Cathy Come Home'. It brought to the mass population for the first time the plight of homeless people and the reality of what having children taken into care actually meant. Probably no documentary or drama has made a similar impact since; one of the upshots of the broadcast was that Rev. Nicholas Stacey and others set up the forerunner of London and Quadrant Housing Trust, which now manages more than 30,000 homes.

London & Quadrant's aims and principles remain fundamentally the same as they were at its inception – to do something about the housing available to families who fall through the net and can't get housed by other means. Its employment practices put it in the Sunday Times 100 Best Companies to Work For in early 2003.

London & Quadrant's rented homes are managed across the regions of London and the south east. There are separate divisions, that provide supported housing and a subsidiary, Tower Homes, which provides low cost home ownership. Tower offers other services such as *There is certainly fun to be had and people enjoy their jobs, but professionalism is a watchword and the company places customer satisfaction above all else* help for key workers (nurses, teachers and other essential workers) who find it increasingly difficult to find somewhere affordable to live in London. London & Quadrant's annual turnover is £104 million, it employs over 600 and staff retention is excellent, particularly at managerial level. It is funded through Government grants, loans raised in the private market and through rent receipts. London & Quadrant believes its people are its greatest asset, ensuring that they are motivated at all times.

## Company Culture and Style

If you are considering applying for a job with London & Quadrant, a good first move is to put away any preconceptions you might have about social housing and the voluntary sector. It would be wrong to say the atmosphere and attitude is strait-laced in any way. There is certainly fun to be had and people enjoy their jobs, but professionalism is a watchword and the company places customer satisfaction above all else. Tom Nicholls, Head of Human Resources, describes the company mission as 'creating places where people want to live...and work'. He and the organisation believe that building a good working atmosphere will ultimately enable staff to deliver excellence in customer service.

The hierarchy is fairly flat and the management team extremely stable – most of the directors have been on board for some years. Communication is a key enabler for the business to do its job – L&Q has won awards for its implementation of technology, not only for internal communications but for its online customer services.

There are no set rules about dress, but people tend to come to work looking smart regardless. Internal communications are good; for example there is an annual conference for staff and other internal events that ensure people are kept up to speed with what's happening, as well as a well-designed intranet. Perhaps crucially, an independent audit suggests that 73 per cent of employees believe London & Quadrant is primarily guided by principles as well as profits. This shouldn't be taken to mean the company is lightweight, though – if you don't believe in going the extra mile to deliver excellence both to the clients and to your colleagues, don't apply.

## Human Resources

The HR department services three areas, HR, facilities and training. In terms of HR the company is dedicated to equal opportunities. Its achievements in keeping staff motivated can be noted in that turnover of staff is around 17 per cent and sickness is down to 2.2 per cent – these are extraordinarily low for what can be a very stressful field.

The stability of the management group means that an unusual amount of the HR team's time is taken up with succession planning – but this doesn't mean it fails to innovate for the rest of the staff in other ways. To begin, HR is at the heart of the organisation rather than on the periphery – a representative sits in on all interviews. The CEO fully supports HR and the 'our people agenda', which accounts for 25 per cent of the five-year plan.

As might be expected from an organisation whose role is primarily in improving the lot of the community, much of the company's HR policy is geared towards being family-friendly in the extreme. It is ahead of the State minimum on family leave, paternity leave, adoption leave, leave for infertility treatment, parental leave, carers leave, flexible working and career breaks. It is aware of the needs of BME (Black and Minority Ethnic) groups and works towards good relations. Among all the companies profiled for this book it was the only one to mention fostering good relations with the unions as one of its aims.

## Career Opportunity and Development

Training is one of the highest priorities of the organisation. Of course every company says this but very few of them give their employees a one-to-one review with their line manager every month without fail – half-yearly often looks generous. At London & Quadrant an annual appraisal is the norm.

L&Q in fact uses training not only to address the individual's needs but also to fill in some of the industry-wide skills gaps that have emerged over the years. For example, as this book went to press, specialist maintenance managers were in short supply and clearly in housing this is very important. Again, the commitment to training is real and not just window-dressing – the company spends a striking £1,200 per head per year on training, both internally and in an alliance with the University of Nottingham, for qualifications in management and another in team leadership.

Even more unusually there is the opportunity for personal development that won't impact the business directly. 'If someone wanted to learn a language, say, they'd do it in their own time but we'd fund it', says Sally Jacobson, Group Director of Human Resources. This ties in with what is obviously an overall commitment to holistic training of employees – at all times they are people rather than economic units, and they are treated accordingly.

People will mostly manage their own career paths, with the organisation fast tracking some individuals where it seems appropriate and particularly when the succession planning becomes involved.

## Remuneration

Remuneration in social housing isn't easily compared to remuneration in the commercial sector, and anyone wanting their salary package to include huge money and attractive share options should check their expectations in this particular area. Indeed, Jacobson is keen to stress that the payback goes beyond money: 'I always tell people that five or six families who would otherwise have remained homeless will have been housed due to their efforts on a particular day', she comments.

However, the standard benefits are impressive. Salaries will be slightly above the norm for the field. Holiday entitlement can reach 31 days per year, there is a pension scheme and non-contributory life insurance and a disability income scheme. Sick pay is above the State's expectations, there is a car loan available in a link with Barclays, eye care vouchers are on offer, there is legal and other counselling available and a 2.5 per cent performance-related bonus for which staff can be nominated by colleagues as well as managers, for outstanding work. Nicholls believes the packages on offer are extremely competitive, which, in a notoriously under-resourced area, they certainly are.

## The Future

London and Quadrant has many plans and wishes for the future. First, says Jacobson, there is the overall image of the housing sector to be addressed. She finds she has to sell the sector to people as much as the individual jobs within L&Q, which makes recruiting less easy than it ought to be. In 2003 the company made the top 100 employer list in the *Sunday Times*; Jacobson wants to crack the top 10.

On a less global scale the organisation will continue to innovate. In 2003 it launched a scheme called Change – a financial service for its residents including the offer of personal loans and other financial products. It will continue to be utterly focused on the customer and to motivate and train its staff to achieve excellence in this aim at all times.

This isn't a company for people wanting loads of personal benefits, glamour and cash. It's a company for someone who wants to finish work, go home and believe they've made a difference. If job satisfaction and benefiting society in general appeals to you, you should give it serious consideration.

Lush sells its hand-made skin, hair and body products both by mail order and through a chain of 151 stores worldwide. Formed in 1994 out of a previous venture, Cosmetics To Go, its projected 2002 turnover is £42 million, and it employs around 400 staff in the UK alone, rising to at least 600 in the busy pre-Christmas season. Lush is privately owned, with founders Mark and Mo Constantine holding a 50 per cent stake.

## Scorecard:

| | |
|---|---|
| Remuneration and benefits | ** |
| Progressive attitude | *** |
| Opportunity for promotion | ***** |
| Training, development and education | *** |
| Working atmosphere and environment | **** |

## Biggest plus:
Plenty of opportunities for growth and progression.

## Biggest minus:
You have to work hard for your money.

Lush Ltd
29 High Street
Poole
Dorset
Tel: 01202 668545
Website: www.lush.co.uk

# Lush

## The Business

Describing itself as a 'cosmetics grocer', Lush produces hand-made skin, hair and body products and sells them by mail order and through a chain of shops around the world. Its unique selling points are fresh ingredients and unorthodox presentation; slabs of soap are laid out like cheese in a deli and sold by weight, and bath bombs are stacked in trays like fruit.

Lush's story begins in 1978, when founder Mark Constantine started supplying products to The Body Shop. When The Body Shop brought its production in house, Constantine set up a mail-order venture, Cosmetics To Go, which collapsed in 1994 from a series of internal and external problems. Lush was set up three months later. In the latest twist in the tale, Lush recently bought back all rights to Cosmetics To Go.

From a single shop in Poole, Lush has now grown to over 150 stores in 20 countries – some wholly-owned and some joint ventures – and its products are made and sold under licence in a further eight countries. It has production facilities in Europe, Canada, Australia, South America, Singapore and Japan. New stores and new countries are being added on a regular basis.

*with a new set of bonus schemes in place, the company believes its salary levels are at least on a par with average High Street levels, with staff able to double their pay for 'achieving the outrageous' (outrageous being defined as, for example, increasing sales in their store by 30 per cent)*

Though Lush made a consolidated loss for the year ending June 2001, it turned in a £3 million profit on revenues of £30 million in the following financial year. The improvement in its fortunes is partly, the company believes, down to its new sales incentive scheme, which enabled it to increase sales by well above average for the market, plus cost savings schemes that streamlined underlying costs. Its projected turnover for the current year is £42 million, of which around 40 per cent will be generated in the UK. It employs around 400 staff in the UK alone, rising to at least 600 in the busy pre-Christmas season, and at least 1,000–1,500 worldwide. The company is privately owned, with founders Mark and Mo Constantine holding a 50 per cent stake.

## Company Culture and Style

In keeping with its unconventional store presentation, Lush offers an open and informal working environment, where suits are most definitely not required. Staff are on first-name terms with the directors and are encouraged to share ideas and air their views both directly, through monthly staff meetings, and through a new online staff forum, set up when it became clear that many staff members were contributing to the customer forum on the public website.

Though Lush has been known to pick staff on the basis of their star signs, the company does not discriminate on grounds of sex, age or race in its recruitment policies. Five out of the nine UK directors are female, and among management generally there's a 50/50 split between men and women. The workforce is, however, predominantly young and white.

Despite its open and unconventional attitude, Lush describes its culture as 'relaxed but not lax', and coasting is not encouraged. Being allowed to fail is part of the company's central philosophy, and indeed enshrined on its carrier bags, but repeated failure is a no-no. In order to increase their earnings and progress in the company, employees have to show results.

Some employees quickly decide the Lush culture is not for them and leave, but in general the company has an impressive record on staff retention, at middle to senior management level at any rate. Of the UK directors, only two have been with the company for less than seven years, and some have been with Lush and its forerunners CTG and C&W since their inception. Some senior staff have even taken pay cuts to join the company.

## Human Resources

Many of Lush's senior people were headhunted from elsewhere; Heather Williams, the company's finance director, for example, was formerly Lush's tax advisor at Ernst & Young. Many others have been promoted from the shop or factory floor. The company also recruits from outside, particularly in the run-up to Christmas – the busiest time of year for any retailer – when its staff levels can increase by up to 50 per cent both in the stores and in its production and fulfilment departments.

Lush has a central payroll department but no central human resources department. Within the company's decentralised structure, managers are given the power, and responsibility, for recruiting staff for their own teams, using their own recruitment methods.

Whether staff are recruited from inside or outside the company, however, the crucial selection factors are attitude, track record and proven performance. Formal qualifications are not a high priority, but ability and willingness to deliver are. Under the company's recently introduced performance incentive scheme, badly-performing staff become a liability not only to themselves but to their manager, encouraging management to be more selective about who they take on and more ruthless about who they keep.

## Career Opportunity and Development

Though there is pressure on Lush staff to perform, the upside is that for those who do, there are plenty of opportunities to progress within the company. Lush is currently expanding rapidly, with new stores opening within the UK. According to

Mark Constantine, the company constantly has more opportunities than people to fill them.

Though some members of the management team have joined from outside, others have worked their way up from the shop floor. The company's current PR manager started out as one of the retail staff and moved on to managing the company's busy Covent Garden store; she is now about to move on to manage one of Lush's overseas operations.

As noted above, the crucial factor in enabling career progression within Lush is not formal qualifications but proven ability to deliver. However, job-specific training is encouraged in all areas of the business. All staff, including temporary Christmas staff, undergo an internal introductory course and the retail staff have formal skin care, hair care and product and quality service training.

Manufacturing staff all train to be what Lush calls Compounders, and when they are trained to make all products, they become Master Compounders, providing a defined career development path with appropriate pay increases and opportunities to progress within management. Members of the perfume team, who make Lush's secret essential oil combinations, are studying for external perfumery exams sponsored by Lush.

Finance staff are also encouraged to study for appropriate exams, and training continues even at the higher levels of management; Williams, for example, is currently studying for an MBA in Entrepreneurship at Manchester Business School.

## Remuneration

Lush freely admits that a year ago, there were rumblings of discontent among its staff over pay. Now, with a new set of bonus schemes in place, the company believes its salary levels are at least on a par with average high street levels, with staff able to double their pay for 'achieving the outrageous' (outrageous being defined as, for example, increasing sales in their store by 30 per cent). Founder Mark Constantine says that he wants to further improve this, so that Lush will offer salary levels in the top 25 per cent for high street staff.

Bonus schemes are being introduced across the board; for example, sales staff can earn an extra £1 an hour for increasing their personal sales. And incentives don't just apply to store employees; product line managers in the production facilities can earn bonuses for increasing production, admin staff can earn bonuses for holding down costs and so on – can, and do, according to Heather Williams, who acknowledges the importance of setting targets that are fair and achievable.

Pay and bonus levels are particularly important at Lush since the company has eschewed other forms of remuneration. Mark Constantine takes the view that he would rather pay staff the most he can afford and let them decide what to spend it on. There are no company cars or company pension scheme, and the idea of an Employee Benefit Scheme was investigated and rejected on the basis that it did not offer significant benefits to staff. Lush is, however, looking into ways of setting up a regular share exchange scheme – what Williams calls a 'share boot sale' – which would allow employees to buy a stake in the company without heavy tax liabilities.

## The Future

Lush has set itself ambitious growth targets. It wants to be five times bigger in five years' time, in terms of both revenue and stores, and 10 times more profitable. An active expansion programme is in place to achieve those aims. As well as opening more UK stores, the company recently appointed an export manager to liaise with country directors and overseas partners and focus specifically on overseas expansion.

Some companies achieve expansion at the expense of quality and focus. As it expands, Lush intends to maintain both its high product quality and its product innovation, both of which are seen as contributing to its already high brand recognition.

Another aim is to continue to recruit high-calibre staff, and offer them the chance to double or treble their salaries based on performance. The new system of incentive schemes is, of course, likely to help Lush achieve this goal.

# MARKS & SPENCER

Marks & Spencer is a British institution; its name a familiar sight on the high street for over 100 years. Its food, clothing and household items have long been a byword for quality. Today, Marks & Spencer employs 60,000 people, mostly in its 300 UK stores. It also has a major franchise operation, with over 100 stores world-wide organised on this basis.

## Scorecard:

| | |
|---|---|
| Remuneration and benefits | **** |
| Progressive attitude | **** |
| Opportunity for promotion | **** |
| Training, development and education | ***** |
| Working atmosphere and environment | **** |

## Biggest plus:
The company's commitment to developing its people.

## Biggest minus:
A danger of being taken for granted on the high street.

Marks & Spencer plc
Michael House
Baker Street
London W1U 8EP
Tel: 020 7935 4422
Website: www.marksandspencer.com

# Marks & Spencer

## The Business

In 1884, a Russian refugee called Michael Marks opened a market stall in Leeds. Ten years later he decided to form a partnership with Tom Spencer, and a British retailing legend was born. From the start, it was an innovative company: before going public in 1926, it was already buying directly from manufacturers. Since the 1930s, Marks & Spencer has been renowned for the high quality of its food, and had the distinction of introducing ready-prepared meals to the UK. It is equally famous for its clothing.

It seemed that nothing could ever go wrong with Marks & Spencer: but it is no secret that serious problems did arise at the end of the 1990s. In a single year, its profits fell from £1.1 billion to less than half that; its share price plummeted; media pundits pronounced its clothing boring, its food products left behind in the innovation stakes and its attitude arrogant; and it was widely regarded as ripe for takeover. One of the triggers of this reaction was the company's involvement with managing stores overseas, which often failed to excite the level of consumer interest seen in Britain. The last two years have been about survival.

> *People can see the results of what they deliver very quickly, and we're highly customer-focused, from the stores to the Head Office buying group*

Happily, much has changed in that time. Marks & Spencer has abandoned its policy of owning stores overseas in favour of franchises. It has revamped its product lines and rekindled its spirit of innovation. Among recent moves, it has introduced its 'Simply Food' stores, aimed at late night or early morning shoppers in strategic locations. It has also announced a partnership with Compass to take its products into major railway stations, offering 'convenience foods convenient to buy'. Recent financial results show that the company's recovery is being sustained.

## Company Culture and Style

Marks & Spencer is a people-centred company, focused on its staff as much as its customers. Its success in the past was due to the skill and motivation apparent throughout the company, and it is determined to regain that.

So, what sort of person thrives at Marks & Spencer? Helena Feltham, HR Director: 'Those who love the immediacy of retailing. People can see the results of what they deliver very quickly, and we're highly customer-focused, from the stores to the Head Office buying group.'

The company has a very clear mission and values, and the culture is definitely shifting back to what it was when the business was at its most successful. For instance, its values are to provide quality, value for money and service – to which have now been added innovation and trust. These last two, while long a part of the Marks & Spencer ethos, had perhaps not been as developed in the recent past. The business is ready to embrace them to the full now.

There is no doubt that Marks & Spencer has taken the lessons of recent years to heart: and this is reflected in its culture. Feltham: 'In the past, we were, if not arrogant, certainly complacent. There was an element of the parent–child relationship in our culture. It's now a much more open place to work, with everyone encouraged to be themselves and use their talents. A key part of our strategy is committed to making Marks & Spencer a great place to work.'

This new culture is manifested in a series of initiatives, including the desire to recognise and respect a job well done, to balance life and work, to be rewarded for superior results, and to canvass the staff for their views. The 'Lifestyles' booklet focuses on the life/work balance, and lists the ways in which staff can make use of this: child breaks, career breaks, flexible working and much more. Local managers have a local budget to reward good performance. There was no staff survey 18 months ago: today, the 'How are we doing?' survey canvasses every member of staff twice a year. There is no doubt further to go; but it is clear that the culture at Marks & Spencer is being transformed.

## Human Resources

HR is an integral part of Marks & Spencer – and it is fully integrated with the business. Helena Feltham: 'HR people are expected to know and enjoy retailing. There isn't an HR strategy but a business/people strategy.'

The bulk of recruitment for the company is for its stores, and for its customer-facing jobs. The policy here is clear-cut: the company wants people who have a passion for people and have inherent skills in building relationships. The message is equally clear for those who can't stand customers: don't bother to apply to Marks & Spencer! The company is happy to train people in work skills but recognises that people skills cannot be taught.

The graduate recruitment scheme, on hold during the company's recent difficulties, is now running again. Marks & Spencer will take around 150 graduates this year. Ideal candidates are those who enjoy retailing and have the potential to be good leaders – people who can deliver success through people and create the conditions for their success.

At every level, though, successful employees are those who are team players yet are able to really take responsibility for their role. Honesty, confidence and the ability to listen and learn are vital, from the newest recruit to the chief executive.

## Career Development and Opportunities

Even in the troubled times of the last two years, no one accused Marks & Spencer of not being excellent at career development, and the company is justifiably proud of this. There are varied opportunities for career development. People are encouraged to move between stores, and across functions within stores. All jobs are advertised online on Vista, the company's career service. It has a careers centre, and training is available to support jobs that come up.

Just as every private in the British army allegedly carries a general's baton in his knapsack, so it is true that any sales assistant at Marks & Spencer could rise to the chief executive's position. There is a carefully planned route from sales adviser to section manager, store manager, area manager and so on, and talented and ambitious individuals could definitely go as far as they wish.

The head office also offers considerable scope for career development, employing as it does 3,000 people. There are opportunities here in IT, marketing, HR and other centralised functions.

Sales advisers are supported by external training programmes, such as the B.Tech course (currently being pursued by 500 employees). There are also links with Middlesex University, which offers a food course equivalent to half a masters' degree, and educational sponsorship for MBAs, Institute of Marketing courses, accountancy qualifications and much more.

In short, there is no lack of training opportunities; however, this is offered as part of self-development. Employees are expected to take responsibility for their own careers, as expressed through personal development reviews. In effect, as the company says, this is 'a learning environment that gives individuals as much opportunity as they want.'

## Remuneration

Marks & Spencer aims to be in the upper quartile in terms of its total benefits package including salary. On top of good base salaries, it offers a competitive package, which reflects individual, team and corporate performance. In 2001, the company added new bonus schemes, which operate from the chief executive down. The thinking here is that everyone has the opportunity to drive the company's results – and should be rewarded accordingly. The management bonus last year amounted to around 20 per cent of salary on average.

In addition, everyone who works for the company is given shares (not share options). This corresponds to one to five per cent of salary. Company cars are offered at a certain management level, with a cash option for those who prefer it. There is also a 20 per cent discount on Marks & Spencer's goods, up to £5,000 in any one year. Holidays can rise to six and a half weeks according to length of service.

Marks & Spencer has retained its final salary pension scheme for existing employees. For new employees, it is introducing a Defined Contribution scheme in April 2003 whereby the company matches their contributions. Benefits also include subsidised health and dental care: and there is an occupational health team of advisers to which everyone has free access.

# The Future

Marks & Spencer has ambitious plans for the future. First, it intends to regain its dominance in the clothing market. Second, it wants to promote its 'Simply Food' stores, increasing the number from 8 to 150 in the next three years by opening new stores in high streets and also in railway stations, through the franchise agreement with Compass. Third, it plans to build a big home business, having perceived a large gap between cheap home stores and department stores and intending to offer everything for the home. And, finally, it wants to expand its financial services, conducting a credit and loyalty card pilot before making a decision to roll this out nationwide.

If these are the tactics, the strategy is to keep building on its fundamental strengths; ensure its locations match the changing face of towns and cities; and above all, to be the standard by which other retailers are measured.

# Masterfoods

Masterfoods is part of Mars Inc, one of the largest privately owned businesses in the world. Its UK and Ireland operation makes up the Western region of Masterfoods in Europe. The company is a leader in the manufacture of snack food, main meal food and petcare products, with brands in its stable including Mars, Snickers, M&Ms, Uncle Ben's, Dolmio, Pedigree and Whiskas.

**Scorecard:**

| | |
|---|---|
| Remuneration and benefits | **** |
| Progressive attitude | *** |
| Opportunity for promotion | **** |
| Training, development and education | **** |
| Working atmosphere and environment | ***** |

**Biggest plus:**
Being a massive global operation, there is unlimited potential for career expansion and growth.

**Biggest minus:**
The biggest plus has negative connotations too, as it's possible to get lost within such a big organisation. Employees need to be able to make their mark.

Masterfoods
Dundee Road
Slough SL1 4JX
Tel: 01753 550055
Fax: 01753 550111
Website: www.mars.com

# Masterfoods

## The business

The creation of Mars Inc is one of those typical rags-to-riches stories. On a visit to the local drugstore in America in 1922, founder Frank Mars and his son, Forrest, had an original idea: to produce a portable version of a chocolate malted milk. The Milky Way bar – known in Europe as the Mars bar – was an immediate success and, together with other famous brands like Snickers, has been the foundation of the global snack food business.

On arriving in Europe 10 years later, Forrest Mars, having established a snack-food facility in Slough, identified pet food as a potential growth market. He became a pioneer in developing the European pet food industry using modern manufacturing techniques coupled with nutritional science. The business rapidly grew to encompass what it is today.

Masterfoods was created in Europe in 2000 to bring together Mars's petcare, snack food and main meal food businesses into a single European organisation. The UK and Ireland organisation, which makes up 40 per cent of the European business sales and profits, has sites in Berkshire, Norfolk, Leicestershire, Yorkshire and Cambridgeshire in the UK, and in Dublin.

*Quality was and still is the foundation of our success. Today, our goal is quality in everything we set out to achieve, the products we make, the services we provide, the people who make up the team*

Worldwide, there are more than 70 factories in over 60 countries operating from more than 150 sites. Today, the total business turns over around $14 billion, around half of which comes from Europe.

## Company Culture and Style

The first thing that strikes visitors to the Slough site is the extent of the open plan floor space. That, and the fact that Western Europe MD, Mike Davies, has his desk right in the middle of the office. The outsider would never guess his seniority and to the insider he is visible and accessible. To describe Masterfoods' working environment as having a distinctive culture would be accurate, and it is completely lacking in hierarchy, as demonstrated by the fact that all employees are known as associates.

The culture is based on five principles – quality, responsibility, mutuality, efficiency and freedom. As Rebecca Snow, Organisation Development Manager, says: 'Quality was and still is the foundation of our success. Today, our goal is quality in everything we set out to achieve, the products we make, the services we provide, the people who make up the team.'

Snow describes the company as a 'fluid organisation', one which has changed significantly in recent times. It incorporates the fourth generation of the Mars family, most of whom play a very strong role in leading the business. There are ongoing activities to monitor and develop the overall 'health' of the company. It commissions Gallup surveys to measure how people feel about the company and to act as a catalyst for change.

Snow says that the change has meant the company culture is now more diverse, though she concedes that there are some people who wouldn't fit in. 'If you like an open plan environment, this is an amazing place to learn and grow and to develop long-lasting working relationships', she explains. 'We have the kind of culture where we walk into any other office in Europe and immediately feel at home.'

Masterfoods takes work/life balance very seriously, so much so there they have established a work/life balance team. This is made up of a representative from each of the various functions of the business. The team has been in operation for about a year and, following extensive research, it is now writing new policies. These include areas such as working hours, sabbaticals, travel, etc. 'An example is our attitude to travel abroad – we always try to have European meetings in the middle of the week so our associates don't find themselves having to travel, say, early on a Monday morning or late Friday night', Snow says.

On the Board in the UK and Ireland there are two women out of a total of eight members, whilst women make up over 30 per cent of senior managers in the region. 'Our record for developing women into senior roles is something we have actively worked at, and achieved considerable success to a point. We recognise that we need to continue our efforts here beyond just "senior management" in particular countries and into the very highest level within the global corporation.'

## Human Resources

Masterfoods has a large presence in the graduate market even though they only recruit 40–50 graduates a year. The graduate recruitment is done in this way so that they can offer individually tailored programmes rather than a treadmill. 'We are relatively lean in terms of people, so we don't have facilities to employ 200 or 300 graduates. We tend to go for quality rather than quantity', Snow says.

The graduates fill an important part of the management pipeline but the company also recruits from a wider market where people have other skills, for which the company usually looks for a minimum of three years' experience. 'Recruiting people from outside stops us from being insular, which is particularly important in a private company', Snow says.

There is a centralised team for external recruitment, a structure that allows for efficiency with benefits in terms of superior candidate care and greater cost effectiveness. Candidate care is vital as Snow says the company wants all people who touch them to have a good experience, even if they don't get job in the end.

A degree is essential for management jobs, although there might be the odd exception. For jobs such as those on the shop floor, candidates would need to have some technical skills.

Masterfoods is a company young at heart and staff can retire at 50. People do rejoin the company at times, mostly, according to research, because they miss the quality of people and the huge amount of opportunity offered.

Apart from so-called hard benefits, the HR department also operates things such as the Associates Assistance Programme, where an outsourced company has been retained to provide any kind of assistance for staff, from sorting out financial issues, to finding a mortgage, to marriage guidance or support for stress, There is also an internal Ombudsman service, which is totally confidential for those staff experiencing line management problems.

## Career Opportunity and Development

Masterfoods has only seven reporting levels, making for a very flat structure but one in which extensive opportunities for progression and development exist.

There is a global learning and development team supporting personal and organisational change through training team coaching and leadership development. Divisions also hold their own events each year to develop functional and technical competence. Line Management Excellence is one of the company's five European priorities and additional focus is being put behind this.

With global operations, opportunities for overseas transfer, particularly at management level, are there for the taking. Snow says staff who take overseas postings are well supported, both financially in terms of being given a house, a car and a salary and pension which remain in the UK, and socially in terms of a spouse support programme.

Staff are also strongly encouraged to manage their own careers – reviews with line managers are regular and personnel support is always there.

'Change can still be scary but it is a way of life now and so we encourage associates to recognise and embrace this. To help them we believe we offer great working conditions and excellent remuneration. We encourage an entrepreneurial spirit because we've learnt that the most successful ideas come from those who know the issues and opportunities best. For their ideas and contribution, associates are rewarded through a global recognition programme. This in turn creates a stimulating and satisfying place to work and it becomes a virtuous circle.'

## Remuneration

There are three sections of any associate's pay that are based on performance. The first is that based on business performance as a whole, secondly that based on growth and profit in a particular area, and finally on a person's own personal development over the year.

Associates are paid weekly and among general benefits are a pension scheme through which Masterfoods will pay up to 18 per cent of a maximum 30 per cent contribution. There is also life assurance, free private healthcare, company cars for sales people only, and a weekly bag of chocolate!

Because Masterfoods is part of a privately-owned company, there are no stock options.

## The Future

Snow says the company's immediate aims are to grow to remain the market leader in both chocolate and petcare in Europe, and to continue the excellent growth in our main meal food business. Internally, they will focus on line management excellence, with Line Management Excellence Week running in the four regions across Europe, and by rolling out a new off-the-shelf competency package for all staff.

Snow concludes: 'We believe that with some of the world's biggest brands, with first class people and excellent line management, we have a real recipe for continued success.'

# *Microsoft*

Microsoft has gone through a process of shedding all the gimmicks and ensuring that its employees are people who share the company vision of making their customers' lives improve through the intelligent application of technology.

Microsoft is the largest PC software company in the world, based in Redmond, and employing thousands. It is behind the celebrated Windows operating system, which, since the mid-1990s, has been the de facto standard for the personal computer, and also the Office suite of office application products. The chances of anyone reading this book not being familiar with at least one Microsoft product is remote. It retains an ethos, however, of being an accessible, flat-structured business that doesn't forget how young it is.

## Scorecard:

| | |
|---|---|
| Remuneration and benefits | **** |
| Progressive attitude | ***** |
| Opportunity for promotion | **** |
| Training, development and education | ***** |
| Working atmosphere and environment | ***** |

## Biggest plus:
The level of empowerment the company offers to its people.

## Biggest minus:
The exhaustion levels – as is the case with many companies that have gone through a growth phase, the employees can get carried away and lose sight of work/life balance.

Microsoft Campus
Thames Valley Park
Reading RG6 1WG
Tel: 0870 6010100
Website: www.microsoft.com/uk

# Microsoft

## The Business

Microsoft is one of the largest software companies in the world, innovating through its Windows software and being one of the principle movers behind the widespread adoption of the Internet as a means of communication and a medium in its own right.

Founded in the 1980s, the company capitalised quickly on the emergence of what was then called the IBM-compatible personal computer – just PC today. It became the market leader in one of the early operating systems, DOS, and based Windows on it to offer an easier-to-use front end. It's easy to forget that this didn't take off initially, but with the emergence of Windows 3 and Windows 3.1, it suddenly became the hottest news in the industry. Windows 95, and later Windows 98 became the standards by which all other desktop technology would be judged, and the latest incarnation, Windows XP, takes the best of these systems and combines it with the robustness of Windows 2000, the professional standard system formerly known as Windows XP.

*Microsoft has gone through a process of shedding all the gimmicks and ensuring that its employees are people who share the company vision of making their customers' lives improve through the intelligent application of technology*

It's tempting to suggest that Microsoft is purely about IT, which is, of course, its core activity, but there are other elements to be borne in mind about the company. It has a deep-seated social conscience and has made huge donations to educational and other trusts. It wants to become a more responsible corporate citizen – more on that in 'The Future' paragraphs.

It is fully listed in the US and has premises in most of the countries around the world.

## Company Culture and Style

When Steve Harvey, UK HR Director, considers the current culture and style at Microsoft he comes out with one word: 'engaged'. There have been a lot of fads in HR policies over the last couple of years – Duvet days (when you call into work and say you can't be bothered to come in and it's accepted) being possibly the most extreme example. For Harvey, Microsoft has gone through a process of shedding all the gimmicks and ensuring that its employees are people who share the company vision of making their customers' lives improve through the intelligent application of technology.

For that reason, the business has a policy of 'eating its own dog food' as it puts it – testing out all of its software on itself as a set of human guinea pigs before sending it out through its distribution channels. The core business values, though, centre around the customer. It is always looking for people with integrity, passion for customers, business partners and technology, openness and respect, willingness to take on challenges and willingness to be accountable. Its website speaks of tenets that propel the business' mission: customer trust, broad customer connection, innovation and responsible leadership, enabling people to do new things and inclusivity for the wider community.

So far, so theoretical, but the business does make an effort to live up to its commitments. Employees, whether they are in Reading or Paris, will find themselves in a pleasant, airy environment. Hard work is a given, and enthusiasm for the technology or more particularly what it can do is essential. An appreciation of the speed at which the technology moves and changes is also an important asset – this can be scary but is also stimulating for the right person. It's an open culture – if you have an idea and want to email it to Bill Gates you can do so and he'll reply.

All manner of people will fit into the company as long as they match those broad criteria, and the HR team has been sufficiently successful in making the business appeal to potential employees to secure the number one spot in the 2003 Sunday Times Best UK Employer list.

## Human Resources

The HR system at Microsoft has been the envy of many corporations for a while now. Inevitably, as an IT company, it was one of the first to operate an intranet, and one through which employees can check their holiday and other entitlements – this is commonplace now but in the late 1990s when MS put it in it was like science fiction. This is still running with developments including 'U' mail, 'U' messaging and 'U' TV – personalised services so that even when sitting in front of an ordinary computer someone feels it's their space.

Technology aside, the HR department sees its mission in traditional terms – to attract, develop and keep the best people. It has a number of specific initiatives to back the project up; a wellbeing centre is full-time in Reading and has a massage clinic and other stress-relieving activities. Harvey, however, is determined to continue putting proactive rather than reactive facilities in place – education on stress management, well man days and well woman days, for example.

## Career Opportunity and Development

Scope for career development is excellent at Microsoft – it's a relatively young organisation and as such unencumbered by old-fashioned notions of the way things should be done. It's happy to promote personal development plans for everyone and if people want to travel the world then there are around 5,000 jobs around the globe to choose from, subject to the right vacancy cropping up at the right time. Moving between disciplines within the organisation is allowed and encouraged, if an individual has a skill gap he or she believes needs addressing.

Internal appointments are frequent, although Harvey is keen to stress the need for external recruitment as well. 'People can be in a job for too short a time and it's not good for the customer – they'd rather have the same account manager for two years than just two months, I'm sure', he comments. He is also aware of the pitfalls of recycling ideas from the same pool of people the whole time.

Nevertheless, if you want to manage your own career and can do so within the parameters of looking after the customer, it's a good place to be. Formal appraisals happen regularly and contact with line managers is open and underpinned by one of the most sophisticated communications infrastructures in the business.

## Remuneration

The good news for Microsoft shareholders – and if you work for the company you will be invited to become one – is that global economic downturn notwithstanding, it announced its first share dividend in early 2003 and the early signs are that this will be the first of many. The financials have been spectacular year on year, but Harvey stresses that the business doesn't plan to stay still as a result. The sales force, for example, was put onto a commission model for the first time in late 2002, and now has a 75/25 per cent model for its pay.

You can take the usual benefits of working for a big company – life assurance, decent holidays etc – as read, and once working for the company you can develop your own benefit package using the intranet. Pay is among the best in the IT sector, mostly because Microsoft can't afford not to attract good people. Other elements – like the crèche at the Reading premises – are being built in as the business develops.

## The Future

Harvey believes Microsoft has done well in the market but has done so possibly at the expense of its employees. When asked about the worst thing about working for Microsoft he considers, and says: 'Seeing everyone so tired. They give so much.' This is an area he wants to address for the workforce before they get much older – and it doesn't mean doing everything the workforce asks. The London team, for example, have suggested putting a crèche in the car park: 'I don't want people dragging their kids across London and putting them in a fume-filled car park for the day', he says. The company will find another way to help.

Another area in which he is keen to see the company develop is as an environmental force. 'Reading council has just put its park-and-ride car park in, built a new one, when we have thousands of places in ours empty at the weekend', he says. 'It's crazy.'

You're left with the impression of a still-new business that's been forced to mature in a very short space of time. Certainly Microsoft has its critics and has been through the courts over some of its commercial practices (and acquitted on most counts); but this is a company that has seen incredibly rapid development and growth and not had time to draw breath. Now that it's issuing dividends and has time to consider its options for further growth, it's encouraging to hear it talking about the well-being of its workforce and the areas it inhabits. Its consolidation should be to the benefit of many.

SOLICITORS

With offices in Birmingham, Cambridge, London and Norwich, Mills & Reeve is a growing profitable law firm building towards a turnover of £40 million by 2004/5. A national reputation has been built up by the firm for the quality of its advice and service to six key areas: businesses and entrepreneurs in the high-tech sector, owners and developers of commercial property, the main carriers of professional indemnity risks, the NHS, higher and further education, and large-scale owners of agricultural land. This is a firm where there's an atmosphere of mutual trust and cooperation, where partners and staff enjoy the fruits of a good quality of life while delivering consistently high standards of service to all clients.

**Scorecard:**

| | |
|---|---|
| Remuneration and benefits | **** |
| Progressive attitude | ***** |
| Opportunity for promotion | **** |
| Training, development and education | **** |
| Working atmosphere and environment | **** |

**Biggest plus:**
The people are great, and it's a good environment to work in, with an exemplary quality of life.

**Biggest minus:**
The ethos that comes from offering the highest quality of advice requires commitment and hard work.

Mills & Reeve
Francis House
112 Hills Road
Cambridge CB2 1PH
Tel: 0870 600 0011
Fax: 01223 355848
Website: www.mills-reeve.com

# Mills & Reeve

## The Business

With offices in Birmingham, Cambridge, Norwich and London, law firm Mills & Reeve's strategy to take it through to 2004 and beyond is clear: focus on achieving a national reputation for the quality of advice and service in six defined market sectors. These sectors are: businesses and entrepreneurs and those who finance them, especially in the technology sector; owners and developers of commercial property; the main carriers of professional indemnity risks; the NHS; higher and further education institutions; and large-scale owners and occupiers of agricultural land.

The firm is led by Senior Partner Jonathan Barclay and Managing Partner Mark Jeffries. Lawyers are members of one of five practice groups: Corporate, Property, Insurance, Private Client and Healthcare. Each group is led by a group leader, with groups divided into teams, each led by a team leader, with 5–10 lawyers per team. Cross-group industry teams ensure a focus is kept on the firm's key markets. There are 63 partners, approximately 250 other lawyers and some 500 staff overall.

*One of our appeals is we are regarded as a high-quality law firm which has a good client base in its chosen sectors and markets, and can offer people high quality, interesting work, but without the arduous working hours of London or City law firms*

Mills & Reeve was founded in 1880 in Norwich by Henry Mills, being joined in 1889 by Edmund Reeve. The firm subsequently acquired a number of small practices in Norwich. A Cambridge office opened in 1986, before a merger with Francis & Co, a firm established in Cambridge for 200 years. The Birmingham office opened in 1998 closely followed by a merger with The Lewington Partnership. A London office opened in January 2000. Turnover to June 2002 was £27.2 million. Target for 2004 is £40 million.

## Company Culture and Style

'One of our appeals is we are regarded as a high-quality law firm which has a good client base in its chosen sectors and markets, and can offer people high quality, interesting work, but without the arduous working hours of London or City law firms', says Sandy Boyle, HR Director. 'We offer an enviable work/life balance. People who work here like hard work but equally appreciate there's more to life than work.'

'In Birmingham we operate the concept of core working hours of 10–4, with people flexing around the beginning and end of the core depending on their own particular circumstances', says Boyle. 'We're considering how we can increase flexibility for everyone generally.'

Across the firm the workforce is split 66 per cent female, 34 per cent male, and of the 63 partners, 49 are male, 14 female. 'There are many legal secretaries in the firm, all of whom are female', says Boyle. 'For high achievers, partnership can be attained in your early 30s.'

Mills & Reeve takes on staff across the board. Two partners were recently appointed in the Birmingham office to handle expansion of the corporate and property teams there. It all depends on the requirements of the business. With support staff, for example, the firm looks for people with the right experience and qualifications, if necessary. New graduate trainees are taken on at Cambridge, Norwich and Birmingham – this is a two-year training contract and represents a 'significant investment'. The most recent two-year intake of 37 comprises 28 females and nine males. 'More females at trainee level could represent their appreciation of work/life balance', says Boyle.

While there is no formal framework regarding haircuts and dress, the legal arena is known for its traditional dress sense. But there are dress-down days for charity. In an opinion survey in 2002, 88 per cent of the staff said they would recommend Mills & Reeve as a good place to work, and 85 per cent said they were satisfied with their jobs (20 per cent above the benchmark for similar organisations).

## Human Resources

'In the summer we run placement schemes where undergraduates spend two weeks at Norwich, Cambridge or Birmingham to get an idea of what it's like working here. We can identify people we're interested in taking on', says Boyle. A recent group of 30 students took up placements of which eight were subsequently selected to join the next intake. The firm also attends various law fairs held at different universities throughout the year, preferring applicants who have an upper second-class honours degree and good 'A' levels.

For other staff positions, these are advertised internally first and on the website. There is also an incentive system of bounty payments where existing employees are rewarded for introducing an applicant who is subsequently employed. 'We agree a specification of what we're looking for in terms of knowledge, experience, skills, different professional qualifications, etc', says Boyle. 'We can sometimes have openings in HR, marketing and IT for example, depending on the needs of the business.'

If people move to other law firms for experience or family moves, there is still the opportunity to rejoin the firm. As a good measure of job satisfaction, staff turnover at Mills & Reeve is 5.6 per cent.

## Career Opportunity and Development

There is seat rotation around the five groups in the two-year training period, where staff look at various aspects of the law, for example, private client or property. Each person decides which area they would like to focus on, and the firm announces newly-qualified positions for September. If for example there is one vacancy in intellectual property and there are four applicants, the best one gets the job. The others must then decide what specialisation to pursue.

The career path for solicitors when they qualify is in five stages: there is newly qualified, solicitor, senior solicitor, associate, and, potentially, partnership. Progression through the different stages is by means of achieving established competences and experiences. Suitable professional qualifications, experience and the ability to be able to demonstrate a proven track record at each stage constitute each staff member's career route map.

The overall direction of the firm and its strategy is the remit of the Partnership Council, which is formed from a number of partners. The Executive Board is responsible for implementing the strategy and running the business, and is composed of the Managing Partner, group leaders and the heads of HR, finance and marketing. The heads of the support services – HR, IT, finance and marketing – each have teams of people reporting to them. These are not all large teams, and while the heads will be responsible for team members' careers, progression will typically be through personal development. Boyle says, 'If there's an HR officer in Norwich for example seeking to progress to a manager's position with no vacancy available, we would look to broaden that person's skills base.'

Everyone has an annual performance review, covering career and personal development and a subsequent salary review. Support staff are reviewed in March/April and receive salary updates in June, while fee earners are reviewed in June and receive salary updates in September.

## Remuneration

'Solicitors are paid at the market rate', says Boyle. 'Salaries are determined according to a complex mix of business performance, individual performance and what's happening in the market. There is a staff bonus scheme for all, linked to the overall performance of the firm. Company cars are offered for business need rather than a perk – with four offices, heads of support services need a car for travel between the offices. There is a defined contribution pension scheme after three months' service, with a minimum of 2.5 per cent of gross pensionable salary. Mills & Reeve contributes 4.5 per cent.'

There are many employee benefits. Immediately on joining, there are 25 days holiday, an extra day at Christmas, bonus week in every 11th continuous year of service; life assurance; car parking; childcare vouchers; ICAS confidential life management support and counselling service; paternity leave; discounted rate BUPA private health subscription; sick pay; discounts with Virgin Wines; wedding leave. After one year, there's free residential conveyancing. After two years, permanent health insurance. After five years' continuous service, there's the option of moving to the higher rate personal pension scheme – four per cent of gross pensionable salary with eight per cent contributions from Mills & Reeve.

Summer 2003 sees the 170 staff in Norwich relocating to new offices, with staff restaurant facilities. Similarly, the facilities at Cambridge are being upgraded to incorporate updated dining and refreshment areas, while Birmingham features break-out rooms, rest areas and refreshment facilities.

## The Future

Mills & Reeve intends to maintain a position in the top 50 UK law firms measured by number of lawyers, turnover and profitability. It will do this by organic growth and increased focus on its chosen sectors, growing both organically and by taking advantage of opportunities to secure teams of specialist lawyers.

Having already seen senior recruits attracted to the firm because of its distinctive culture, the firm wants to build on that culture to enable it to compete for the best available talent. 'The work/life balance here provides the opportunity', says Boyle. 'With the male:female ratio in the workplace changing, we have found we can respond and adapt relatively easily.'

Mills & Reeve has no stated objective to seek a merger nor to open overseas offices. It intends to build on its policy of 'best friends' with firms such as Trask Britt and its membership of an international law group.

Summing up? 'We're a leading regional law firm with ambitious growth plans', says Boyle. Neatly put.

Pinnacle psg is the UK's leading provider in the small but fast-growing field of outsourced housing management and related services. It currently manages or provides services to around 100,000 homes, mostly in London. The privately-owned company employs more than 460 staff, and estimates its turnover for 2002–3 at £18 million (up from £9.9 million in 2001–2 and £8.7 million in 2000–1).

**Scorecard:**

| | |
|---|---|
| Remuneration and benefits | *** |
| Progressive attitude | **** |
| Opportunity for promotion | ***** |
| Training, development and education | **** |
| Working atmosphere and environment | *** |

**Biggest plus:**
A fast-growing, progressive company with a big mission and plenty of opportunity.

**Biggest minus:**
The immaturity of the market means Pinnacle must work hard to justify itself and satisfy demanding customers.

Pinnacle psg
4th Floor
Charter House
2 Farringdon Rd
London EC1M 3HN
Tel: 020 7017 2000
Fax: 020 7017 2099
Website: www.pinnacle-psg.com

# Pinnacle

## The Business

Pinnacle psg is the UK's leading provider of outsourced housing management and related services, managing around 40,000 homes and providing services to a further 60,000. Founded in 1988 to manage private sector housing, the company formed a social housing operation in 1994 to manage council and housing association properties. Since then it has grown rapidly, and now employs more than 460 people, and estimates its turnover for 2002–3 at around £18 million. The company has projects in Edinburgh, Milton Keynes and Kent and is planning further expansion, but so far the great majority of its business has been in London.

*Pinnacle aims to change the way public sector services are delivered by making them more accountable and more relevant to the individual or community*

Pinnacle works for local authorities and housing associations as well as universities, schools, hospital trusts and developers. Its services include housing and neighbourhood management (collecting rent, managing empty properties, dealing with tenant enquiries, handling budgets and repairs, etc), estate services (eg cleaning and grounds maintenance), community development (including sports coaching, youth clubs, arts projects and trips for the elderly), call centres, professional services (eg surveying, architectural and planning supervision), consultancy, and technology outsourcing.

Although some forms of outsourcing are commonplace in the public sector, outsourcing of housing management is only just beginning, and Pinnacle is at the forefront of the revolution. 'We're the only public sector outsourcing company dealing directly with the community', says Pinnacle's chief operating officer, John Swinney. 'We're trying to change the way services are delivered in the public sector.'

## Company Culture and Style

Pinnacle aims to change the way public sector services are delivered by making them more accountable and more relevant to the individual or community. This can be a hard task, both physically (40 per cent of employees are manual workers) and because some local authorities are not yet used to the give-and-take which a successful outsourcing relationship entails. But it is also a rewarding task, says Swinney. 'People enjoy working for us', he says. 'It's hard graft, but we encourage them to feel empowered to do things the way they want. When we take on existing employees as part of a new contract, our ability make them our biggest advocates is testimony to the success of our approach.'

The company is egalitarian. Several directors have worked their way up from the shop floor, there are no private offices with plush carpets, and everyone gets virtually the same holidays and benefits. 'People often talk about Pinnacle as a family', says Swinney.

Its customers feel the same way. 'When you visit an estate, the tenant representatives sometimes come up and give you a kiss, because they're so grateful that you're making a difference to their lives', says Swinney. 'We've got cleaners who do the shopping for the old people on their estates and groundsmen who do old people's gardens in their spare time.'

Asked about the typical Pinnacle employee, Swinney says: 'People who want to work hard, grow, take the initiative and do things.' Nor is the company afraid to employ a few 'characters' or mavericks.

Rapid growth is putting pressure on the company's organisation, and the raw enthusiasm of the directors and senior management will soon need to be supported by a more formal, procedural approach. But the company is very hot on communication and innovation, and although 80 per cent of staff have a public sector background, the culture is entrepreneurial. 'People joining us from the public sector find us a breath of fresh air', says Swinney.

The company is happy with flexible working hours and home-working, dress codes are relaxed, and ethnic and social diversity are encouraged. The gender balance is about 50/50, although the frequency of evening meetings seems to have made women reluctant to serve as directors.

## Human Resources

Most of the work done by Pinnacle is fairly straightforward, so the company sets more store by attitude and aptitude than paper qualifications or direct experience, since the latter can be trained in or acquired on the job. Some staff have MSc's in housing from London University, others are school-leavers. A number have been recruited through Pinnacle's Brighter Futures initiative, a six-month community programme aimed at getting long-term unemployed people skilled and into work; begun in the London Borough of Haringey, Brighter Futures is being extended to other London boroughs and to Edinburgh.

Brighter Futures is typical of Pinnacle's approach. 'We'd much rather employ local people, because they're more committed and stay with us longer, and we have very few temporary staff', says Swinney. Staff turnover is about average for the sector at 22 per cent (17 per cent for white-collar workers), but it is falling, and Pinnacle aims to get the figure down to 15 per cent during 2003.

People usually join Pinnacle to work on a particular contract, and receive induction training locally. After a month or two, they attend a one-day induction course at head office, meeting the Board for a drink, as well as more recently-joined staff working at the sharp end.

# Career Opportunity and Development

More than half of Pinnacle's staff work in its housing offices, collecting rent, managing empty properties, dealing with tenant enquiries, handling budgets and repairs, etc. There are also consultants and professionals such as surveyors, as well as cleaners and groundsmen. Promotion opportunities are good. Three of the directors have risen from the 'shop floor' level of housing manager, and almost all senior managers have been promoted at least twice during their time with Pinnacle.

The company likes to empower staff to develop their careers. People who want to move jobs – whether to gain promotion, to learn new skills, or for personal reasons are either encouraged to apply for new posts through the Internal Staff Vacancy Scheme or can join the Staff Transfer List. These initiatives account for around 95 per cent of all moves within the company. 'The transfer list has been one of our best innovations', says Swinney, 'and together with our commitment to advertising every vacancy internally, people can feel they have control over their own destiny.'

There is a formal Performance Management Scheme for all staff, who receive twice-yearly reviews with their line manager, and there are development and training plans for both individuals and teams. Staff are helped to gain further qualifications, including MSc, MBA and professional qualifications such as housing management or accountancy. Training is given in personal and business skills, and top-tier managers are groomed for potential places on the Board through the Management Development Programme.

People who prefer to be 'doers' rather than managers are also supported – this is not a company where you are written off if you don't just want to shin up the greasy pole, and technical expertise is prized as highly as management ability. The company has a Knowledge Management Scheme to enable staff to publicise their skills, knowledge and interests across the company; if you want to pick someone's brains on a business problem, or find the other Wimbledon supporter, the knowledge management database will tell you where to look. Pinnacle has had Investors in People certification since 1997.

# Remuneration

Salaries at Pinnacle are similar to those in the public sector and housing associations, since these are the main points of reference, and around 25 per cent of Pinnacle's staff are still on public sector pay scales, having joined the company under TUPE (Transfer of Undertakings Protection of Employment) legislation. On top of this the company pays bonuses, usually related to performance against client contracts. Directors receive bonuses based on the whole company's performance.

Everyone gets 25 days' holiday (unless they qualify for more under TUPE). Health insurance and death in service benefits are available to all staff, and everyone gets a pension. This is final salary if guaranteed under TUPE, otherwise money-purchase with the company contributing 7 per cent (or 10 per cent for directors – their only 'perk'). Company cars are very rare. Employment contracts can be flexible, for example allowing people to take sabbaticals, adjust their hours during school holidays, etc.

Share ownership is encouraged, and around a quarter of staff now own options or shares, including many manual workers. Overall, around five per cent of Pinnacle is owned by its staff. 'We'd like everybody to own shares in the company; it can really change their attitude to their work', says Swinney. Each year the company sets aside share options for staff at all levels who 'go the extra mile' – with excellent customer service, new ideas, excellent performance, or simply showing a passion for their job. Because Pinnacle is a private company, staff who leave must sell their shares.

## The Future

The market for housing and neighbourhood management in the public sector is still in its infancy. According to Pinnacle, the number of homes where management has been outsourced is just 55,000, out of a potential market of 2.8 million council homes and 1.4 million housing association properties. So although Pinnacle is the largest company of its kind in the UK, it is aiming for rapid expansion – including branching out from its London heartland – and hopes to be managing 250–300,000 homes in 3–5 years. 'We're operating in a massive market that's only just starting to happen', says Swinney.

Pinnacle's aim is to become the local authority's agent in an area, not just managing housing but providing a fully integrated service for the community, potentially including education, social services and health. 'For everything that touches residents, we will be able to deliver the service, or we will know someone who does', says Swinney. 'We want to make a profound difference to the way public services are offered in this country.'

# PriceWaterhouseCoopers

PricewaterhouseCoopers is the world's largest professional services organisation, serving the whole range of blue chip corporate marketplaces, mid-tier and non-profit organisations, public sector and governments worldwide. PwC operates in over 140 countries and employs 125,000 people in many professional disciplines. There are many career paths possible within the UK firm, and options available to suit people with a variety of strengths and aspirations. If you wish to rise to partner status, the firm will welcome you – but if family or personal commitments are a greater priority, or if your career plans do not include admission to partnership, then as long as you can match your career plans and talents to PwC's business needs, there will be a place for you at PricewaterhouseCoopers.

**Scorecard:**

| | |
|---|---|
| Remuneration and benefits | **** |
| Progressive attitude | ***** |
| Opportunity for promotion | **** |
| Training, development and education | **** |
| Working atmosphere and environment | **** |

**Biggest plus:**
The opportunity to develop business skills rapidly, through varied, challenging work and early responsibility, supported by unrivalled training and coaching support – with the ultimate goal of partnership for those willing and able to go for it.

**Biggest minus:**
Not for the faint-hearted or for those shy of taking ownership of their own career development.

PricewaterhouseCoopers
1, Embankment Place
London WC2N 6NN
Tel: 020 7583 5000
Website: www.pwcglobal.com/uk/careers/

# PricewaterhouseCoopers

## The Business

PricewaterhouseCoopers is one of the longest-established professional services organisations in business, with its origins dating back to 1849. The current structure is the result of a merger between Price Waterhouse and Coopers and Lybrand in 1998.

Its status as a leading player is confirmed by the fact that it serves 70 per cent of the FTSE companies. In the UK it employs some 15,000 people. The services it offers its clients include audit, tax, merger and acquisition management, business advisory services, human resource consulting and, through a tie-up with its correspondent law firm, Landwell, legal services. It sold its stand-alone IT consultancy in 2002 to IBM.

*On visiting one of the firm's premises at Embankment Place in London it is refreshing to see the emphasis being so firmly on people rather than solely on their output. This in turn leads to positive business results*

Significant emphasis is placed on the needs of the clients, which might mean working extended hours for periods of time, or work schedules changing at short notice. Flexibility is the key and this expected level of commitment is balanced with flexible working, which allows employees to take time off to compensate for this.

## Organisation Culture and Style

The above section may make the firm sound a pretty serious, hard-working organisation – and indeed in terms of delivering results for clients, it's a highly charged environment. On visiting one of the firm's premises at Embankment Place in London, however, it is refreshing to see the emphasis being so firmly on people rather than solely on their output. This in turn leads to positive business results.

Jackie Gittens, head of PwC's professional HR team, explains that the firm's core values are Excellence, Leadership and Teamwork. The scope for people with different skills is of course substantial; the skills of the people who are working in IT may share little in common with those of the Human Resource Consulting staff, for example, who in turn will be different from those in the auditing and business advisory practice. Perhaps more interesting is the recognition that different employees will want different things from PwC. 'There will be some people to whom nothing is more important than becoming a partner, so they'll want to concentrate on rapid career advancement.' says Gittens. 'Others will find other aspects of their lives are more of a priority, so they'll want a different work/life balance, without being any less dedicated to their job. We want to accommodate people of both sorts, as long as they can add value to our business and our clients.'

This approach involves a renewed emphasis on results rather than actual hours worked in the office, and an allowance for flexible working, which has been made possible by technology advances in recent years. The bottom line is that the business must grow and be served by its staff, but if someone can achieve that in a nine-day fortnight (to use an actual example) or through working some of the time from home, that's fine. Essentially, if someone wants to work in a particular way, and can make a business case for doing so, the firm can be flexible.

The result is a high level of employee satisfaction; the business leaders commission quarterly independent surveys on how people feel, and the results have been encouragingly positive. Staff retention is high as a result.

## Human Resources

PricewaterhouseCoopers recruits at all levels, starting not with graduates but with work placements for schoolchildren of 16–17 over the summer holidays so that people can get an idea of the firm and its values as early as possible – during 2002 there were some 200 'A' level students on the premises. Student entry works with PwC visiting colleges, as might be expected of any substantial concern. More mature, experienced entrants to the business are also welcome, and the firm recruits from a huge range of skills and backgrounds.

The focus on the needs of each individual is a key theme in how PwC cares for its people. For example there is a confidential counselling telephone line for employees who need advice on any personal or work-related issues; many staff work part-time or flexible hours, or take extended leave or career breaks to focus on family responsibilities, to travel or to achieve other goals; there are opportunities to work overseas at appropriate stages in your career; and when people leave PwC, that's not seen as a barrier to coming back: over 600 people returned to PwC during 2002, having tested the water outside – a figure of which Gittens is proud.

## Career Opportunities and Development

The opportunities for advancement within this, one of the world's biggest business service concerns, is simply vast. Some may see their natural role as heading up PwC in Australia. If so, they must make the case for it, talk to their career counsellor, partners and HR, and build towards it. It won't be out of the question, although clearly the top jobs attract the most competition. Equally, of course, individuals who are not performing, and who fail to improve after due counselling, will find their prospects with the firm distinctly limited.

The firm is very much geared up to attract self-starters, and the people who flourish will be those who think about the sort of niche in which they want to operate and who are willing to find out about opportunities, link their own career aspirations to the needs of the business, and go for it. A considerable investment is made in training and developing people to meet business needs, and staff are expected to seek out the most appropriate learning opportunities from a vast range of options. This is part of the firm's philosophy of self-awareness; employees from the entry-level staff up to and including partners are encouraged to be aware of their position within the business and how they fit into it in terms of asking for help and input where necessary, and to take the role of coach for less-experienced colleagues as required: there is little place for solo stars in PricewaterhouseCoopers.

It is therefore possible to structure your own career development within PwC and to get the training necessary for whatever your objective may be. More than most businesses, PwC is about people, and these living assets are encouraged to make the most of themselves!

## Remuneration

PwC strives to keep its salaries and its overall package competitive, and to differentiate remuneration as much as possible based on performance. The package includes a flexible benefits scheme, which allows individuals to choose from a range of options the benefits that will be of most value to them. This includes the option to take a slightly lower salary and increase your core holiday allowance of four weeks up to a maximum of six weeks. With flexible benefits, a 21-year-old might want an extra week's holiday or a car and not care very much about the various insurance arrangements available. A 40-year-old may have very different priorities, and can tailor his or her benefits package to allow for this.

## Future

PricewaterhouseCoopers sees its future very much in continuing its market lead and widening the gap with its competitors. So, in spite of difficult economic conditions and the need (in common with most organisations) to make some tough decisions about redundancies, PwC has never stopped actively recruiting, but has remained focused on the need to renew itself continuously with fresh energy, diverse skills and new talent to secure its long-term profitability.

PwC does not simply employ people – it *is* the people who work there, and its success depends upon its ability to continue attracting the largest cadre of the brightest and best graduates in the UK, and then giving them the best training and experience available, so that they will want to stay and be a part of PwC's ongoing success story. To do that, PricewaterhouseCoopers is committed to continuous improvement in providing the challenge, variety, development opportunities, support, autonomy, recognition and reward that their diverse and highly talented people crave.

# REUTERS

Reuters is one of the world's leading providers of financial intelligence and news on a worldwide basis, supplying written, video and Web-based stories to the leading news outlets of the world, including the BBC, CNN and others. Quoted in London and on the Nasdaq market, it has an organisational structure that ensures its complete independence and ability to adhere to a specific set of values at all times and it doesn't fight shy of controversy – refusing to refer to the 11 September attackers as terrorists, for example, since this is a value judgement it believes a neutral service shouldn't take.

**Scorecard:**

| | |
|---|---|
| Remuneration and benefits | **** |
| Progressive attitude | *** |
| Opportunity for promotion | **** |
| Training, development and education | *** |
| Working atmosphere and environment | *** |

**Biggest plus:**
The people and the brand.

**Biggest minus:**
The company's success is often dependent on that of the financial markets it serves.

Reuters
85 Fleet Street
London EC4P 4AJ
Tel: 020 7250 1122
Fax: 020 7542 9055
Website: www.reuters.com

# Reuters

## The Business

Reuters is identified in the public eye as a news gatherer, but it's worth noting that 90 per cent of its revenues actually derive from its information service offered to the financial and media sectors. The general news service has recently been extended to appear on the company's website for public consumption – until November 2002 this website consisted mostly of corporate profiling.

Some 2,400 editorial people work for the company, which is just over a century and a half old. It is the world's largest news and television agency, comprising 197 bureaux in 130 countries. Taking into account the non-editorial staff as well, the company employs 16,000 people.

The numbers concerning its productivity are impressive. It generates 30,000 headlines (including those from third parties) and eight million words in 16 languages, daily. 511,000 professionals use the service, spread over 52,900 locations. It provides information on over 960,000 shares, bonds and other financial instruments, and information on 40,000 companies. It draws financial information from 244 exchanges and OTC markets and updates its financial data 8,000 times per second.

> *If one word were to sum up the feel of Reuters then it's 'multicultural' – the parochial needn't consider applying for any vacancies*

It's serious about what it does and its brand reputation is such that it cannot afford to do it other than perfectly. It is quoted on the London Stock Exchange and Nasdaq and has a Founder Share Company owning a single Founder's Share that can be used to overrule any others in the event of someone else trying to introduce any bias; the result is that its 150 million data records and 3,000 billion data fields therein are among the most highly-regarded in the world. It supplies news to the people the public think of as the news gatherers.

## Company Culture and Style

If one word were to sum up the feel of Reuters then it's 'multicultural' – the parochial needn't consider applying for any vacancies. Fluency in a second language is an absolute must for journalist graduate entrants and this does mean fluency – GCSE French won't cut it. It's a business that is proud of the highest standards of independence so anyone not buying into this completely will not fit.

Like a lot of large companies it has some overtly stated values, which include: independence, accuracy, and the speed with which it reports on things.

It therefore feels a lot like a privately-owned company and the speed makes it feel like a smaller one, when in fact it went public in 1984. It retains an informal feeling as long as the results are being achieved. Dress is best described as business casual unless a major client is about to be met, in which case common sense tends to prevail.

The biggest buzz staff get out of working for the company, though, has to be the one that arises from the brand. 'The brand is fantastic', says Mark Sandham, HR Director. 'It has global reach and is extremely well-known and well-regarded in the marketplace.' No book written by professional journalists is going to disagree with that. Reuters supplies news to the people who write the news and remains fiercely proud of its reputation.

It is forward-looking in many respects. At director level, 23 per cent are female, and throughout the company 18 per cent of the top 300 people are female. The company wants to build this up and considers that the next wave of female management is now coming through the ranks. The approach to flexible working is, to an extent, dictated by the work; if the news is happening at a given time then, no, clearly you can't work when you feel like it; home working is an option, though, and of course many of the service elements of the company (IT etc) are not constrained in the same way as the editorial team might be.

## Human Resources

Getting into the company to enjoy the benefits isn't a pushover, though. A second and preferably third language is a must for editorial graduate entrants; the minimum degree level for people on the graduate recruitment scheme is a 2.1. Overseas readers will want to note that excellent English is obligatory for working in the UK, and people need three 'B's at 'A' level to be considered without a degree.

Those without academic qualifications but with relevant experience will, of course, be considered on their merits. Outside of the editorial community there isn't a 'typical Reuters' profile as there is with some other companies; the jobs will dictate the skills required and those needed by the IT staff, for example, will differ widely from those in the HR and other service departments.

## Career Opportunity and Development

Once a candidate has accepted the stringent criteria for entry into one of the world's top news agencies, the scope for personal development and indeed moving between disciplines is considerable. As this book went to press, the acting HR Director worldwide had a background in litigation, for example, and employees wanting experience of other areas within the company need only ask their line managers for advice. Clearly there needs to be a business case for the extra training that will be required but Reuters is pleased to provide it once the need has been established. The structure is open enough for people to move up within the organisation but it's also open at all levels to outsiders – the management combines Reuters veterans with people with backgrounds from other companies.

Training is done both in-house and in partnership with the University of Michigan. Positions that occur are always advertised on the company Intranet, but employees should be well aware that competition is frequently fierce and there is no culture of 'jobs for the boys' at this equal opportunities employer. There is definite scope for international travel; the company sees itself as global in nature and staff wanting to take advantage of this are encouraged to do so.

There is an extensive section on careers on the company website, containing not only information on vacancies but also frequently asked questions and information on the current management team.

## Remuneration

Many of the benefits on offer to Reuters employees are common to all major companies – health insurance, pension and the 'usual suspects' are all present and correct. Share savings schemes run throughout the company – whilst compiling this profile the Corporate Research Foundation's man jokingly said 'what, so the receptionist's a shareholder' – and was told, politely, that indeed she was. Options and other benefits kick in at different levels depending on the job and indeed the territory in which an individual is working; different legislations will apply to stock benefits in different countries.

There is a lot of performance-related pay and this benefits most of the staff since the business attracts self-starters and people who pride themselves on working at an optimum level most of the time.

## Future

The tricky thing about talking of the future for a company like Reuters is that it is already effectively where it wants to be, as a world leader in its field. Sandham talks about continuing to be at the forefront of providing information to the financial marketplace, but this is hardly a revelation since it's already happening.

A number of things can be said with some certainty. In HR terms it will always aim to be ahead of any employment legislation and treat its employees better than its legal obligations say it must. It has won awards from *HR Magazine* already and plans to add more of those. More globally, the business aims to continue growing. It will remain steadfastly independent and guard its reputation for accuracy and timeliness in its reportage.

Overwhelmingly, Reuters is a brand for excellence in reportage and it plans to continue this, whilst growing its financial reports for corporate customers. There seems to be no reason to doubt it should succeed in doing so.

In less than 25 years, Richer Sounds has grown from a standing start to become the largest retailer of hi-fi equipment in the UK with an annual turnover of more than £100 million. Remarkably, for the last 11 years it has been the company with the world's highest volume of sales per square foot – as testified by the Guinness Book of Records. It has 49 stores in the UK and two in the Republic of Ireland, and employs 400 people. Not surprisingly, *Business Age* has called the company's founder Julian Richer 'a marketing legend'.

### Scorecard:

| | |
|---|---|
| Remuneration and benefits | **** |
| Progressive attitude | ***** |
| Opportunity for promotion | **** |
| Training, development and education | ***** |
| Working atmosphere and environment | **** |

### Biggest plus:
'It's fast moving, it's dynamic and it's fun – we take the business seriously but not ourselves.'

### Biggest minus:
'It's demanding, it's hard work and there's nowhere to hide.'


Richer Sounds Plc
Recruitment House
1a New Street
City of London
London EC2M 4TP
Tel: 020 7626 8006
Website: www.richersounds.co.uk

# Richer Sounds

## The Business

A number of companies in this book have set their industry alight by transforming the concept of customer service. Richer Sounds is another example. In 1978, Julian Richer was just 19 years old and had a limited amount of funds behind him. What he also had, though, was far more valuable: a belief that people wanted to buy good hi-fi equipment, and an understanding that customer service was often sadly lacking in the hi-fi business.

He therefore set about putting his principles into practice. His start was modest: he bought a small shop in the London Bridge area and piled stocks of hi-fi units into it. But while the shop may have been unprepossessing, the customer service was impressive. Word soon spread that here were people who knew about hi-fi – and, even more importantly, treated customers with friendly respect and professional standards, not with the disdain sometimes shown in hi-fi stores. Richer Sounds had arrived.

*Julian Richer's concept of customer service is paralleled by a similar concept of employee treatment. His famous saying, 'We are into the twenty-first century and most employers are in the stone age' has been widely quoted and attracted considerable media interest*

Richer Sounds is now the UK's largest and most profitable retailer of hi-fi equipment. The company has 49 stores in the UK, with two in the Republic of Ireland organised on a franchise basis. The philosophy of its UK store placements is that every city with a population of over 250,000 has access to a Richer Sounds store within half an hour's drive. Over one million people use the company's stores every year, and its product range has expanded to include budget audio, high quality reference products, home cinema equipment and lifestyle systems.

## Company Culture and Style

There is no denying that Richer Sounds is a great place to work. This is the view of its people, backed up by external accolades. The latest of these was when the company was placed third in the Sunday Times Top 100 UK Companies to Work For – and first in terms of British-owned companies.

The reason for this is simple. Julian Richer's concept of customer service is paralleled by a similar concept of employee treatment. His famous saying, 'We are into the twenty-first century and most employers are in the stone age' has been widely quoted and attracted considerable media interest.

Richer wants his shops to be fun, non-intimidating and characterised by the feel of a club that is free to join. Browsers are welcome. To achieve all this, though, requires treating the employees in a special way. As Richer says, 'We spend a fortune doing things for colleagues that you need to do so they will put themselves out for customers.' That word 'colleagues' sums up a great deal of the philosophy.

Richer's colleagues have carte blanche when it comes to assisting customers. As he puts it, 'when it comes to sorting out a customer's problem, there are no rules.' *Business Age* lauded Richer Sounds as 'leading a revolution in staff culture and customer service', and the key to both would seem to be colleague stimulation. People enjoy working for Richer Sounds because they are well-treated and empowered. They can make a difference and are encouraged to do so – for the past seven years, Richer Sounds has won the UKASS award for the largest number of suggestions per head.

As you might expect, there are no specific dress rules apart from 'not looking scruffy': here, as elsewhere, Richer expects his colleagues to use their common sense and treat people as they themselves would like to be treated. Similarly, staff need to avoid strong-smelling food and drink for at least 12 hours before starting work. In general, it seems, colleagues are happy to comply with these hardly-rigorous requirements in return for working in a fun, enjoyable and rewarding environment.

## Human Resources

When it comes to recruiting people, the same kind of fresh approach is to be found as characterises the rest of the business. Richer: 'We want friendliness and love of hi-fi – not good looks or selling experience.' In the same way, paper qualifications count for nothing at Richer Sounds. Personality is the key.

People would be welcome to rejoin the business – but there are very few in a position to do so, for the simple reason that most are still working for the company! Richer Sounds has a very low staff turnover rate: not surprisingly, given its excellent rewards and the 'twenty-first century' way it treats its people. There are five-year and ten-year clubs, for instance, and there are many in the company with considerably longer service.

The company is an equal opportunities employer. The aim of its policy in this area is 'to ensure that no job applicant or employee receives less favourable treatment on the grounds of their sex or sexual orientation, race, colour, nationality or ethnic or national origins, or is disadvantaged by conditions or requirements which cannot be shown to be justifiable'. This is part of a code of conduct that applies similarly rigorous tenets throughout the company's operations.

## Career Opportunity and Development

The distinctive treatment of Richer Sounds' colleagues begins the moment they join the company: they are sent on a three-day induction course, and there is further training for everyone later down the line. This attitude underlines Richer's philosophy that 'our people are our most prized asset'.

In some businesses, appointments from outside the company can cause tension and frustration, and even result in disgruntled employees leaving the company altogether. This never happens at Richer Sounds, for the simple reason that all promotions are made from within the company! Job vacancies are disseminated throughout the business, and people are encouraged to move between jobs and between stores. With such a wide UK network, the company finds that when people move home, perhaps because of their partner's job, there is often an opportunity to transfer to another Richer Sounds store.

Colleagues are encouraged to take responsibility for their self-development, and for those who want to progress there is really no limit to the possibilities offered at Richer Sounds – always provided that their enthusiasm, attitude and customer focus remain in place. Additional training is offered to those who want it, to help them develop their product skills.

Another distinctive aspect of Richer Sounds is its career counselling approach, something that is enshrined within the company's philosophy. Basically, anyone in the company can go to anyone within Richer Sounds for career counselling – and this includes going to Julian Richer himself.

All performance and salary reviews are conducted regularly, and certainly more frequently than the annual basis favoured by some employers. As Richer says, 'If you want to know what your people think, which we do, then you need to listen to them – and once a year just isn't good enough.'

# Remuneration

Considering the often lowly-paid nature of retailing, Richer Sounds' remuneration is very good: an 18-year-old sales assistant can make over £20,000 a year. It is also scrupulously fair. One of the things that makes Richer Sounds fun to work for, though, is the system of rewards available on top of the good pay. This approach is summed up on the company's website: 'We reward good old-fashioned hard graft with an excellent salary, generous incentives, a host of exciting benefits and unparalleled career opportunities.'

Those incentives include company-owned holiday homes, which all staff can use, entirely free of charge. These include ten homes in the UK and even in Spain, Holland, Italy and France. The five-year staff club mentioned earlier can also enjoy a range of rewards including lunch at London's Ritz Hotel.

The policy on incentives is summed up by Richer: 'They're many and varied – because it makes sense to spread smallish rewards around rather than to dispirit and annoy almost everyone because a few people have scooped the pool.'

Holidays start at 20 days a year. This increases by a day for each year served above five years, up to a maximum of 25 days.

## The Future

The company has grown its success on stores that have tended to be crammed with hi-fi units and somewhat cramped, in favour of outstanding service by the colleagues. This 'cheap and cheerful' image has been in line with Julian Richer's declared belief that he would rather spend money on his people. Certainly, feedback shows that most staff have been happy with this approach. Nevertheless, it is now a Richer Sounds aim to improve the working environment of its stores.

This could be a challenge; creating barriers and potentially alienating customers, and indeed coming to resemble some of the more traditional stores that Richer set out to replace. However, Richer is determined to achieve some middle way. 'Just because it's difficult doesn't mean it can't be done.'

Continued expansion is the other main ambition for Richer Sounds. The company plans to have up to another ten stores in the UK by the end of 2003.

Many high-street retailers have encountered problems in expanding, or even surviving, in the testing economic climate of recent years. However, Richer Sounds' special feel, good value, and, above all, excellent customer service standards look to stand it in good stead for further growth.

Backed with a prestigious brand pedigree, Rolls-Royce is a world-leading power systems provider, designing, manufacturing and supporting a range of products and services for air, sea and land applications. Some 37,000 employees are located in over 30 countries, servicing the company's key markets of civil aerospace, defence aerospace, marine and energy. Highlights of the company's results in 2002 were underlying profits of £255 million on a turnover of just under £6 billion and a record order book of £17.1 billion. Rolls-Royce operates in four growth markets and has introduced online services to ease business transactions and increase the speed and quantity of information available to customers and suppliers.

**Scorecard:**

Remuneration and benefits ★★★★
Progressive attitude ★★★★
Opportunity for promotion ★★★★★
Training, development and education ★★★★★
Working atmosphere and environment ★★★★

**Biggest plus:**
A UK-based global leader in high-tech industry, this is an exciting and challenging company to work for, with a great future.

**Biggest minus:**
Not for those who don't like change and challenge.

Rolls-Royce plc
65 Buckingham Gate
London SW1 6AT
Tel: 020 7222 9020
Fax: 020 7227 9170
Website: www.rolls-royce.com

# Rolls-Royce

## The Business

Rolls-Royce will soon be 100 years old. Much has changed in the century that's passed. Today, this is a global company providing power for land, sea and air. The company has a balanced business portfolio with leading positions in civil aerospace, defence, marine and energy markets. There are now over 53,000 Rolls-Royce gas turbines in service, generating high-value services throughout their 25 to 40-year operational lives. Rolls-Royce is a technology company, to differentiate it from just an engineering company, and it is furthermore a leading technology concern. The engines it develops, manufactures and sells have a value by weight that's equivalent to the same weight of platinum. It takes base metals and produces valuable products through applying knowledge and technology. To do this, there are 39,000 people operating from over 30 countries across all continents.

*We have a robust business based on a strategic approach that builds on the common characteristics of power systems and an understanding of customers' service needs. We have excellent technology, products, services and people, and are well positioned for further growth*

Key financials are impressive – the 2002 interim results show profit before tax of £104 million, a record order book of £16.7 billion, and strong aftermarket services representing 41 per cent of sales and 29 per cent of the order book. With a coherent business model, there is a consistent strategy addressing four growth markets and investing in technology, capability and infrastructure.

In civil aerospace, Rolls-Royce is ranked world number two, powering 38 of the world's top 50 airlines. Its market share has tripled since the 1980s, notching up 32 per cent in the first half of 2002. Service revenues have more than doubled and repair and overhaul tripled over the past decade.

## Company Culture and Style

Chief Executive, John Rose, positions Rolls-Royce as a customer-focused organisation: 'We have a robust business based on a strategic approach that builds on the common characteristics of power systems and an understanding of customers' service needs. We have excellent technology, products, services and people, and are well positioned for further growth.'

Margaret Gildea, Director of Career Development, says, 'Rolls-Royce is driven to provide a working climate that enables freedom, energy and the ability to get the task done well and quickly.' Indeed, internal moves since strategic actions rooted in 1997 have been towards placing greater emphasis on trust and teamwork, with decisions taken in the best interests of Rolls-Royce. 'This all represents significant cultural change, and has necessitated a lot of internal education and communication.'

While customers, shareholders and suppliers are three of the four key constituents to financial success, the fourth is employees. 'Rolls-Royce recognises this and links the future of the company closely to its employees because it is they who will drive the continuing success of the company', says Gildea. This is a company operating at the cutting edge of advanced power technology, where the gifted scientist is able to stretch his or her skills and talents to the limit, assisted by the practical engineering, teamwork and entrepreneurial skills of all the company's employees, including the general managers and other specialists.

There are no rules on what to wear. Most people, however, are smartly dressed. As Gildea points out, 'we fit in with local culture because we are a global company'. There are a lot of talented people here and because of the company's long history, there are high-quality people of all ages. Common to all is the sense of pride. Engineering has long had a male image, which is reflected in the composition of the board of directors. But Rolls-Royce actively welcomes diversity and women in the company have every chance to achieve. 'There are no glass ceilings', says Gildea. 'We don't seek one personality type, but everyone must be capable of teamwork.' Rolls-Royce received the Investors in People accreditation at the end of 2001.

## Human Resources

'We have a large graduate and apprentice intake, and we operate a strong policy and tradition of promoting from within', says Gildea. 'It's quite possible to move from the bottom to the top. But while the company fosters long-term service, it's equally prepared to learn from outside too. If you're a world-leading company, you have to have world-leading people – and that means having the right balance between your own and expertise recruited from outside.'

If anyone leaves the company, it's always possible for them to rejoin, the view being that this can enrich the knowledge base and experience of the business, as well as adding an extra strategic dimension. Training is offered, linked to business needs. 'In 2001 our spend on training was £25 million', says Gildea. 'This is viewed as growing talent and capability from within.' All major Rolls-Royce sites have training centres. In the UK, the company's Derby site boasts the recently-built state-of-the-art Learning and Development Centre, which assists in propagating Rolls-Royce's culture of continuous learning. Rolls-Royce is investing increasing amounts of time and money in developing its employees to support the company's drive for quality and excellence. 'The people running Rolls-Royce have achieved tremendous results and demonstrated qualities such as self-confidence, integrity, innovation and judgement', says Gildea.

# Career Opportunity and Development

Everyone manages their own careers and the company shares with staff the responsibility for implementing individual plans. 'Remember we have a good order book. We are addressing four growth markets and thus have an excellent future. People want our products, whether it's for electricity, cruise ships, flying or defence', says Gildea. 'You could say we supply the infrastructure for living.'

Rolls-Royce has the know-how in technology business and a lot of investment in financial business. Its business is very long-term. Engines being sold today have minimum 25 to 40 year life spans, so the more being sold today, the greater the opportunity for selling services and spare parts. Some 41 per cent of overall revenues currently are sourced from services, and with more total care packages and joint ventures with airlines being initiated, this figure is expected to increase significantly in the years ahead. One of the fastest growth businesses for the company is in condition monitoring and predictive maintenance – diagnosing conditions in engines before they occur. Rolls-Royce will provide engines and technical capability for airlines in a 'power by the hour' scheme – for every hour an aircraft is in the air, the airline pays a fixed fee and Rolls-Royce ensures the engine will operate at maximum efficiency. Similar opportunities present themselves in the power, oil and gas pipeline, and ships businesses. All this presents a need for a new set of skills, a service mentality and exceptional customer focus.

HR teams within the company's business units offer support and advice on career opportunities. There is a personal development planning process, plus regular assessment and appraisal. There are opportunities to work overseas (key locations are in the US, Canada, Germany, Nordic countries, South America, and Australasia) and to move between the company's businesses. There is a parallel emphasis on general management and technical specialism.

# Remuneration

Rolls-Royce carefully monitors remuneration levels in other companies and makes sure that it is always able to offer attractive pay and progression to talented individuals. Extensive use is made of performance-related increases to base pay and employees are eligible each year for a bonus plan delivering up to two weeks' pay. Rolls-Royce provides all the benefits that would be expected of a company of its reputation and standing, ranging from sports and welfare facilities to support for education and training. Employees are encouraged to become shareholders in the company and there are currently three different share ownership plans, which all employees can choose to join. These plans offer ways of buying shares at a discount or receiving them free of income tax.

A Save As You Earn Sharesave plan, made available to all UK employees and those of the company's wholly-owned subsidiaries worldwide in September 2001, had a positive response from nearly 50 per cent of those eligible.

Across the whole of the company, Rolls-Royce's pension schemes are up with best practice. In the UK, company cars are viewed as a reward for certain levels of job. All employees have access to the company's car lease scheme, to lease chosen cars at favourable rates. There are various reward and incentive schemes running across the UK company. The fact that this must be a happy workforce is mirrored in the statistic that the average length of service per employee is over 25 years. Most people do stay with the company for a very long time.

## The Future

The future will see a move to services – more diagnosis, predictive maintenance and condition monitoring – with a continuing emphasis on the evolution of gas turbine technology in the company's four growth sectors. Rolls-Royce is ranked number two globally within its peer group, which also includes General Electric and Pratt & Witney.

To pick up on Chief Executive, John Rose's core message, the underpinning of the company's future strategy rests firmly on keeping all its customers satisfied. Currently, Rolls-Royce excels here. Being the company that it is, there is a keen awareness that technological leaders are judged by their weakest product and/or system. The brand pedigree associated with Rolls-Royce is legendary, and will remain so as long as the company's values continue to be embraced by its people. Indeed Rolls-Royce looks set to be a company that is 'trusted to deliver excellence' for a considerable time to come.

*The Royal Bank of Scotland Group*

The Royal Bank of Scotland Group, founded in 1727, is one of the UK's top 10 companies and is Scotland's largest company, Britain's largest corporate bank, the second largest bank in the UK and Europe and the fifth largest bank in the world. The superlatives continue – it is also the fastest-growing bank in the UK.

Its takeover of NatWest in 2000 has catapulted it into world prominence. It has worked hard and successfully at bringing NatWest comfortably into the fold, merging operations and IT systems, protecting and enhancing the individual brands, whilst continuing to acquire on a more modest scale. It is undoubtedly the jewel in Scotland's financial crown.

**Scorecard:**

| | |
|---|---|
| Remuneration and benefits | **** |
| Progressive attitude | **** |
| Opportunity for promotion | **** |
| Training, development and education | **** |
| Working atmosphere and environment | *** |

**Biggest plus:**
Matching ambition with prudence.

**Biggest minus:**
Liable to get so big that it is seen as being too big to care.

The Royal Bank of Scotland Group
42 St Andrew Square
Edinburgh EH2 2YE
Tel: 0131 556 8555
Fax: 0131 557 6565
Website: www.rbs.co.uk

# The Royal Bank of Scotland Group

## The Business

Royal Charter founded the Royal Bank of Scotland on May 31, 1727. The new bank opened for business in December 1727 and immediately began issuing its own bank notes. And it was the bank that invented the overdraft.

It has grown throughout the years by a series of mergers and acquisitions, with names like the Drummonds Bank, Williams Deacon's Bank and Child & Co. coming into its grasp.

The highlight was its successful bid in 2000 for the London-based National Westminster but its acquisitions have not been confined to these shores. In 1988 it acquired the Citizens Financial Group in New England, USA. Over the years Citizens has expanded and is now one of the 20 largest commercial bank holding companies in the USA. One observer noted: 'It is clear that the Royal Bank's expansion will be in the United States. This has never been a happy hunting ground for UK financial institutions but the Royal seems to be writing a different book', says Professor Charles Munn of the Chartered Institute of Scottish Bankers, quoted in *The Scotsman* newspaper.

*Key to its success is an entrepreneurial drive coupled with innovation and flexibility. Steering clear of unnecessary bureaucracy reinforces this and this approach is used internally and externally*

As Britain's largest corporate bank and one of Europe's oldest banking names, with over 114,000 employees world-wide and its head office in Edinburgh, it now employees more people in North America than in Scotland.

Individual parts of the Group have received a wide variety of accolades. Through its Corporate Finance Division it is one of the country's largest owners of aircraft, ships and trains. And through its Global Travel Money Services it is one of the world's largest bank note dealing operators.

## Company Culture and Style

The culture is based on growth, innovation and developing methods of securing the continued success of the Group. This approach is not typical of other financial services organisations. Individual businesses within the Group have also created cultures that are meaningful and motivating for their employees.

For example, the cultural environment in a major insurance call centre differs considerably from that in a corporate Group office. There remains, nevertheless, a single, overarching objective: to deliver sustainable value to shareholders, which the Group believes can be achieved by adding value to its customers.

The Group has a strong business ethos. Resources are focused on achieving against stretching performance measures and targets. Key to its success is an entrepreneurial drive coupled with innovation and flexibility. Steering clear of unnecessary bureaucracy reinforces this and this approach is used internally and externally. The Group's commercial success is gained through its responsiveness to customer needs and being speedy in its decision-making.

Employees are encouraged to take responsibility and to be accountable for their actions, to be open to new ideas and to be flexible in their approach to work. Employee development is regarded as critical to ensure that everyone is equipped to take the Group forward in its success. There has been heavy investment in e-learning and the Group has Europe's largest online learning platform, which will be developed further during 2003.

The Group regards all its decisions and ways of doing business as being fair, objective and based on ethical considerations and it declares that its aim is to treat employees with respect and consideration.

## Human Resources

The Group's new recruitment literature is being developed to highlight the inclusive approach towards recruiting for roles within the Group. It was designed with the help of all businesses in the Group and therefore targets a wide and diverse audience. All recruitment practices have been designed to ensure that they can easily be adapted to meet the individual needs of applicants where required.

The successful integration of NatWest employees and the development of the tools, platforms and equipment to support this has been a big task. This integration has not just been about employee terms and conditions or about computer systems, but more it has focused on dealing sensitively and appropriately with employees who have experienced a massive change.

Redundancies across the enlarged Group were inevitable and employees faced new management practices, busy colleagues with little time to spare and fresh faces joining old teams. It has been a huge challenge, which the Group has succeeded in.

The Group believes that one of its greatest challenges is to ensure that its workforce has the knowledge, experience and skills vital for its future. It is investigating opportunities to enhance its training and development programmes by working in partnership with major, internationally recognised business schools.

## Career Opportunity and Development

The integration of NatWest into the Group was in itself a great opportunity, with the creation of a new marketplace and employees being given a chance to shine.

Internal promotion opportunities have been significant as the Group continues to take advantage of its enhanced power and reputation.

The self-management of careers is strongly encouraged and there is a philosophy of individuals being responsible for their own development. There is a strong focus on job-related training and development, with the Group providing world-class learning opportunities.

The Group invests substantially in developing processes that identify high-potential talent at various stages in their career. The emphasis on development activities from these interventions has a major motivational impact on the talent across the Group.

Employees at all levels in the Group are given the chance to develop their career by seeking examinations or qualifications (eg up to and including MBAs) that are relevant to their role. The Group's role in employee development is to support appropriate learning. This can be in a number of ways, eg meeting the entire cost of the course or qualification and offering time off for study, revision and exams. This encouragement takes a step in a new direction in 2003 with the offer of financial incentives to employees who gain banking professional qualifications.

Career opportunity and development is seen as an important tool in the attraction and retention of the best people. This is possibly because of the complexity of the businesses, brands and divisions that make up the Group as a whole. The diverse nature of businesses and the wide geographical spread bring long-term career opportunities, that few organisations can match.

# Remuneration

The Group offers what it calls a 'results-driven reward structure, which recognises the different pay drivers of both the market and the individual'. This includes a market-related reward structure and a number of performance-based incentive and bonus schemes.

In addition to competitive salary and the opportunity to participate in an incentive or bonus scheme, benefits include Profit Sharing, a Sharesave scheme, and a non-contributory, final salary pension scheme. This is the last such scheme in the financial sector open to new employees and the Group regards it as a 'unique and significant benefit'. On average, the value of this pension is 17.5 per cent of annual salary. Additional voluntary contributions can be made, with the Group adding an extra five per cent on top of what the employee elects to put forward.

Furthermore, in 1998 the Group introduced a pioneering flexible benefits scheme with a wide range of benefit products such as competitive healthcare, discounted shopping vouchers, insurance-based protection, reduced childcare vouchers and the opportunity to buy or sell holiday entitlement.

Following the acquisition of NatWest, over 72,000 employees are now eligible to take part, making this one of the largest flexible benefit schemes in Europe. The Group-wide employee opinion survey shows that staff strongly appreciate this benefits package. There is a constant programme of review and improvement, the latest new options being telephone legal advice and a PC or laptop and improvements to dental and healthcare options. Alterations were also made to the calculations for buying and selling holidays to be more flexible for staff working non-standard hours, and greater discounts were negotiated so that the retail vouchers now offer typical savings of 5–10 per cent.

## The Future

The Group has well-developed succession plans and talent spotting programmes in place, and it believes that one of its greatest challenges is to ensure that it retains its workforce with the knowledge, experience and skills that will be vital to its future.

With NatWest successfully integrated, the Group has both acquisition and organic growth in mind. Ambition is not in short supply – its target growth areas include Europe and the United States.

In the US the Group is likely to make a significant impact. Group Chief Executive, Fred Goodwin, has turned his sights on further acquisitions and will make full use of his end-of-2002 accolade of being named by Forbes Global magazine as businessman of the year.

Forbes said: 'Fred Goodwin is hardly known in the States but he is definitely somebody Americans should be aware of.' America – you have been warned.

# *Saffery Champness*

## C H A R T E R E D    A C C O U N T A N T S

One of the UK's top twenty accountancy firms, specialising in providing expert financial and business advice to private clients and owner-manager businesses, Saffery Champness employs more than 400 people in ten offices, including two in Scotland and one in Guernsey. It has fostered a 'one firm' culture, offering hands-on, personal service, and takes a leading role in SC International, a worldwide association of accountants and business consultants.

**Scorecard:**

| | |
|---|---|
| Remuneration and benefits | ***** |
| Progressive attitude | **** |
| Opportunity for promotion | **** |
| Training, development and education | ***** |
| Working atmosphere and environment | **** |

**Biggest plus:**
The chance to work for diverse and interesting clients in a relatively relaxed but hands-on environment.

**Biggest minus:**
Small-scale operations limit career development for some.

Saffery Champness
Lion House
Red Lion Street
London WC1R 4GB
Tel: 020 7841 4000
Fax: 020 7841 4100
Website: www.saffery.com

# Saffery Champness

## The Business

John Joseph Saffery started his practice in the City in the mid-19th century and over ensuing years the firm has managed to remain strongly independent. Its last merger occurred in 1988 when it took over and renamed parts of rival firm Armitage & Norton.

Now the UK's 19th largest accountancy practice, Saffery Champness moved last year into new six-storey headquarters in central London, where client work is handled in three main groups: business advisory, investment and land, and tax.

In 2003, the number of partners will rise from 47 to more than 50. The firm serves mostly owner-managed businesses employing up to 300 people; consequently the firm's fee-earners tend to work on interesting but short-term projects, with considerable partner involvement.

*Although many of the firm's clients come from the higher echelons of British society, the firm aims to be a classless, relaxed meritocracy, placing an emphasis on supporting, training and delegating to others in a team setting*

Among clients are members of the aristocracy, barristers, Chelsea Football Club and more than 400 charities. The firm also has strong rural links. Many organisations have a longstanding connection with the firm, according to Jon Young, Head of Human Resources and HR Consultancy Services.

Saffery Champness plays a leading role in SC International, a global network of 140 firms in 50 countries. It has facilitated individual secondments, for example to the United States, Australia and South Africa.

Growing areas of business in the United Kingdom include corporate finance and work for charities. The tough economic climate has worked in the firm's favour: profits in the financial year ending in March 2003 are significantly up on a turnover of some £28 million. 'This year we have progressed on every financial measure', said Young.

## Company Culture and Style

Saffery recognises its most important asset to be its people, and welcomes a 'wide variety of backgrounds', which 'accordingly bring a diversity of knowledge and experience'. Although many of the firm's clients come from the higher echelons of British society, the firm aims to be a classless, relaxed meritocracy, placing an emphasis on supporting, training and delegating to others in a team setting. Employees cite its happy and stimulating working environment and the fact that 'the work is different every day'.

'The people we take on will have relatively fun-loving, friendly personalities. They tend to enjoy socialising, and they are not particularly ambitious. Boffins and nerds will not usually fit into our culture', said Young. Employees tend not to work long hours except for short bursts of intense activity on specific deals. Longstanding relationships with clients enable work to be planned in advance, enabling staff to maintain a sensible work/life balance.

Since 1994 the firm has conducted a regular attitude survey in which employees are given the opportunity to rate communication within their own units and within the firm, as well as management style, delegation and coaching, feedback and opportunities for professional development. In 1997, Saffery was only the second UK accountancy firm to gain Investors in People accreditation for all its operations.

Briefing meetings are held quarterly in every office, in which partners will give presentations, highlight key issues and answer questions. On a lighter note, each office holds an annual 'fun day' and other social events such as quiz nights.

While more than half of last year's intake of graduate trainees were female, just a quarter of senior managers in the firm are women. However, Saffery Champness strives to be flexible about working hours, taking pains to accommodate employees' choices. Young estimated that up to 20 per cent of people working for the firm have negotiated with local managers to agree patterns of work that vary from the norm.

Every employee is given his or her own desk as a private 'space' in which to work, and partners are linked to the office by broadband internet, enabling them to work from home.

## Human Resources

Saffery Champness takes on between 12 and 15 graduate trainees each year, but only participates to a limited degree in the milk-round of universities. Two years ago it launched an online selection process to pre-screen graduate applicants. Those who get through the personality, numeracy and other tests are invited for an assessment day: successful candidates are offered a job the same evening. Last year the rate of acceptance was 95 per cent.

'People come to us because they know we have a good name for training and they know that they are going to get a high degree of variability in clients. There is diversity, a lot of opportunity and more interesting work', said Young.

The new system has cut months and considerable cost out of the recruitment process, and also provides a safeguard against discrimination of candidates from ethnic minority backgrounds.

When seeking to recruit other accountants, the firm usually employs people who have specific technical expertise in markets where it is active. The firm has estimated it will need to recruit a new partner every three months to keep pace with its growth objectives – fortunately more people are now applying to join the firm at senior manager level or above.

# Career Opportunity and Development

Over the past few years, the firm has moved away from investment in external tutelage and now provides most of its courses, including student, technical and personal skills training, in-house.

The firm runs a 'performance and development' (PAD) review procedure annually, in which all partners and employees are asked to complete a lengthy assessment of their role and performance, supplemented by a six-month check to assess whether objectives are being achieved.

In due course this material will be updated and stored on an intranet system; some IT modules, as well as human resources policies and briefings, are already available to employees online.

All graduate trainees participate in a formalised coaching and mentoring system, alongside their three-year technical training that leads to accountancy qualifications. At a higher level, the firm has links with the Academy for Chief Executives and uses external mentors where appropriate.

There is a budget for each employee to attend training conferences, but most management skills training takes place in-house. Employees from manager level upwards are expected to participate in a two-day career development workshop, providing an opportunity to explore skills and strengthen weaknesses in support of their development, and in some cases preparation for partnership. Support staff are also encouraged to gain professional qualifications, sponsored by the firm.

Not many employees choose to study for further qualifications, such as the Masters in Business Administration, although the firm has been supportive of such requests when asked.

Partners are nominated and selected on the basis of a variety of skill areas. Upon achieving partnership status, individuals are encouraged to identify and develop work in niche interest areas and because of this, sectors such as entertainment and film are now a growing source of income for the firm.

# Remuneration

While other larger firms have been forced to freeze employee salaries, Saffery Champness's successes have meant it has continued to increase pay for staff. It now finds itself among the industry's better remunerators.

Salaries for staff are established via a complex set of calculations, incorporating advice from external advisers to create a salary range for each job position. Partners 'spend hours discussing every proposal to make sure that everyone is treated fairly', said Young.

Bonuses for senior managers are calculated on an individual basis and are rated against a set of five criteria. They can be as much as 20 per cent of pay. All staff share equally in a firm-wide profit-sharing plan, based on firm-wide performance.

The firm might be too small to offer an in-house gym or canteen, but instead it has pioneered a benefits package called Select, through which employees can choose to spend their allowance on a range of interchangeable benefits, including pension and holiday provision, private medical insurance, childcare vouchers, travel, dental and home insurance, health club membership, a car scheme and even a tax-efficient home computer purchase.

Last year, 70 per cent of Saffery Champness's employees used the package to vary their benefits.

## The Future

Broadly, Saffery Champness's aims are to remain independent and to continue to grow, as well as consolidate, its secure client base.

Internally, the firm will continue to innovate in the area of technology to increase value in the business. The focus in the near future is for the human resources function to migrate performance appraisal reviews to an electronically-based system, which can be streamlined and applied more effectively.

The plan for the firm as a whole is to grow by 35 per cent over a three-year period. 'We don't want to merge with anyone unless we come out on top', said Young. 'Over the years we have talked to most of the top twenty firms but if we want to retain our independence and people enjoy working here, why would we want to merge? Independence is an important cultural element for us.'

Sage is a publicly-quoted software house, which produces business software solutions – accounts, payroll, ebusiness, CRM – for 500,000 UK customers, from self-employed individuals to medium-sized companies, allowing those customers to grow without needing to change their supplier. It is fiercely committed to the community around its Newcastle HQ and turns over around £400 million per year.

**Scorecard:**

| | |
|---|---|
| Remuneration and benefits | *** |
| Progressive attitude | *** |
| Opportunity for promotion | **** |
| Training, development and education | **** |
| Working atmosphere and environment | *** |

**Biggest plus:**
Fast-changing environment will be stimulating to many.

**Biggest minus:**
Fast-changing environment will be extremely stressful to people wanting a stable routine – if this is you, don't apply.

Sage
Sage House
Benton Park Road
Gosforth
Newcastle Upon Tyne NE7 7LZ
Tel: 0191 255 3000
Fax: 0191 255 0308
Website: www.sage.co.uk

# Sage

## The Business

Sage is a business software house that has been in existence since 1981. It began when founder the late David Goldman wanted to develop an accounts system for his printing operation. He swiftly realised his customers would benefit from something similar and set to work on marketing his product. The organisation has now grown beyond recognition from those early beginnings, although recurring sales from printed forms such as invoices are still important to the business. During 2004 it will move into new premises at a newly-developed business park in Newcastle with Sage at the centre (it is hoped that the company will attract more technology businesses to the area). At the end of the same year Newcastle's newest and largest music centre – with recording studios, meeting halls and concert halls – will open under heavy sponsorship from the company, and will simply be called The Sage Gateshead.

*Sage's Newcastle head office has traditionally served the small business, which is a different customer to that served by the Thames Valley-based Enterprise division, and making everyone feel part of the team is an issue of which the directors have been made aware. Staff feedback remains positive, and the unification of at least the Newcastle end into a single building will help in this goal*

The business has grown both organically and through an aggressive acquisition policy. In recent years it has bought small business accounting specialist TAS Books and plans to maintain this separate product line alongside its own Instant Accounts product. At the upper end of the scale it bought Tetra Systems, now Sage Enterprise, and it has also made a strategic investment in buying Interact, a supplier of CRM and contact management software. These apparent departures will help flesh out the company's offerings in Customer Relationship Management systems, which allow a company to track every transaction with a customer so that any member of staff can be fully briefed at any time.

The company employs some 1,400 people and recruits around 150 per year.

## Company Culture and Style

Although growing and maturing, Sage retains the feel of a young and exciting company to work for, at least in part due to the efforts of HR Director, Karen Geary. She has spent some time in formalising the informal so that meetings and feedback sessions with directors, which used to happen spontaneously and informally, happen as a matter of routine.

Indeed, the whole company ethos and culture was undergoing something of a revamp as this book went to press. Focus on the customer and the employee and the balance between the two has always been vital to Sage, but only in late 2002 did the need to state some core values explicitly emerge. 'When you reach a certain size people expect you to have a formal statement about your values', explains Geary. The statement will focus on delivery of excellence to customers above all else and it's important to stress that this is a change in form rather than substance.

Another change is in the appointment of an internal communications manager, whose role is to ensure consistency of messages throughout the business and particularly to ensure feedback and comments can happen at all levels without engendering a blame culture. Staff focus groups have been set up and take place frequently to ensure people are feeling fulfilled, and the feedback has been positive to date.

Other issues have included the disparity of the companies within the Group. Sage's Newcastle head office has traditionally served the small business, which is a different customer to that served by the Thames Valley-based Enterprise division, and making everyone feel part of the team is an issue of which the directors have been made aware. Staff feedback remains positive, and the unification of at least the Newcastle end into a single building will help in this goal. Technology has also done a lot in this respect, in that people can log onto the corporate intranet, which is geared very much as an interactive guide and knowledge sharing resource, rather than the company rule book.

Most of the positions in Sage will involve working at one of its premises. There are some people in Research and Development working remotely but the take-up has not been great, and the culture remains very much biased towards being on the spot rather than working remotely.

## Human Resources

The HR team has seen its role alter from focusing on recruitment from the outside a few years ago to balancing this with staff development. Spending on internal development has all but quadrupled in 24 months, including the appointment of full-time staff with the brief of improving the lot of the team who are in place already. It is also looking into what to do about childcare – vouchers are among the options under consideration – and the continued auditing of employee feedback.

'We used to be very much based on a growth model, whereas now we're as focused on the people we have', says Geary. This increased focus was put to the test when during financial downturns across all industries Sage had to make redundancies for the first time in 2002: 'We limited it to managers', says Geary. 'I think everyone was a bit shocked because it hadn't happened before, but we handled it pretty well.'

As well as increasing the development of existing staff, recruitment to add to the skills available to the company continues apace. Graduate recruitment is ongoing and job vacancy information is always available on the website.

## Career Opportunity and Development

As has been stated already, the company is launching a number of initiatives to develop the skills of its employees to a greater extent than ever. One recent scheme involved taking some 'high fliers' out to work exclusively on new projects for a few days. 'That went down well', says Geary; 'There was an appreciation that the best new talents we had were on the front line; they know the products and the customers best and it's not always easy to find them.' Not that they should always need finding – making yourself known as a self-starter and a planner of your own career is key to successful employment at Sage.

To this end the company has launched a workshop for managers and employees entitled 'Managing Your Own Career', which offers an interactive session on developing career goals and personal ownership of your aspirations. Geary is adamant that the company will not encourage a spoon-fed culture. Reviews are another area to enjoy an overhaul and these now happen in a more structured way with a greater focus on development and achievement than before.

## Remuneration

Performance-related pay happens through around 70 per cent of the organisation and share ownership is open to everyone and option offers happen once you're in junior management; pay rates are healthy according to which region an employee is in (those in the North East do well as compared to the local market average; those in the South, though not underpaid, will notice less of a differential). Pay structures are likely to be a continuing issue in the light of Sage's policy of buying companies, since clearly pay structures prior to an acquisition by Sage will be beyond the company's control, but the money will need harmonising afterwards.

Health insurance, pensions and the raft of benefits one might call 'the usual suspects' are all in place. Although Sage continues to seek to offer its employees a better deal, it isn't a company that gets a lot of complaints about terms from those already in place.

## Future

Sage is making the transition between being a little start-up company to a more substantial operation and is putting management strategies in place accordingly. This includes a constant reappraisal of its pay structure and incentives to staff including those outside the obviously commission-driven sales area.

In terms of people, the company will continue to invest in its personnel, and the renewed focus on their development isn't going to go away. Encouraging the right people to come forward to grow the company both from within and externally is an equal priority for the moment, says Geary: 'The only thing holding the company back from growing more quickly is getting the talent in the right place where it can make a real difference.'

Looking at the business' growth and its ambitions not only for itself but for its local community you could be forgiven for wondering whether that's overly critical. One of the more consistent performers on the Stock Exchange and now in the arts, Sage's brand looks set to be around for some time.

# J Sainsbury plc

Sainsbury's is the UK's second-largest supermarket chain, with around 500 stores nationwide, ranging from out-of-town superstores to high street shops. The group, which also has interests in property and banking, a growing online business and a large US subsidiary, is in the middle of an ambitious corporate change programme. Sainsbury's employs about 170,000 people, and pre-tax profit in 2002 was £679 million on turnover of £18.2 billion.

**Scorecard:**

| | |
|---|---|
| Remuneration and benefits | **** |
| Progressive attitude | **** |
| Opportunity for promotion | ***** |
| Training, development and education | **** |
| Working atmosphere and environment | *** |

**Biggest plus:**
A strong sense of purpose and an ambitious change programme should make for an interesting and challenging career.

**Biggest minus:**
The tough grocery market is getting even tougher, with strengthening competition.

J Sainsbury plc
33 Holborn
London EC1N 2HT
Tel: 020 7695 6000
Fax: 020 7695 7610
Website: www.j-sainsbury.co.uk

# Sainsbury's

## The Business

John James and Mary Ann Sainsbury opened their first grocer's shop in Drury Lane, London in 1869, making the group, which still bears their name, the oldest supermarket chain in the UK. It was the biggest, too, until overtaken by Tesco in the 1990s – a blow to its self-esteem, and the catalyst for some serious soul-searching and streamlining.

This culminated in a mammoth business transformation programme – the largest in the UK, says Sainsbury's, and led by Chief Executive, Peter Davis – which is radically changing the group's stores, head office and supply chain operation. The company's mission is to be 'first for food', and much of the change programme is about building on the company's reputation for quality, service and competitive price in food, and transferring these values to the rest of its business.

*There are three basic streams – the stores (much the largest, of course), supply chain, and the business centre – but the company has deliberately made these more integrated. 'We believe our future leaders will have cross-business experience'*

Sainsbury's is no vanilla brand. The largest superstores can employ 800 people and turn over £80 million a year, while the growing number of in-town Sainsbury's Local stores offer more of a traditional experience, both in attitude and customer service as well as size.

In addition to around 500 UK stores, Sainsbury's has more than 200 stores in the USA under the Shaws brand, making it the second-largest food retailer in New England. It has one of the UK's largest property companies, with assets of around £4.5 billion, which develops mixed-use sites that include homes and leisure facilities as well as stores. Sainsbury's Bank, a joint venture with HBOS, is small but growing. And Sainsbury's To You is the UK's second-largest online grocery business, with sales of £110 million in 2002.

## Company Culture and Style

Sainsbury's new business centre in the heart of London is not what you would expect of a grocer's headquarters. Yet in many ways it symbolises the rebirth the company is working towards. Seven different offices were deliberately rolled into one to promote cross-functional cooperation between the 2,500 people who work there, and the open-plan layout is full of breakout areas. Even the staff restaurant next to the vast atrium is used for product promotion and testing new lines – almost a metaphor for the core values of excellence in and passion about food, which Sainsbury's is trying to duplicate into all its operations.

Similarly fundamental changes are affecting the other areas of the business, with 40–50 stores being transformed every year, and the supply chain operation increasingly concerned with long-term relationships and environmental issues as well as core values such as quality and price.

'All great organisations go through cycles of rebirth, that's how they survive, and at the moment we're embracing change at an enormous rate', says Imelda Walsh, Sainsbury's Human Resources Director. 'The kind of people who flourish here are those who want to grab at opportunities. Most of us are juggling a lot of balls at a time.'

Retail is hard work, a fiercely competitive, 24-hour, 363-day business. 'When other companies are easing down on the last Friday before Christmas, we're gearing up for our busiest weekend of the year', says Walsh. And it goes without saying that Sainsbury's people need a passion for customer service.

Despite the inevitable shift work necessary to serve our customers, Sainsbury's is not a long-hours culture. Sir Peter Davis, CEO, is a founder member of the Employers Forum for Work-Life Balance, and the leadership of the Company understand people's need to balance their home and work commitments. Where possible, flexible working solutions are encouraged to help support this.

Two-thirds of staff are women, and Sainsbury's has one of the highest ratios of women in top jobs, with a near 50:50 balance in management and two women on the Board. Twelve per cent of staff come from ethnic minorities, and Sainsbury's gay and lesbian colleagues are well supported through the GALAS (Gay & Lesbian at Sainsbury's Group)

## Human Resources

With around 500 stores to manage, Sainsbury's needs large numbers of leaders, and recruits up to 150 new graduates a year, mostly into stores. Some have specific degrees, such as food technology, and disciplines such as human resources are so competitive that you may need a further degree. But the company also recruits at 'A' level, modern apprenticeship and NVQ level, and some people join at the bottom and work their way up. Overall the company recruits tens of thousands of people a year.

Undergraduates can request summer and full year placements, whilst many other students enjoy their first taste of Sainsbury's through weekend or vacation work. Sainsbury's also welcomes experienced people, not necessarily with retail backgrounds (around half of senior managers have less than three years' service), and former staff are encouraged to rejoin – including Peter Davis, who had worked at Sainsbury's before becoming 'the man from the Pru'.

Last year, Sainsbury's invested heavily in its formal induction process. The graduate training programme lasts from a year (for marketing, buying and supply chain) to three years (for retail and finance).

Walsh believes the message about Sainsbury's new image is getting through. 'I interviewed someone the other day, and he said "I want to work here because I feel I can really contribute to changing things"', she says.

## Career Opportunity and Development

Sainsbury's employs buyers, marketers, food technologists, media professionals, HR and IT specialists, project managers, lawyers and surveyors, as well as retail specialists, so there is no shortage of possible careers. There are three basic streams – the stores (much the largest, of course), supply chain, and the business centre – but the company has deliberately made these more integrated. 'We believe our future leaders will have cross-business experience', says Walsh.

The company is keen to promote from within, and quickly, so there are lots of opportunities, and able people can be store managers by their late 20s. Senior-level succession planning is a regular aspect of board meetings, and managers are conscientious about developing career paths for all staff. 'We like to combine using people's existing skills with stretching them and promoting them based on their ability', says Walsh.

In 2003, Sainsbury's is introducing a two-year Corporate Leadership Programme, a fast-track graduate training scheme offered to 30–40 high-performing graduate recruits after about nine months' service. It aims to develop generalists with a broad company and business perspective, with experience in the corporate change programme.

Staff (Sainsbury's always calls them 'colleagues') get to manage their own careers, but with a lot of support and advice, and the biannual formal reviews are increasingly looking at 'soft' measures of capability as well as hard achievements. 'We're interested in not just what you deliver, but how you deliver it', says Walsh.

In 2001, Sainsbury's was the first major food retailer to achieve Investors in People certification. 'Our training offer is reputed as the best in the industry', says Walsh. The learning@Sainsbury's site on the company intranet has extensive training materials, supplemented by classroom training, and support for staff taking vocational qualifications such as CIM, CIPD, NVQ and the certificate in retail management.

## Remuneration

Sainsbury's aims to be in the top quartile for total cash remuneration. Bonuses and performance-related elements are increasing in size and importance for all managers, not just those in sales roles. For example, in stores with top mystery shopper ratings, special bonuses are paid to all staff.

The company has a long history of share ownership by staff, with share options down to middle management level, save-as-you-earn schemes, etc. Like many corporates, the company had to close entry to its final-salary pension scheme in 2002 after nearly 70 years, and now has a defined-contribution scheme with Legal & General, which all staff are eligible to join.

Middle managers and above qualify for BUPA health cover, while store managers and equivalent grades get a choice of company car. Everyone gets a 10 per cent staff discount after six months' service, and staff can also get discounts on insurance, banking services and leisure items. Most sites have subsidised restaurants, and the Sainsbury's staff association offers anything from sports and social events to discounted holidays.

Holiday allowance starts at 22 days, rising to 25 days after five years' service, and up to 27 days for middle and senior managers. Maternity benefits are good, and include higher maternity pay for women with more than one year's service.

## The Future

The tough retail environment is getting even tougher, and Sainsbury's knows it must maintain a delicate balancing act – flexible enough to stay competitive, but resisting the temptation to over-diversify. 'We need to be very aware of the competition', says Walsh.

The Sainsbury's Local convenience stores are growing fast, and online sales are increasingly important, but these represent new channels rather than changes of direction. The most interesting new venture is Sainsbury's Bank, where the company sees significant growth potential in a selective set of financial services products.

The company is also proud of the early success of its Nectar customer loyalty card, in partnership with Barclaycard, BP and Debenhams. Nectar promises to be an excellent source of customer data for planning new stores and marketing campaigns. It will be a vital weapon in the contest to be food retail's top dog in the coming decade.

# Samworth Brothers

QUALITY FOODS

Samworth Brothers makes good quality food for the top end of the market, mainly for the leading high-street retailers. It also owns the Cornish-based company Ginsters, the market's premier 'food for people on the move brand', Walkers, a quality producer of pork pies in Leicester, and the Beeton brand. The company name stands for quality in the food industry as well as excellent treatment of employees and good working relationships with its customers. Samworth Brothers employs around 5,000 people (with some seasonal variations) and had a turnover in 2002 of £350 million.

## Scorecard:

| | |
|---|---|
| Remuneration and benefits | *** |
| Progressive attitude | **** |
| Opportunity for promotion | *** |
| Training, development and education | **** |
| Working atmosphere and environment | *** |

## Biggest plus:
A hands-on style with lots of freedom.

## Biggest minus:
A lean, mean structure without a cushion.

Samworth Brothers Ltd
Chetwode House
Leicester Road
Melton Mowbray
Leicestershire LE13 1GA
Tel: 01664 414500
Website: www.samworthbrothers.co.uk

# Samworth Brothers

## The Business

Samworth Brothers Limited is a privately-owned business specialising in fresh, chilled food manufacturing. It supplies virtually all the major food retailers, including Asda, Safeway, Sainsbury's, Somerfield, Tesco and Waitrose. It has its own distribution business to assist in serving these customers. As Chief Executive, Brian Stein says, 'There is no such thing as contracts in this industry; it's all about service. We provide the best food manufacturing facilities in the UK and we are as responsive as our fast-moving customers demand. That's why they stick with us.'

The company's roots go back to a business founded in Birmingham by George Samworth over 100 years ago. Samworth Brothers as it currently exists was formed in the 1950s. Three generations of Samworths have created one of the leading businesses in the British food industry, yet it remains little known outside it. Stein: 'It's probably true that we have hidden our light under a bushel. It's also true that we've been totally focused on doing what we do.'

*Each company is sharply focused on its own market place: each has its own marketing department, its own HR department, and so on. Such central control as there is concentrates on giving each company its objectives rather than the route to achieving those objectives: strategy rather than tactics*

That strategy has certainly paid off. In 1995 it employed around 1,500 people and had a turnover of £150 million. Now employees are up to around 5,000 and turnover is £350 million – a highly impressive rate of growth.

Today, Samworth Brothers comprises 11 operating companies based in Cornwall and Leicestershire, producing a wide range of products from pork pies and Cornish pasties to sausages, sandwiches, desserts and ready meals. It is a major player in sandwiches on motorway forecourts. And, as stated above, it supplies an impressive range of customers, principally the major multiples.

## Company Culture and Style

The first thing to know about the companies within Samworth Brothers is that they are highly autonomous in the way they operate. There is very little central organisation. Each company is sharply focused on its own marketplace: each has its own marketing department, its own HR department, and so on. Such central control as there is concentrates on giving each company its objectives rather than the route to achieving those objectives: strategy rather than tactics.

This gives the management of each company lots of freedom to manage their own business. Stein: 'Managers who want to run their own show and are good at it will find they have a virtually free hand here.'

Workers and management are encouraged to identify with their company first and Samworth Brothers second. Having said that, there is a group umbrella. Managers come together for regular conventions and meet their opposite numbers elsewhere in the group. There is also a group magazine.

Despite their differences, the companies share several principles, chief of which are a pursuit of excellence and great treatment of their people. Stein tells the story of the group's Bradgate bakery, which is a company dedicated to serving one of its high street retailers. Another customer, interested in expanding its range, had a tour of Bradgate and came back saying that he wanted Samworth Brothers to build him a facility just like this one! Stein: 'The staff sold him. Anyone can build a building – but creating that culture is another thing.'

That culture is summed up by excellent working practices and treatment of staff that is the envy of its competitors. Interestingly, the company's staff have no union affiliation. Stein: 'Unions were created, and exist, to look after workers who get a poor deal. I say to our staff: if we treat you badly, join a union. If we treat you well, don't.' The fact that no one on the staff has joined speaks volumes about the culture – and, the company believes, allows it to respond far more rapidly.

## Human Resources

All vacancies are advertised throughout the group as well as externally. The phenomenal growth of Samworth Brothers meant that, for some years, most posts were filled from outside; this was a function of the lack of resource inside rather than any preference. In fact, the group prefers to recruit and promote from within.

Samworth Brothers has been recruiting graduates for five years and has a good retention level of these individuals, the earliest of whom are now supervisors, junior managers or managers. It currently takes on from six to eight graduates annually. Graduates, and a selection of non-graduates, go on a fast track, exploring the various companies and job options, which usually lasts two years. At the end of that period, they can apply for a post or be appointed to one. Top candidates may have two or three opportunities.

Retention levels in the group as a whole are 80–90 per cent, which is very high for the industry. Inevitably, some people move on – but often decide they want to return. Increasingly, there are also lots of people from Samworth Brothers' competitors who want to come on board!

## Career Opportunity and Development

Given the large number of companies within the group and the excellent growth rates of those companies, there are excellent opportunities for promotion, both by moving within the group and by staying in the same company.

Some Samworth Brothers companies provide career reviews for everyone down to team leaders, while others review all staff. (The group is encouraging the development of the latter trend.) This includes a discussion of each person's career development, and can last from two minutes to two hours! The aim is to match the right people to the right jobs. Some areas, such as IT, have grown considerably in recent years and have extra opportunity for promotion.

There are many examples of impressive career development. One former shop worker is now a sales director of one of the Samworth Brothers companies, and this is by no means unique. Numerous directors are female, and there are other high-level posts occupied by women. Stein: 'We promote the best, irrespective of sex, creed or colour.'

Samworth Brothers has its own Training Academy, with a considerable resource of training materials. These can foster both personal and work-related development: everything from health and safety and food hygiene to French and fly-fishing!

Those on the fast track are encouraged to manage their own careers, assisted by mentors. Indeed, self-development is fostered throughout the company. Stein: 'the inherent skills you need are hard work, common sense and a good attention to detail. We can train in all the technical areas but we can't train those. If you have them, and want to get on at Samworth Brothers, you will. Our industry is tough and demanding, and we need people who can cope with that pressure while having a good rapport with both customers and staff. Anyone with those skills will find that the sky is the limit here.'

## Remuneration

The group aims to pay as well if not better than its rivals, and conducts regular surveys to see how competitive its salaries are. The surveys cover the whole range of employee roles from the shop floor to managers to directors.

Being a private company, there are no share options or share-save schemes. There is, however, a bonus programme: each business puts eight per cent of its profits into a pool which is paid to those employed in that business.

In these days of dwindling final salary schemes, it is refreshing to see that Samworth Brothers remains committed to its own such scheme. It currently pays from 12 per cent to 14 per cent into the scheme for all staff, and finds that this is now frequently recognised as a real benefit rather than being taken for granted as in the old days. In staff surveys, this often comes in at the top of the agenda. Staff contribute just five per cent into the scheme.

All Samworth Brothers staff are covered by a healthcare plan. Stein: 'I believe that covering the entire staff in the healthcare plan is unique not only in the UK food manufacturing industry but in UK manufacturing as a whole.'

There is a company car scheme that again is competitive for the industry. This covers technical managers/personnel managers and above. The scheme is reviewed regularly.

# The Future

At a time when many manufacturers are performing sluggishly if not disappearing altogether, Samworth Brothers habitually records double-digit turnover growth. What is the secret of this success? One factor is undoubtedly its policy of organic growth: apart from its Ginsters and Walkers acquisitions in 1977 and 1986 respectively, virtually all its growth has been from within. Stein: 'Some companies have a good culture; others don't – and it takes a huge effort to change a bad culture. The right culture is vital, and we find that the best way is to develop it ourselves.'

Given this background, it is not surprising that Samworth Brothers plans to continue to grow at a similar rate. Against a backdrop of tremendous change in UK food retailing, the company has invested enormously in its facilities (£12 million in Ginsters alone), in low-cost production methods, and in ways to motivate its staff.

Stein: 'This is a tough industry, but the fittest will survive. By continuing to do a very good job for our retailer customers, we believe that more business will come our way.'

# Severn Trent Water

Severn Trent Limited is a privately-owned environmental services company, which runs a water, waste and utility service called Severn Trent Water (STW). STW is UK-based and provides services to over seven million domestic and business users, and sewerage services to over eight million.

**Scorecard:**

| | |
|---|---|
| Remuneration and benefits | **** |
| Progressive attitude | *** |
| Opportunity for promotion | *** |
| Training, development and education | **** |
| Working atmosphere and environment | **** |

**Biggest plus:**
Its secure status and outlook for both its staff and customers.

**Biggest minus:**
As a utility business providing a core service the Company is highly regulated with performance monitored by OFWAT, the Drinking Water Inspectorate, Watervoice, the Environment Agency, politicians, media and other interested groups. This environment won't suit everyone.

Severn Trent Limited
2297 Coventry Road
Sheldon
Birmingham B26 3PU
Tel: 0121 722 4000
Fax: 0121 722 4800
Email: www.stwater.co.uk

# Severn Trent

## The Business

Severn Trent Water is the largest company within the Severn Trent Group, which is made up of a variety of businesses providing products and services world-wide, and is the fourth largest privatised water company in the world.

Formed in October 1989, the company evolved out of the creation of the water authority in 1974: over 28 years ago, 137 local authorities, 2 river boards, 14 joint water boards and 2 joint sewerage boards were merged to create the Severn Trent Water Authority. Since privatisation is has invested over £5.7 billion to improve resources, quality and services.

Collectively, STW boasts total UK revenues of £900 million, and total UK pre-tax profits reached £201 million. Headquartered in Birmingham, it also has offices in Derby and Coventry. These locations combine a number of departments and functions within the business, which collectively employ over 4,600 staff in total. Severn Trent Water also has two sister companies: Severn Trent Retail Services, which can save customers money on gas, electricity, phone bills and insurance cover, as well as Severn Trent Utility Services, which make their skills and experience available to other business organisations.

*the way it supplies work-related resources and its approach to health and safety ... are as important as maintaining its brand and reputation*

As a closely and well-scrutinised regulated monopoly business, STW is required to provide regular reports to OFWAT, the water industry's regulator, the Drinking Water Inspectorate, public health doctors and environmental health officers who scrutinise their performance, although to date, STW has achieved commendably good results.

## Company Culture and Style

As the firm's core product is water supply, by nature, it is at times quite a conservative organisation. It generally sets long-terms goals rather than focusing on reacting quickly to changing market conditions. But being highly regulated, any quick fire reactions would be impractical and unlikely.

Its values pivot around its colleagues, its company, customers and communities and these are reflected in the company's day-to-day dealings. Regarding colleagues, the way it supplies work-related resources and its approach to health and safety are as important as maintaining its brand and reputation. Customer-related values are reflected through its customer promise initiative: a series of initiatives around which it operates and delivers customer services such as confirming appointments within a agreed time frame, and agreeing compensation for agreed shortfalls of service. Special policies for the elderly and disabled, such as bills written in Braille, also exist. Its community values are also important and include its fair trade policies and extensive work for charitable trusts.

In terms of dress codes for workers, protective clothing and uniforms for many of its operational staff are provided, as they often need to deal with sewage and chemicals. Within customer facing roles, when security could be an issue, staff wear uniforms. For other roles, smart dress is usually the case.

Although STW recognises equal opportunities are 'key business measures' and aims to have at least three per cent of employees from ethnic minorities, it still remains a white, male-dominated company.

A similar trend can be seen with its female staff, who are significantly outnumbered by male staff, and this is also the case in regards to senior management roles where men outnumber women 13:1. There is only one area where women outnumber men and that is within customer relations and human resources. However, STW points out that many of the jobs on offer at the company involve heavy manual labour tasks and these traditionally attract more men than women. Its approach to diversity is actively being addressed.

The firm adopts a flexible approach to those who have just given birth or have small children and offers packages above the statutory requirements. Upon their return, women may choose to work flexible hours and share contracts that have flexibility with start and finish times. The firm also recently introduced a career break scheme.

## Human Resources

During the recruitment process the company takes into account how well the candidates would 'fit within the company culture'. Apart from this, the firm looks for specific characteristics, qualifications or experience for the very different roles its offers. Staff recruitment is through agencies, internal and external advertising, word of mouth and promotions, but with a staff turnover at less than four per cent per annum, its generally has few opportunities for recruitment. Its undergraduate activity is particularly attractive, and in the last three years it has recruited on average 20 graduates on to its central scheme.

For existing employees, the HR department works with line managers to ensure that the company is operating in accordance with its values and procedures. With an HR department of 40 assisting a workforce of over 4,500 employees, it feels the most effective way to deploy its resources is through formulating policies with regard to staff feedback. For example, it is currently reviewing its approach to pay and rewards to allow greater pay progression as a direct result of staff feedback.

Overall the HR department ensures staff are recruited and inducted properly; that staff receive appropriate training and development to do their job, and where there are issues in the workplace such as harassment, that policies are in place to help resolve these. The HR department look to motivate staff through perform-ance-related bonuses and review schemes, training and developing staff to ensure care is available during difficult times.

## Career Opportunity and Development

In terms of career development STW has a comprehensive management develop-ment framework which ranges from the use of business schools for senior managers through to IT-based learning packages, a learning resource centre and company library as well as self-managed career development and training. STW has a range of technical training – both in terms of health and safety and how to do particular jobs, as many of the roles are highly specific – BTECs, NVQs and tech-nical qualifications to ensure staff capabilities in these areas. During the last few years, HR has held a staff training budget of £1.4 million, with over £300,000 held in line departments towards training activity.

In terms of planning and career development, STW offers a formal planning process which covers the top 2,000 people in its business and is based on a series of appraisals and presentations to management boards and executives. This identi-fies training and development needs, and successors for all posts for a period of up to five years. One-to-one appraisals are carried out annually at all levels of the company. Employees have the opportunity to directly influence their own careers through the sort of information that is put forward to these panels. STW also advertises all jobs internally (outside the management population) and has a series of in-house secondments where people can be transferred for further experience. STW also sponsors a number of MBA/MSc programmes.

Graduates are offered an intensive one-year programme designed to give them an overall introduction to the business and the skills required for their chosen career or profession. They are encouraged to gain professional qualifications and receive a benefits package and mentoring as well as regular feedback on their progress.

## Remuneration

Staff grade structures are established on the basis of an agreed grading scheme with the trade unions, that represent them. Salaries are negotiated annually and employees in the staff bands have the opportunity to move through bands depend-ing on their performance. Where performance is exceptional, staff in the higher bands have the opportunity to be paid outside of the band and personal 'packages' are awarded to highly-valued individuals whose skills may be at a market premium.

To ensure its approach to pay and reward is fair in view of both the market forces and the company, an external agency, Haypaynet, compares STW with 23 other UK major utility businesses to ensure its salaries are appropriate. Management salaries typically range from £35k upwards and all managers are on a bonus scheme of at least 20 per cent of their salary. STW also provides an employee share save scheme and encourages share ownership amongst its employee base.

Employees can get non-monetary bonuses as a way of 'saying thanks', and these come in the form of leisure or retail vouchers. In terms of company cars, only senior managers or those joining management teams are eligible. Healthcare is also offered, with the firm operating private healthcare schemes, full-time employees are eligible for free private healthcare. The company also offers life insurance to its employees through its pension scheme, and the value of cover is three times salary. All permanent employees with at least six months' service are entitled.

In terms of pensions, the company operates a 'final salary' scheme, which is available to all employees with greater than a six-month contract, except for non-final salary employees.

## The Future

As the business is firmly routed in the water industry, it is restricted to being highly regulated and therefore the prospects of acquisition are constrained by the regulator, who has disallowed any UK water company from merging or taking over another.

Within the next five years, STW hopes to have moved into what it terms as 'the next regulatory cycle' through which it will have agreed a series of improvements to its environment and customer services.

It also hopes to continuing growing like it has over the past three years, whereby it has developed two new business streams which sit outside the core regulated base: Severn Trent Utility Services provides utility contract management to a range of businesses including Scottish Water and London Underground. In addition, it hopes to grow its embryonic business in the areas of gas and electricity retailing, telecoms, land searches and a range of other products.

Ten years on, and the company hopes that its growth will continue. It keeps its fingers crossed for the regulator to change its approach to mergers and acquisitions, allowing it to further grow through consolidation of other UK businesses and perhaps through an integration of its other environmental services companies under the Severn Trent Group, to include, for example, BIFFA Waste Services.

# SIGNET

Signet is the world's largest speciality retail jeweller with operations in the US and UK. In the UK it trades under three brands: H.Samuel, Ernest Jones and Leslie Davis. With currently 610 stores across Britain and Ireland, Signet has a 17 per cent share of the total UK jewellery market and annual sales of £474 million. It employs 6,000 people in its retail outlets and a further 1,000 in service operations in London and Birmingham.

## Scorecard:

| | |
|---|---|
| Remuneration and benefits | **** |
| Progressive attitude | *** |
| Opportunity for promotion | **** |
| Training, development and education | ***** |
| Working atmosphere and environment | ***** |

## Biggest plus:
A fun, team-oriented work environment.

## Biggest minus:
Will not suit individualistic types.

Signet Group plc
Zenith House
The Hyde
London NW9 6EW
Tel: 0870 90 90 301
Fax: 020 8242 8588
Website: www.signetgroupplc.com

# Signet Group

## The Business

Signet is well-established in the jewellery market, with H.Samuel in existence as long ago as the 19th century. In spite of having a large share of the total UK jewellery market, the sector remains highly fragmented, with a large number of independent traders, and local and regional chains. The same is true of jewellery suppliers. Unlike wholesalers involved in other areas of retail, jewellery suppliers, manufacturers and designers are often small and consequently business is very much driven by relationships.

Listed on the London Stock Exchange and the NASDAQ National Market in the US, the Group trades under two main retail brands in the UK, aimed at different markets. H.Samuel is aimed at the mass market with higher volumes of sale and lower value purchases, while Ernest Jones/Leslie Davis is aimed at customers with more money to spend on special purchases. Each is effectively run as a separate business but Signet's integrated supply chain processes, distribution and warehousing, benefit both operations equally.

*Signet's own research has found repeatedly that staff identify teamwork as the company's defining characteristic*

The jewellery sector has enjoyed continued growth for some time and Signet has performed particularly well over the last four years. Though jewellery is not an essential item, shoppers have shown a willingness to spend money on it, particularly on special occasions. Within the industry, the biggest change in recent years has been that jewellers are having to adopt a more retail-orientated mindset. Customer expectations have also risen and shoppers now want the kind of personalised service from multiples they have come to expect from the small local jeweller.

## Company Culture and Style

Signet's own research has found repeatedly that staff identify teamwork as the Company's defining characteristic. Mike Povall, Director of HR, says, 'People can see the business. Whether it be at one of our stores or whether you are looking at the business in total, it's not so big that you can't feel a part of it.' The attractiveness of Signet as a place to work is enhanced by the nature of the product being sold. People find it a lot easier to get enthusiastic about selling jewellery than they do about many other kinds of retail merchandise, Povall believes.

Teamwork is key to the success of each of the retail stores. The performance of the store is planned down to individual sales associates, all of whom will have their daily targets to achieve. Consistency in the offer is achieved with store designs across the country looking very similar, and defined product ranges from each size of store. The largest stores are run by up to 35 people, who are employed at different times throughout the week. Smaller stores, by contrast, may have no more than four or five staff. Regardless of the store's size, all the products and customers should always be visible wherever you are in the store.

Employees need to be energetic and proactive and want to learn about new aspects of the business, according to Povall. Taken as a whole, the workforce is relatively young; 60 per cent of employees are under 40. Field workers must acquire a comprehensive knowledge of retail work; not only how to serve and sell to customers, but also with regard to stock control, security and other aspects of running a store. Strong communication skills are obviously vital. Alongside this, a level of emotional intelligence is desirable, in order that staff know to adapt their sales technique to suit different types of customer and transactions. Clearly, the 'hard sell' approach is not appropriate and could damage repeat business.

# Human Resources

Signet's biggest recruitment phase takes place in October and November when up to 3,000 extra staff are taken on for the Christmas period. Many of these are retained each year; the experience of working during the busiest retail period gives new recruits an excellent insight into the business and the importance of teamwork within it. From the Company's point of view, the specialist training it gives to prepare them for this, adds to their value.

However, not all recruitment is seasonal. In fact, Signet hires managers all year round through a range of channels, including the Internet, career centres, local press and via national advertising campaigns. Vacancies in the buying departments or central business areas are advertised under the Signet brand; all field work opportunities, on the other hand, are advertised under the banner of the relevant retail brand name.

The Company continuously strives to improve its practices and is becoming more sophisticated in its approach to find the right type of personality for its store management. Where once there was a reliance on an interview for selection, the company is now placing greater emphasis on psychometrics and role-play to find people with the raw talent who, with the right training, will thrive in the industry.

Because of its dominant market position, Signet rarely recruits people with existing jewellery experience for its managers. Currently, around 40 per cent of management vacancies are filled internally and this proportion is set to rise further. For central departmental positions, such as logistics or buying, there is greater emphasis on finding people with the right technical skills and experience.

# Career Development and Training

Signet offers plenty of career opportunities to employees both in retail and Head Office. Flexibility on location and brand can increase promotional prospects, with many employees developing their career across the brand fascias and within Head Office. According to Povall, 'People who like the jewellery business tend to stay with us a long time. We encourage that because we don't want to lose their experience to another company.'

No doubt about it, Signet takes the training of its people seriously. Three months initial training for new management recruits encompasses an induction process and the acquisition of basic product knowledge. This takes place as the first stage of the Signet Jewellery Academy, within which technical or operational training runs alongside behavioural and managerial courses.

Technical knowledge is acquired through JET I, an externally managed qualification run by the National Association of Goldsmiths. Applicants are required to complete a largely distance learning-based study programme. The programme usually requires six months' study and combines written work with applied knowledge, such as how to recognise different types of precious and semi-precious stones. Signet also runs a number of other accredited courses on jewellery products for those who want to acquire knowledge on specific items or brands. Managers can develop their specialist knowledge further through JET II, which encompasses product valuation and repair skills among other things. By contrast, behavioural skills are taught as part of in-store training programmes. These include 'Sell, sell, sell', which focuses on customer service, along with a number of other management programmes. The Company is aiming to develop all staff at Ernest Jones/Leslie Davis stores to be JET I proficient and a fair proportion of staff in H.Samuel.

# Remuneration

The reward package offered to Signet employees is a combination of base pay, bonuses and incentives, which vary in size according to seniority and business area. If, for example, an employee is employed in a high-footfall store in a major retail location, it is possible to earn significantly more than a comparable role in a smaller store.

Other benefits include above statutory holidays, staff discount of 30 per cent and pension scheme subject to eligibility.

The Company recently introduced a scheme to incentivise skills acquisition through base pay. This means that job title and grade are now much less a driver of the reward policy than basic individual performance and competencies.

# The Future

Signet is currently rolling out a modernisation programme for all its UK stores. The aim is to make the existing premises more inviting and accessible, to encourage customers to come inside and browse, and to improve staff interaction with the customer. The refurbishments underscore the fact that the Group already owns prime sites in most towns and cities and cannot acquire many more without competing against itself. Instead, the strategy to ensure a good retail environment, allied to a strong customer service ethic, consolidates and builds on Signet's existing market dominance. Not to say that there isn't competition out there: there is, more than ever before, in fact – most recently from supermarkets and fashion outlets. However, the level of product knowledge and quality of service are seen as key differentiators and reasons why there is a belief that the consistent sales growth of the last few years can be sustained.

## Sodexho
### Catering and Support Services

Sodexho Alliance was founded in Marseille in 1966 by Pierre Bellon, who remains its Chairman and Chief Executive Officer. It is the world's leading provider of food and management services, with operations in 74 countries and annual turnover of 12.6 billion Euro (£8.6 billion). Its £1 billion UK and Ireland operation dates to 1995, when it acquired contract catering specialist Gardner Merchant. Sodexho's 52,000 UK and Ireland employees represent one-sixth of corporate total, and provide catering and support services to clients in the business and industry, education, healthcare, leisure and defence sectors. Sodexho Alliance is listed on the Paris Bourse and the New York Stock Exchange.

**Scorecard:**

| | |
|---|---|
| Remuneration and benefits | *** |
| Progressive attitude | ***** |
| Opportunity for promotion | ***** |
| Training, development and education | **** |
| Working atmosphere and environment | *** |

**Biggest plus:**
A diverse business with an open culture and management style that allows people to develop.

**Biggest minus**
Having to balance the needs of clients and end-customers can be challenging, as can the broad range of business activities, which means that it can take time for external entrants to familiarise themselves with all parts of the company.

Sodexho Alliance
Resourcing Manager
The Merchant Centre
1 New Street Square
London EC4A 3BF
Tel: 020 7815 0610
Website: www.sodexho.co.uk

# Sodexho Alliance

## The Business

The core of Sodexho in the UK and Ireland is the provision of food services to the key market segments of Business & Industry, Education, Healthcare, Defence and Leisure. However, in some divisions, up to half of the business is now support service; for example, the company operates retail shops on client sites, and provides cleaning, reception, portering, reprographic and grounds maintenance services.

The catering side has evolved greatly too, and covers everything from fine dining in the City of London to staff restaurants in offices, schools and hospitals. 'The influence of the high street has been notable in the last ten years', says Martin Gash, Sodexho's HR Director for their Business and Industry Sector.

There are five main operating segments within the company. The largest is Business and Industry, which mainly provides services across different sectors, eg Banking, Insurance, and Manufacturing. The other segments are Education, which covers both state and private schools, universities and colleges of education; Healthcare – services to the NHS and PFI hospitals; Defence services to all three services; and the Leisure sector responsible for event catering at some of the largest race courses, events and heritage sites. Sodexho in the UK also has a division that specialises in vending services, and an independent business arm (Tillery Valley Foods), which produces high-quality cook-chilled food for hospitals, schools and commercial businesses. Each of Sodexho's 3,500 clients is an operating unit, with its own Unit Manager. The smallest of sites may only employ two or three staff, whereas certain locations such as large hospitals may employ several hundred staff operating in a range of service environments.

*The skills, experience and attitude of our staff and managers is paramount. This, in turn, must be supported by effective business procedures behind the scenes*

## Company Culture and Style

Sodexho's mission is to supply services that improve the quality of daily life for its customers. This means satisfying both the end-customer and the client who is actually paying for the service provision.

Gash says that this influences the type of staff that Sodexho looks for in its recruitment activities: 'We're always striving to ensure high and consistent standards of service delivery. To achieve this, the skills, experience and attitude of our staff and managers is paramount. This, in turn, must be supported by effective business procedures behind the scenes – an area where the company has made significant advances in the recent past.'

It can be hard for people joining the company from other sectors to cope with the range of client environments and cultures within which we operate on a daily basis. 'You need a very flexible attitude', Gash says.

Sodexho employs roughly equal numbers of men and women, with slightly more women at unit and divisional level, and some very senior female executives in the company. Its approach as regards working hours is a flexible one which has long supported its efforts in the past to retain and develop its people.

'We have been trialing a formal homeworking policy involving 30 managers recently and numerous others have expressed an interest in taking up this option', Martin Gash says. 'The company can benefit in terms of costs associated with office space and travel. Importantly, homeworking, where appropriate, can have a significant impact on the quality of working life as far as our staff are concerned. However, we are conscious that it suits some people and jobs more than others and we apply assessment criteria therefore in implementing our homeworking policy. In considering the suitability of an individual for homeworking we look at their personality profile, management style, personal circumstances and the nature of their responsibilities at work.'

The company nominates a charity every two years for fundraising purposes and sets a target amount for the organisation to achieve. The last appeal raised £400,000 versus a target of £250,000: a significant achievement, which was the result of all parts of the company contributing with a large number of different fundraising initiatives. 'Community Concern' is the main vehicle to support the company's Corporate Social Responsibility Programme. The scheme encourages employees to support local community projects across key towns in the UK.

## Human Resources

As its range of services has broadened and the company has grown, it has improved its college and university links and revamped its graduate development programme accordingly.

'At graduate level', says Gash, 'new entrants will be expected to pass from the structured development programme that the company offers, on to middle and senior management positions. We are therefore targeting universities/degree courses that can offer capable candidates with some business and commercial understanding (via academic studies and work experience) and a genuine interest in our business sector.'

Beyond its graduate recruitment activity Sodexho has established recruitment processes at every level in the business to support its requirements as regards succession planning.

The company is working with an external provider to ensure a more consistent and effective approach in particular areas such as Internet-based recruitment. Sodexho's own intranet system also provides a broad range of company-related information ranging from compensation and benefits to the latest company news. It also provides a confidential way for employees to ask questions and make suggestions in relation to broader business issues, although Gash notes that it can never replace face-to-face communication and team meetings.

There is a big part-time contingent in Sodexho's workforce, which is a common feature of the service sector. It is also connected with the fact that the company actively seeks to maintain links with staff who leave to have families, encouraging them to return to part-time work or to short-term assignments and therefore continue working with the company. 'It is common for people to leave and return. We always aim to be as flexible as possible in this regard as it can enable us to hold on to some of our best people. Equally where we recruit people into new positions we try to balance internal promotion with external recruitment', Gash notes. 'This ensures in terms of succession planning we have an appropriate balance of "home-grown talent" and new ideas and energy from outside of the business.'

## Career Opportunity and Development

The company operates established 'management development programmes' at every level. These are linked to management competency frameworks, which underpin assessment and development planning.

Psychometric testing is also used in both recruitment and staff development programmes. At the same time of writing, 360-degree appraisal is being introduced at middle and senior management level to support development activities and provide a more objective basis for performance management.

There are opportunities across the organisation for individual secondment. Given Sodexho, like many of its clients, is a global company, increasingly managers in the UK and Ireland will have to work closely with colleagues abroad to support larger internationally-based contracts and/or contract opportunities.

## Remuneration

Sodexho extended its divisional bonus scheme to include all unit managers last year. Its ability to do this is linked to the successful implementation of new systems, which allow it to analyse its business and financial performance at unit level in much greater depth than before. It aims to keep the scheme simple with realistic targets that enable managers to earn bonuses of up to 10 per cent of their salary based on measurements such as financial performance and quality of service delivery. The scheme is monitored and publicised quarterly and Gash says that the company intends to develop it further in the future. 'We are keen to do more in rewarding exceptional performance', he said.

The company has also extended its flexible benefits scheme down to unit level. This allows unit managers to tailor their own benefits to meet their particular personal needs.

There is a company car scheme, which is mainly for managers whose jobs demand that they travel. A cash alternative is available, if preferred.

# The Future

'Sodexho increasingly differentiates itself from its competitors based on its multi-service capability. The company wants to be seen more as a partner than a supplier, which is realistic when you consider the range and quality of services which we offer to clients. We are not just providing the non-core services', says Martin Gash, 'a multi-service contract can be integral to a client facility and can have a big impact on the attitude, morale and performance of the client staff.'

To deliver an effective service in this environment, however, you have to be quite sophisticated in the way in which you understand and respond to clients needs.

As well as the inevitable economic factors, Government policy is an important external influence on the service sector in which Sodexho operates. For example, an increase in the number of PFIs (Private Finance Initiatives) in the future in various sectors will affect the way in which the company manages and structures its business. Generally speaking, contracts are likely to become larger in the future with more being multi-service in nature.

The future is one of continuing change but great opportunity for people working in this business environment.

## TENCEL®

Tencel produces Lyocell, an environmentally-friendly cellulosic fibre, under the Tencel brand name. There are two main markets for Tencel fibre – textiles and garments, and nonwoven materials – and both are growing rapidly. Tencel employs 360 staff worldwide, 200 of them in the UK. It has manufacturing units in the UK and US, and offices in seven countries. Most staff work in development and manufacturing, but there are also growing opportunities in marketing. Tencel is part of the Acordis group, which specialises in man-made fibres and speciality materials. Its turnover is Euro 100 million and rising fast.

**Scorecard:**

| | |
|---|---|
| Remuneration and benefits | *** |
| Progressive attitude | **** |
| Opportunity for promotion | **** |
| Training, development and education | **** |
| Working atmosphere and environment | **** |

**Biggest plus:**
The challenge of working for a fast-growing company with unique, innovative technology.

**Biggest minus:**
Not for those only in it for the money – pay and benefits are only average.

Tencel
PO Box 5
1 Holme Lane
Spondon
Derby DE21 7BP
Tel: 01332 681829
Fax: 01332 281705
Website: www.tencel.com

# Tencel

## The Business

Tencel's business is the revolutionary fibre from which it takes its name. Tencel fibre started life in the research labs of Courtaulds plc back in the mid-1980s, and went into commercial production under the Tencel brand in1992.

Invented as an alternative to viscose – which Courtaulds also created – Tencel was a big breakthrough in fibre technology. Like viscose, it is made from natural materials (wood pulp) and is biodegradable, but unlike viscose it uses an environmentally-friendly production process and is also much faster to produce. Made into fabric, it has a number of advantages: it's breathable, drapes well, and has a soft finish.

Tencel can also be made into non-woven materials where its combination of strength and absorption make it ideal for applications such as disposable wipes, disposable garments and filters. Nonwovens currently account for a minority of turnover but are growing fast, and the market potential is huge.

*For those with an interest in textiles or high-performance materials, Tencel is an exciting and challenging place to work. It develops leading-edge technology, carries out its manufacturing in state-of-the-art plants, and has succeeded in turning Tencel into a premium brand that employees are proud to be associated with*

In 1998, Courtaulds plc was acquired by Akzo Nobel, a Dutch multinational specialising in coatings, chemicals, pharmaceuticals and man-made fibres. Akzo Nobel merged its fibre activities with Courtaulds' to create the Acordis fibre operation, which was divested at the end of 1999. Tencel is one of the operating companies within the Acordis group.

Tencel is the dominant force in Lyocell production, with only one competitor – Austrian company Lenzing. It sells Lyocell under the Tencel brand name into two markets for Tencel fibre: textiles and garments, and nonwoven material for use in applications such as disposable wipes and filters.

Of Tencel's 360 staff worldwide, 200 are based in the UK, where it has one manufacturing unit, R&D laboratories, administration offices and a marketing office/showroom in London. It also has two more manufacturing plants in Mobile, Alabama, and offices in New York, Hong Kong, Tokyo, Bangalore, São Paulo, and Shanghai.

## Company Culture and Style

Tencel's main business is development and production of high-performance fibre and it is, by its nature, a highly-technical organisation. It employs a mix of people from chemical engineers in its research labs through to technicians on its factory floors and creative types in its marketing department, but the vast majority of its employees are on the technical side.

It has around 45 researchers carrying out fibre and fabric research at its labs in Derby, plus 300 manufacturing staff in its plants in Grimsby and Mobile. The remaining staff work in marketing, sales and merchandising – and will generally have a background in textiles. However, Tencel aims to be market-driven rather than product-led, and marketing skills will become increasingly important as the business grows.

For those with an interest in textiles or high-performance materials, Tencel is an exciting and challenging place to work. It develops leading-edge technology, carries out its manufacturing in state-of-the-art plants, and has succeeded in turning Tencel into a premium brand that employees are proud to be associated with.

Tencel's extremely low staff turnover is a testimony to the rewards of working there. In 2002 only around 20 people worldwide left the company, and the year before that only two people left. 'We don't have a turnover issue,' says Mike Proctor, the company's Human Resources and Business Development Director. The company has a good working relationship with the trade unions both in the UK and US.

As a manufacturing company, Tencel is unsurprisingly fairly male-dominated overall, since fewer women tend to apply for technical jobs. The company does, however, regard itself as 'completely equal opportunities'. It does have some female technical employees and on the marketing side the male:female ratio is 50:50.

Though customer-facing staff in the offices wear suits and (in the case of men) ties, the atmosphere within the company generally is informal but orderly, with manufacturing teams wearing a casual uniform they chose for themselves.

For the 300 manufacturing staff who keep the plants running, flexible working is obviously not really an option. But the five-shift system worked is highly popular with employees, meaning they only work three or four days before having a break and giving them regular breaks of around 18 days.

## Human Resources

Given the nature of its business and the nature of its workforce, it's to be expected that Tencel looks to take on mainly people with a technical background. In its Derby labs, researchers will have a postgraduate or higher degree in a relevant subject, such as chemistry, physics or chemical engineering; many of them have doctorates.

Manufacturing workers do not need a degree, but Tencel is looking for evidence of technical ability and, ideally, experience in the fibre or chemical industries. Its major UK manufacturing plant in Grimsby is located on the Humber

Bank, where a wide range of chemical companies are based, and Tencel can draw on a large pool of trained staff.

Recruitment for manufacturing staff is generally carried out via ads in the local paper; the company's clean, pleasant, ultra-modern working environment and five-shift system mean it has no trouble filling jobs.

Researchers and marketing staff are generally recruited via ads in the national press. The company does not generally get involved in the university milk-round but will sometimes approach local universities with a strong track record in science subjects if it has specific technical jobs it needs to fill.

## Career Opportunity and Development

Tencel has a very stable and long-standing senior management team. Many of the senior managers are employees from the Courtaulds days; at board level, average length of service is 21 years and one member has 40 years' service.

But this doesn't mean there are no opportunities for career development. Below board level a lot of new talent is bubbling up. Tencel is growing fast, and many employees have been with the company only two or three years (though as noted above, once they've joined few people seem to leave).

On the manufacturing side, there are opportunities to rise to shift operations manager – a key role involving running the factory and taking production decisions – and production manager. A highly-skilled workforce is essential to Tencel's business and it invests heavily in training for its manufacturing staff, with the aim of bringing them to NVQ Level 3 standard.

Most of the company's senior management, however, are graduates who have risen from the research and marketing side. Tencel emphasises internal promotion, and all jobs below board level are advertised internally to begin with. It also believes in internal development and each year will plan one or two key moves in each location, to keep the flow of ideas within the company moving.

This includes moves overseas: Tencel has a presence in seven countries around the world and tries to create opportunities for sales, marketing and manufacturing staff to work in other countries on a short- or long-term basis.

## Remuneration

People want to work for Tencel because it's a dynamic, growing company, not because of the money: the company is the first to admit that its UK pay is currently only average for the industry, and it offers very few other frills.

UK employees, however, do benefit from an excellent pension plan, carried over from the Courtaulds days, when it was one of the top five schemes in the country.

At the moment, bonus schemes are only available to senior managers, though the company is about to introduce a performance-related bonus scheme that will apply to everyone in the organisation.

For UK employees, private health insurance starts at the £40,000 pa level. As this level has been fixed for several years, the net effect has been to extend this benefit further down the company structure. Company cars are given to staff who need them.

Elsewhere in the world, pay and benefits are commensurate with market rates, though the package of benefits offered to the workforce in Alabama is regarded as above average for the area.

## The Future

Tencel has ambitious growth plans for the future. It has innovative, patented fibre technology and intends to capitalise on its market leadership by developing new Tencel products. For example, in the textile business it has introduced a version with natural stretch – like Lycra but with the advantage of breathability.

Tencel is also actively developing its nonwovens business, which it intends will account for 50 per cent of turnover in a few years' time. There is a large potential market for biodegradeable nonwoven materials in a wide range of applications that require strength and absorbancy, and Tencel is researching new applications. In the year 2000, Tencel produced 2000 tonnes of nonwoven material; in 2003 it expects to produce 17,000 tonnes with growth continuing rapidly.

To take advantage of these emerging opportunities Tencel will continue to need both excellent technical and development staff, and talented, creative marketing people to identify and exploit new market opportunities.

# TESCO

Founded in 1919 as a tea supplier by Jack Cohen in the East End of London, Tesco took its name from Cohen and T.E. Stockwell, one of Cohen's partners. Today, Tesco is Britain's number one food retailer and controls more than 15 per cent of the country's food market through its 730 UK stores and online operations. It employs over 200,000 people in the UK alone. It also has 77 stores in the Republic of Ireland, 142 in Central Europe and over 70 in South East Asia. In its latest financial year, the Group made operating profits of £1.2 billion on sales of £25.6 billion.

**Scorecard:**

| | |
|---|---|
| Remuneration and benefits | **** |
| Progressive attitude | ***** |
| Opportunity for promotion | ***** |
| Training, development and education | **** |
| Working atmosphere and environment | *** |

**Biggest plus:**
People's contribution receives full recognition.

**Biggest minus:**
A demanding place to work with high expectations on management and above.

Tesco Stores Ltd
Tesco House
Delamare Road
Cheshunt
Hertfordshire EN8 9SL
Tel: 01992 632222
Website: www.tesco.com

# Tesco

## The Business

Jack Cohen pioneered many concepts of food retailing throughout the last century. Since his death in 1979, the company has continued his innovative traditions. It was the first major food retailer to introduce home shopping, and it remains the biggest and most profitable.

The group has four main components to its strategy: its main UK stores, its retailing services (Tesco.com, Tesco Personal Finance), non-food, and international. Within this overall framework it has developed four formats: the superstore, the Tesco Extra hypermarket, the Metro high street store and the smaller Express convenience store.

In 1996 it established an e-commerce arm, and more recently set up a joint venture to form the women's website iVillage. The group's personal finance arm, a joint venture with the Royal Bank of Scotland, now has over three million customers.

*Its philosophy is straightforward, summed up in its mantra 'better, simpler, cheaper'. This can be expanded into 'better for customers, simpler for staff and value for money throughout its operations'*

At the end of 2002 it acquired T&S Stores which owns the One Stop and Day & Nite fascias. It plans to convert 450 of the 862 stores to the Tesco Express format over the next three years.

Since the 1990s, Tesco has been expanding rapidly overseas. It now has 50 stores in Thailand, three in Taiwan, four in Malaysia and 22 in South Korea. In Europe, it has a major presence in the Republic of Ireland, Hungary and Poland, the Czech Republic and Slovakia. In Calais, France, the Tesco Vin Plus store sells beers, wines and spirits.

## Company Culture and Style

The core purpose of the company is expressed in its model called The Tesco Way. This has a number of segments, but its core purpose is 'to create value for customers to earn their lifetime loyalty.'

Its philosophy is straightforward, summed up in its mantra 'better, simpler, cheaper'. This can be expanded into 'better for customers, simpler for staff and value for money throughout its operations'. This philosophy breaks down into a stringent checklist, and any new service, operation or product should meet all three criteria. The company's 'steering wheel' allows it to track its performance against these goals.

So what is Tesco like to work for? Tough but rewarding is a good way to describe it. Miranda Clarke is the group's Head of Resourcing and has been with the company for over 15 years. As with most jobs, she has considered moving at various times – and at each time, something has come up to dissuade her from leaving. 'There are just so many opportunities here,' she says. 'Openings are coming up all the time.'

Feedback from new starters, including those in senior roles (£50,000 remuneration package and above) is telling: the company is described as challenging, fun, and not afraid to chill out and celebrate success. It is also a company with as little hierarchy as possible. Clarke describes a recent advertising awards ceremony she attended: 'With many of the other award winners, the trophy was collected by the HR Director or similar. When it came to Tesco, the person who went up to take the award was the one responsible for the ad campaign. And that's found right across the group.'

A key part of the company style is the concept of One Team. This means that, wherever you work in the group, you are one. This takes practical form in initiatives such as the one introduced in the Autumn of 2002 where each manager at a certain level spent a week in a store seeing exactly how things went at the shop level. Tesco is certainly the opposite of ivory-tower thinking!

## Human Resources

The company operates a graduate recruitment scheme, taking around 50 graduates for its head office operation and another 50 elsewhere in the group. This represents a significant resource for Tesco, although with a UK staff roll of over 200,000 it is clearly not the be-all and end-all. Indeed, more than 90 per cent of store managers within the group are recruited from within. Clare Chapman, Group Human Resources Director, comments: 'We recognise that we have people from very different places, and that what matters is what they do, not where they come from.'

As well as graduates, the group has an 'A' level entrance scheme as well as a basic entry course for those starting at or near the bottom. There is certainly no stigma attached to that, however; Tesco is definitely a company where each employee carries a manager's or director's baton in his or her knapsack. Miranda Clarke's husband, for instance, decided to drop his 'A' level studies and join Tesco instead, and is now a Regional Manager responsible for 15 stores. One of the group's Board Directors started as a part-timer. And there are many other examples throughout Tesco. There is a high level of staff loyalty within the group.

## Career Opportunity and Development

When it comes to getting on, Tesco has an exceptionally impressive set of programmes. Its Options Programme is an accelerated training suite. Its various levels help people to move upwards, according to their ability and ambition.

One of its levels produces store managers. This is a 12-week course with up to six or seven days of training back-to-back. It takes a mix of 50 people, both internal and external, and at the end of the course each is given control of a shop! The success of this programme has led the group to set up a similar programme to create store directors, and will take around 10 such candidates in 2003.

The group also has a programme called Select. This recruits both graduates and 'A' level candidates from outside Tesco.

Then there is a set of bronze, silver and gold awards. These can best be explained by an example. Take a cashier, for instance. Many of these are happy in their roles and are not interested in progressing, at least at present (fortunately for the group, since they provide a vital resource). The bronze level provides the basic must-haves of the job: legal, hygiene, etc. Once these are mastered, that cashier might take the silver award, providing the skills for additional responsibilities. Then the gold award would go further, allowing him or her to become a trainer of future cashiers. Those who wanted to progress further up the ladder can then embark on an appropriate level of the Options scheme.

There are many opportunities for progression, and over 1,000 management roles are advertised within Tesco each year. With the group's overseas presence, these opportunities include many in Europe and the Far East. Anyone interested in this type of progression would be 'talent spotted' in the career management interview and, if suitable, would be taken forward to a talent planning meeting, involving feedback from various managers. The successful candidates would then be matched to a job when available, and offered massive assistance in areas such as childcare, language training and moving help.

# Remuneration

The group operates a performance-related pay scheme, whereby employees are appraised annually and given quarterly updates. Pay may be regionally weighted.

Tesco has all the additional remuneration elements one would expect of a leading British company. These include a save-as-you-earn and buy-as-you-earn share schemes, whereby staff members can set aside a proportion of their wages to buy shares in the company. Over 80,000 employees now hold shares in Tesco, cementing their loyalty to the group.

All employees can join the company's award-winning defined-benefit pension scheme, Pension Builder, which is based on career average earnings.

There is a company car scheme for certain levels, which in recent years has become highly flexible. Employees can now keep the fuel allowance instead of the car, or vice versa, or both. There is also the option to take a cash alternative.

Another incentive is the Record Breakers scheme. Every six months, the board nominates ten products, and stores compete in promoting them. The winning stores win a specified amount for their store fund, which can be spent on sports and social activities.

Staff also benefit from a staff discount card, low-cost membership of the group's Extra Choices Club, which offers great deals on short breaks and holidays, and discounted gym membership at clubs across the country.

## The Future

For Tesco, the focus for the future remains firmly on the customer. Miranda Clarke: 'We need to meet customer needs and, wherever possible, anticipate those needs.' She points out that, of the Tesco creed of 'better, simpler, cheaper', the best for the customer element is still paramount.

Tesco sees no problem with the fierce level of competition in the marketplace at the moment: indeed, it provides an additional spur to the company to clarify its thinking and maximise its delivery. Clarke: 'Competition is good for the customer, and we're behind anything that falls into that category.'

Chapman agrees with this, and points out the importance of innovation in this area. 'If you are going to follow the customer, you have to understand the customer. A lot of our innovations are going to come from recognising their differing lifestyle choices and needs.' Given Tesco's past successes, staying on top of customer needs does not look like posing too great a problem for the group.

TNT UK Ltd is a customer-focused, staff-dedicated company in the express delivery, logistics and mail industry. It has established itself as a dominant player in this field by encouraging total commitment to service excellence and by employing committed sales and results-driven achievers. Its success in an intensely competitive environment has also been achieved via progressive and innovative business strategies, which include the clever use of technology while maintaining old-fashioned beliefs and personal touches from the MD down.

**Scorecard:**

| | |
|---|---|
| Remuneration and benefits | **** |
| Progressive attitude | ***** |
| Opportunity for promotion | ***** |
| Training, development and education | ***** |
| Working atmosphere and environment | **** |

**Biggest plus:**
TNT prides itself on its lack of hierarchical structure and of maintaining a 'no barriers' open door policy for both staff and customers.

**Biggest minus:**
The incredibly aggressive, sales-driven working environment won't suit people who aren't completely dedicated to the company.

TNT Express House
Holly Lane
Atherstone
Warwickshire CV9 2RY
Tel: 01827 303030
Fax: 01827 301301
Email: info@tnt.co.uk
Website: www.tnt.co.uk

# TNT

## The Business

TNT first entered the UK market in 1978, buying out Inter-County Express which, at the time, had a few hundred employees and turnover of less than £5 million per annum. Since then, TNT UK Ltd has grown organically to become known as one of the country's leading express delivery companies, with sales of nearly £1 billion per year. It now employs nearly 14,000 people around the UK and in Ireland, and operates more than 6,000 vehicles from over 100 locations.

Growth year-on-year has outgrown the market and this year, the company will again record a profit – the ninth successive year of doing so.

Parent company, TPG, with headquarters in Amsterdam, is a global provider of mail, express and logistics services.

*One of the greatest advantages about working for TNT is that there is always room for promotion, especially considering that the company is opening new depots all the time, employing around 250 people in each*

TNT UK comprises three principal businesses, each specialising in a particular sector or market: TNT Express Services provides national and international door-to-door express delivery services for businesses, TNT Logistics delivers a wide range of supply chain activities to major blue-chip companies, TNT Newsfast is the market-leading carrier of national newspapers and magazines in the UK.

All that the company does is underlined by its determination to make a positive impact on society. This manifests itself not only in its strong belief in corporate social responsibility, but also in the way the company respects its staff. TNT received recognition as an 'Investor in People' in 1994 and is now considered by the industry as the benchmark for staff training.

## Company Culture and Style

The crux of TNT's values in terms of staff can be found in the emphasis it places on its 'home-grown timber' policy. As Tom Bell, MD of TNT Express Services, explains: 'Because we have grown organically, we've brought people in as the business has grown, and these people have grown with us. Of the 18 directors who report to me, only one was brought in from the outside – all the others have progressed from lower levels within the company.'

The overall company culture very much hinges on that philosophy but also operates in an environment of aggressive competitiveness. Bell is very direct about the kind of people he's looking for – keen, young, bright, with a good attitude and a commitment to bettering themselves. 'You're either a TNT person or you're not,' he says. Those who get through their first six months at the company tend to stay for many years – this year 64 staff received recognition for 25 years' service, while next year this will reach 111.

So, definitely no shrinking violets in this company, but for those who do thrive, there is very much an open-door policy instituted from top management down. 'I am very careful to foster a 'no barriers' culture. If a customer or a staff member phones me, there is no secretary screening my calls and I believe in my staff – no matter who they are – calling me by my first name,' Bell says.

Another indication of the lack of hierarchy is that staff who have performed well can expect a personal, hand-written note from Bell – email is too impersonal for this important gesture, he believes.

Working at TNT is all about flexibility and, by extension, trust. This means staff aren't penalised for arriving at work five minutes late, or for having to take care of personal business during working hours, but in return, they are expected to give their best at all times. Performance measurements are held in high regard and take place regularly.

Allied to this is the emphasis the company places on training. With about 4,000 similar businesses in the UK alone, TNT has to maintain its position of being one of the big four globally in its industry and, explains Suzie Theobald, Group Personnel Director, the differentiator lies in its people.

A high percentage of the team is female, right from depot managers to director level, where the IT, financial and personnel directors are all women.

## Human Resources

All vacancies are advertised around the globe and key to staff loyalty to TNT is its home-grown timber policy, where current staff are encouraged to grow within the organisation. This works well, as indicated by the fact that there have been 2,400 'positive development moves' in the past 12 months.

There are no minimum criteria to promotion and, indeed, Bell himself climbed the ranks from driver to current MD, as did Theobald, who started her career at TNT as a Site Manager for the company's same-day delivery service.

Because of the type of business TNT is in, the HR department is very much focused on providing a safe working environment. The UK company has been awarded a British Safety Council five-star rating as well as earning 4 Swords of Honour, recognising them as one of the top 40 safest companies in the world.

'The Swords of Honour are very prestigious, and internally recognise that we do provide a safe and secure environment and that our people are involved in the safety process. It also projects a good image externally and has created much goodwill within the company,' Bell says.

Retention of staff is vital and although 20 per cent of new starters move on in their first six months, Theobald is quick to explain that the majority of these are telesales staff, who are notoriously fickle. Management turnover stands at four per cent, a figure that is more indicative of TNT's situation, she believes.

## Career Opportunity and Development

One of the greatest advantages about working for TNT is that there is always room for promotion, especially considering that the company is opening new depots all the time, employing around 250 people in each.

Because TNT is part of a worldwide business, the opportunities to work abroad are extensive. Seven people from the UK have, in the past year, been transferred to locations including Australia, the US and Holland.

There is a fairly strong graduate recruitment programme, which each year takes in up to 14 students for a year. 'This enables us to find out where their strengths are and whether they are the kind of people we are looking for,' explains Theobald. In addition, every 18 months, 24 staff are chosen by external selectors to undertake a general management programme designed by Nottingham University. Ninety-five per cent of the first intake have already been promoted and, of those, 64 per cent received their promotion while still on the course.

As demonstrated by its IIP status, TNT places great emphasis on training, over 90 per cent of which is done internally. All staff members are appraised at least once a year, after which they discuss their training needs with their line manager. 'This helps the individual to manage his or her own career and, once the manager has concurred, the training is automatically undertaken,' Theobald says. 'When we track a career path and related training needs, we work on the current job role and bear in mind what will be essential to the next job.

'Our aim is to provide a work environment that is conducive to multi-skilling; to enable people throughout the business to use practical techniques and skills acquired through company training schemes,' she explains.

## Remuneration

Theobald believes salaries are in the upper quartile for the industry, and include a basic plus an incentive. For example, a good depot manager could be earning around £70,000 when bonuses are taken into account. Everyone in the company, even those in the finance and administration departments, is on a bonus scheme of some form or other and certain staff can earn up to 50 per cent of their salaries in this way. Drivers are on a productivity incentive, sales staff on the usual bonus and commission, while management are all on quarterly bonuses linked to profit. Senior management bonuses are linked to the annual profit figure.

TNT also provides a pension scheme, contributing seven per cent, with staff adding in three per cent. Annual leave is set at 26 days.

Company cars, usually Audi, Volvo or Rover models, are a common perk within the company, with staff from the sales, depot management, finance and administration departments accounting for the 1,800 company cars.

To add rewards further down the line, managers are provided with unlimited 'Tommy Trucker' awards – £5 Marks & Spencer vouchers, which they can hand out to staff as incentives for any good deed. Then there are the quarterly 'Make It Happen' awards which are given to people who have done something really special, eg a driver who might have apprehended a thief.

## The Future

'We will continue to outgrow the market, produce record results, maintain the healthy financial state of the company and provide wonderful opportunities to people who want to be in an international business,' is how Bell sums up aims and goals for the next five years.

'For any young person who wants a career, the service industry is the way to go,' he believes. 'We are a quality organisation offering opportunities that are beyond belief if you've got get up and go and a desire to win. Although we are considered a role model in our industry at the moment and the UK is TPG's top-performing division, we are not inward focused or too proud to learn from other companies.'

All laudable aims and, with TNT's current focus on its staff and on customer service, ones which should be sustainable for the next 10 years and longer.

The Travel Inn chain is part of Whitbread Group Plc and operates at the budget rather than luxury end of the accommodation market. This isn't a comment on its commitment to excellence or the dedication of its staff, however, which is paramount. It operates throughout the UK, mostly with accommodation adjacent to other Whitbread premises, although it does have a number of stand-alone properties, which contain a Travel Inn branded restaurant called Slice.

## Scorecard:
| | |
|---|---|
| Remuneration and benefits | **** |
| Progressive attitude | **** |
| Opportunity for promotion | ***** |
| Training, development and education | **** |
| Working atmosphere and environment | **** |

## Biggest plus:
The people – a survey showed that 94 per cent of the staff had good friends at work, which tells you something about the atmosphere.

## Biggest minus:
The organisation's reputation as a budget service can bring out the snob in some job applicants, who believe they can't be taught much by such an organisation. They are wrong.

Travel Inn
Oakley House
Oakley Road
Leagrave
Luton, LU4 9QH
Tel: 01582 499297
Fax: 01582 499413
Websites: www.travelinn.co.uk
www.travelinnjobs.co.uk

# Travel Inn

## The Business

Travel Inn is part of the Whitbread group and exists as a joint venture between two companies within the group, Whitbread Hotels and Whitbread Restaurants. Typically you'll find them next to a Beefeater or other restaurant outlet owned by the group, except in some cases where they have independent managed facilities. It remains in the UK, although is considering expansion overseas; there were no firm plans in this area to announce at the time of writing.

Established 15 years ago, the organisation's attachment to Whitbread gives the staff many of the benefits of working for a substantial public quoted company (see page 430 for Whitbread's profile) without feeling they are employed by some faceless conglomerate. It employs some 7,000 people working across 300 premises, and this includes 17,000 rooms. Jobs exist both in customer service and in management, and there will be considerable expansion over the next few years – by 2008 the organisation aims to have 25,000 rooms. Given that it has taken 15 years to reach 17,000 it can be seen that its growth targets are aggressive in the extreme.

Staff turnover, in common with most of the hospitality industry, is heavy – but this largest hotel network in the UK is sufficiently well thought of to have earned a place in the 2003 Sunday Times 100 Best Companies to Work For survey.

*The company operates 100 per cent Satisfaction Guarantee; if a customer doesn't get a good night's sleep they can get a refund and many members of staff are trained and authorised to give it on the spot – there's no reference to managers above and no writing to head office*

## Company Culture and Style

The values, or beliefs as Travel Inn calls them, to which the organisation subscribes are perhaps not astonishing but are no less worthy for that. These beliefs are 'Dare to Care', 'Keep it Simple' and 'Right First Time', and underpin everything that the company does, both from a customer perspective, and a team perspective.

For such a substantial business, though, the approach is deceptively informal (not to be confused with lax or uncompetitive – more on that later). Clearly, customer-facing staff will be wearing uniforms as the customers will expect, and equally clearly the senior executives visiting shareholder events and City analysts will do them the minimal courtesy of wearing a suit. However, beyond that there are no hard and fast dress rules and this non-hierarchical attitude is reflected in the day-to-day running of the company. 'There's a lot of good humour,' says HR manager Kevin Rhodes. 'You can share a laugh and a joke with senior executives.'

This apparently relaxed attitude, however, masks an intense seriousness about putting the customer first and empowering staff so that they can do so. The company operates 100 per cent Satisfaction Guarantee; if a customer doesn't get a good night's sleep they can get a refund and many members of staff are trained and authorised to give it on the spot – there's no reference to managers above and no writing to head office. The banter and relaxed attitude also masks competition between the different premises – it's friendly competition but everyone wants their hotel to be the best and there are annual awards to reflect this.

As well as an openness to this sort of culture and hard work, an ideal employee will be meticulous with attention to detail – this is true of everyone from the managers to the housekeeping staff. It is also aware of equal opportunities issues and is pleased to note that at least 33 per cent of the senior managers are women, as audited independently by the *Sunday Times*.

## Human Resources

Recruitment happens in a number of different ways depending on the level of the vacancy being filled. Housekeeping, reception, and food and beverage staff will be sought locally by site managers who are allocated a budget and given autonomy to recruit as they believe appropriate. Recruiting the managers centres mostly around the graduate market, beginning with work experience placements while candidates are still at college. 'There's a huge market to be tapped, you hear about graduates being unable to get jobs so we talk to them at an early stage,' says Rhodes. Anyone interested in working for the company who has been missed out of that particular loop could do worse than to check the dedicated recruitment website, which also has links to other vacancies within the Whitbread Group.

It is down to the management teams within Travel Inn that credit lies for the fun and informal atmosphere within the units. An indicator of this is that 74 per cent of the people are confident in their management and 70 per cent felt their work/life balance was being catered for (source, once again, the *Sunday Times* survey). The hotel trade is notorious for long hours and poor social life; Travel Inn is aware of this and discourages excessive hours, preferring to have an effective workforce for their core time.

The other area in which HR is extremely active is succession planning. Rhodes estimates that 70 per cent of management jobs are filled through internal promotion.

## Career Opportunity and Development

Moving about within Travel Inn is encouraged as long as it fits with the aims of building the business, and to achieve an individual's career aims they have a year-end appraisal as well as a half-yearly meeting with their line manager. If someone is looking for a move, their first natural calling point would be the Travel Inn intranet. They then need to talk to their line manager, who will sponsor their application if the person is ready for their next move

The annual training budget is a hefty £3 million, and most staff confirm that they are well sponsored to acquire new skills, up to and including sponsorship for formal qualifications such as an MBA. Rhodes' aim is to get everybody working to a personal development plan to enable team members to identify their own goals and skills gaps, which happens for the majority already.

## Remuneration

Employment candidates and new staff are often pleased to note that Travel Inn pay levels are ahead of the competition in most cases. A London-based General Manager can be earning above £40,000 per annum. Pay increases are at the discretion of line managers, who will have a budget within which to work, that they may allocate according to performance if they wish.

Rewards are not simply financial, however. A good pension scheme is provided as would be expected with any substantial business; there are also incentives such as the annual 'award trip' for annual award winners within Managed Travel Inn (in late 2002 a group of 14 employees were sent to Dubai for four days). Incentives are also given for achieving 100 per cent occupancy, and outstanding brand audit scores. Bonuses are allocated on the basis of a balanced scorecard system that assesses a manager's impact on the customers, his or her team, and the shareholders. Inevitably, everyone gets a Whitbread discount card immediately when they join.

## The Future

The business' aggressive growth targets have already been stated and will inevitably mean the future will involve a lot of recruitment in the medium term. Other possible growth areas may include further business services; in 2001 the company opened its first Touchbase centre, which is a purpose built meeting rooms concept. As of March 2003 they have three Touchbases in operation, and the plan for 2003/4 is to open another 15 of these.

Rhodes' personal ambition is to continue building the company's reputation as one of the best employers in the UK. Given the hot-house environment that has traditionally been the hotel trade and contrasting this with the company's track record in employee satisfaction to date, you get the distinct impression that he and his team are succeeding.

# United Business Media

United Business Media provides business information services principally to the technology, healthcare, media, automotive and financial services industries. The services are provided by its leading market research, news distribution, publishing and events organising businesses. United Business Media has market-leading positions in professional media, news distribution and market research, and also has a specialist classified advertising publication business.

**Scorecard:**

Remuneration and benefits                    ****
Progressive attitude                         ****
Opportunity for promotion                    ****
Training, development and education:         ****
Working atmosphere and environment:          ****

**Biggest plus:**
Its dynamism and fast pace mean that you're never bored.

**Biggest minus:**
It's hard and demanding work, so won't appeal to everyone.


United Business Media
Ludgate House
245 Blackfriars Road
London SE1 9UY
Tel: 020 7921 5090
Website: www.unitedbusinessmedia.com

# United Business Media

## The Business

United Business Media (UBM) came into being as the result of a merger between United News & Media plc and MAI plc. The former company specialised in newspaper publishing, including *The Daily Express*, *The Daily Star* and regional titles: these were sold following the merger. MAI focused on TV and market research: the TV interests have recently been divested from the group. What remains is an organisation dedicated to providing business information services – through trade shows, exhibitions, and the publishing of literally hundreds of magazines.

UBM has three core divisions: professional media, market research and news distribution. In its latest financial results, the professional media division produced a turnover of £533 million, operating profit of £32 million and had 3,163 employees. The division includes CMP Media, the leading US high-tech B2B media company, and provider of healthcare information and education; CMP information, a UK-headquartered magazine and events business; and CMP Asia, with exhibitions and publications in key Asian markets.

*Despite its scale, the company has clearly retained the friendly, smaller company feel; perhaps assisted by its divisional structure and also by its ability and desire to take decisions quickly in an exceptionally fast-moving industry*

The market research division had a turnover of £194 million, operating profit of £23 million and 1,471 employees. NOP World is the ninth largest market research company globally, with brands including NOP Research, Strategic Marketing Corporation, Mediamark Research Inc and Roper/ASW.

The news distribution division had a turnover of £125 million, operating profit of £35 million and 975 employees. PR Newswire and PR Newswire Europe provide comprehensive communications services for PR and investor relations people.

UBM also has a specialist classified advertising publication business that includes *Exchange & Mart*, *Auto Exchange*, *Industrial Exchange & Mart* and *Dalton's Weekly*.

## Company Culture and Style

When it comes to its culture, UBM's watchword is 'dynamic'. As Jane Stables, UBM's Group Legal and Personnel Director, puts it, 'We have a small company environment in a big company'. UBM certainly is big: it has over 6,000 employees and is listed on the London Stock Exchange (just falling out of the FTSE 100 last year). Despite this scale, the company has clearly retained the friendly, smaller company feel; perhaps assisted by its divisional structure and also by its ability and desire to take decisions quickly in an exceptionally fast-moving industry. The FT's Lex Column described UBM several years ago as having a 'fleet-footed and nimble management', and this remains true today.

The structure is the opposite of bureaucratic, and there is no sense of it being boxed into rules or traditions. There is a flat management structure, a fluidity, an informality – and a sense that anyone can rewrite its approach at any time.

So who flourishes at UBM – and who doesn't? The winners are those capable of thinking outside the box; of employing creativity; and of working hard. The losers are those best described by the opposite of those qualities.

The company has an exceptionally flexible working policy, recognising that the work/life balance has changed radically in recent years. Unlike some companies that only pay lip service to this fact, however, UBM practises what it preaches. Any employee can apply to work flexibly – and currently, over half of the head office workforce does so in some shape or form: varying hours, working from home, job sharing, part-time working, and more. Jane Stables: 'We train our managers to manage people in this pattern. The key is that employees have to convince us that they can cope with the flexible aspect, such as fitting in meetings if working from home.'

In terms of its people, UBM aims to have a wide mix of people from a diversity of backgrounds. Critically, there is no strict need to have worked in media before joining the company. What is needed is the ability to demonstrate creativity and commitment to work.

## Human Resources

UBM regards the HR function as a business partner. As a result, its HR people are highly business-oriented. Jane Stables: 'We recognise that our business is knowledge-based and our people are our business opportunity. We are constantly in partnership with the business managers to make sure people are looked after as they would want to be.'

A demonstration of the importance the company allots to HR is Stable's own position: she reports directly to the Chief Executive Officer and has a place on the company's informal executive committee.

Perhaps surprisingly for a media-related company, there is no sign of the ageism prevalent in some areas of industry; indeed, people of any age are welcome to apply to UBM as long as they can demonstrate ability, creativity and flexibility. A dynamic quality, a hands-on attitude and a practical rather than a theoretical approach are the only requirements. Similarly, a degree is not necessary, although graduates can be given a fast-track to succeed.

## Career Opportunity and Development

Given the company's three main divisions, there is plenty of opportunity to move within UBM to further one's career. As Stables says, skills are transferable at UBM. In the same way, there are opportunities to move to other countries: over half of its 6,000+ employees are in the USA, with the remainder spread between the UK, Continental Europe and the Far East. All vacancies are advertised internally and anyone can apply for a job within UBM.

There is a formal appraisal process that includes an opportunity for each employee to discuss his or her training needs. There is also a set of internal and external mentoring programmes.

UBM operates a programme whereby potential leaders are brought together. These are of different ages, background and aspirations, the only shared criterion being that they have been singled out as having leadership potential. In 2002, the programme numbered 20 employees. They are examined individually at the beginning of the year and then given formal training as a group. Stables: 'This programme is all about leadership. It's designed to help you equip yourself as a leader.' The programme frequently enlists the aid of some high-ranking mentors: in 2002, the programme was run by a former head of Cranfield's Management Development School.

Some companies within UBM operate a graduate recruitment programme. This numbered around 20 individuals in 2002. Successful entrants receive a fast track to management and an overview of the company's various functions.

## Remuneration

UBM measures itself against its market and aims to be around a median payer. On top of salary, there is an annual bonus scheme based on profitability and the individual's personal business plan. Stables: 'These plans may have more than just financial elements. An individual might be given a specific project, for instance, and be measured against how well this is achieved.'

The company operates a defined contribution salary scheme for all employees. There is also life cover and PHI cover. It has moved away from company cars to offering cash allowances.

## The Future

The company plans to extend the range of its services to its key business sectors by investing in new products, by providing its services globally and by acquiring companies that extend its range of products and enhance its growth prospects.

Stables summed up her view of UBM's future as follows: 'We want each division to be number one in its market place. At the moment, for instance, our market research division is the ninth largest in the world. Some companies might be content with this, but we don't intend to rest until we've established genuine leadership for every part of UBM. That means being consistently better than the competition, all the time.'

This self-assigned goal will be demanding; given UBM's strength in dynamic, creative achievers, however, it looks perfectly achievable.

## UNIVERSAL MUSIC UK

Universal Music is the largest recording company in the UK, employing 1,250 people (including Britannia Music) and with sales of £517 million in 2002. A public company, Universal is home to many record labels, including Polydor, Universal – Island Mercury, Philips, MCA, and Decca.

**Scorecard:**

| | |
|---|---|
| Remuneration and benefits | ***** |
| Progressive attitude | **** |
| Opportunity for promotion | **** |
| Training, development and education | **** |
| Working atmosphere and environment | ***** |

**Biggest plus:**
The opportunity to work in an industry about which many people are passionate.

**Biggest minus:**
Pressure to perform all the time.

Universal Music
1 Sussex Place
Hammersmith
London W6 9XS
Tel: 020 8910 5000
Website: www.umusic.com

# Universal Music

## The Business

The Universal Music story originally began in 1898 with the foundation of Deutsche Grammophon by Siemens. That company would eventually become Polygram, which in turn would be acquired by the Seagram-owned MCA-Universal in 1998. The Universal Music Group was formed a year later, and the year after that became a division of media conglomerate Vivendi Universal.

The consolidation that took place was deemed necessary in the face both of increased competition within the media and entertainment industry and of contraction of the market for new recorded music. Falling sales of CDs and the impact of music piracy have hit small and large music businesses alike and seen many a share price dip as a result.

## Company Culture and Style

An informal work culture prevails throughout Universal; one that is creatively-driven, rather than led by accountants. Much of this is down to chairman Lucian Grange who has extended the range and genre of artists signed to the business, since being appointed two years ago. According to Malcolm Swatton, HR Director, the enthusiasm for new musical talent is as strong at the top of the organisation as it is anywhere else. 'At board meetings, at least 50 per cent of the time is taken up with talking about new signings and potential signings, playing and listening to new releases, and reviewing and critiquing videos and TV commercials being produced,' he says.

*Universal deliberately accommodates and supports the right of the managing director of each label to run the business according to their own vision. At a sales level this has to be managed carefully, but overall this diversity is seen as a positive asset*

It is also a highly competitive environment. Naturally, Universal is in competition with other manufacturers and suppliers of published music, but the record labels within the group are also in competition with one another. The likes of Mercury and Polydor operate quite separately and feel different places in which to work. Universal deliberately accommodates and supports the right of the managing director of each label to run the business according to their own vision. At a sales level this has to be managed carefully, but overall this diversity is seen as a positive asset. It certainly adds to the fun element. In an industry where success is measured weekly, the workplace is fast-moving and sometimes highly charged.

Marketing of product is a key aspect of the business. Each label has its own marketing department, which is responsible for campaign and front-line marketing of current music releases. Alongside this label-based activity there is a strategic and catalogue marketing department. Here, the focus is on repackaging and remarketing older material. Other marketing is coordinated around film soundtracks, compilation albums and TV programmes.

Another important area of activity is artist and repertoire (A&R). Again, there is a dedicated team at each label that is geared towards managing the relationship with the music acts. Scouts regularly check out music venues for new talent, while managers take responsibility for finding producers and songwriters with which their artists can collaborate.

## Human Resources

There is a definite cachet to working in the music industry and at the biggest company in the industry this is enhanced still further. Small wonder then that Universal does not have a recruitment problem. In fact, on average it receives between 100 and 150 speculative CVs each week. Most applicants do not pass the pre-sift but those that do are interviewed in the first instance by HR. In practice, even those that are rejected at the earliest stage may be successful later on, since many applicants send CVs direct to music labels. If a manager there sees something they like they will pass it back to HR and an interview may eventually be arranged.

Even though Universal is clearly a place people want to work, it advertises in trade publications for professional vacancies and uses search firms for senior appointments. It has also recently introduced a graduate recruitment programme. In these areas, qualifications matter; in the creative areas of the business, they are less significant. There, according to Swatton, 'It's passion, it's vision, it's energy, it's drive and it's experience that count.'

With this in mind, a good deal of importance is attached to face-to-face interviewing. Two or three interviews will take place in order to get a sense of the individual and the kind of relationship they would have with existing team members. In A&R, for example, the current managing director sees nine out of ten of all new recruits before they are hired.

## Career Opportunity and Development

'We don't run courses in this organisation for everyone. When you join you'll go through an induction process, like everyone else – what we call 'Introduction to Music'. But outside of that the only training you'll receive is relevant to your performance, relevant to plug a skills gap or relevant to prepare you for a promotion,' explains Swatton.

In such a highly competitive environment targets feature prominently. Everyone has a regular career review with their line manager and sometimes also with HR. In identifying the skills gaps present in each individual, employees have the opportunity to take a wide variety of technical and competency-based workshops. There are four kinds of training activity: department specific events; residential events for key performers; one-day courses and short skills courses for junior staff.

Outside the appraisal process, managers at Universal grade staff on a 'traffic light' basis. About 10 per cent are high-performing greens: these are the managers of the future and will be nurtured accordingly. Most of the rest are amber: they are performing adequately but are not dynamic enough to be classed as green. Reds are low performers and these will be moved on if they cannot improve their performance. If possible they may be found a more suitable position for their abilities elsewhere in the business, but otherwise they will need to seek alternative employment. With demand to work at Universal so high there is never any shortage of replacements.

## Remuneration

Reward strategy at Universal is highly incentivised. Base pay is upper quartile but it is the supplementary bonuses that help create and motivate the high performers so prized within the business. The bonus scheme for managers is an amalgam of personal performance, business unit performance, UK performance and Universal's global performance. It can lead to pay-outs of up to 200 per cent of on-target bonus earnings. A&R has a specific bonus scheme based on artist royalties and sales, while sales staff have a commission-based bonus structure. Every individual receives a guaranteed bonus payment at the end of the year – last year this amounted to three per cent of base pay.

There are also a number of discretionary bonus schemes. Usually, this applies to people who have performed exceptionally well over a period of time or for a particular project. All employees are eligible for two free Universal products each month, while at Britannia good attendance can be rewarded with free concert tickets or a cash reward.

At a time of cutbacks in the pensions industry, the company has recently upped the contribution it makes to its money-purchase scheme, to which everyone has access. Life assurance and permanent health insurance is also available to all. Managers are immediately eligible for private medical cover, which is extended to other employees after two years' service.

## The Future

Although Universal enjoyed record turnover and record profits in 2002, there are major challenges to its immediate future and that of the music industry as a whole. The two main ongoing concerns are piracy and Internet file-sharing, and the advent of Broadband is set to deepen the impact of the latter still further.

According to Swatton, a number of initiatives are in the pipeline to combat piracy – both company-led and industry-wide. Universal has also established a new media department to grab a larger slice of online activity. He adds, 'From an HR perspective we've got to do everything we can to manage expectations but also not to make people feel too insecure or worried at the change happening in the marketplace or the business. In some ways it's a double-edged sword because if you are in a business that is contracting, you frighten off the people you want to attract and retain the people who are worried about their security and future and who should really be thinking about other career moves.'

THE **Human** NETWORK

Vanco is a global virtual network operator, which has been rated one of the world's 500 fastest-growing technology companies. Treating telecommunications infrastructure as a commodity, it designs, implements and manages corporate data networks, and prides itself on its ability to provide quick, reliable and secure communications for companies across the globe. It now employs some 350 people and its products are to be found in nearly 200 countries. Clients include Pilkington Compass Group, Virgin Megastores, Staples, Tibbett & Britten and Ford. At January 2002 pre-tax profits were £3.1 million on turnover of £37.1 million

**Scorecard:**

| | |
|---|---|
| Remuneration and benefits | ***** |
| Progressive attitude | ***** |
| Opportunity for promotion | **** |
| Training, development and education | ***** |
| Working atmosphere and environment | **** |

**Biggest plus:**
The chance to work in a truly multicultural team and operate within a pioneering 'challenger' company that benefits from plc status.

**Biggest minus:**
The isolated location of its head office, and an often pressurised environment with nowhere to hide if you don't perform.

Vanco
John Busch House
277 London Road
Isleworth
Middlesex TW7 5AX
Tel: 020 8380 1000
Fax: 020 8380 1001
Website: www.vanco.info

# Vanco

## The Business

Vanco has been a pioneer since the early 1990s, when liberalisation of telecoms monopolies across Europe gave rise to the development of competing carriers. As a virtual network operator it does not own infrastructure: it is 'an independent broker of connections' which relies on many different operators. By treating bandwidth as a commodity, it provides customers with access to best prices and solutions using the most appropriate technology.

Chief Executive, Allen Timpany, bought the then loss-making company in 1988 and shifted its focus from bureau services to the provision of managed data networks. The company broke even two years later. In 1993 Vanco opened its first international office in Madrid; it now has bases in cities including Paris, Hong Kong, Singapore, Sydney, Dubai, Johannesburg and Buenos Aires. With an active presence in more than 50 countries, its solutions are available in some 190 countries.

In 2000 Vanco earned a place in Deloitte & Touche's Hot 500 list of global growth IT companies, with continued growth in profits and turnover of around 40 per cent. In November 2001 the company floated on London's main Stock Exchange. It was the only main listing of Q4 and went ahead very successfully despite the aftermath of September 11.

*If you want to join a company where you can have an input in improving – and creating – ways of working, you will thrive*

The company positions itself at the forefront of new technologies and creates bespoke solutions. With the aim of providing a top quality customer experience, it recently recruited its first 'quality director' from the Hilton hotel chain. In a tough climate for telecoms, Vanco continues to grow, and has increased revenues year-on-year for a decade. Its success stems from its cohesive and highly-motivated team, an in-depth understanding of customer needs, and the establishment of offices and network management capability in the US and Asia.

## Company Culture and Style

Vanco puts customers and staff at the heart of its mission, declaring itself 'the human network'. It looks for intelligent and energetic employees who are likely to be systems-oriented and to enjoy efficiency and refining processes. 'If you want to join a company where you can have an input in improving – and creating – ways of working, you will thrive,' says Ciaran Roche, Technical Consultant, who points to the company's focus on quality and service.

While the culture is fast-moving and pressurised, Vanco is keen to ensure a healthy work/life balance. Indeed, one of the company's stated aims is to encourage people to go home at night, and to encourage cross-function socialising, it operates a regular dining club, called 'Foods of the world' which entertains groups of employees at local restaurants. At present just 20 per cent of the senior management is female but the company is looking to increase this figure and, as it recruits in continental Europe, to embrace multinational diversity.

Employees are very pro-active at an individual level. For example, while the company raises money on a corporate level for CARE International and sponsors the popular Three Peaks Challenge, community initiatives are often generated by members of staff. 'We support dozens of things that people believe in,' says Andy Brown, Vanco's PR Manager. 'Some of that is structured, but a lot is by making it clear that if you come with a sensible proposition, it will receive a warm welcome.'

Vanco has a flat management framework in which teams 'tend to grow underneath people as they take more on. It's not a case of being promoted as such – it's a case of your role developing, and that is how you develop,' says Brown. Structurally, the company is divided into small business groups, each with their own finance, sales and administration teams. Small forums also meet regularly to discuss how to improve internal processes.

Overall, Vanco benefits from a consistent, strategic approach to decision-making, which stems from having had the same owner, Allen Timpany, in the driving seat for 14 years. 'I have employed powerful people around me,' he says, 'and that combination of power with responsibility is, I believe, a good formula for business.'

## Human Resources

The difficulties afflicting many telecoms operators have worked in Vanco's favour: hiring became noticeably easier in 2002 amid a tough climate for telecoms, easing worries that recruitment could not keep pace with growth. The company uses agencies to find top quality recruits, who do not necessarily need a background in computer networking but will probably possess at least an upper second degree.

The human resources function advises departments on best practice but recruitment is usually carried out by senior line managers. Vanco recruits up to 15 graduates annually but also looks for more experienced hires aged 50-plus. Timpany explains: 'I believe that in growing a business quickly, if you can hire people who have been through that learning process before, it brings a calmness and maturity to operations, which is invaluable.'

There is no system in Vanco for taking a career break: cases are managed on an individual basis, but the company accepts that it will need to look at more structured systems in the future. There is no provision for flexible working, although employees can log into Vanco's system from a different location in order to work remotely.

# Career Opportunity and Development

One of the advantages of working for this company, given its small size, fierce ambitions, established credentials and leading position in the field, is the opportunity to take a leading role in a growing office abroad. 'We don't have as many departments and places for people to go to as a larger company, but the opportunities for taking responsibility and moving around are greater,' says Timpany.

Generally, employees will work at head office in Isleworth for at least six months before moving elsewhere. If someone expresses an interest in working in a particular country, senior management might work with that employee over several months to facilitate the move and build it into that individual's career plan. Because of a lack of language skills in Britain, Vanco now also actively recruits in continental Europe for positions in the UK.

The company is developing further training structures and systems such as self-managed e-learning, and plans to roll these out over the next 12 months. At present, new hires are given a week's induction and supplementary training occurs later. Within each job role, skill areas both hard and soft are identified, and training is given in 90-minute slots. However, in order to progress within the company, employees must demonstrate good business awareness and management skills as well as mastery of specific skills.

The company runs a business executive scheme, of which one perk is the opportunity to borrow one of Vanco's sports cars for a weekend. Senior management in the company meets for strategy days three or four times each year, sometimes with outside facilitation, and mentoring and development are given according to the needs of an individual. In addition, the company is willing to look at sponsoring employees who wish to continue their learning on MBA or other professional courses, or in areas such as language skills. Succession planning within Vanco consists of training up deputies in departments and carrying out formal reviews twice a year to look at specific training needs.

# Remuneration

While other companies have been forced to make cutbacks, Vanco has continued to pay its employees competitive, above-average salaries. In addition, it relies heavily on performance-based bonuses, with almost every employee on some kind of incentive scheme. At its network management centre, for example, employees can be eligible for a bonus if they achieve a greater than 70 per cent success rate in pre-emptive fault notification. 'These schemes are linked to us achieving noticeably superior service,' says Brown.

Employees receive company cars depending on whether or not a car is relevant to their job role. Vanco has also developed a cafeteria-style benefits package, which enables employees to exchange one benefit for another, up to a certain monetary value, and which it will roll out in all offices except in countries with prohibitive regulations.

More than two-thirds of employees are shareholders in the company. 'The ability for people to share in the financial wealth that they are creating is an absolute cornerstone and it has provided a stability for us throughout turbulent times of shortage of labour,' says Timpany. 'We have had a very strong workforce, because they have had an investment and a share in the success of it.'

In addition, Vanco takes all employees and their partners on a four-day overseas break, the 'Kick Off' conference, which is held in a top hotel in continental Europe. The event 'welds the company into a single team', says Timpany. 'If you are going to offer global solutions to big companies, it's got to be evident that your company works together, and you must do more than the minimum.'

## The Future

Vanco is growing from a medium-sized company into a large business: it is coming of age, and its immediate aim is to improve what it does within a scaleable, efficient and secure framework. The market in which the company operates is currently worth some $50 billion per annum. 'Our business model is recognised internationally and we have established ourselves as a leading global provider. Now we have to make sure that we can maintain the quality of what we do internally in order to enhance the quality of service externally,' says Timpany.

His aim is to create a global brand that is 100 per cent service focused. In the long term, he predicts that Vanco will become one of the world's largest specialist global corporate data network service providers. He believes that, far from being squeezed out by multinational systems integrators such as EDS or IBM, and with the increased use of data networking and reliance by big companies, Vanco will continue to build a substantial business and reputation as a valued specialist supplier.

Virgin is the largest group of private companies in the UK, employing some 23,000 people in Britain and a further 8,000 overseas. Its business interests around the world include planes, trains, finance, music, mobile phones, soft drinks, holidays, cars, wines, publishing and bridal wear. Its total worldwide revenues in 2003 are expected to be in excess of £4.8 billion.

### Scorecard:

| | |
|---|---|
| Remuneration and benefits | **** |
| Progressive attitude | **** |
| Opportunity for promotion | **** |
| Training, development and education | *** |
| Working atmosphere and environment | ***** |

### Biggest plus:
The chance to be judged on your merits rather than fitting a mould.

### Biggest minus:
A highly-entrepreneurial, fast-moving culture that won't suit slackers.


Virgin Management Ltd
120 Campden Hill Road
London W8 7AR
Tel: 020 7313 2000
Fax: 020 7727 8200
Website: www.virgin.com

# Virgin

## The Business

Sir Richard Branson is arguably Britain's best-known entrepreneur. In 1967, as a teenager, he started *Student* magazine. This led to a mail-order business, recording studios and a chain of record shops: Virgin profited, in particular, by the success of Mike Oldfield's bestselling album *Tubular Bells* throughout the 1970s.

Branson leased his first aeroplane and launched Virgin Atlantic in 1984, offering scheduled flights between Gatwick and New York. Two years later Virgin floated on the stock market – a move that proved unsatisfactory – and in 1988 Branson announced a management buyout. Around this time, the Virgin Charter was drawn up to enshrine the agreement with partner companies. By 1990, the group had trebled its turnover over three years.

Today Virgin operates as a branded venture capital organisation, raising capital through strategic partnerships. Its structure is that of 'a family, rather than a hierarchy'; some functions such as human resources are central, and play a role in incubating businesses at early stages. Companies operate from various locations including Norwich, Crawley and Trowbridge.

*Staff are expected to 'get their hands dirty and not expect other people to do what they don't do themselves', but while the group is flexible about working patterns and encourages all employees to work at their own pace, no one should come to Virgin expecting an easy ride*

Common to all Virgin companies are qualities such as flexibility and a drive to improve on existing standards. Virgin's innovations in distribution and direct selling have revolutionised industry practice.

Virgin Management is the company that manages Branson's interests in the group. Branson himself still takes an operational role, although a small group of senior executives represents him on many company boards. As a general rule, Virgin Management likes to own at least half the equity in its businesses. Opportunities also exist for employee ownership: Rowan Gormley, the former head of the pioneering Virgin Direct (now renamed Virgin Money), founded and has a 50 per cent stake in Virgin Wines.

Since 2000 Virgin has been driven by the swift expansion of its mobile phone business and rapid growth of its businesses internationally.

## Company Culture and Style

Research shows Virgin to be the UK's third most admired brand. People outside the organisation associate Virgin with ambition, popularity and friendliness.

Since the mid-1980s, the general public has also linked the brand with the extraordinary energy and seemingly unshakeable confidence of the group's founder.

Inside Virgin, remarkably for such a diverse group, cohesion is fostered by a shared affinity for Virgin 'values' and an emphasis on direct lines of communication. The group began as a team effort (in the late sixties, staff producing *Student* magazine were all paid the same on a shift system) and today, even within one of the group's more beleaguered companies, Virgin Trains, teamworking and morale remain strong. Will Whitehorn, Virgin's Brand Development and Corporate Affairs Director, says: 'It is still the only train operating company that hasn't had a strike since 1997, because our relationships with staff are better. They know that Richard has taken a battering but has supported them throughout.'

Virgin staff are surveyed on a confidential basis, but are also encouraged to talk directly to the boss if they have a problem or complaint. 'Richard has an open-door policy and believes that people should not be criticised for communicating with him or telling him about something that is happening in the company,' says Whitehorn. 'He is a figurehead with attitude – he is, without doubt, one of the main reasons why a lot of people work here.' However, Virgin's founder has also set the task of creating a culture that can thrive without him.

The working environment, like Branson himself, is extremely hands-on. Staff are expected to 'get their hands dirty and not expect other people to do what they don't do themselves', but while the group is flexible about working patterns and encourages all employees to work at their own pace, no one should come to Virgin expecting an easy ride. Women as well as men are appointed to the top jobs: several senior executives are female and although 'it is no easier to get on at Virgin than elsewhere', the group claims there is no prejudice.

## Human Resources

In 1999, during the dot.com boom, Virgin found some of its best people were being poached because of their skills in brand development, and so a new generation of management moved up to fill in the gaps. Three years on, a job with Virgin is far tougher to come by and the group predicts that the climate is unlikely to change in the near future.

Sir Richard Branson became an entrepreneur upon leaving school, and traditionally Virgin has preferred to recruit people from the industry rather than straight from university. In 2000 it introduced a graduate training scheme, intending to recruit a dozen recent university-leavers onto a structured development programme. But it hired just six graduates in 2002 and is presently only looking for candidates with experience in relevant markets. The best advice for those who want to join the organisation, says Whitehorn, is to get to know someone who works at Virgin and find out about opportunities, rather than send an unsolicited job application. The group advertises vacancies on its internal intranet, and is working to improve and facilitate the transfer of existing employees between businesses. The human resources function at Virgin also works with individual businesses to locate high achievers and identify management development needs.

## Career Opportunity and Development

Virgin's fluctuating evolution and expansion into a series of new business areas has enabled it to develop and retain talent in a way that few other businesses have been able to manage. A continual challenge is to meet the expectations of employees who want to exercise entrepreneurial flair. 'One desire Richard has always had is to create more entrepreneurs out of the people he works with,' says Whitehorn. 'And in the longer term, people can make career moves that they couldn't elsewhere.' Brett Godfrey, for example, initially came to work for Virgin in Europe but in 2000 he took the brand back to Australia, spearheading the launch of Virgin Blue, a low-cost airline which is now publicly quoted.

The group has always sought to identify people within the organisation who possess sufficient ambition, vision and drive to take it to new levels. Each company has its own succession plan, and while the commonly-quoted maxim is that people join Virgin 'for six months or for life', senior executives are constantly looking to locate and groom successors.

At the time of writing, Virgin plans no major expansion in Britain beyond natural growth in the areas it currently trades in, though overseas expansion is likely to produce more opportunities in the UK.

The group runs several training and development schemes, mostly in-house. Occasionally employees are sponsored or released to do MBA courses. Managing directors of the various Virgin businesses meet frequently for briefings, and once every six months, senior managers in every business are sent 'back to the floor' – an approach pioneered by Virgin Atlantic in the early 1990s. 'We think one of the best ways to train senior managers is to put them into the front line of their own business on a regular basis,' says Whitehorn.

Each business is also given a free hand to develop corporate social responsibility initiatives. Virgin Atlantic, for example, is involved with a number of community projects in the Crawley and Gatwick area. In addition, a proportion of profits from the businesses go to Branson's charitable foundation, which is one of the founders of what has now become Comic Relief.

## Remuneration

The group does not tend to operate grading structures except in specialised functions; instead it operates as a meritocracy, with the opportunity to reap large rewards. Each Virgin company differs but all operate bonus and profit-share schemes of some kind, and some offer equity involvement. As with most large companies, senior management are offered equity incentives. Over the next decade, Virgin plans to take six or more of its companies public, and aims to offer share schemes accordingly.

Most of the group's biggest businesses are unionised and generally Virgin enjoys a good record on industrial relations. While Virgin Atlantic is a less generous payer than British Airways, its bonuses are 'remarkably competitive' and salaries are higher than at competitors such as British Midland and EasyJet. 'We probably have a greater range of benefits than the average company,' adds Whitehorn.

Perks of working for Virgin include a range of benefits and discounts such as cheap travel, entertainment products such as CDs and DVDs, and, in some companies, free lunches, as well as subsidised membership of Virgin Active gyms. Healthcare and pension arrangements vary from company to company; some, but not all, are administered centrally.

## The Future

Virgin Mobile launched in November 1999 with 90 staff. It now employs more than 2,000 people, has more than 2.4 million customers and is Virgin's fastest-growing business in North America. While other companies have also been rapidly expanding (Virgin Active, for example, opened more than 100 gyms in its first two years), the group's airline remains the other strong engine of growth. Cabin crew and pilots opted to unionise in 2001, and when Virgin Atlantic had to act fast and make redundancies post September 11, staff themselves decided who would stay and go. The redundancy programme was completed within eight weeks.

Virgin predicts it will have £8 billion of revenue by 2006, and one of the main ways it plans to achieve this is by enhancing and leveraging the strength of its brand around the world. By the year 2010, Virgin believes it will be a leading global brand. Over the next five years it will continue expanding around the world in core business areas: the group plans to treble the number of Virgin Megastores in the States, for example. Tough times are ahead, but Virgin, says Whitehorn, remains undaunted. 'I believe our model comes into its own in difficult economic circumstances.'

# enjoy!Whitbread

Whitbread's brands hold strong positions in three of the fastest-growing sectors of the £172 billion UK leisure market – hotels, eating out, and health and fitness. The company intends to be the UK's leading hotel company by 2005, through its brands Travel Inn and Marriott, while each week about 1.5 million people pass through one of its 1,300 restaurants, which include Beefeater, Brewers Fayre, Brewsters, Costa, TGI Friday's and Pizza Hut. The final element in the company's trio is David Lloyd Leisure, already the UK's largest health and fitness club brand, with 290,000 members.

**Scorecard:**

| | |
|---|---|
| Remuneration and benefits | *** |
| Progressive attitude | **** |
| Opportunity for promotion | **** |
| Training, development and education | **** |
| Working atmosphere and environment | **** |

**Biggest plus:**
The dynamic nature of the businesses Whitbread is in means its employees have unlimited possibilities and are constantly stimulated and encouraged to find new and better ways of dealing with customers.

**Biggest minus:**
Because of the very nature of the industry Whitbread is in, its performance is at the whim of market forces and unforeseen events such as September 11.

Whitbread plc
Citypoint
One Ropemaker Street
London EC2Y 9HX
Tel: 020 7606 4455
Fax: 020 7806 5444
Email: info@whitbread.com
Website: www.whitbread.co.uk

# Whitbread

## The Business

Whitbread is one of the oldest independent companies in UK, dating back to 1742 when Samuel Whitbread, a brewer, founded the original company. Since then, it has survived several face lifts, the most dramatic of which came in 2000 when Whitbread sold its breweries and exited its pubs and bars business to concentrate on competing for leisure spend. After several decades of diversification, Whitbread re-focused its business on the growth areas of hotels, restaurants and health and fitness clubs. Its reinvention as a leading light in the leisure business coincided with the end of the brewing and pub-owning tradition that Samuel Whitbread had begun over 250 years earlier.

Director of Corporate Affairs, David Reed, explains that the reason behind this watershed in the company's history came about when directors realised its future lay in the high-growth markets where it was already a leader, rather than in the traditional, low-return businesses upon which the company had been founded. Today, the company is a market leader in all three of its industries, employing more than 60,000 people across 2,000 locations.

*Training is of enormous importance within all of the company's divisions. Not only does this ensure that staff are better able to do their jobs, it also means that they are better equipped to progress in a chosen career*

Being a public company, Whitbread has a range of important shareholders, including Prudential Assurance Company, Standard Life funds, Legal & General Pooled Index Fund and Lloyds Bank.

Up to 99.5 per cent of Whitbread's operations are based in the UK, but international expansion is on the cards within the next five years. The company continues to have overseas interests in Germany and through franchised Costa businesses in the Middle East. Reed says that Whitbread will continue to explore overseas options but only if they are convinced these will produce attractive and sustainable returns.

## Company Culture and Style

Company culture changed dramatically when Whitbread underwent its transformation two years ago. HR Director Angie Risley explains that they were able to retain the good from the past, and build on it to 'create what Whitbread will be like for the next 250 years'.

'Values are the rock upon which we base our decisions', she explains. 'We used to described our values as pride, respect and teamwork, but we are shifting those to reflect today's environment, to caring for customers, challenging the status quo, maintaining a belief in people, and exuding a passion for winning.'

Friendliness and helpfulness are at the core of all Whitbread's people. Feedback from a variety of sources, including recruitment companies, analysts and suppliers, all reinforce this. Risley says this is important to the company because, if they look after their own people, their staff will look after their customers and create the correct kinds of experiences for them.

Unit managers form the bedrock of how Whitbread manages its extensive staff numbers. A balanced scorecard measures employees' performances each month and they, in turn, participate in a regular employee survey called VIEWS. Conducted anonymously, respondents are able to provide opinions and feedback on issues ranging from the company's strategy to belief in management decision-making. The results are communicated – in full – to Whitbread's people, along with the actions to be taken by management to address the issues raised.

Being in such a customer-focused industry, a particular sort of personality is needed to thrive – friendly, people and customer focused, and an enjoyment of the industry. Having said that, however, Risley is quick to emphasise that even introverts do well within the company, as it's more about empathy with colleagues and customers – an attitude that pervades the entire organisation – rather than an outgoing, confident personality that people need to have.

Within senior management, Whitbread's female staff count is sitting at around 40 per cent. There is also a high percentage of part-time employees who are able to juggle their lives, choose shifts, and enjoy flexibility in their work patterns. A lot of time and effort has been spent on developing its intranet specifically so people can log in and catch up easily.

## Human Resources

Recruitment varies depending on employee groups, but the majority of recruitment is done through unit managers in the local employment market. Head office offers extensive help to each unit manager with recruitment decisions, providing toolkits and job centre contacts. Recruitment at national level also takes place – primarily for senior staff appointments – and Whitbread recently launched an Internet recruitment service, which it believes will grow significantly over the next year. Recruitment fairs, schools and colleges are also popular recruiting venues.

There are no minimum qualifications criteria for staff. Says Risley: 'One of our strengths is that we can offer opportunities to the right people, no matter what their background. We prefer to test for an ability to think, and look for commercial, numeracy and verbal skills.'

She adds that research has shown that it's rare for their staff to leave to go to a competitor – instead, they might go into a different industry. They've also found that people who get past the initial 12-week probation period stay with the company for more than two years.

Whitbread has a good staff retention reputation, and is striving to be better than the industry average of 60 per cent. According to Risley, a number of their brands already exceed that. Marriott, in particular, is recognised in the *Sunday Times'* 100 Best Companies to Work For as a leading hotel employer.

'We believe strongly in the principle that it's much more effective and better for customer relations to try to retain staff rather than having to recruit new people and retrain them – this forms the fundamental focus of our people policy.'

## Career Opportunity and Development

Training is of enormous importance within all of the company's divisions. Not only does this ensure that staff are better able to do their jobs, it also means that they are better equipped to progress in a chosen career. An example of this is the Chef's Modern Apprenticeship Scheme, where Whitbread works with colleges around the country to provide students with both a job and a college education.

A wide range of external executive programmes, from leadership skills to the Whitbread MBA programme in conjunction with Oxford Brookes University, is available for senior staff, while training for new staff is emphasised, especially within the first 90 days of employment. Once again, training using the Internet is a new but growing medium, and a key element of the company's new ERP, due to go live by the end of 2003, will be via e-learning.

An advantage of a company like Whitbread, which has such diverse opera-tions, is that there are numerous opportunities for people to move around the various businesses and to develop their careers. Risley says there is good move-ment across Whitbread's brands and it is encouraged as it provides broadened experience.

With the Whitbread brands' international affiliations, the prospect of an over-seas transfer is strong within the Marriott group.

Career paths for employees are mapped out from day one, and Whitbread has found that a great source of new management comes from those who go from being a team member to unit leader.

'People feel as though they're in control of their careers,' says Reed. 'They are encouraged to communicate with their line managers and discover what they need to do in their current job in order to be promoted.'

The company's Organisation and People Review identifies high-potential people and plans out a succession route from them, starting from unit manager level. Another way that employees can chart their progress is via performance manage-ment. 'What we have is a 360-degree review of anyone's career', explains Reed.

## Remuneration

Remuneration is based on performance and the company drives much of what it expects through bonus schemes. These are based on achievements from the balance scorecard. At individual team member level, there are added incentives for the team. All bonuses are currently cash-based but Whitbread plans to introduce share ownership as part of this.

All staff who have worked for Whitbread for at least a year are eligible to buy shares in the company. There is also health insurance, although access to this does vary depending on which part of the organisation you work for. Life plans, opportunities to buy and save Whitbread shares after a year's service and staff discounts across all brands are also part of all staff packages.

Company cars kick in automatically when employees hit the appropriate management grade.

'We believe that loyalty is a two-way street. In our experience, what you get out of a relationship approximates to what you put in. We believe in putting a great deal of effort into creating and maintaining a working environment where high quality, committed people can grow and prosper', says Risley.

## The Future

Whitbread is aiming for a double-digit growth in profit every year, and hopes to extrapolate this to new units. For example, says Reed, they hope to grow DLL from the current 50 units to 100, the budget and travel business from 17,000 rooms to 25,000, Pizza Hut outlets from 400 to 700, and Brewsters from 130 to 220 over the next five years.

Beyond that, Whitbread will look to see what it can do outside the UK, particularly the Western European market. In the shorter term, a major acquisition in a similar industry will take place within next 12 months.

'We have real ambition to take the entity we've created in two years and expand it exponentially', Reed says.

Xansa is an international business process and IT services company that creates and delivers process and technology solutions that significantly improve its clients' business performance. How it achieves this will vary from client to client; the constants are strong relationships, a dedicated team, attention to detail and listening to the customer rather than telling them how to work. It specialises in four services: business and technology consulting, IT implementation, IT outsourcing and business process management, and is a publicly-quoted, company.

**Scorecard:**

| | |
|---|---|
| Remuneration and benefits | **** |
| Progressive attitude | ***** |
| Opportunity for promotion | ***** |
| Training, development and education | **** |
| Working atmosphere and environment | **** |

**Biggest plus:**
The culture and the people. The workforce and its Trusts own around 30 per cent of the equity.

**Biggest minus:**
Extremely tough market conditions in the IT services sector in 2002 forced Xansa to operate in an environment characterised by cutbacks in IT development spend.

Xansa
420 Thames Valley Park Drive
Thames Valley Park
Reading RG6 1PU
Tel: 08702 416181
Fax: 08702 426282
Website: www.xansa.com

# Xansa

## The Business

Xansa was one of the first businesses to introduce flexible working practices back in the early 1960s. Four decades later, flexibility and innovation remain watchwords for this progressive company. Now an international player, Xansa focuses on delivering business process and technology solutions to significantly improve its clients' business performance. Around 55 per cent of Xansa's clients have worked in partnership with Xansa for more than five years. The company's blue chip client list includes AXA Sun Life, Barclays, BT, Boots, The Co-Operative Bank, Diageo, and mmO2.

In the mid-1990s it adopted a policy of acquiring other companies to enhance its skills and services portfolio; these have included OSI in 1998 and Druid in 1999. In 2001 the company consolidated all its businesses under one brand, Xansa. More recently it has welcomed a new Chief Executive – Alistair Cox. As anticipated following his arrival, Xansa has undergone a root and branch overhaul resulting in a more mature and realistic business outlook.

## Company Culture and Style

Like any major progressive company, Xansa finds that its style and feel changes often. This is partly because of its beginnings as an entrepreneurial flexible and family-friendly employer, but it leads in visionary ethos too, as an organisation wanting to make a difference for its employees and clients. It is this attitude permeating throughout the organisation that leads to clients telling HR Director, Mike Harling, that they have noticed Xansa people appear to enjoy working where they do and are proud to be part of it. At the company's UK-based HQ in Reading, Berkshire, this is very much in evidence around the offices. Facilities are good, the atmosphere is friendly and there are no hard and fast rules about dress – the company employs adults who, it believes, understand that turning up to a meeting with a potential blue-chip client in jeans and pink hair is probably not a good idea.

*it is the client rather than the company that dictates the culture and style in many ways. As a major player in the outsourcing market, Xansa will send its people to work full time on a client's site or simply take over the client's IT staff, so fitting in with the client is paramount*

In fact it is the client rather than the company that dictates the culture and style in many ways. As a major player in the outsourcing market, Xansa will send its people to work full time on a client's site or simply take over the client's IT staff, so fitting in with the client is paramount. Harling comments that clients often note the good match the company makes with them; this is because part of the organisation's mission is to listen to how a client business works and not to impose its own model of working.

It should also be understood that Xansa is aware of the environmental impact its activities can have. Its annual report has a section devoted to what it's doing to improve its performance in this area – this isn't just top show, the company retains a commitment to perform well in areas outside the pure financials on the balance sheet, as well as to make money.

# Human Resources

As a company that specialises in managing change and other issues for its clients, Xansa is as aware as anyone that its people are its primary resource. For that reason it tailors its packages and career development paths carefully along individual lines. The HR department's contribution has been to put in place well-defined competencies and skill requirements for each position, so staff will know exactly where they're aiming.

In terms of applicants and finding the job for which you may be qualified, the website at www.xansa.com is a good starting point as current vacancies are posted online almost religiously.

Employee satisfaction is important to the company. In December 2001 it completed the first of its employee satisfaction surveys, in which 3,000 employees took part. 74 per cent of them were pleased to be working for Xansa and over 80 per cent were aware of the company's desire to continue to unite its different activities under a single banner, with three quarters appreciating the impact this would have at local level. The HR team is committed to keeping employees aware of international policies and the way these will affect staff, and will do this through the company intranet and other means.

# Career Opportunity and Development

As the company website says, individuals are encouraged in Xansa to manage their own careers within a transparent framework. In other words, if you want to move across different disciplines and learn different skills then, as long as suitable opportunities exist, you'll be supported to do it. Harling believes this is overwhelmingly a positive thing: 'People might be excellent in, say, a technical capacity. Instead of pigeonholing them we're pleased to empower them to move into a role that might offer them new opportunities for development. However, this can occasionally involve telling people they don't appear to have the aptitude for the role to which they aspire, an element of the job Harling admits is not always pleasant. Managers will always attempt to handle situations like this sensitively or better, to head them off through realistic appraisals at all times so, say, a shrinking violet appreciates early on that they're not going to be Sales or Client director.

Opportunities for training are therefore many, and the business is keen to apply the principles it uses for its clients for its own needs – any methodologies it works on during a client project will more than likely surface when appropriate to Xansa itself.

Supporting this, there are the formal career frameworks put in place by the HR team – working in conjunction with the reward philosophy there should be much to appeal to the right person.

## Remuneration

Xansa's philosophy is very much about looking at an individual's entire package rather than simply the salary, but unlike a number of companies making that claim this isn't a blind for low pay. Harling and his team take part in regular salary surveys across the market to ensure that the pay on offer is above average, but the overall package reflects non-financial elements as well – the official formula for total reward is Salary + Benefits + Bonus/Commission + Share/Stock Options.

Much of the salary structure is self-explanatory. Bonuses are offered on performance while commissions clearly apply to sales activities. Stock options kick in at senior levels but share-based savings schemes are widespread throughout the company, and for which Xansa is renowned as a pioneering organisation. These schemes also win awards.

Through its Flexible Benefits Plan, other benefits can be tailored to a person's needs – pensions, holidays, life assurance, car or car allowance can be mixed and weighted according to an individual's preference.

## The Future

Xansa has had an interesting recent past that augurs well for its future. Specifically it has had to face its first major redundancy programme for as long as most of the current directors can remember. This will sound less than positive at first but oddly it's not. The reason is the reaction of the staff, whose view had less to do with the understandable insecurities a time like that might bring and more to do with pragmatism and a will to taking the company forward. 'Nobody likes having to lose colleagues,' says Harling, 'but the view was very much, OK, if this has to happen then so be it, how do we handle it sensitively, build for tomorrow and stop it happening again?'

The answer is that you can't stop it from happening again. A company like Xansa will always be at the mercy of the good fortune of its clients, and during the opening years of the 21st century most of those have also faced challenging markets. Nevertheless, the support of a motivated staff, as noted by so many of the clients, speaks of a mature and realistic, as well as optimistic, company. It should be well placed to ride out any difficulties in the future and move forward with confidence.